Alexander Pope
and His
Eighteenth-Century
Women Readers

Claudia N. Thomas

Southern Illinois University Press
Carbondale and Edwardsville

Frontispiece: Alexander Pope by Charles Jervas (ca. 1717).
Reprinted by permission of the National Portrait Gallery, London.

Library of Congress Cataloging-in-Publication Data

Thomas, Claudia N.
    Alexander Pope and his eighteenth-century women readers / Claudia
N. Thomas.
        p. cm.
    Includes bibliographical references and index.
    1. Pope, Alexander, 1688–1744—Criticism and interpretation—
History—18th century.   2. Women—Great Britain—Books and
reading—History—18th century.   3. Women and literature—Great
Britain—History—18th century.   4. Authors and readers—Great
Britain—History—18th century.   5. Pope, Alexander, 1688–1744—
Appreciation—Great Britain.   6. English poetry—Women authors—
History and criticism.   7. English poetry—18th century—History and
criticism.   8. Pope, Alexander, 1688–1744—Influence. 9. Influence
(Literary, artistic, etc.)   I. Title.
PR3637.W6T48   1994
821'.5—dc20   92-42647
ISBN 0-8093-1886-5   CIP

The paper used in this publication meets the minimum requirements of
American National Standard for Information Sciences—Permanence
of Paper for Printed Library Materials, ANSI Z39.48-1984. ♾

To my parents,
Belle Dodds Thomas
and
John J. Thomas, Jr.

Contents

Preface   ix

Introduction: Alexander Pope, Literary
    Creativity, and Eighteenth-Century Women   1
1. "Appeals to the Ladies": Pope and His *Iliad* Readers   19
2. Women's Prose Responses to Pope's Writings   68
3. Women's Poetic Addresses to Pope   118
4. Eighteenth-Century Women and Pope's Early Poetry   160
5. Pope and Women's Poems "Something like Horace"   194
    Conclusion: Pope's Influence on
        Eighteenth-Century Women's Poetry   227

Notes   249
Bibliography   281
Index   297

Preface

Alexander Pope and His Eighteenth-Century Women Readers is not a
catchy title, but I hope it suggests a study not merely of Pope's influence on women writers but of the complex interactions between Pope
and women readers and between women and Pope's writings
throughout the century. Pope's attitude toward women is not simple
to define; nor did women often receive his texts passively. I have
tried to elucidate some of the choices Pope made in addressing women
readers and some of the strategies women used in responding to him.
Their imitations, appropriations, and repudiations of Pope constitute
part of the history of women's entrance into the literary marketplace.

Alexander Pope did not function, to his contemporary women
readers, as the bogey he sometimes appears to be in current criticism.
For reasons both professional and personal, young Pope courted
(some might say exploited) a newly identified female readership. His
maneuvers succeeded; Pope's Homeric translations and such poems
as "Eloisa to Abelard" remained favorites among women for generations. But Pope's inclusion of women had another, perhaps unantici-
pated, result: from his earliest readers on, women responded in kind
to his writings. During his lifetime, women addressed themselves to
Pope, some assuming his genuine interest in their welfare, others
outraged by his affronts. To most, Pope was a potential correspondent
rather than a distant inhabitant of Mount Olympus.

After his death, Pope increasingly took on the role of forefather
to women writers, in a feminized version of what Harold Bloom has
described as the struggle between an aspiring writer and a chosen
predecessor. Since her death in 1689, Aphra Behn had been all but
banished as an admissible foremother, and few women seemed eligible for that status until Elizabeth Rowe's death in 1737. In Pope,
however, women discerned a male precursor not only sympathetic
to their cultural predicament but in some ways sharing it, due to his
physical, religious, and political liabilities. Pope's writings—unlike

those of most female precursors—were abundantly available to women. And most women poets' techniques reveal close study of his poems.

For all these reasons, replies to and imitations of Pope appear in most women's poetic miscellanies. For the same reasons, women responded freely to Pope in prose—for example, critiquing his reasoning in *The Essay on Man*, although that poem had not explicitly sought a female audience. And when not reflecting on Pope at length, women alluded to him in their prose and poetry. Denied direct access to the classics, women were nevertheless conversant with Pope's canon—Pope was their classic writer, his sentiments apt for quotation in letters, novels, and essays.

Of the many women whose writings I consider in this study, I found few who merely mimic Pope. Most reveal the subtle connections between writing as women—that is, either consciously or unconsciously adhering to gender roles sanctioned by their culture—and "writing woman" in the feminist sense of disrupting masculine systems. As chapter 4 explains in more detail, even the most decorous of women's revisions of Pope tend to reveal the flaws in his constructions of femininity, while nudging readers toward a broader conception of womanhood.

Because the significance of women's adjustments often lies in nuances rather than in overt confrontations, I have included more close readings than generalizations in this study. Moreover, many of the texts I treat have not been reprinted, and I prefer to present my evidence rather than ask my readers to agree with unsubstantiated conclusions. More importantly, however, I wish to honor these eighteenth-century women writers—those foremothers that Elizabeth Barrett Browning and even Virginia Woolf sought in vain—by quoting their writings rather than merely describing or generalizing about them. Even the least accomplished of these writers, such as Elizabeth Boyd or Mary Chandler, appears cleverer when responding to Pope than we might have supposed. Pope not only challenged but inspired his women readers. And in rising to the occasion of talking back to Pope, the most recent inhabitant of a very masculine Parnassus, eighteenth-century women set a precedent for every woman writer who has followed.

Throughout the text, my citations to poetry refer to line numbers and my citations to prose refer to page numbers.

I began researching *Alexander Pope and His Eighteenth-Century Women Readers* in 1989, as a summer postdoctoral fellow at the William Andrews Clark Memorial Library of UCLA. Robert Folkenflik, who headed that summer's program, supported and encouraged me, although my pursuit fit very loosely into our seminar on "The Artist as Hero." Thanks to Professor Folkenflik and the Clark's wonderful staff, this book occurred to me while I walked one evening along the beach at Pacific Palisades.

I thank the NEH Travel to Collections Fund and Wake Forest University's William C. Archie Fund for Faculty Excellence for enabling additional research at the British Library in July and August 1990. I wrote most of the book during a Z. Smith Reynolds leave from my teaching duties at Wake Forest University. Elen Knott and William Ach particularly facilitated my research in Wake Forest's Z. Smith Reynolds Library. I also thank the staffs of the Huntington Library, the Bancroft Library at Berkeley, and UCLA Special Collections.

Many colleagues in the Wake Forest English Department have been supportive. To former provost Edwin Wilson and Chair Barry Maine I owe my leave. Nancy Cotton deserves my deepest thanks for reading each draft as it materialized; her comments were invaluable. Robert Lovett shared his extensive knowledge of the eighteenth-century novel and the book trade; Andrew Ettin, his expertise in the pastoral; and Dillon Johnston, his grasp of poetics. I also thank Gale Sigal, Anne Boyle, Gillian Overing, Dolly McPherson, Mary DeShazer, and Elizabeth Phillips for the lively discussions, not to mention the friendship, that buoyed me through this project. Thanks, too, to Dee Perry, department secretary, for both friendship and crucial practical assistance and to Carol Burns of Southern Illinois University Press and Jill Butler for editorial assistance.

Among colleagues at other universities, Charles Hinnant kindly read my discussion of Anne Finch—now stronger, I believe, after his response. Generously, James Winn thoroughly critiqued early drafts. His knowledge of Dryden particularly benefited my first chapter. Robert Folkenflik has continued his support and criticism, suggesting to me, for example, where Johnson as well as Pope were implicated in women's texts. My readers at Southern Illinois University Press offered valuable criticism. Above all, I thank Susan Staves for her advice and encouragement. *Alexander Pope and His Eighteenth-Century Readers* was fundamentally inspired by her analyses of women's place in eighteenth-century English society and culture.

Portions of chapters 1 and 2 appeared in *Eighteenth-Century Life* 14 (1990) and in *The Age of Johnson* 4 (1991), respectively. I thank the editors for permission to include revised versions of those articles. I am also grateful to the National Portrait Gallery of Great Britain for permission to reproduce Charles Jervas's enigmatic portrait of Alexander Pope.

To David L. Faber I owe thanks for years of friendship and inspiration. Finally, I wish to thank my parents for a lifetime of loving encouragement. I dedicate this book to them.

Alexander Pope
and His
Eighteenth-Century
Women Readers

Introduction: Alexander Pope, Literary Creativity, and Eighteenth-Century Women

Alexander Pope's rhetorical constructions of femininity have stimulated recent critical debate. Such studies as Laura Brown's Marxist *Alexander Pope* (1985) and Ellen Pollak's feminist *The Poetics of Sexual Myth: Gender and Ideology in the Verse of Swift and Pope* (1985) have analyzed Pope's poems from specific, late twentieth-century points of view.[1] Their perspectives emphasize Pope's role as a spokesperson for his culture, both writers arraigning him for opinions less defensible today than 250 years ago. Pope appears a straightforward misogynist in both studies: according to Brown, he trivialized and commodified women; in Pollak's account, he insulted and oppressed them.

Brown's and Pollak's books have inspired provocative rereadings of Pope and his contemporaries. Ruth Salvaggio's *Enlightened Absence* (1988), for example, has applied French feminist theory to works by Newton, Swift, Pope, and Anne Finch, although Salvaggio regards the male poets with more pity than anger.[2] All three studies raise questions about the sufficiency of modern insight to elucidate eighteenth-century texts. If Pope was a brutal misogynist, why did contemporary enemies dismiss him as a women's toy, and his writings as a ladies' pastime? If Pope deemed women inconsequential, why did he bother to cultivate a female audience? Why did he sympathize with women's limitations in such poems as "Epistle to Miss Blount, with the Works of Voiture" (1712)? And how did eighteenth-century women readers receive his writings? These questions demand a more extensive and accurate context than current opinions provide.

The women who read and responded to Pope's writings formed a prominent aspect of that context. In "Engendering the Reader: 'Wit and Poetry and Pope' Once More" (1988), Penelope Wilson has advocated a reader-response approach to the sexual politics of Pope's rhetoric. Complaining that few contemporary women readers' responses to Pope survive, Wilson nevertheless argues that the most fruitful area for feminist studies of eighteenth-century writings examines images of the woman reader.[3] Wilson observes that applications of current theory to Pope's poetry risk anachronism. She claims, however, that without a significant sample of women's responses, reader-response criticism will remain confined to studies of textual images and gendered rhetoric. More recent studies have moved beyond this impasse. Valerie Rumbold's *Women's Place in Pope's World* (1989) has studied Pope's relationships with women, observing their responses while filling some of the lacunae in Maynard Mack's *Alexander Pope: A Life* (1986).[4] Several inconsistencies in Pope's attitude toward women become coherent in Rumbold's context. His frequent blend of sympathy and disdain, for example, grew from volatile relationships with particular women rather than from philosophical dismission of womankind. Donna Landry's *The Muses of Resistance: Laboring-Class Women's Poetry in Britain, 1739–1796* (1990) includes a Marxist analysis of Pope's significance to laboring-class women poets.[5] Rumbold's and Landry's books demonstrate that, as Wilson predicted, contemporary women's responses uniquely illuminate Pope's writings, but also that, contrary to Wilson's fears, those responses are eminently recoverable.

A surprising amount of testimony survives to illustrate the ways eighteenth-century women read Pope. The poet courted their responses: contemporaries identified Pope's work with the growing audience of female readers, and Pope sometimes chose genres conventionally associated with women, such as the heroic epistle. Women referred to, quoted, and commented on Pope's poems and letters in diaries, letters, travel books, translations, essays, and novels. Women addressed poems commendatory or critical to Pope and designed companion pieces to his poems. Women poets learned their craft by studying English poets, especially Pope. Their poems refract his themes, language, and imagery through feminine experience and opinion. Pope's women readers, moreover, ranged from laborers to aristocrats, encompassing responses influenced not only by gender but by social and economic status.

These responses should prove crucial to feminist analyses of Pope's writings. They confirm the extent to which Pope's poems and prose merely reiterated feminine stereotypes or expanded the contemporary horizon of expectations. They determine whether women received Pope's work passively or resisted its constructions of femininity. Women's responses reveal which aspects of or possibilities latent in Pope's work caught their attention—sometimes unpredictable from a late twentieth-century point of view. Contemporary women's responses clarify both Pope's work and its relation to cultural history. Equally important, they advance feminist criticism and women's literary history and help to reconstruct the female experience and perception of eighteenth-century culture. As I hope to demonstrate throughout *Alexander Pope and His Eighteenth-Century Women Readers*, a response to Pope was, for many women, a response to cultural issues ranging from women's emotional and intellectual qualities to their creative capacity.

Intruders in the Garden:
Eighteenth-Century Women and Literary Creativity

Pope, at least in his youth, associated romantic or sexual feelings for women with creativity, and both with natural settings. His poignant "Hymn Written in Windsor Forest" (1717) bids farewell to both his home and the romantic aspirations of his youth.[6] Pope commemorates Windsor's woods as the "Scene of my youthful Loves" (2), then as the scene of his dedication to poetry after realizing that he might "love the brightest eyes, but love in vain!" (8). Henceforth, the energy other men might direct toward business, political preferment, or love would be lavished on his muse, a creative spirit emanating in this hymn from the natural world that inspired his earliest published poems.

Five years later, having completed his initial landscaping at Twickenham, he confided in "Epistle to Mr. [John] Gay" his identification of the garden with romantic or sexual longing.

> Joy lives not here; to happier seats it flies,
> And only dwells where *Wortley* casts her eyes.
>
> What are the gay parterre, the chequer'd shade,
> The morning bower, the ev'ning colonade,
> But soft recesses of uneasy minds,
> To sigh unheard in, to the passing winds?
>
> (5–10)

Hopelessly attached to Lady Mary Wortley Montagu, Pope claimed to have created a bower in which "to die" like a wounded deer, "the arrow at his heart" (12). But literally, he had created a retreat in which to craft poems expressing his emotions. As Pope aged, his emotions were most often stimulated by friendships, ethics, and politics, rather than by romantic love. But his garden and grotto remained the site of creative inspiration, haunt of the same muses who pressed his hand in Windsor Forest "and said, Be Ours!" ("Hymn," 4).[7]

This relationship between Pope and his natural surroundings was understood by generations of Pope's readers, who donated sparkling stones to pave his grotto during the poet's life, and who made so many pilgrimages to Twickenham after his death that Baroness Sophia Howe, its weary proprietor, tore down the villa and defaced the grotto and garden in 1807.[8] What Mack has called "a Pope-and-Twickenham legend" evoked such poetic tributes as Robert Dodsley's to "the solemn Place, / From whence [Pope's] Genius soar'd to Nature's God" (*Garden*, 266–67). Women readers, too, identified Pope's garden with his genius, as well as with their own relation to creativity.

But women's responses to Pope's garden were necessarily more complicated than, for example, that of the Frenchman who identified with Pope ("Comme toi, je chéris ma noble indépendance") and invoked him as muse "dans ces bosquets par ta muse habités."[9] Twickenham enshrined the association between "husbanding" a landscape and "fathering" verse, recognized at some level by Pope himself in his Windsor "Hymn" and "Epistle to Mr. Gay." Pope cultivated the image of Horatian philosopher, determined to write poems that "pleas'd by manly ways" ("Epistle to Dr. Arbuthnot," 337). While women admired Pope's writings as avidly, their identification with the poet was never as straightforward as men's. Their relation to Twickenham as a symbol of creativity likewise required considerable adjustment. Pope's home represented not just a particular poet's achievement but a gendered conception of genius that discouraged female emulation. It is not surprising, therefore, that of responses written by two prominent women during Pope's lifetime, one was inimical; the other, covertly ambitious.

Lady Mary Wortley Montagu was simultaneously complimented and embarrassed by Pope's tribute in "Epistle to Mr. Gay." She sent a copy of the verses to her sister in Paris, but she explained she had "stiffle'd them" in England, and she requested that Lady Mar do the same. Lady Mary characteristically felt the impropriety as much as the flattery of Pope's admiration. She informed Lady Mar that Pope, whom she saw "very seldom," had "made a subterrenean Grotto, which he has furnish'd with Looking Glass, and they tell me it has a very good Effect." Twickenham gossip contradicted Lady Mary, reporting that the pair were very close.[10] If so, Lady Mary was probably among the first visitors to the new grotto.

Pope and Lady Mary quarreled, however, not long after he composed "Epistle to Mr. Gay." In 1728, he ridiculed her in the *Dunciad* as the bane of a "hapless Monsieur . . . at Paris" (2.127). Pope referred to Lady Mary's unfortunate management of Nicolas-François Rémond's South Sea investment, but in the *Dunciad*'s context his remark suggests sexual misconduct. Lady Mary retaliated for this assault on her reputation by attacking Pope's poetic reputation. "Her Palace placed beneath a muddy road" (1729) installs Pope as crown prince of dullness.[11] The poem opens with a startling description of the very "subterrenean grotto" Lady Mary had praised to her sister seven years before.

Lady Mary mocks Pope's selection of a cave for creative meditation, recalling instead his vivid evocations of the caves of Spleen (*The Rape of the Lock*) and Dulness (*Dunciad*). In her poem, Pope's grotto exercises a gravitational pull downward, impeding packhorses on the road above. Lady Mary subverts Pope's architectural metaphors.

> Here chose the Goddess her belov'd Retreat
> Which Phoebus trys in vain to penetrate,
> Adorn'd within by Shells of small expence
> (Emblems of tinsel Rhime, and triffleing Sense),
> Perpetual fogs enclose the sacred Cave,
> The neighboring Sinks their fragrant Odours gave.
>
> (4–9)

Lady Mary replaces an ancient tradition, the cave as site of prophetic vision, with her own observation that the god of poetry cannot penetrate its walls. Pope paved his grotto with shells, mirrors, and sparkling minerals, a glittering ambience for meditation. While Pope evidently associated the spars and shells with poetic inspiration, they seemed cheap "Emblems of tinsel Rhyme" to his adversary.

Lady Mary finally condemns the grotto's unhealthy proximity to the river, not to mention local cesspools. Her description suggests Pope's affinity with the filthy antics of his dunces in book 2 of the *Dunciad*, in which Dulness inspires Curll with "ordure's sympathetic force" (95) but then awards him a mere phantom poet for winning the booksellers' race. Dulness consoles Curll, however, by suggesting he mislead the public with a similar ploy, attributing scurrilous publications to distinguished authors just as a bawd dubs her prostitutes

"Duchesses and Lady Mary's" (*Dunciad*, 2.128). Lady Mary's response implies that a correspondingly literal association with excrement inspired Pope's slander. But Pope's grotto was not endangered by cesspools, though a damp cave was hardly the ideal environment for a frail man. Pope thought less of this inconvenience than of the grotto's associations with wisdom and philosophical simplicity. Lady Mary's satire ignores these ideas, rejecting not only Pope's claim to poetic inspiration but the poet himself. In his poem to Gay, Pope had implicitly dedicated his landscape projects—including the new grotto—to Lady Mary. "Her Palace placed beneath a muddy road" emphatically repudiates that gesture, denying Pope's worthiness as a lover, as a poet, and even as a landscape architect.

Elizabeth Carter enjoyed a happier venture into Pope's garden in July 1738. The poet was not at home when her party visited, but his servant John Serle permitted them to view Pope's grounds. Carter was impressed enough to write her father that "of all the Things I have yet seen of this sort none ever suited my own Fancy so well."[12] Like most tourists, Carter desired a souvenir: she evidently plucked a sprig of laurel as an appropriate token of her visit to the poet's garden. However she intended the gesture, Samuel Johnson detected its professional significance. He published a Latin epigram on the incident in July's *Gentleman's Magazine*, declaring that "dulcis Elisa" had no need to steal the laurel; "Si neget *Popus, Apollo* dabit."[13] Pope, of course, had not denied Carter the laurel; she undoubtedly "stole" the sprig because her host was not present to grant her request. But several *Gentleman's Magazine* contributors were charmed by the young woman's "theft"; the August *Gentleman's Magazine* contained three translations of Johnson's epigram.[14] Each contributor's epigram suggested "Eliza's" longing for the laurel wreath of poetic fame and the injustice were Pope to refuse this deserving female aspirant. As Johnson expressed it in his translation, "Were *Pope* once void of wonted candour found, / Just *Phoebus* would devote his plant to thee" (7–8).

These gallant epigrams probably display the writers' wit and prowess in translating Latin (Stephen Duck, the "thresher poet," was one contributor) as much as the writers' admiration of Elizabeth Carter's poetry. Carter had just published her first volume of poems that month. Her contributions to *Gentleman's Magazine* had been enthusiastically received, but she had not courted the role of Pope's female rival. The three men's epigrams in the August *Gentleman's Magazine* nevertheless develop the image of Carter as an ambitious interloper in Pope's garden. "Alexis" imagines her "rapt with eager hand . . . snatch[ing] the bay" (3). In Duck's version, "Desirous of the laurel bough, / She crops it to adorn her brow" (3–4). Carter's gesture thus appears an aggressive assertion of her poetic achievement. All three epigrams also cast Pope as the jealous guardian of Parnassus by speculating whether he might refuse "a wreath so due" ("Alexis," 4). The image suggests that Pope is aware of and threatened by Carter—an idea that might have occurred to Johnson because he knew she was translating Crousaz's hostile *Examen* of the *Essay on Man*. The epigrams bear little relation to Carter's personality or her actual visit to Twickenham, but they record a contemporary impression of Carter's gifts. Her literary career was barely established, but at least three literate men considered her a potential feminine rival to masculine poetic hegemony. Although constrained to trespass in Pope's domain, she deserved to share his laurel wreath.

Sharing the page with these tributes, Carter answered Johnson's epigram in both Latin and English. The responses disclaim false modesty, acknowledging both her literacy and her wit. But she abjures any pretense to rival Pope.

> In vain *Eliza*'s daring hand
> Usurp'd the laurel bough;
> Remov'd from *Pope*'s, the wreath must fade
> On ev'ry meaner brow.
>
> (1–4)

Rather than contradict her male admirers' account of the visit, she chastizes herself for usurping Pope's laurel. Carter gracefully accepts their compliment, but she defuses any potential offense to the Wasp of Twickenham. Perhaps, worried that her translation of Crousaz might anger Pope when published, she wished to avoid prior offense. Carter entertained ambivalent feelings about Pope's verse. By accepting Johnson's conceit, she acknowledges her literary ambition. She even describes herself grabbing the laurel wreath from Pope's head. But the theft is foolish and ineffectual; Carter simultaneously owns her ambition and denies her ability to achieve it. Concerned to appear modest as well as accomplished, Carter was not what modern feminists call a "voleuse de langue"—a woman who steals, then flees with, masculine language.[15] Although the garden that reflected Pope's imagination suited her fancy, she makes no move to appropriate his property, either the laurel or the claim to poetic excellence it represents. Instead, Carter describes her visit to Twickenham as a bungled theft, a doomed attempt to transplant Pope's laurels "to climates not their own" (6). A child not of Phoebus but of "a paler sun" (8), she cannot sustain the wreath. Carter's response epitomizes what proved to be her fitful career. Torn between awareness of her gifts and a nearly insurmountable shyness about pursuing literary projects, she never seriously competed for literary fame. The *Gentleman's Magazine* epigrams suggest both her youthful aspirations and the fear that prevented her outright quest. Carter fancied Pope's garden, but she contented herself with a surreptitious visit.

Elizabeth Carter's deference, like Lady Mary's repudiation, regarded a living contemporary. Lady Mary confined her poem to manuscript, emphasizing the personal nature of her grievance with Pope. Her retaliation against his boasted grotto intends a reciprocal wound. Carter's epigrams defer to a poet feared for installing critics and would-be competitors in successive editions of the *Dunciad*.[16] When she criticized Pope's poems, she did so subtly.

Women writing after Pope's death more freely described the garden's personal significance, identifying it with their personalities and aspirations. When Jael Henrietta Pye published *A short account, of the principal seats and gardens, in and about Twickenham* in 1760, she prefaced her little guide with an apologetic introduction.

> These little Excursions being commonly the only Travels permitted to our Sex, & the only Way we have of becoming at all acquainted with the Progress of Arts, I thought it might not be improper, to throw together on Paper, such Remarks as occured to me, never intending they should appear: but the Partiality of some of my Friends have call'd them to Light.[17]

She concludes by soliciting constructive criticism, but she adds "that it is my Ambition, to appear to [my readers], in every agreeable Light but that of an Author" (xi–xii).

When Pye approaches Pope's garden, now owned by Sir William Stanhope, the sole object of her description is the poet's obelisk commemorating his mother.

> This is a Circumstance of more Credit to him, than all his Works; for the Beauties of Poetry are tasted only by a few, but the Language of the Heart is understood by all.

Nor does the Author of the *Essay on Man*, surrounded by the Muses, and invoking his *St. John*, appear half so amiable, as the pious Son, lamenting over the Remains of his aged Parent. (18–19)

Pye evidently found in Pope's garden a kindred spirit, more disposed to appear a man of sentiment than an author. After confessing her ignorance and limited experience, Pye rejoices that Pope's most remarkable garden ornament appealed not to the privileged few—aristocratic men, such as Bolingbroke—but to the many. Pope's reverential gesture appealed to this young lady, who found his filial devotion more accessible than his poetic ethical system.

Pye's younger but more distinguished contemporary Hannah More recorded her response to Pope's garden in greater detail. More's letter to Mrs. Gwatkin is undated, but her visit must have taken place between Sir William Stanhope's additions to Pope's house (ca. 1760) and his death in 1772.[18] The visit thus predated More's first publication (*The Search After Happiness*, 1773) and her first visit to London. More declares that although she could not attend the recent birthnight in town, her loss has been more than compensated: "I have visited the mansion of the tuneful Alexander." Although More later became skeptical of Pope's verse, this early letter all but deifies the poet: "I have rambled through the immortal shades of Twickenham; I have trodden the haunts of the swan of Thames." Having announced her adventure, however, More descends abruptly into reality.

You know, my dear madam, what an enthusiastic ardour I have ever had to see this almost sacred spot, and how many times have I created to myself an imaginary Thames: but, enthusiasm apart, there is very little merit either in the grotto, house, or gardens, but that they once belonged to one of the greatest poets on earth. (Roberts, 1:34)

In a critical manner prophetic of her later prose, More explains that Pope's house must have been "very small" before Sir William added two wings. Sir William's decor, however, is "only genteel," and his library "contemptibly small." More's dream of Pope's immortal haunts confronts mundane reality: "The grotto is very large, very little ornamented, with but little spar or glittering stones" (1:35).

More finds Twickenham's failure to match her expectations disconcerting. Her long-awaited view of the Thames was foiled; its "noble current was frozen quite over." But she produces a compensatory myth. The Thames' frozen condition explains "why we saw no naiads. Every Hamadryad was also congealed in its parent tree." Soothed by this fiction, More confesses, "I could not be honest for the life of me: from the grotto I stole two bits of stones, from the garden a sprig of laurel, and from one of the bed-chambers a pen" (1:35). The filched souvenirs jar with More's reputation for scrupulous honesty. In 1785, for example, she was outraged when Ann Yearsley accused her of withholding subscription money. But More was no different from Elizabeth Carter or any tourist coveting a token remembrance; that Pope's grotto seemed "very little ornamented" fewer than thirty years after his death suggests hundreds of previous depredations.[19]

More's stolen souvenirs are less revealing than her letter's ambivalence. She recalls her anticipatory rapture as an established attitude ("You know . . . what an . . . ardor I have ever had to see this . . . spot"), taxed by her encounter with the small, plainly furnished house and somber grotto. By imagining the temporary flight of resident naiads and hamadryads, More preserves a cherished ideal. Only Pope's *Pastorals* feature naiads, although More may also have recalled the nymph Lodona in "Windsor Forest," or the sylphs in *The Rape of the Lock*. More's fable suggests that she, like many eighteenth-century women, preferred Pope's early, less controversial poetry. Or she may have wished simply to reinstate a literary ambience in the frozen landscape. But by inventing a fanciful explanation for Twickenham's uninspiring reality, More maintains her youthful rapture. Her selection of relics—the laurel, the pen, the stones from Pope's grotto— seeks communion with the poet by removing bits of his "haunts" for personal meditation. Away from the house and grotto, More can satisfactorily reconstruct their "immortal shades." This impulse contrasts significantly with More's later attitude. As a mature writer, More could no longer reconcile her delight in "tuneful Alexander" with what she considered dangerous about his verse. This early visit anticipates her eventual disillusionment, but it also suggests why More later warned young readers against Pope's poetry: as a young woman, Hannah More had overlooked reality for the sake of Pope's aesthetic pleasures.

Lady Mary dismissed Pope's "Shells of small expence," while Elizabeth Carter and Hannah More—typical middle-class tourists— coveted souvenirs. More's laboring-class nemesis, Ann Yearsley, responded quite differently to Twickenham in "Written on a Visit," from her second volume (1787).[20] Yearsley's poem expresses no proprietary relation to the poet's garden. She rather distinguishes between Pope's verse, written solely to please his muse, and her own, sponsored by patrons. Yearsley does not approach the garden with impunity as an invited guest or even as a member of a touring party, but as a self-conscious "rustic" unsure of her welcome.

> Delightful Twick'nham! may a rustic hail
>   Thy leafy shades, where Pope in rapture stray'd,
> Clasp young-ey'd Ecstasy amid the vale,
>   And soar, full-pinion'd, with the buoyant maid?
>
> Ah! no, I droop! her fav'rite Bard she mourns;
>   Yet Twick'nham, shall thy groves assist my song;
> For while, with grateful love my bosom burns,
>   Soft Zephyr bears the artless strain along.
>
> (1–8)

Yearsley's late-century apotheosis contrasts poignantly with Pope's account of the "kind Muses" who met him as he "stray'd" in Windsor Forest. Those had "gently press'd [his] hand, and said, Be Ours" ("Hymn," 4), a chaste simulacrum of the marriage or love affair he might long for but would always be denied. Pope's somber version of his union with the muse acknowledges the severe limitations imposed by his body and his adherence to Catholicism. Yearsley, writing forty-three years after his death, imagines only the poet's blissful freedom to stray untrammelled over his own property, accompanied by a muse more like a concubine than the wife-substitute of Pope's "Hymn." Where Pope had forsaken dreams of power, property, and romantic love for poetry, Yearsley imagines him ravished by unlimited creative power, clasping his ecstatic muse and soaring above the landscape.

Yearsley's glance strains upward in her first stanza, hoping to glimpse the soaring bard. Her second "droops" back, first into Twickenham's reality: Pope died long ago, and the leafy shades now mourn rather than inspire their favorite poet. Yearsley also subsides into her own predicament. She must not aspire to Pope's unlimited heights but must write "with grateful love" in strains blown horizontally by breezes, toward her patrons, rather than upward over Twickenham's groves. The rest of the 52-line poem develops Yearsley's situation. She is evidently the guest of a wealthy couple, Maro and Emma, names redolent of his classical learning and her leisured sensibility.

Emma's pet lamb, spared from preying dogs or human slaughter (lines 9–16), represents their pastoral existence. Yearsley imagines both Maro and Emma weeping over the lamb's eventual death, "Nor will the pang Lactilla's bosom spare" (20). A kind of private laureate, Yearsley will celebrate the pair's exquisite sensibilities. Dismissing her premonition of the lamb's tragic death, however, Yearsley concentrates on the friendship she feels privileged to share and inspired to sing (lines 21–32). Unlike Pope's, who clasped his muse and soared upward at will, Yearsley's poetic flight is monitored by her learned patron, Maro. Maro graciously encourages her untaught "native Genius" (32).

> See, Maro points the vast, the spacious way,
>   Where strong Idea may on Rapture spring:
> I mount!—Wild Ardour shall ungovern'd stray;
>   Nor dare the mimic pedant clip my wing.
>
> (33–36)

Maro permits Yearsley to "stray," like her imagined Pope, into the poetic sky. That acquired permission, however, distinguishes Yearsley from her Twickenham predecessor. Her defiance of pedants, moreover, reminds readers of her deficient education. When Yearsley cries, "*Rule*! what art *thou*? Thy limits I disown!" (37), hers is not the sentiment of Pope, who blasted such critics secure in his mastery of "those *Rules* of old *discover'd*, not *devis'd*" ("Essay on Criticism," 89), the rules of classical Greece and Rome. Yearsley's is the defiance of a self-taught milkwoman, sanctioned by her patron's indulgence.

Maro invites Yearsley to soar, just as a conscientious host might invite his guest to ride. She soars on not "full-pinion'd" but borrowed wings. Yearsley concludes by assuring readers that, while she may not know the classical rules of composition, her verse is nevertheless guided by ethical precepts (line 45). Lest anyone misconstrue her delight in creativity, she pledges that "when soft'ning pleasure would invade my breast; / To [precept] my struggling spirit shall resign" (46–47). This promise, again, differentiates Yearsley from Pope. While the genteel male poet achieved fame by "clasp[ing] young-ey'd Ecstasy amid the vale," the laboring-class female must maintain her reputation by sinking to rest "on [precept's] cold bosom" (48). While no pedant may clip her wings, Yearsley's prudent wish not to offend readers effactually checks her creative flight. She finally bids farewell to Twickenham's groves, enjoining local maidens who stroll there to "reflect how soon / Lactilla saw, and sighing left the scene" (51–52). Not for Yearsley are either Lady Mary's scorn or Carter's and More's acquisitive impulse. After reflecting on the relation between her career and Pope's, Yearsley relinquishes the scene that inspired her comparison. Her poem abjures furtive ambition like Carter's or imaginative escape like More's, for frank acknowledgment that a milkwoman-poet has no business in Pope's garden.

Anna Seward, writing to Mrs. Childers in 1804, completes the spectrum of women's responses to Pope's garden and its creative associations.[21] Seward had been reading a five-volume edition of Lady Mary Wortley Montagu's letters, and she had confessed her irritation with Lady Mary's avowed contempt for Pope. Seward assures Mrs. Childers that Pope's anger with Lady Mary was justified, "since, in the zenith of his admiration, it reached his ear, that she had lyingly called him 'the thing of sound without sense.' Where was her own sense so to call the more than Horace of his time?" (*Letters*, 6:146). Seward finds particularly exasperating Lady Mary's description of Pope's grotto "in her pointless satire, the Court of Dulness" (6:149). Seward persistently defended the literary glories of Queen Anne's reign, often to preface her claim that England currently boasted even greater poetic riches. Lady Mary's dismissal of a site frequented by "all the brightness of the famous poetic galaxy" thus affronted both Seward's critical judgment and, by extension, her stature as heir to the Augustan poets.

But Lady Mary's cynicism most distresses Seward. "With what different ideas did I, in my youthful years, meditate the same scene," Seward cries. She produces, as illustration, a sonnet "On Reading A Description of Pope's Gardens at Twickenham." She claims she wrote the poem in her "youthful years," although undoubtedly she revised it to convey her mature perspective.[22]

> Ah! might I range each hallow'd bower and glade
>   Museus cultur'd, many a raptur'd sigh
>   Would that dear local consciousness supply
>   Beneath his willow, in his grotto's shade,
> Whose roof his hand with ores and shells inlaid!
>   How sweet to watch, with reverential eye,
>   Through the sparr'd arch, the streams he oft survey'd,
>   Thine, blue Thamesis, gently wandering by?

This is the poet's triumph, and it towers
  O'er life's pale ills, his consciousness of powers
  That lift his memory from oblivion's gloom;
Secure a train of these recording hours,
  By his idea deck'd with tender bloom,
  For spirits rightly touch'd, through ages yet to come.

Lady Mary's spirit, by contrast, was not "rightly touched"; her inability to appreciate Pope's grotto seems comparatively corrupt. "These innocent and delightful enthusiasms are real blessings to the mind in which they spring," comments Seward (*Letters*, 6:149). But the sonnet records more than Seward's championship of her predecessor against his (in her estimate) mean-spirited adversary. It also reveals Seward's competitive estimate of Pope's gifts, her almost literal longing to stand in his creative shoes.

Ann Yearsley gazed skyward toward the soaring poet, only to murmur "Ah, no." Her sigh acknowledged the ineradicable distance between herself and Pope. Anna Seward's octave recreates Twickenham from Pope's personal vantage. She imagines roaming from bower to willow to grotto, sighing because Pope himself stood in these precise spots and enjoyed the same view of the Thames. Seward's "local consciousness" impresses her not with Pope's absence or superiority but with the delightful prospect of becoming Pope, or at least sharing his perspective, while she surveys his domain.

The sonnet's concluding sestet is more ambiguous. "This is the poet's triumph" ostensibly refers to the consoling thoughts Pope enjoyed while contemplating the Thames from his grotto. Secure in his immortal gifts, Pope knew that "spirits rightly touch'd, through ages yet to come" would revere his memory. Seward's demonstrative "this," however, also refers back to the particular experience described in her octave: Anna Seward's imaginary visit to Pope's garden. "The poet's triumph," in this reading, is his reincarnation in Seward's consciousness. Anna Seward materializes in Pope's garden as his heir, destined not only to defend his reputation but, as his creative disciple, to extend Pope's triumph. Such a reading of this sonnet seems strained only outside the context of Seward's lifelong relation to Pope. Throughout her career, she quarreled with, analyzed, defended, appropriated, and revised Pope's poems. With "On Reading a Description of Pope's Gardens," she may intend only a lyrical tribute to his enduring appeal. The ambiguous syntax of her sonnet's central turn, however, undermines Seward's purpose. By assimilating Pope's "local consciousness" to the favored poetic form of her mature career, Seward suggests the magnitude of her aspiration.

This brief survey indicates the complexity of eighteenth-century women's responses to Alexander Pope. Pope and his garden represented the relation between artist and creative power, a vexed issue for contemporary women. They were uncertain, at first, of their right to "attempt the pen."[23] But later, emerging cautiously into the literary marketplace, eighteenth-century women probed Twickenham's metaphorical implications. Their assessments suggest the range of possible female responses to Pope, by readers variously educated and of different social and economic status. Individual gifts and temperaments, changing literary tastes, and women's growing share in the literary market throughout the century preclude a static definition of Pope's relation to his eighteenth-century women readers. Women's responses to Pope's garden also belie any conclusion that women passively received Pope's gender ideology. Carter's and Yearsley's wistful poems, for example, announce but finally cancel feminine ambitions. Both poems, while conciliatory, indicate painful awareness that cultural demands for feminine submission and propriety exacerbate masculine poetic hegemony. That Carter and Yearsley accede does not prove that they sanctioned these constraints. Their poems intimate resistance as well as submission. That Pope and his garden represent a locus of struggle to all these writers does not prove he was women's oppressor. Pope often figures in women's writings because he appears, as to Lady Mary, vulnerable; as to More, pleasurable; and as to Seward, an eligible predecessor.

Women's responses also do not indicate—as Joseph Wittreich has concluded of Milton—that Pope was really a feminist.[24] Rather, Pope's attitude toward women tempered complex experience with reductive contemporary ideas. We may gauge, from the result, one important boundary of Pope's creative imagination. Pope also struggled, in his *Iliad* translation, to fulfill the role of scholarly classical translator, while assimilating women into a traditionally male audience. To the modern reader, Pope's notes directed toward women segregate and stigmatize his female readers. To contemporaries, the same notes encouraged women's unprecedented familiarity with Homer. His critics attempted to sabotage Pope's literary reputation by branding him a ladies' poet. But women rewarded Pope's gesture by cherishing his *Iliad* throughout the century. Many also developed a rather proprietary attitude toward his canon, scrutinizing Pope's constructions of femininity with proportionate interest. Their responses encompassed many issues besides gender, ranging from Pope's possible function as mentor, to his ethical and political philosophies. Women refused to abide by Pope's definition of their interests in the *Iliad*, although some modern scholars assume that Pope's significance, for eighteenth-century women readers, inhered in his constructions of gender. By forgetting the range and perspicuity of contemporary women's responses, we have not only abridged the rich history of Pope's critical reception but unwittingly abetted his representations of a shallow, passive femininity.

Pope's eighteenth-century women readers, their opinions finally enriching critical discussion, have long been shadowy figures. Although information about them is increasingly available,[25] their group portrait remains unsketched. Or perhaps a portrait of Pope's typical woman reader exists but its significance has gone unrecognized. While fanciful, such an identification would solve the mystery of Pope's most enigmatic portrait, painted by Charles Jervas while Pope was translating the *Iliad* (see frontispiece). In this portrait, Pope sits in an armchair wearing a blue-gray suit, pensively daydreaming beneath a bust of Homer. Behind the poet's chair, a shoeless young woman in a dark gold satin dress stretches on tiptoe, grasping a large book in her left hand while, with her right, pulling aside the heavy green drapery that obstructs a high shelf.[26] As Mack has observed, the woman resembles neither Blount sister (*Pope*, 343), although the painting was traditionally said to represent Pope and Martha Blount (Wimsatt, 21). If Jervas intended her as an allegorical figure, a representation of Pope's muse or even of life's distractions, her purpose remains obscure (Mack, *Pope*, 343).

Whatever her original function in the painting, this young woman suggests several characteristics of Pope's eighteenth-century women readers. Her shoelessness and her glance over her shoulder toward Pope and the viewer intimate deference; she evidently wishes to avoid disturbing the poet from his reverie. These characteristics may also indicate stealth, in a literal rendering of women's circumstances. Women often read poetry in snatches during precious leisure hours, sometimes despite parents' or husbands' disapproval. The painting's figure, moreover, must stretch while pushing aside a heavy curtain to reach the book, most likely a volume of Pope's Homer. Although Pope encouraged women to read his Homer, many cultural obstacles impeded women's familiarity with classical literature. Richard Steele and Joseph Addison, for example, reiterated women's domestic priorities and intellectual deficiency throughout their periodicals. Although the *Tatler* and *Spectator* condemned educational programs that refined women's bodies while neglecting their minds, reading was clearly reserved for rare intervals of leisure between household chores.[27] Perhaps this young woman fears that, just as she grasps her prize, a stern parent or tutor—or even Pope—will interrupt and demand that she complete her needlework before indulging in Homeric reading.

The postures and expressions of the two figures also delineate the distinct attitudes of contemporary men and women toward literature. The poet sits at ease, oblivious to the young woman as he dreams of Homer. Although Pope appears tiny in proportion to his chair, the viewer focuses on him instantly not only because of his central position but because his face, wig, hands, and linen are bathed in light. The poet's abstraction thus appears a holy or visionary experience, the vital creativity that produced Pope's Homer. Even the poet's gleaming armchair suggests that gentlemanly leisure promotes genius. Pope's pose might represent masculine domination of early eighteenth-century English literature. Proud of their superior educations, complacent in their possession of leisure, genteel and aristocratic men presided over most genres. Women resembled the figure in Jervas's painting: preferably engaged in household tasks, they tiptoed behind the masculine throne.

Such projects as Pope's translation, however, were steadily making classical masterpieces available to the unlettered. Timorously but persistently, women approached texts previously reserved for privileged men. Their responses would be overshadowed by masculine achievements, even as this young woman is obscured by Pope's chair. But Pope himself, secure in his domination of the portrait and of the literary scene, facilitated women's conditional access to classical translations, and he later encouraged several as professional writers. In Jervas's painting, the poet's expression is serene and gentle; if he is aware of the young woman behind him, her activity does not irritate him. If this painting intentionally represented Pope and a woman reader, his pose would suggest toleration, at worst benign neglect.

The poet refrains from interrupting her surreptitious activity, as the woman grasps a volume disclosing to her a portion of the cultural riches that have palpably enraptured their translator. If the moment dramatized continued, we might see this satin-clad woman glide away with Pope's Homer, and perhaps—after slipping on her shoes—steal into the poet's garden to read his *Iliad*.

1

"Appeals to the Ladies":
Pope and His Iliad Readers

After praising Alexander Pope's translation of Homer's *Iliad* as a "poetical wonder,"[1] Samuel Johnson censured one aspect of Pope's commentary.

> It has, however, been objected with sufficient reason, that there is in the commentary too much of unseasonable levity and affected gaiety; that too many appeals are made to the ladies, and the ease which is so carefully preserved is sometimes the ease of a trifler. Every art has its terms and every kind of instruction its proper style; the gravity of common critics may be tedious, but is less despicable than childish merriment. (*Lives*, 3:240)

Johnson's remark illustrates the predicament of any scholar analyzing a text at a distance from its historic context. Our late twentieth-century response to Johnson's comment is likely to compound the difficulty. Approaching Pope's commentary from his late eighteenth-century perspective, Johnson was baffled by Pope's avoidance of scholarly "gravity." At first glance, Johnson's stricture seems to anticipate current feminist responses. He appears repulsed by Pope's attempt to usher women readers through the epics by diverting them with "childish merriment." The friend of such women as Elizabeth Carter, Charlotte Lennox, and Hester Lynch Thrale must have understood that "unseasonable levity and affected gaiety" were not necessary to engage women in Homer.

A reading mindful of context diminishes the feminist tendency of Johnson's criticism. Just before discussing Pope's *Iliad*, Johnson prefers Pope's *The Rape of the Lock* to Boileau's *Le Lutrin* because "the freaks, and humours, and spleen, and vanity of women . . . do more to obstruct the happiness of life in a year than the ambition of the clergy in many centuries" (*Lives*, 3:234). His remark about Pope's commentary reflects less sympathy for women readers than the dismay of a conservative scholar confronted with outrageous departures from critical style. Pope had addressed unlearned women in an unscholarly manner in his notes. By failing to observe the "proper style" of a grave "kind of instruction," Pope had transgressed the fundamental principle of decorum.

A deconstructionist might observe that the anomalous levity of Pope's commentary reveals a gap in his text, exposing many of his assumptions as poet, translator, and cultural commentator. I share this perception, but my feminist-historical focus suggests a different approach to Pope's translations, through his constructions of femininity and his relation to women readers. In her preface to *Women's Place in Pope's World* (1989), Valerie Rumbold regretted that she "had to leave out . . . the question of women as subject and audience in Pope's major translations" and most "of the comments on his work by contemporary women readers" (xv). I take these omissions from Rumbold's fine study as an opportunity for my own, because Pope's Homer epitomizes his early relation to women readers.

During his lifetime, Pope's enemies derided him as "the ladies' play-thing" because he directed some of his verse, including his translations, to female as well as male readers.[2] Critics from John Ozell to Joseph Weston considered couplets less "masculine" than blank verse. Furthermore, Pope threatened some contemporaries because he invited women to participate, albeit as consumers, in their male-dominated culture. In the late twentieth century, however, Pope's writings have attracted severe analyses by scholars, such as Laura Brown and Ellen Pollak, who have numbered his constructions of femininity among the worst examples of enlightenment misogyny; to some Pope appears dangerous because he defined women's role as passive participants in that culture.[3] Such contradictory perceptions warrant investigation of the historical context in which Pope produced his translations and his readers received them. Johnson's opinion, expressed sixty-one years after Pope completed the *Iliad* (1715–20), suggests that the expectations that guided and greeted Pope's translations had already faded, to the extent that Johnson found Pope's "appeals to the ladies" perplexing.

Hans-Robert Jauss's suggestion that we consider the public horizon of expectations when assessing an older text is particularly appropriate in the case of Pope's Homer. In "Literary History as a Challenge to Literary Theory," Jauss has reasserted the importance of readers' aesthetic expectations to literary history.[4] Any work must conform somewhat to cultural expectations, generic and ideological, or risk appearing outrageous or even unintelligible to its audience. According to Jauss, mediocre or "culinary" writings tend to remain entirely within the boundaries of dominant cultural assumptions, and "classic" writings struggle against those boundaries, questioning current tastes and values. Jauss's theory helps explain the contradictory reception of Pope's feminine constructions by contemporaries and modern readers. Though conforming to early eighteenth-century expectations of the epic in most areas (for example, in his use of the heroic couplet and of elevated diction and in his scholarly apparatus), Pope departed noticeably from convention in his direct appeals to women readers. Despite his many concessions to convention, the mere fact that Pope sought and addressed women readers gratified some contemporaries and shocked others. But to modern feminists Pope's adherence to convention in the tone and content of those "appeals to the ladies" obliterates any appearance of iconoclasm. The horizon apparent to Pope's earliest readers has long since melted from view, leaving a different horizon of expectations in its place.

Jauss's argument directs us back toward the context in which Pope produced his translation, to the expectations of his earliest audiences, as the basis for a study of the poet's relationship with his women readers. The eighteenth century had its own feminist agenda, according to which Pope's choices may be assessed. With Jauss's suggestion in mind, we perceive that Samuel Johnson's comment raises several pertinent issues, perhaps more discernible to us than to Johnson. As a young poet, why and how did Pope direct his publications to an audience that included women? Which cultural influences prompted Pope to adopt a certain tone and style when addressing women readers? To what extent, if any, did Pope modify the attitudes he learned? Finally, how did women readers themselves respond to Pope's translations: Were they effectively confined to a "childish" interpretation of Homer? Did they detect and resent Pope's condescension? The answers to these questions clarify Pope's attitudes and suggest certain trends in women's responses that persisted throughout the century.

Because Pope both translated and commented on the *Iliad* but contributed only twelve books and the postscript to the *Odyssey*, I confine my analysis to the former epic. But eighteenth-century readers were uncertain about the extent of collaboration involved in the translation of the *Odyssey*, and they usually considered both epics Pope's work. For that reason, we will find several women referring to "Mr. Pope's *Odyssey*," remarks I have included as responses to Pope's Homer. These remarks also suggest that William Broome and Elijah Fenton (doubtless with Pope's aid) successfully duplicated certain aspects of the *Iliad*—such as refined imagery and elevated diction— appreciated by contemporary readers.

Dryden: Pope's Epic Predecessor

That Pope intended his translation's audience to include women at all is significant. Translations had been appearing in increasing numbers since the late seventeenth century, but most of them were directed to literate male readers. In the preface to his edition of *Terence's Comedies and Plautus's Comedies* (1694), a random but representative example, Lawrence Echard lists his intended readers as "the Dramatick Poets," "Schoolboys and Learners," and "Men of Sense and Learning."[5] Women are not invoked at all, and "the more ordinary sort of People" are mentioned only for the salutary effect that reading these plays might have on their morals. Pope's great predecessor and model, John Dryden, was certainly cognizant that his audience would include women longing for a fine English Virgil; his subscribers included a number of women aristocrats, actresses, and relatives.[6] Nevertheless, he addressed a select group of peers in the preface to his translation of Virgil's *Aeneid* (1697), dedicating his work to "Souls of the highest Rank, and truest Understanding," distinguished from those "warm young Men, who are not arriv'd so far as to discern the difference betwixt Fustian . . . and the true sublime."[7] When Pope boasted in his preface, "If my Author had the Wits of After Ages for his Defenders, his Translator has had the Beauties of the Present for his Advocates,"[8] he was not merely indulging in flattery but confirming his unprecedented courtship of women readers and subscribers for what he intended as a cultural monument.

We may grasp Pope's intention by comparing his commentary with that of John Dryden. In his preface to the *Iliad*, Pope devotes a paragraph to his disappointment "that Mr. Dryden did not live to translate the *Iliad*." He acknowledges Dryden's *Virgil* as the best of all previous translations into English, except for some flaws that "ought to be excused on account of the Haste he was obliged to write in" (*Poems*, 7:22). Dryden had translated Virgil's *Pastorals*, his *Georgics*, and the *Aeneid* in just three years, from 1694–97, under a contract with his publisher, Jacob Tonson. Like Pope's, Dryden's translation was supported by much of the aristocracy and the most distinguished society of his day. Unfortunately, dogged throughout the project by sickness and by business and financial worries, the aging poet had become embroiled in a bitter argument with Tonson over the distribution of subscription money. Partly from anger, partly from sheer weariness, Dryden retaliated by abridging his projected commentary.[9] He wrote Tonson in February 1696, declaring that his notes would now "be onely Marginall to help the unlearned, who understand not the poeti- call Fables. The Prefaces, as I intend them, will be somewhat more learned."[10] When the handsome folio was published, each of Dryden's original five-guinea subscribers was honored with an illustration fea- turing his or her title and coat of arms. As for the mere "vulgar" reader, Dryden explained in his postscript

> that the few Notes which follow, are *par maniere d'acquit*, because I had oblig'd myself by Articles, to do somewhat of that kind. . . . The Unlearn'd may have recourse to any Poetical Dictionary in *English*, for the Names of Persons, Places, or Fables, which the Learned need not. (*Works*, 6:810)

Dryden's ambivalence toward his unlearned readers is evident from the beginning of his observations.

In contrast, Dryden's dedicatory epistles are gracious, leisurely, even flattering. Here and elsewhere, the difference between the two poets' circumstances influenced their commentaries. Pope wrote at the commencement of his career. When he composed his preface in 1715, the Tories had not yet sunk into the disarray that characterized that party throughout the rest of his life. He could afford to invoke the magnanimous and fashionable opinion that parties were now obsolete. As John Aden and others have suggested, Pope's translation seems often to solicit toleration, sympathy, and national broad-mind- edness.[11] In his preface, Pope acknowledged the support of men and women, Tories and Whigs, Hanoverians and Jacobites. Even his pref- erence for domestic scenes appears to be an Addisonian campaign for reformed manners. Dryden, however, wrote as a defeated Jacobite at the unfortunate conclusion of a long career. As he confessed to

Lord Clifford in his dedication to the *Pastorals*, "I have found it not more difficult to Translate *Virgil*, than to find such Patrons as I desire" (*Works*, 6:3). In the essay dedicating the *Aeneid* to the Marquess of Normanby, Dryden insisted on addressing a small, select audience. This requirement suggests the tense relationship among the displaced old Jacobite, his subscribers, and the general public. His claim to appeal only to "souls of the . . . truest understanding" applied to readers with similar political sympathies, as well as to those with classical learning.

While Pope's preface introduces his readers to the "Beauties" of Homer's "wild Paradise" (*Poems*, 7:3), Dryden's dedication considers several controversies surrounding the *Aeneid*. As Stephen Zwicker has observed, lengthy digressions provided Dryden with opportunities for political allusions.[12] This emphasis accounts for much of the difference between Pope's treatment of women throughout the *Iliad* and Dryden's characterizations of Dido and Lavinia: Dryden was more interested in evoking political responses than in flattering female readers. Dryden devotes a substantial proportion of his dedication to a defense of Aeneas against "the Ladies; who will make a numerous Party against him, for being false to Love, in forsaking *Dido*. And I cannot much blame them. . . . Yet if I can bring him off, with Flying Colours, they may learn experience at her cost" (*Works*, 5:294). Dryden grants that Aeneas was indeed guilty of ingratitude, "for *Dido* had not only receiv'd his weather-beaten Troops before she saw him, and given them her protection, but had also offer'd them an equal share in her Dominion" (5:295). But Dido was "ungrateful to the Memory of her first Husband, doting on a Stranger; enjoyed, and afterwards forsaken by him" (5:298).

Aeneas's desertion at the command of Jupiter was Dido's punishment for folly and faithlessness. Dryden finds Aeneas's behavior insensitive and speculates that Virgil resorted to Jupiter's intervention to justify his hero's departure. By this point, however, the reader cognizant of Dryden's political sympathies might have recognized in Dido a veiled warning to England.[13] The nation that had proved faithless to its "first husband," doting on a "stranger" after hospitably receiving his troops, might find itself in a similar predicament. Like Aeneas, whose troops "plunder'd" Carthage before escaping to new conquests (Dryden, *Aeneid* 4.580–90), William was criticized for depleting England's wealth to support his foreign wars. The analogy is imperfect but suggestive, and it indicates that Dryden's attitude toward Dido resulted from the political interpretation underlying his analysis of "this Noble Episode" (*Works*, 5:297). The British people, not merely ladies, were the objects of his scorn. They resembled the people of Carthage, "naturally perfidious; for [Virgil] gives their Character in their Queen" (5:299).

Dryden refers to the feminine character only once in his notes, describing Lavinia's mourning for Turnus at the end of the *Aeneid*.

> This Fable of *Lavinia* includes a secret Moral; that Women in their choice of Husbands, prefer the younger of their Suitors to the Elder; are insensible of Merit, fond of Handsomeness; and generally speaking, rather hurried away by their Appetite, than govern'd by their Reason. (*Works*, 6:834)

And this is from the writer characterized by Jean Hagstrum as "the poet of both erotic and ideal love"![14] Perhaps Dryden again alludes to the political faithlessness of James II's people, but he offers the remark without mitigation or sympathy.

Dryden's commentary here invites comparison with, for example, Pope's introduction of Helen in Book 3 of the *Iliad*, in which he grants that "the Reader has naturally an Aversion to this pernicious Beauty" but counters that Helen's personality is so sympathetically portrayed by Homer "as to make every Reader no less than *Menelaus* himself, inclin'd to forgive her at least, if not to love her. We are afterwards confirm'd in this partiality" (*Poems*, 7:199 n. 165). Pope's graciousness toward Helen not only confirms Hagstrum's sense of him as a prime mover toward the "age of sensibility" but must also have pleased many women readers, unaccustomed to seeing their sex treated so tenderly in an imposing literary work. Compared to Dryden's treatment of Dido and Lavinia, Pope's characterization of Helen is compassionate and open-minded, if in retrospect contributing to a current fashion for pitiful fallen women. It is no wonder that an enemy sneered in 1719 that Pope had made Homer "*fine*—the *Beaus* and *Belles* to please."[15]

Bringing Homer to the Tea Table: Addison and Steele's Periodicals and Pope's **Iliad**

Like Lawrence Echard, Pope intended his epic to have an edifying effect on "more ordinary" people, but such readers figured as an important part of his prospective audience. Just eighteen years after

Dryden published the *Aeneid* (1697), Pope addressed an expanded reading public, including not only aristocrats and literate gentry but prosperous merchants, professionals, and women. This was the generation of readers primed by *The Tatler* and *The Spectator* to seek entertainment both refined and refining. In their pioneering essays, Addison and Steele had instructed men to cherish their wives, and women to become engaging companions for their husbands. One pleasure the sexes could share was reading; Addison trained his audience in the cultivation of imagination and the principles of literary criticism. When Pope sought the support of a wide spectrum of wealthy and influential people, he had in mind a project that would appeal to the readership of both sexes that was encouraged by Steele and Addison. According to Pat Rogers, of the 574 *Iliad* subscribers, 8 percent were women. For the *Odyssey*, 13 percent of 609 subscribers were women, a percentage only surpassed in that era by the 15 percent female subscribers to John Gay's *Poems* (1720).[16] Pope's 8 percent, rising to 13 percent, may reflect only the traditional belief that Homer had composed the *Iliad* for men, the *Odyssey* for women. But it may also indicate Pope's relative success in pleasing women readers of the *Iliad*, which persuaded even more of his well-connected women friends to patronize the *Odyssey*. Pope's search for female subscribers may be reflected in one of the few surviving advertisements of his subscription campaign, which appears on a leaf of the five-canto *Rape of the Lock* (1714),[17] that poem dedicated to a belle and "intended only to divert a few young Ladies."

Pope appealed to women readers of the *Iliad* in two ways, one of which conformed to the expectations of both male and female readers. This first technique capitalized on a trend reflected in England since the success of Colley Cibber's *Love's Last Shift* (1696) and most recently gratified by Nicholas Rowe's *Jane Shore* (1713). Cibber's genteel comedies and Rowe's she-tragedies attracted audiences enjoying a cultural movement away from cynical wit and toward fine feeling. Instead of heartless rakes, these new dramas featured long-suffering heroines. Their male characters were heroic or villainous according to whether they reformed themselves or continued to persecute their wives. Addison and Steele encouraged the trend in such essays as *Spectator* 142 (Addison et al., 2:60–64), in which Steele published his love letters to his wife.

Pope participated in this trend by sentimentalizing the *Iliad* in ways that evoke pity for the heroic characters rather than more stereotypically masculine responses, such as anger or martial fervor.[18] In the scenes between Hector and Andromache, especially, Pope presented "an amiable Picture of conjugal Love, as oppos'd to that of unlawful Passion" (*Poems*, 7:349 n. 462). Pope's concern with the Trojan couple confirms his effort to guide contemporary taste; in 1749, in the second edition of his popular *Letters . . . by Sir Thomas Fitzosborne, Bart.*, William Melmoth declared that "the most pleasing picture in the whole Iliad, is, I think, the parting of Hector and Andromache."[19] Juxtaposing passages from Pope's translation with selections from Dryden's, Melmoth disparaged Dryden's "cold and unpoetical fidelity to the mere letter of the original," compared with Pope's license, which "by heightening the piece with a few judicious touches, has wrought it up in all the affecting spirit of tenderness and poetry" (Cronin and Doyle, 40). Melmoth's response suggests that by midcentury Pope had persuaded several generations of readers not only to accept his interpretation of Homeric values but also to find those values pertinent and instructive.

A comparison of Pope's rendering of the parting of Hector and Andromache in book 6 with the versions of John Dryden, Anne Dacier, and Richmond Lattimore illustrates Pope's appeal to contemporary taste. In Lattimore's modern, literal translation of the scene, Hector consoles Andromache by imagining a glorious future for their son: "Some day let them say of him: 'He is better by far than his father,' / as he comes in from the fighting; and let him kill his enemy / and bring home the blooded spoils, and delight the heart of his mother."[20] In Dryden's translation of the scene (1693), Hector predicts that, after Astyanax's first battle,

> Some aged Man, who lives this act to see,
>
> . . . .
> May say the Son in Fortitude and Fame
> Out-goes the Mark; and drowns his Father's Name:
> That at the words his Mother may rejoyce:
> And add her Suffrage to the publick Voice.
>
> (6.164–69)

While Dryden's Astyanax will "bring his *Trojans* Peace and Triumph home" (163), Madame Dacier's, like Lattimore's, brings home more tangible trophies in her *L'Iliade d'Homere* (1st ed., 1711). Hector implores "Puissant Jupiter, & tous les autres Dieux de l'Olympe" that when "ses peuples en le voyant revenir vainqueur de ses ennemies,

& chargé des sanglantes despouïlles de leurs braves chefs, s'escrient sur son passage ce Prince est beaucoup plus vaillant que son pere: & puisse sa mere, tesmoin de ses éloges, sentir toutes la joye d'avoir un fils si grand & si vertueux."[21] In Pope's version, Hector prays for Astyanax,

> So when triumphant from successful Toils,
> Of Heroes slain he bears the reeking Spoils,
> Whole Hosts may hail him with deserv'd Acclaim,
> And say, This Chief transcends his Father's Fame:
> While pleas'd amidst the gen'ral Shouts of *Troy*,
> His Mother's conscious Heart o'erflows with Joy.

(6.610–15)

Of the four versions, Dryden's is the grandest; the son's accomplishments—his restoration of civic ideals—will be celebrated by the admiring public, of which Andromache is only a part, adding her voice to the general acclamations. Lattimore's Astyanax, however, comes home to delight his mother's heart, but Hector imagines her pleasure at the sight of his "blooded spoils." Dacier's interpretation falls between these two: Astyanax returns burdened with "des sanglantes despouïlles de leurs braves chefs," but his mother's "joye" is caused by the peoples' "éloges," not by the sight of bloody spoils. Dacier specifies that Andromache will feel all the joy of having a son "si grand & si vertueux," and similarly in Dryden's text, Andromache admires her son's civic achievements.

Pope's translation differs from all these. Astyanax is imagined the hero of "Whole Hosts" after capturing the "reeking Spoils" of a pile of slain enemies, an image more princely than Lattimore's and less euphemistic than Dryden's. As in Dacier's text, the heart of Pope's Andromache "o'erflows with Joy" at the shouts, not at the sight of the "blooded spoils." But Pope refrains from defining the cause of Andromache's joy; her heart is merely "conscious," which suggests a generalized vulnerability or tenderness as much as it does awareness of popular acclaim or pride in her son's strength. In his note to the scene, Pope is quite explicit about what he considers admirable in Hector's speech.

> Tho' the chief Beauty of this Prayer consists in the paternal Piety shown by *Hector*, yet it wants not a fine Stroake at the end, to continue him in the Character of a tender Lover of his Wife, when

he makes one of the motives of his Wish, to be the Joy she shall receive on hearing her Son applauded. (*Poems*, 7:357 n.615)

Hector and Andromache exemplify the "passionate friendship" that was beginning to be extolled as the basis of the ideal marriage (Hagstrum, 132). Pope further suggests that the gladdening of a woman's "conscious Heart" is a most desirable goal for her husband and children.

A second comparison of the same scene with Knightly Chetwood's version (1693) further illustrates Pope's contemporary idealization of the Trojan couple.[22] Chetwood's Hector and Andromache embody the seventeenth-century ideal of heroic love. Hector prophesies that his son will "equal me, wear, and deserve the Crown" (6.102).

> Then in the Mother's Arms he puts the Child,
> With *troubl'd* Joy, in flowing *Tears* she *smil'd*.
> *Beauty* and *Grief* shew'd all their Pomp and Pride,
> Whilst those soft Passions did her Looks divide.
> This Scene even Hector's Courage melted down,
> But soon recovering, with a *Lover*'s Frown:
> *Madam* (says he) *these Fancies put away*.
>
> (6.109–15)

Chetwood's translation abounds in the kinds of paradox featured in the love and honor debates of heroic drama. Andromache's passionate beauty tempts the Almanzor in Hector to abandon his role as warrior. He is "melted" by the "Pomp and Pride" of that irresistible combination, "Beauty and Grief," viewed as a "Scene" in "her Looks." Hector's stern rejoinder seems as much a reminder to himself to repress his amorous fancies as a command to his wife to suppress her sorrowful ones.

In Pope's version, Hector does not melt. His compassion, not his lust, is moved by Andromache's maternal fears.

> He spoke, and fondly gazing on her Charms
> Restor'd the pleasing Burden to her Arms;
> Soft on her fragrant Breast the Babe she laid,
> Hush'd to repose, and with a Smile survey'd.
> The troubl'd Pleasure soon chastis'd by Fear,
> She mingled with the Smile a tender Tear.
> The soften'd Chief with kind Compassion view'd
> And dry'd the falling Drops, and thus pursu'd.

> *Andromache*! my Soul's far better part,
> Why with untimely Sorrow heaves thy Heart?
>
> (6.616–25)

Pope's emphasis is clearly on a different kind of love. Andromache's distress arouses not amorous passion but kindness and tenderness in her husband, a gratifying advance in sympathy as far as many of Pope's genteel contemporaries were concerned. Hector's address to his wife as his "better part"—his spiritual part—also reflects a more exalted notion of the wife's role in a marriage.[23] Such anachronistic complaisance toward women indicates that Pope deliberately interpreted his characters in ways that would appeal to readers interested in the concept of affectionate marriage.

One further example illustrates the various ways Pope's commentary functions with his text to insinuate values edifying for all readers but perhaps particularly welcome to women. In book 11, Agamemnon leads the Greeks to a near rout of the Trojans. Pope's introductory comment explains that Agamemnon's exploits in this book complete the hero's rehabilitation, in the reader's estimate, from the despot of book 1 to a paradigm of kingly valor. Pope nevertheless qualifies his readers' response to Agamemnon's onslaught. In the midst of the battle, as Hector attempts to rally his troops, Agamemnon performs a fresh burst of mayhem.

> Ye sacred Nine, Celestial Muses! tell,
> Who fac'd him first, and by his Prowess fell?
> The great *Iphidamas*, the bold and young,
> From sage *Antenor* and *Theano* sprung;
> Whom from his Youth his Grandsire *Cisseus* bred,
> And nurs'd in Thrace, where snowy flocks are fed.
> Scarce did the Down his rosy Cheeks invest,
> And early Honour warm his gen'rous Breast,
> When the kind Sire consign'd his Daughter's Charms
> (*Theano*'s Sister) to his youthful Arms.
> But call'd to Glory by the Wars of *Troy*,
> He leaves untasted the first Fruits of Joy;
> From his lov'd Bride departs with melting Eyes,
> And swift to aid his dearer Country flies.
> . . . .
> Oh worthy better Fate! oh early slain!
> Thy Country's Friend; and virtuous, tho' in vain!
> No more the Youth shall join his Consort's side,
> At once a Virgin, and at once a Bride!

No more with Presents her Embraces meet,
Or lay the Spoils of Conquest at her Feet,
On whom his Passion, lavish of his Store,
Bestow'd so much, and vainly promis'd more!

(11.281–94, 311–18)

Pope composed three notes for this passage. At the invocation of the Muses, he observes the dramatic effect of Homer's use of this device: "By means of this Apostrophe, the Imagination of the Reader is so fill'd, that he seems not only present, but Active in the Scene to which the skill of the Poet has transported him" (*Poems*, 8:47 n. 281). Given this cue, Pope works to evoke an emotional response from his reader. Yet Homer has skillfully focused the reader's attention on a digression. Pope observes that "Homer here gives us the History of this Iphidamas, his Parentage, the Place of his Birth, and many Circumstances of his private Life. This he does to diversify his Poetry, and to soften with some amiable Embellishments the continual Horrors that must of Necessity strike the Imagination in an uninterrupted Narration of Blood and Slaughter" (8:47–48 n. 283). Finally, lest modern propriety interfere with sympathy for this young hero, Pope cautions, "That the Reader may not be shock'd at the marriage of *Iphidamas* with his Mother's Sister, it may not be amiss to observe from *Eustathius*, that Consanguinity was no Impediment in Greece in the Days of Homer" (8:48 n. 290).

Pope tempers the glory of Agamemnon's deed by enlisting the reader's heartfelt sympathy for young Iphidamas. Further, he regards the story of Iphidamas's civilian life as a kind of pastoral or romantic interlude, encouraging the reader to weep over this tale of patriotic virtue leading to unfulfilled love. Homer had achieved poignancy by contrasting his death with the magnificent good fortune of Iphidamas in Thrace. Although orphaned, he had been raised by his royal grandfather and married to a princess worthy an enormous dowry. But all this felicity cannot prevent Iphidamas's brutal death at Agamemnon's hands. Pope focuses instead on Iphidamas's marriage, described as a great love affair. His bride's personal charms are given to his passionate embrace, and he leaves her "with melting Eyes," only because his country is even "dearer." The dowry with which Homer's Iphidamas won his wife becomes the "Presents" of an enamored lover, the "lavish . . . Store" of a grand passion.

Pope's exclamatory grief over the fruitless death of Iphidamas, an affectionate bridegroom and virtuous patriot, and over the cruel fate of his "Virgin . . . Bride" invites from the reader not only tears but assent to Pope's opinion of the nature of this tragedy. The "Blood and Slaughter" that constitute the *Iliad* are horrible because they deprive innocent young men, such as Iphidamas, of their expectations of love and marriage—the "Fruits of Joy." Iphidamas deserves a long and peaceful life in the arms of his "lov'd Bride." Instead, "unwept, uncover'd, on the Plain he lay, / While the proud Victor bore his Arms away" (11.320–21). Pope may have been translating a narration of military exploits, but the author of "Windsor Forest" never hesitates to suggest the inestimable value of domestic happiness in times of peace.

A literal rendering of the Iphidamas episode reveals quite a different emphasis. In John Ogilby's version (1660), similar to those of such chronologically disparate translators as George Chapman, Thomas Hobbes, and Richmond Lattimore, Iphidamas marries Theano's sister; "But Her he soon forsook to purchase Fame, / And with twelve Ships to help the Trojans came."[24] (Lattimore's Iphidamas goes "looking for glory / from the Achaians," 11.227–28.) The Homeric hero ventures not for pure love of his country but in hope of personal glory, or fame. Iphidamas is tragic in the Homeric sense because he dies before achieving a great reputation. Despite his prospects and ambitions, he is left a naked corpse on the battlefield. His name will linger only in the recitation of Agamemnon's victims. Pope's Iphidamas leaves for war in a different state of mind. The bridegroom "departs with melting eyes," torn between love and patriotism. Chapman's Renaissance hero's "grandsire gave his daughter to his love, / who straight his bridall chamber left."[25] Although in Chapman's translation, "Fame with affection strove, / And made him furnish twelve faire ships to lend faire Troy his hand" (11.195–96), in no version except Pope's is there the suggestion that Iphidamas's love for his bride presents even a momentary obstacle to his departure.

All other versions of the episode stress the irony of Iphidamas's death as a waste of material possessions; his marriage proved a poor bargain.

> Thus fell'st Thou hapless Youth! assisting *Troy*,
> Before thou didst thy beauteous Wife enjoy;
> Though thou a hundred Beeves on her bestow'dst
> And thousand Goates and Sheep by promise ow'dst.
>
> (Ogilby, 11.259–62)

To this, John Ogilby adds a marginal comment that dowries were given by bridegrooms to their brides' families in Homer's time. Of all the passages under comparison, Ogilby's is the only other translation to invite an emotional response ("Thus fell'st Thou hapless Youth!"), and yet the rationale for grief in Ogilby's text differs from that in Pope's translation. The implication of the passage, that Iphidamas will never be able to redeem his vast investment, bears little relation to Pope's image of the tragic lover, whose "Presents" (nothing so vulgar as "Beeves" or "Goates and Sheep") were tokens of his boundless affection. Once again, Pope moves toward a sentimental view of courtship and marriage. He romanticizes such institutions as the dowry, which here becomes a measure of affection. Theano is not merely another of Iphidamas's "unenjoyed" possessions but his "Consort." Pope suggests a loving bond absent from Homer and all other versions. By insisting on the importance of this digression, Pope draws his readers' attention to a highly personal interpretation of the original episode, carefully embroidered to present his timely ideal of gallant youth and marriage.

Such scenes as this one represent Pope's attempt to produce an epic pleasing and instructive to discriminating men and women. As Catherine Talbot later remarked of the *Odyssey*, "Mr. Pope's verse can give dignity to a *peg* or a *pig*, and the divine Eumaeus is so worthy a man, that I overlook the unlucky circumstance of his being a hogherd."[26] Pope's commentary continues his appeal to fastidious readers, as he carefully explains away even the appearance of lowness in his characters. Moreover, because the events of the last twenty years had left many people weary of martial aggression, Pope composed such notes as those about Iphidamas to maintain their attention during lengthy battle scenes. In book 11, Pope comments on Nestor's brief respite from battle (763–87), explaining that "the Poet here steals the Reader from the Battel, and relieves him by the Description of Nestor's Entertainment. . . . Without this piece of Conduct, the Frequency and Length of his Battels might fatigue the Reader, who could not so long be delighted with continued Scenes of Blood" (*Poems*, 8:69 n. 763). In book 15 in a note directed to readers whose interests are more domestic than martial, Pope compares Homer's epics to conduct books, "whereby his Reader may be inform'd how to regulate his own Affairs" (*Poems*, 8:202 n. 164). And in book 9, he transcribes Madame Dacier's comparison of ancient and modern modes of cookery (*Poems*, 7:446 n. 271), though Pope's representation of ancient cooking methods in his text is not as precise as hers.

Pope also includes sympathetic interpretations of Paris and Helen that are sure to appeal to contemporary beaus and belles. In book 6, Paris is characterized not as a monster but as "a *Bel-Esprit* and a *fine Genius*" overwhelmed by an unfortunate passion (*Poems*, 7:345 n. 390). Helen's characterization particularly demonstrates Pope's affinity with current culture. In book 6, Pope calls attention to "the Repentance of *Helena*" in a speech where she blames heaven for permitting her to live and describes Paris as her cursed fate. Pope comments that "she fairly gets quit of the Infamy of her Lover, and shews she has higher Sentiments of Honour than he. How very natural is all this in the like Characters to this day?" (*Poems*, 7:348 n. 432). "Characters," as in dramatic characters, is the key word in Pope's evocation of Helen's plight as a she-tragedy. In the English version of Dacier's *L'Iliade d'Homere* that Pope frequently consulted, John Ozell translates her comment on the same passage. Dacier argues that by complaints of divine intervention, "it seems that *Helen* wou'd thereby excuse, or diminish her Fault, as if it had not been in her Power to hinder what the Gods had resolv'd."[27] Pope eschews Dacier's skepticism, creating a Helen who resembles the victimized heroines of recent drama.

Pope's observations of Helen throughout the *Iliad* recall the epilogue he contributed to *Jane Shore* (1713), written by his friend Nicholas Rowe. In that poem (*Poems*, 6:113–15), Pope teased the ladies of the audience into sympathizing with Jane, the play's tragic heroine: "Prodigious this! the Frail one of our Play / From her own Sex should mercy find today!" (1–2). Pope's Helen resembles Jane, whom he had described as a "piece of failing flesh and blood, / In all the rest so impudently good" (47–48), more than she does Dacier's self-extenuating sinner. His characterization of the epic's "unfortunate Beauty" (*Poems*, 7:348 n. 432) capitalizes on popular fascination with doomed heroines, fallen but ennobled by repentance.

Pope made his *Iliad* appealing to contemporaries by adjusting certain scenes and characters to resemble the patterns of refinement suggested by genteel culture, such as plays and periodical essays. He instinctively shunned such models as the opera and fledgling novel. Still, his "high" text had been accused of barbarity by recent commentators.[28] By turning to such moderate arbiters of manners as Rowe, Steele, and Addison, Pope invested his translation and commentary with the most current available ideals of male and female behavior, not to mention a neutral political position calculated to attract patrons from both parties. He could then interpret Homer either as a moral exemplar or as a reflection of ancient crudity, as occasion offered. By rejecting such sources of psychology and manners as the novel, however, Pope did more than avoid scandalous associations. Such novelists as Aphra Behn and Delarivière Manley might have suggested alternative ways of characterizing or addressing women. Instead, Pope consciously aligned himself with a group of writers engaged in defining the nature and role of women in ever-narrowing terms, even as they invited women to expand their notions of themselves as cultural consumers. By doing so, he diminished the apparent novelty of his overt appeals to women readers of epic by framing those addresses in a conventional style. The horizon of expectations remained undisturbed, although Pope had inserted a new stratum in his implied female readership.

Laura Brown has observed that the "defenseless woman" of late seventeenth-century and early eighteenth-century tragedy was crucial to the evolution from aristocratic heroic drama to bourgeois domestic drama.[29] Dramatists demanded "sympathy, not judgment," from audiences witnessing the plight of heroines who were "economically impotent but dramatically vital" (442–43). In his epilogue to *Jane Shore*, for example, Pope directs the genteel women in the audience merely to pity Jane and amend their own hypocrisy. He does not address the problem of ameliorating similar predicaments in contemporary London, which would imply an adverse judgment of his culture. Real abandoned mistresses remained ciphers despite the enormous popularity of their fictional counterparts. In *Women and Print Culture*, Kathryn Shevelow has traced a similar process.[30] Women were invited into the readerships of early periodicals, but their roles were gradually transformed. Women readers of John Dunton's *Athenian Mercury* (1691–97) had been invited to participate in the journal's question-and-answer format, although their queries were often treated harshly. Steele and Addison edited or fabricated female correspondence, gradually all but eliminating participation by women (with the significant exception of Lady Mary Wortley Montagu), while promoting their own concepts of femininity. Ruth Salvaggio has described this phenomenon as "enlightened absence": configurations of femininity appeared everywhere in a culture drained of actual women's qualities or personalities.[31]

Although Pope, like Dunton, Steele, and Addison, was engaged in adapting a high cultural artifact to emerging bourgeois tastes and values, his choice of theatrical and essay models for his conceptions of women in the epic was not inevitable. His choice may seem surprising given his familiarity with the most recent French prose translation of Homer by Anne Dacier. In *Des Causes de la Corruption du Goust*, an essay defending Homer from "modern" criticism of his primitivism and barbarity, Dacier had insisted on an interpretation of the epics as moral allegory still relevant to contemporary Christians. As all of the characters, male and female, human and divine, respond to Jove, they represent plausible relationships between humanity and the Deity. Their behavior illustrates moral growth or decay. Dacier suggests, for example, that Helen's repeated self-incriminations demonstrate "une morale excellente; elle voit l'horreur de son crime, elle le déteste, & elle l'attribuë à son peu de vertu."[32] Her analysis renders Helen a representative sinner, not the specifically feminine penitent of Pope's version. Pope, avowedly "[fighting] under Madam *Dacier*'s banner" ("Postscript," *Poems*, 10:392), appropriated Dacier's interpretations where convenient, elaborating the "Remarques" that accompany her translation where they served his purposes. For example, he refines the domestic strife between Jove and Juno in book 1 to defend women against "those old Fellows," the critics, who "fall so hard upon Womankind" while ostensibly criticizing Juno. Refusing to take part in "this general Defection from Complaisance," he prefers Madame Dacier's interpretation of Juno's behavior as representative of humankind's. Not only is such an interpretation "more noble and instructive in general, but . . . it is more respectful of the Ladies in particular" (*Poems*, 7:120 n. 698).

In practice, Pope relied on the English translation of Dacier's text into loose English blank verse by John Ozell with William Broome and William Oldisworth (1712). He often paraphrased and developed Dacier's remarks, but he acknowledged only direct quotations. For example, when Venus entices a reluctant Helen into Paris's bed in book 3, Dacier comments, "*Helen*, notwithstanding her Repentance, cannot forbear loving Paris: What *Venus* says of the Beauty of that Prince, revives her Passion on a sudden; *Homer* thereby perfectly shews what a Woman is capable of, that has once lov'd" (*Iliad*, 1:143 n. l). In his note on the same scene, Pope elaborates Dacier's remark into a study of female psychology.

> Nothing is more fine than this; the first thought of *Paris*'s Beauty overcomes (unawares to herself) the Contempt she had that Moment conceiv'd of him upon his Overthrow. This Motion is but natural,

and before she perceives the Deity. When the Affections of a Woman have been thoroughly gained, tho' they may be alienated for a while, they soon return upon her. Homer *knew* (says Madam *Dacier*) *what a Woman is capable of, who had once lov'd.* (*Poems*, 7:215 n. 487)

Dacier's suggestion that a woman is "capable of" resuming a former passion becomes in Pope's comment an inexorable process—the conventional weakness of the "fallen woman"—and his final quotation of Dacier claims her authority for his characterization of Helen.

Dacier's conception of femininity is more complex than Pope's. She changes the lion who finds his cubs slaughtered, Homer's simile for Achilles in book 18, to a scientifically more accurate "grisly Lioness" (18.120). Pope follows Homer and compares Achilles to a lion, no doubt considering the propriety rather than the accuracy of the epithet. In another instance, Dacier uses Vulcan's account of his fall in the same book as an opportunity to chastise "those Worldly Mothers who having ill-favour'd Children do no longer preserve a Mother's Tenderness towards them, and seek only to conceal them" (4:125 n. z). Pope omits any animadversion against Vulcan's "proud Mother" (18.463), which would have marred his translation's more simplistic emphasis on maternal tenderness.

Pope's role in creating his culture, including its narrow conception of femininity, has been labeled misogynistic by scholars who identify him with one extreme pole of contemporary thought. Misogyny, a prominent trope in late seventeenth-century and early eighteenth-century writing,[33] held that women were the debased opposites of men: fragile instead of strong, unstable instead of consistent, irrational instead of reasonable. Antithetically, Mary Astell claimed in her *Reflections Upon Marriage* that "Sense is a Portion that God Himself has been pleas'd to distribute to both Sexes with an Impartial Hand, but Learning is what Men have engross'd to themselves."[34] Women throughout the eighteenth century, from Lady Mary Wortley Montagu to Mary Wollstonecraft, insisted that women were not essentially different from men but had been deformed through lack of education. Though few besides Maynard Mack have compared him to a modern feminist,[35] Pope espoused a third alternative, available through Steele and Addison as a compromise between misogyny and feminism. Throughout the *Tatler*, *Spectator*, and *Guardian*, women are characterized as both different from men (vain, trivial, giddy) and capable of instruction for their vital roles as wives and mothers. Positing a narrow, domestic nature for women, Steele and Addison nevertheless championed women's right to a more useful education than the lessons in dress and deportment often considered sufficient. Pope's addresses to women readers throughout the *Iliad* demonstrate that he had precisely this compromise in mind.

Pope's appeals to the ladies are actually rare, but they invariably contain specifically feminine information or reflect feminine preoccupations, even at the expense of elucidating the passage. Perhaps the clearest example occurs in book 22, where Pope interrupts his description of Andromache's frantic grief with a painstaking reconstruction of her headdress. "The Ladies cannot but be pleas'd to see so much learning and Greek upon this important Subject," he concludes smugly, before continuing his discussion of Hector's mourners (*Poems*, 8:481 n. 600). (In her remarks on the same passage in *L'Iliad d'Homere*, Madame Dacier says little about Andromache's ornaments except that nobody knows exactly what they looked like.) Pope's tone is condescending in this as in other comments, the implied reader of which is female. He suggests that women are interested in trivia and defers to their demand for it. As both gentleman and professional writer, Pope goes to great lengths to satisfy "the Ladies."

Another example is his treatment of Jupiter's seduction by Juno (book 14), which Pope at first dismisses: "I don't know a bolder Fiction in all Antiquity . . . or [one] that has a greater Air of Impiety and Absurdity" (*Poems*, 7:165–66 n. 179). He determines to interpret it, on second thought, as a moral fable suggesting "abundance of Instruction to a Woman who has a mind to preserve or recall the Affection of her Husband," as Joseph Addison had observed in *Tatler* 147. Pope quotes at length Addison's contention that Juno's "Care of her Person and Dress, with the particular Blandishments woven in the *Cestus*, are so plainly recommended by this Fable, and so indispensibly necessary in every Female who desires to please, that they need no further Explanation." Following Addison's lead, Pope manages to transform Homer's low episode into an allegory providing practical instruction for women. Unlike Belinda's toilette, where her charms rise in proportion to the amount of powder and brocade she layers on herself (*The Rape of the Lock*), Juno's grooming and costume are models of simplicity and wholesomeness. Pope finally complains, however, that "one may preach till Doomsday on this Subject, but all the Commentators in the World will never prevail upon a Lady to stick one Pin the less in her Gown, except she can be convinced, that the ancient Dress will better set off her Person" (*Poems*, 8:169 n. 203).

Pope then musters his rhetorical powers to promote classical fashions. Through such banter, he attempts both to refine Homer and to improve the manners and taste of his readers, in conformity with his conception of the Homeric ideal. Like Addison in his periodicals, Pope refers to specific contemporary fashions. Having satirized formal dress in *The Rape of the Lock*, where Belinda sports a low-cut bodice and brocade mantua with furbelowed, hooped petticoat, Pope describes Juno's attire as a simple, sashed robe with little jewelry—perhaps resembling the informal closed robes worn by the Blount sisters in the portrait Charles Jervas painted for Pope in 1716.[36] Ladies frequently chose closed robes or wrapping gowns for their portraits, evidently associating such undress with classical drapery. With his painter's eye, Pope here champions the prototype of this mode.

In addition to offering such practical advice, Pope's addresses to women in his commentary sometimes approach moral problems by appealing to women's responses. In book 24, Thetis's advice to Achilles to "indulge the am'rous Hour" with Briseïs becomes Pope's opportunity to question what was sometimes considered a male prerogative. He refuses to accept Madame Dacier's extenuating interpretation of what he describes as an "almost obscene" passage.

> Madam *Dacier* . . . has recourse to the Lawfulness of such a Practise between *Achilles* and *Briseïs*; and because such Commerces in those times were reputed honest, therefore she thinks the Advice was decent: the married Ladies are oblig'd to her for this Observation, and I hope all tender Mothers, when their Sons are afflicted, will advise them to comfort themselves in this manner. (*Poems*, 8:542 n. 168)

Pope's sneer at Dacier, like his earlier pride in supplying the details of Greek millinery, betrays his sense of rivalry with the French woman, whose translation appeared just four years before his first volume. His appeal to wives and mothers to justify his stricture is meant to demonstrate his comparative sympathy for mothers. A digression from the main issues of the epic provides Pope with an occasion to ingratiate himself with women while providing moral instruction for all contemporary readers.

Notes drawing attention to ancient grooming, cookery, and mother-child relationships encouraged women to find the *Iliad* pertinent to their concerns. Although he considered reading epics a salutary female activity, Pope also assumed that women required appeals to feminine emotions and activities to maintain their interest. Both beliefs resemble those suggested by Richard Steele and Joseph Addison throughout their essays. Addison's essay on "The Utility of Learning to the Female Sex" in *The Guardian* 155 (8 September 1713) recommends the pursuit of knowledge to women because they have so much spare time, because their husbands are often ignorant ("great pity there should be no knowledge in a family"), and because learning might bring them "honour and fortune." Studying keeps women out of mischief ("a female philosopher" is "not so absurd . . . as a female gamester") and enables them to teach their children. Addison pronounces himself diverted by a conversation among learned women: "It was very entertaining to me to see them dividing their speculations between jellies and stars, and making a sudden transition from the sun to an apricot, or from the Copernican system to the figure of a cheesecake."[37] Like Samuel Johnson, who many years later extolled Elizabeth Carter because she could make a pudding and translate Epictetus from the Greek, Addison considered women's priorities ultimately domestic. As long as women did not lose this sense of their priorities and pursue learning to the prejudice of such primary feminine occupations as cookery (and, as ladies, rather frivolous cookery at that), Addison preferred learning to such thoughtless or even dangerous avocations as gambling.

Because refined gentlemen were not expected to indulge in the impassioned pursuit of any one art or science, the young women whom Addison imagined chatting about the stars while concocting cheesecakes were their ideal feminine counterparts. Steele assumed that women's narrow interests would prevent their absorption in, or even comprehension of, such esoteric matters as literary criticism. In *Spectator* 66, after his essays on true and false wit, Addison observed that "I have several Letters which complain to me that my Female Readers have not understood me for some Days past, and take themselves to be unconcerned in the present Turn of my Writings" (Addison et al., 1:282). In the event of her marriage to a lout, however, Addison admitted that a woman might become the sole repository of knowledge, and consequently of refinement, in her family. Given their leisure to learn and their opportunity to inculcate knowledge in children and even husbands, women actually occupied a pivotal position in Addison and Steele's campaign to refine British morals and manners. That role was narrowly circumscribed. Their attention had to be focused on the home, and their family duties justified their education. Jellies and stars, the sun and an apricot—a woman's "Copernican system" revolved around a cheesecake. In his early letters and poems, Pope also imagined a genteel feminine way of life, sequestered and thus necessarily centered on the tasks and recreations of the family home and garden. But Pope also understood, in a more sympathetic way than Addison ever expressed it, women's longing for involvement in the "great world," in which they could usually participate only through public social amusements.

To Martha and Teresa Blount, Pope complained in 1715 that their insatiable appetite for news while they resided at Mapledurham had reduced him to a mere newsmonger—a "Brother of Dyer & Dawkes."[38] He understood, however, that reading was one way for a woman both to pass time and to enjoy vicariously the experience denied her by seclusion. He obliged Martha Blount by supplying her with books, imploring her on one occasion "to stay her Stomach with these half hundred Plays, till I can procure her a Romance big enough to satisfie her great Soul with Adventures" (*Corr.*, 1:252). The remark, contemporary with *The Rape of the Lock*, suggests a similar condescending amusement: a "great-Souled"—that is, heroic—woman will be satisfied with literary adventures, even as Belinda the heroic belle longs for flirtatious conquests. While Addison assumed feminine nature was properly absorbed in domestic cares, Pope recognized that reading was also a relief from domestic boredom. Moreover, reading encouraged that cheerful, philosophical nature that alone enabled a woman to bear her inevitably frustrating social position—as he explained in both *The Rape of the Lock* and "To a Lady. Of the Characters of Women." His "Epistle to Miss Blount, With the Works of Voiture" (1710) stresses that "*Good Humour* only teaches Charms to last" (61), a good humor to be inculcated by Voiture's book. Beyond the condescension lurks some acknowledgment that female good humor is a heroic response to the circumscribed routines and relationships available to women.

Both Addison and Pope encouraged women readers to pursue knowledge, but with different emphases. If Teresa Blount had married the boorish Squire who, in "On Her Leaving the Town, After the Coronation," loved her "best of all things—but his horse" (30), Addison's Mr. Spectator would have promised that at least, if she read and studied between household chores, she could still maintain a genteel household. Pope might have responded that reading would enable her to bear the tedium of daily routine and to maintain a cheerful temper. Perhaps because his closest women friends, the

Blounts, were not married and did not manage their home, Pope could envision women reading for their pleasure and enrichment— reading without one hand in the jelly jar.

Given his more complex understanding and sympathy, Pope's choice of an Addisonian tone and style for his addresses to women in the *Iliad* notes is perplexing. Pope's decision may have been motivated by tensions similar to those that characterized his letters to women. As James Winn has explained, the gallant mode of address to women was commonplace in the early eighteenth century, but Pope improved upon the popular complimentary style by adding his own facetious humor.[39] But letters to women he loved, or whose love he coveted, posed a special problem. A crippled dwarf, Pope had reason to fear that any serious declaration of love for a lady would be ridiculed or scorned. Consequently, his letters to such women as the Blounts or Lady Mary Wortley Montagu abound in "confessions of love . . . disguised by . . . comical strategies" (Winn, *Window*, 106). Wit became not only his weapon for competing with other admirers but his way of avoiding the pain of rejection were he to confess his love directly.

Tensions similar to those in his letters surface in *The Rape of the Lock*, written while Pope was commencing his translation. Maynard Mack has argued that *Rape* owes its "deep currents of affection and sexual attraction, not to mention its finely observed particulars both teasing and admiring" to Pope's relationship with the Blounts (Mack, *Pope*, 257). Valerie Rumbold has posited a specific comment on the Catholic social circle of both Belle Fermor and the Blounts, with particular reference to Teresa's flirtatious activities (48–82). Ellen Pollak, however, has found *Rape* distasteful, an insulting assertion of "the myth of passive womanhood" (77–107). Perhaps Pope intended both affection and insult. The poem and its equivocal dedication resemble Pope's most facetious letters, such as those to the Marriots, friendly letters sprinkled with mock insults, double entendres, and outrageous compliments.[40] When Pope sent Mrs. Marriot and her daughter an advance copy of *The Rape of the Lock*, he declared that "this whimsical piece of work . . . is at once the most a satire, and the most inoffensive, of anything of mine. . . . 'Tis a sort of writing very like tickling" (*Corr.*, 1:211). His opposition of the terms "satire" and "inoffensive" suggests that Pope was well aware of the offensive potential of his poem. Yet he evidently assumed that these ladies, and others like them, would appreciate the humor of both poem and dedication, while apprehending his satirical intention.

If Pope intended his facetious epistolary style to entertain his female correspondents while deflecting their potential scorn for his more serious sentiments, he may have devised the similar style of his *Iliad* notes to accomplish analogous purposes. By including material intended for women's exclusive entertainment, he established his desire to serve them, according to a conventional understanding of their domestic and emotional priorities. But Pope's condescending tone enabled him to affirm his masculine superiority amidst the details of millinery and cookery he compiled for the ladies' satisfaction. Finally, and similarly to his correspondence and *Rape*, Pope courted women readers, but with less potential risk to his ego in the event of rejection by readers characterized as vapid belles rather than, for example, avid classicists. When choosing his style, Pope was eminently aware of Steele and Addison as successful predecessors in adjusting the gallant style to a broad audience. A *Guardian* contributor, seeking to attract approximately the same readers drawn to Steele and Addison's publications, Pope adopted a similar approach to women. In doing so, he chose for his own enterprise a tested, successful style, familiar to that relatively new segment of the reading public. The undertones of compassion and admiration present in many of Pope's letters and poems were eliminated for the epic's broader audience.

Pope's style may also have been motivated by his need to characterize the opposite sex after inviting from his general public many traditionally feminine responses, such as parental love and lack of interest in battles. Like Addison in *Spectator* 10, Pope conveniently distinguished a class of readers for whom "the Toilet is their great Scene of Business, and the right adjusting of their Hair the principal Employment of their Lives" (Addison et al., 1:46). As in Addison's essays and his own most playful letters, Pope then directed comments to this imaginary constituency, employing raillery to persuade women to avoid feminine foibles. One example is the Addison-inspired notes on Juno's toilette. A darker result of Pope's adoption of a hypothetical female reader occurs in book 22 of the *Iliad*, where Pope describes Homer's description of the widowed Andromache's grief as "far beyond all the Praises that can be given it" (*Poems*, 8:479 n. 562). Yet even this dramatic passage, which exemplifies familial affection and particularly celebrates the devotion of wives and mothers, must be recommended to female attention by a note describing Andromache's coiffure. Notwithstanding his sympathy with women and conviction that they should be encouraged to read, Pope, for reasons ranging from self-protection to expediency, addressed them in terms of conventional assumptions about women's interests and attention spans and focused on the benefits of reading.

The *Iliad*'s ambiguous attitude toward women originated in Pope's mingled sympathy and condescension, influenced by his pragmatic choice of a successful model. Not only modern readers have voiced concern over Pope's apparent assumption that the female is trivial. John Dennis, censuring another of Pope's early poems, asked in 1717, "Are there really no Women who are Worthy to appear in the Temple of Fame?"

> Heroick Virtue is certainly more Admirable in Women, than it is in Men, on account of the Defects in their Educations, the Tenderness of their Constitutions, and the extreme Violence of their Passions. And therefore both Homer and Virgil introduced Female Warriors into their Poems, to render their Works the more admirable.[41]

Despite Dennis's praise of female warriors, however, his notion of female difference was very close to Pope's. Women have been imperfectly educated, more regrettably because of their fragile health and volatile temperaments; and female heroism is, therefore, more admirable than male because it is anomalous, not to say abnormal. Dennis does not suggest that women are as heroic as men, or even that female heroism is the same as male heroism. Pope's translation was directed to a conception of women much like Dennis's. The *Iliad*'s few allusions to Amazons are passed over without comment, perhaps in deference to women readers. Pope tactfully ignored popular contemporary references to Amazons as, to borrow Howard Weinbrot's observation, "types both of the aggressive and sexually hungry woman" (37).

Pope's translation fulfilled Addison's wish for more edifying entertainment for women. In "Catalogue of a Lady's Library" in *Spectator* 37 (12 April 1711), Addison ridicules one woman's (Leonora's) undisciplined approach to learning. Leonora amasses a conglomeration of books, "either because she had heard them praised, or because she had seen the authors of them." She prefers to read romances, however, which gives her "a very particular turn of thinking"—an inability to cope with life's practical aspects. Comparing Leonora's fanciful garden to her mind, Addison laments,

> What improvements would a woman have made, who is so suscepti-
> ble of impressions from what she reads, had she been guided to
> such books as have a tendency to enlighten the understanding and
> rectify the passions, as well as to those which are of little more use
> than to divert the imagination! (Addison et al., 1:152–59)

Studied from this perspective, Pope's addresses to women appeal to such ladies as Leonora, an audience conventionally perceived as frivolous, for whom the *Iliad* would be at once entertaining, instructive, and morally uplifting. Reduced in some respects to a conduct book, the epic would nevertheless far surpass their usual reading material.

Yet partly because he addressed women at all, and in a fairly common style, Pope was maligned by various contemporaries. In *Homerides; or, A Letter to Mr. Pope, by Sir Iliad Doggerel* (1715), Thomas Burnet and George Duckett ridiculed Pope's subscription as a design to attract illiterate readers. "Sir Iliad" proposes that Pope commission a puppet show at Bath, to drum up subscribers for his translation "among the Beaux and Ladies there." "And, I suppose," he adds, "'tis only for such as them, who do not understand the Greek, that you design your Translation." Sir Iliad's snobbery becomes more apparent when he recommends that Pope modernize his epic "in such a manner, that every Country Milkmaid may understand the *Iliad* as well as you or I." Once ladies are admitted to the privileged male circle of those familiar with Homer, who knows where the havoc wreaked on patriarchal culture might end? But Sir Iliad warns Pope that his task will be difficult; even "the Names used in the Original can never sound prettily in English Verse, and will be fitter to frighten Children than to divert Ladies."[42] Pope's appeals to women, which appear insulting today, were evidently considered iconoclastic by some of Pope's contemporaries.

Burnet and Duckett were part of a curious Whig conspiracy to discredit Pope's translation, a campaign probably initiated by Addison himself. The reasons behind Addison's insidious activity, ranging from professional jealousy to political animosity, have been traced by many scholars,[43] but a curious aspect of Pope's enemies' detraction is their repeated insinuations that he might mislead Addison's assiduously courted female Whig sympathizers. For example, in the wake of the abortive 1715 rebellion, Addison began publishing *The Freeholder* to carry on the Whig "successes over the minds of men, and [to reconcile] them to the cause of their king, their country, and their religion."[44] *Freeholder* 26 (19 March 1716) featured "considerations offered to the disaffected part of the Fair Sex." Tory ladies, or "angry stateswomen," are asked to consider

> the great sufferings and persecutions to which they expose themselves by the obstinacy of their behavior. . . . They are obliged by their principles to stick a patch on the most unbecoming side of their foreheads. They forego the advantage of birth-day suits. . . . They are forced to live in the country and feed their chickens; at the same time that they might show themselves at court, and appear in brocade, if they behaved themselves well. (143–44)

Such coaxing might persuade a child—or Belinda of *The Rape of the Lock*. More sober-minded ladies—such as, perhaps, Belinda's admonisher, Clarissa—

> should consider, that they cannot signalize themselves as malecontents, without breaking through all the amiable instincts and softer virtues, which are peculiarly ornamental to womankind. Their timorous, gentle, modest behavior . . . must be sacrificed to a blind and furious zeal for they know not what. (144)

The anomalous zeal that constituted Dennis's notion of female heroism becomes in Addison's view an unsexed, even deranged, fury.

Addison finally threatens these Tory sympathizers: "The worst character a female could formerly arrive at, was of being an ill woman; but by their present conduct, she may likewise deserve the character of an ill subject" (145). Addison's thrusts become less and less chivalrous, as he first affectionately teases the ladies with loss of beaus and brocades, then accuses them of poor breeding and bad manners, and finally frightens them by equating the loss of political reputation with the loss of moral reputation. Few eighteenth-century women dared toy with their reputations. Thus this advice from the kindly monitor of *The Tatler*, *Spectator*, and *Guardian* seems hostile, as if the pose of gallantry could no longer be maintained before these political enemies. Addison appears to have felt that extreme measures might be necessary to convert disaffected women. Could he have been taking seriously his earlier pleasantry in *Freeholder* 4 (2 January 1716) that "Ladies are always of great use to the party they espouse, and never fail to win over numbers to it" (17)? Addison's acknowledgment of a female segment of readers/consumers seems also to have rendered their political opinions more valuable, or potentially more dangerous.

Addison followed this sermon to "the fair ones of the adverse party" with an obvious parody of Pope's "Temple of Fame" in *Freeholder* 27 (23 March 1716). In this essay, "Second-Sighted Sawney," a highland malcontent of dubious origins, is granted a vision of the "Temple of Rebellion." (Pope, as "Sawny Dapper," had been taunted for his allegedly obscure family origins in Charles Gildon's *New Rehearsal* [1714], part of the pre-*Iliad* anti-Pope campaign.) This edifice is remarkably like Pope's temple, except that it is not built on a rock of ice but is made of snow, and it contains statues commemorating Ambition, Envy, Disgrace, Poverty, and even Passive Obedience. The vision melts at the appearance of the blazing star of "Religion, Loyalty, and Valour," compelling the temple's votaries to "disperse themselves by flight . . . among the mountains" (150). This identification of Pope with the rebellion of 1715, papism, and cowardly political tactics recalls Gildon's *New Rehearsal*. In that parody, the only defense of Sawny is that he "has a very pretty Genius, is very harmonious, and Writes a great many fine things, ask the Ladies else."[45] The *Freeholder* essay, replete with damaging associations, implies that the Tory literary lion might be capable of leading astray Addison's carefully tended flock.

A year later, in his *Remarks upon Mr. Pope's Translation of Homer*, John Dennis was still declaiming against the "Vagary of Fortune . . . and the epidemical Madness of the Times" that have "given [Pope] Reputation."

> And Reputation, as Hobbes says, is Power, and that has made him dangerous; therefore, I look upon it as my Duty to King George, ... to my Country . . . which this Vile Scribbler . . . has been so industrious to destroy, and to the Liberty of my Country . . . to pull the Lyon's Skin from this little Ass. (ii–iii)

Dennis's tirade makes explicit what Addison's allegory had implied: a Tory Catholic had no business educating beaus, belles, or milkmaids. When the Whigs accused Pope of subverting his country and jeopardizing liberty, they really objected to his attempting precisely what Steele and Addison had intended in their papers: introducing culture to a wider audience. Pope himself perceived the irony of their complaints when he compared the first volume of the *Iliad* with that of Thomas Tickell, his Addison-coached Whig competitor: "[If] our Principles be well consider'd, I must appear a brave *Whig*, and Mr. *Tickel* a rank *Tory*; I translated Homer for the publick in general, he to gratify the inordinate desires of One man only [Addison]" (*Corr.*, 1:306). Years before, in his introduction to *The Tatler*, Richard Steele had explained that his journal would "offer something, whereby . . . worthy and well-affected Members of the Commonwealth may be instructed . . . what to think. . . . I resolve also to have something which may be of Entertainment to the Fair Sex."[46] Pope sought to accomplish an identical goal in his *Iliad* translation and notes.

Addison had long since terminated his efforts at detraction. Perhaps he simply realized the uselessness of continuing them throughout all six installments of Pope's translation, especially after the clear public approbation of the initial 1715 volume. Tickell also declined translating any further books of the *Iliad*. More important, perhaps, was the total demoralization of the Tory party following the Northern Rebellion. Although Dennis had still to write his *Remarks* accusing Pope of undermining the nation, by spring 1716 the Whig party no longer had any immediate reason to fear the Tories, much less to persecute a prominent Tory sympathizer for his classical translation. In *Freeholder* 40 (7 May 1716), Addison commended Pope's *Iliad* for its inimitable service to the "illiterate among our countrymen" (234). As Thomas Burnet put it, "Addison and his 'gang' had 'dropt their resentment' against Pope," and the poet's share in the enterprise of filtering culture to women and "the middling sort" could be acknowledged.[47] By the time Johnson wrote his *Life of Pope* (1781), the political dimensions of Pope's undertaking, the lurking hazards of his address to women and "the vulgar," had been forgotten.

Women's Responses to Pope's Appeals

Long after the original imbroglio, Pope's addresses to women readers invited controversy. In 1729, Edward Ward published "Durgen," a poem begging women's support for Lewis Theobald's projected edition of Shakespeare. He warned them not to "doat . . . so much on one proud epick Muse" but to "lend [their] hands to the deserving Task."[48]

Then may you, charming Students, justly boast
An useful Treasure, bought at little cost,
And *Shakespeare's* faithful Friend more honour gain,
Than *Homer's* Ape by his Translating Pen.

(959–62)

Ward's appeal to women's instinctive desire, as consumers, for a bargain—"an useful Treasure, bought at little cost"—recalls another convention established by the early periodicals. Ward contrasts Theobald's quest for honor with Pope's presumably sordid subscription; Pope's translation was a cheat. While warning women against Pope, Ward adheres to a stereotypical image of his female readers as passive consumers vulnerable to false advertising claims. Another of Pope's "dunces," Aaron Hill, composed "The Progress of Wit: A Caveat," recalling the pastorals as he evoked Pope's career.

Tuneful Alexis, on the Thame's fair Side,
The Ladies Play-thing, and the Muses Pride,
With *Merit*, popular, with *Wit*, polite,
Easy, tho' vain, and elegant, tho' light.[49]

Hill's criticism of Pope's appeal to women readers is equally insulting to those women themselves. These lines conflate Pope and his verse; both are "Play-things" for the ladies, as if women were children incapable of taking an artist or his work seriously. Moreover, Hill describes Pope and his poetry as "easy," "vain," "elegant," and "light," further aspersing women's tastes, while adhering to conventional conceptions of women as frivolous and easily captivated by appearances.

While men's responses to Pope's appeals to the ladies were often politically motivated and did little justice to those ladies themselves, women's responses to Pope's Homer were more complex. Their less secure position as critics often necessitated obliquity. Anne Dacier, however—by this time an elderly and renowned scholar—could afford to be more direct. She replied scathingly to Pope's unacknowledged borrowings from her own commentary.

Dacier appended her comments to the second edition of *L'Iliade d'Homere* (1719), after reading a translation of the first part of Pope's preface. In her "Reflexions sur la premiere Partie de la Preface de M. Pope," Dacier is most concerned to correct Pope's assertions of Homer's primitive morality and luxuriant style. In her opinion, the *Iliad* resembles André le Nôtre's Versailles more than Pope's wild Paradise, and she reiterates her opinion that Homer's heroes parallel the biblical patriarchs. Pope had commented that "it must be a strange Partiality to Antiquity to think with Madam *Dacier*, 'that those Times and Manners are so much the more excellent, as they are more contrary to ours,' " although "there is a Pleasure in taking a view of that Simplicity in Opposition to the luxury of succeeding Ages; in beholding . . . Princes tending their flocks, and Princesses drawing Water from the Springs" (*Poems*, 7:14). Furious that Pope had claimed to disagree with her while paraphrasing her sentiments about the princes and princesses, Dacier complained:

> J'avouë que je n'aurois pas crû me voir attaquée par M. *Pope*, dans une Preface ou j'aurois dû attendre de sa part quelque petite marque de reconnaissance, ou dumoins quelque legere approbation de ce que j'avais eû le bonheur de penser comme luy en plusiers choses, par example, sur les moeurs anciennes, aprés avoir dit dans ma Preface que les Princes gardoient les troupeaux, que les Princesses alloient puiser de l'eau à la fontaine.[50]

A few years later, an anonymous translator working for Edmund Curll observed of this passage that "the Lady is very modest when he uses her own Words, to say she was happy in having *Thought* as he did; tho' it is plain he borrowed this *Thought* from her."[51] But Dacier's response is more ironic than modest. Her condescension reflects the security of an established reputation. Fearful that Pope might damage not only her own but Homer's reputation among unlearned readers, Dacier demonstrates the circularity of an argument that simultaneously ridiculed her preference for ancient manners and claimed to view with pleasure the simplicity of ancient times. While eschewing her translator's clumsy sarcasm, she reminds her young competitor of his indebtedness.

Dacier's conclusion is equally double-edged. She has been most concerned, throughout her critique, with Pope's efforts to "refine" Homer, compared with her impulse to revere the *Iliad* as a kind of Scriptural analogue.

> Un homme si habile ne se bornera pas à perfectionner l'art du poëme Epique; ce seroit peu de chose, il perfectionnera l'art de la politique, bien plus estimable & plus important que ce-luy de l'Epopée; un homme capable de corriger Homere, sera capable de former des hommes. . . . Voilà une grande resource pour un Estat![52]

Given Dacier's reverence, it is unlikely she believed that the man who had "corrected" Homer would prove invaluable to the English nation. The anecdote she uses to support her prediction, in which Alcibiades exclaims to a bragging grammarian, "*Eh mon ami, . . . tu es capable de corriger Homere, & tu t'amuses à enseigner des enfants, que ne t'occupes-tu à former des hommes!*" suggests contempt.[53] Dacier must have regarded Pope as sacrilegious, particularly as she formed her opinion of his *Iliad* preface from an inaccurate French translation. Her reduction of Pope to an overweening grammarian recalls the young translator to the proper humility of their shared profession. But Dacier unwittingly predicts the future course of Pope's career, after he "stoop'd to Truth, and moralized his Song." In 1719, Pope was years away from *The Dunciad*, his *Essay on Man*, and the *Moral Essays*, yet Dacier ironically intuits his ambition to "former des hommes." Dacier's conclusion seems in retrospect to prophesy Pope's mature writings. The bravura that tempted Pope to affect originality in his critical assessments later inspired his persona as the self-confident moralist. Intending to wound by a slighting reference to his pretensions, Pope's shrewd adversary noted the pride that constituted a chief motivation of his career.

When he first read this passage, Pope was unnerved by the political implications of Dacier's conclusion. Brean Hammond has reminded us that Pope first encountered the "Reflexions" in 1723, amidst the scandal over his edition of the late duke of Buckingham's *Works* and shortly before Bishop Atterbury's trial (33–36). Pope eventually had the last word in this exchange, responding in a postscript to the *Odyssey* six years after Dacier's death. He claims his intention "to pay some part of [the] debt" owed Dacier's memory by all admirers of Homer, but he wastes no time before declaring, "I think her Reasoning very bad" (*Poems*, 10:392).

Pope explains that Dacier's misconstructions of his claims arose from her use of a translation, the very source of error she frequently criticized in her writings on Homer. As for her insinuation that he plagiarized her ideas, Pope sinks to misogyny to extricate himself.

The truth is she might have said *her words*, for I used them on purpose, being then professedly citing from her: tho' I might have done the same without intending that compliment, for they are also to be found in *Eustathius*. . . . I cannot really tell what to say to this whole Remark, only that in the first part of it Madam *Dacier* is displeased that I don't agree with her, and in the last that I do: But this is a temper which every polite man should over-look in a Lady. (*Poems*, 10:394)

This patronizing remark manifests Pope's anxieties over the critique of a woman he had just claimed to "respect [for] her Authority" (10:392). The passage is thoroughly sophistic; there had been no indication in Pope's *Iliad* preface that the phrases about the pastoral princes and princesses were drawn from Dacier. His reminder that she had borrowed from Eustathius merely extenuates his own practice. We are also reminded of Pope's vulnerability to such charges, as he worked to obscure the extent of his *Odyssey* collaboration from the public. Pope reveals the primary source of his discomfiture, however, in his conclusion, abjuring Dacier's claim that having "corrected" Homer he will inevitably attempt political reform: "Far . . . from the Genius for which Madam *Dacier* mistook me, my whole desire is but to preserve the humble character of a faithful Translator, and a quiet Subject" (10:397). If Dacier, wounded by Pope's lack of respect for her opinions, had intended to make her Tory, Catholic English rival writhe a bit in return, she succeeded from beyond the grave.

More pleasant to Pope were his exchanges with Lady Mary Wortley Montagu during her sojourn in Turkey. Judging from her literary activities, Lady Mary dazzled her contemporaries. Joseph Addison revised his *Cato* after perusing the critique she wrote at his request. Later, Addison printed her response to his essay on the "Club of Widows" as *Spectator* 573 (Addison et al., 4:556–61), a rare gesture to one of his women readers. Lady Mary also enjoyed the friendship and confidence of John Gay, collaborating with him on versions of her *Town Eclogues* (1715–16). Later, Henry Fielding's lifelong esteem for his second cousin blossomed when she critiqued and encouraged his first play, *Love in Several Masques*.[54] Pope was infatuated with her, pursuing her with a series of manipulative but futile love letters throughout her diplomatic travels. Her responses, measured and often deliberately opaque, contain one of the earliest recorded female responses to Pope's *Iliad*.

In 1717, Lady Mary wrote to Pope from Adrianople about his first two volumes of the *Iliad*:

I read over your *Homer* here, with an infinite pleasure, and find several little passages explained, that I did not before entirely comprehend the beauty of: Many of the customs, and much of the dress then in fashion, being yet retained . . . I can assure you, that the Princesses and great ladies pass their time at their looms, embroidering veils and robes, surrounded by their maids, which are always very numerous, in the same manner as we find *Andromache* and *Helen* described. . . . The snowy veil, that Helen throws over her face, is still fashionable, and I never see half a dozen of old Bashaws . . . but I recollect good King Priam and his counsellors. (Pope, *Corr.*, 1:398)

Miriam Kramnick's remark that Lady Mary was always "careful to tailor her philosophy to suit her correspondent"[55] suggests that Lady Mary's strategy may have been to reassure Pope that she had noticed the correct feminine aspects of the translation before proceeding with a topic of more intellectual interest, the comparison of English and Turkish versification with which she concluded her letter. Such a reading suggests an early instance of what Lady Mary called concealing her "Learning . . . with as much solicitude as she would hide crookedness or lameness" (*Letters*, 3:22).

But Lady Mary had no motive to conceal her intelligence from Pope. He admired her poetic ability, consoling himself in her absence by copying her *Eclogues* into a leather-bound album.[56] A simpler conclusion is that Lady Mary, absorbed in her observations of the exotic Turkish culture, responded immediately to the colorful details of classic dress and customs with which Pope intended to captivate his women readers. Lady Mary's letters abound in descriptions of Turkish dress and domestic life, particularly in her accounts to female correspondents, indicating that she too thought such information interesting. Moreover, Pope claimed that Lady Mary's observations would illuminate Homer's text. In June 1717, he wrote to her, "I make not the least question but you could give me great Eclaircissements upon many passages in Homer, since you have been enlightend by the same Sun that inspired the Father of Poetry." The suggestion is not merely gallant: Pope explains that her imagination must be enhanced by her ancient environs, where she may "read the Fall of Troy in the Shade of a Trojan Ruin" (*Corr.*, 1:406) However, Lady Mary chose to comment first on the feminine customs recorded in the translation and to recall the scene that introduces Helen. Her remarks may simply indicate the perceived relevance of Pope's appeals to women readers, or perhaps they reveal Pope's incisive appraisal of contemporary women's interests.

Another of Lady Mary's statements may have influenced Pope's commentary. In a letter from Constantinople dated 1 September 1717, Lady Mary praised Pope for having "touched the mantle of the divine Bard, and imbibed his spirit." She hoped, however, that the *Odyssey* would quickly succeed Pope's *Iliad*.

> I love [Odysseus] much better than the hot-headed son of Peleus, who bullied his general, cried for his mistress, and so on. It is true, the excellence of the Iliad does not depend upon his merit or dignity, but I wish nevertheless that Homer had chosen a hero somewhat less pettish and less fantastick; a perfect hero is chimerical and unnatural, and consequently uninstructive; but it is also true that while the epic hero ought to be drawn with the infirmities that are the lot of humanity, he ought never to be represented as extremely absurd. But it becomes me ill to play the critick. (*Corr.*, 1:423–24)

Though George Sherburn warns that Lady Mary's letter is possibly inauthentic, the extent to which Pope exonerates Achilles' character and behavior in his last three volumes is remarkable. In book 16, for example, when Achilles sacrifices to Jove after sending Patroclus into battle, Pope observes that "tho' the Character of Achilles every where shews a Mind sway'd with unbounded Passions . . . yet he preserves a constant Respect to the Gods, and appears as zealous in the Sentiments and Actions of Piety as any Hero of the Iliad" (*Poems*, 8:250 n. 283). Pope's desire to rehabilitate Achilles is most pronounced in book 24. Of Achilles' speech to Priam on the inevitable sorrows of human life, Pope notes:

> There is not a more beautiful Passage in the whole Ilias than this. . . . *Homer* to shew *Achilles* was not a mere Soldier, here draws him as a Person of excellent Sense and sound reason: . . . And it was a piece of great Judgment thus to describe him; for the Reader would have retain'd but a very indifferent Opinion of the Hero of a Poem, that had no Qualification but mere Strength. . . . By these means he fixes an Idea of [Achilles'] greatness upon our Minds, and makes his Hero go off the Stage with Applause. (*Poems*, 8:564 n. 653)

Pope's comments seem designed to answer Lady Mary's objection to "the hot-headed son of Peleus." Her diction had lowered Achilles in the manner of contemporary burlesques of Homer; he "bullied his general, cried for his mistress, and so on." Pope's translation ennobles

Achilles' speech and gestures, while his commentary reinforces the hero's "Endowments of Mind and Body" (*Poems*, 8:570 n. 798). His efforts demonstrate that Pope took the opinions of such readers as Lady Mary seriously, despite her disclaimer that "it becomes me ill to play the critick." Nevertheless, the contrast in their attitudes—hers cynical, his earnest—is characteristic and foreshadows their inevitable break.

Madame Dacier's and Lady Mary's responses to Pope savor of potential dialogue. Dacier's irony is designed to evoke consideration from an aggressive young author. Lady Mary's cynical wit holds Pope's earnest flattery at arm's length, while her discussion of Homer in relation to Turkish social customs deflects attention from her tendency to "play the critick." Other women readers throughout the century, unconstrained by the possibility of Pope's response, confided their opinions of Pope's Homer in letters, journals, and poems. Their comments ranged from casual mentions to considered criticism, but all reveal that Pope drew women into an inclusive experience of the epic, even inspiring emulation. Intending perhaps an Addisonian arrangement by which women were invited to participate but then were implicitly excluded from certain aspects of the reading experience (as when Steele claimed his lady readers failed to comprehend the *Spectator*'s literary criticism), Pope had instead crafted a translation that delighted women. For example, Mary Delany, then Mrs. Pendarves, wrote Ann Granville on 1 April 1729 asking her mother and cousins to "muster up my books that they have got among them, and let me have them, if they have done with them; there is Homer's Iliad and the Belle Assemblée, I don't remember if they have any others of mine.[57] The casual recollection of what was almost certainly Pope's *Iliad* along with a fashionable French romance suggests Pope had reached the audience he referred to in *The Rape of the Lock* dedication— the same ladies who might have read "*Le Comte de Gabalis*, which both in its Title and Size is so like a *Novel*, that many of the Fair Sex have read it for one by Mistake." Mrs. Delany, not only a lively and intelligent woman but a botanical artist whose love of design made her an indefatigable reporter of court fashions, may have enjoyed Pope's descriptions of ancient dress.

A thoughtful exchange between Catherine Talbot and Elizabeth Carter in 1746 illustrates the appeal Pope's translations held to discriminating women. Carter, an accomplished Greek scholar, wrote her friend that

> I . . . have been reading Memoirs, namely the Memoirs of Ulysses,
> which in pure reverence to the name of Homer, I have with some
> difficulty just got through; . . . really it does not seem of any great
> importance to the reader whether Telemachus (like a notable house-
> wifely young man as he was) hung his cloaths upon a peg, or was
> sloven enough to throw them on the floor. . . . If it was not an
> incontestible fact that Milton wrote Paradise Regained, one could
> never believe Homer wrote the Odyssey. (*Letters*, 1:166–67)

Carter found "tedious" those details that she supposed were "to be
admired for their noble simplicity" yet seemed merely ignoble. Why
should a genteel reader's attention be given to Telemachus's
housekeeping, "or whether Mr. Trulliber (I have forgot his Greek
name) took exact care of the hogs?" (*Letters*, 1:166).[58] Carter's strictures
echo the "modern" objections to Homer's primitivism that Pope attempted to obviate by refining his text. For Talbot, his effort had been
successful. She responded to Carter:

> I cannot possibly agree in your sentiments of the Odyssey, for it has
> been always a very favorite poem of mine. See the benefit of igno-
> rance! perhaps you too, if you had never read any Odyssey but Mr.
> Pope's, would be fond of it. I read it last year in very agreeable
> society, and very great amusement it gave us. Mr. Pope's verse can
> give dignity to a *peg* or a *pig*, and the divine Eumaeus is so worthy
> a man, that I overlook the unlucky circumstance of his being a hog-
> herd. . . . Some time or other (for I do not utterly despair) when I
> have the happiness of seeing you often, we will read the Odyssey
> together. (Carter, *Letters*, 1:170–71)

Talbot's defense of the *Odyssey* evokes the communal life of genteel eighteenth-century women. Literature was often read in "agreeable society." Perhaps Talbot had been regaled with a reading of
Pope's *Odyssey* while doing needlework in the evenings at her "foster
father" Bishop Secker's palace.[59] To be acceptable entertainment for
a mixed circle of ladies and gentlemen, a work had to be suitably
refined. Talbot's description also reminds us that poetry and novels
were still read aloud in the eighteenth century, and that the mellifluous
dignity of Pope's diction probably helped keep hearers' minds away
from the epic's "low" images; the description of Eumaeus as "the
careful master of the swine" (4.593) is one of his version's few direct
allusions to Eumaeus's livelihood. Neither Carter's nor Talbot's concern with decorum was particularly feminine. Talbot describes the

contemporary ideal of domestic entertainment: literature purged of any grossness that might prove embarrassing in mixed company.[60] But because ladies did not usually retire to their closets to read Latin or Greek ("See the benefit of ignorance!"), their encounters with crucial classical texts might be confined to those translations that were read in the drawing room after supper. Talbot's pleasure in the *Odyssey* indicates that Pope succeeded in rendering Homer quite accessible to women in a culture with ever-narrowing conceptions of appropriate reading.

Both Carter and Talbot were avid readers and critics of contemporary writings. As a classical scholar, Carter tended to have broader notions of decorum for both texts and women. For example, when Talbot found Mary Jones's miscellany, with her Swiftian poems, unbearable in 1752, Carter rejoined that she still found the collection commendable because of Jones's letters (*Letters*, 2:86–87, 101). Carter's objection to the *Odyssey* suggests a scholar's boredom with "housewifely" details. Her response to Talbot's defense admits, ironically, "the benefit of ignorance": "I am heartily ashamed of the abuse I have thrown upon the Odyssey. My only excuse is that I have never seen Mr Pope's. In justice to Homer I will fully agree in every fine thing you will say about the Iliad" (*Letters*, 1:180).

Carter's subtle reminder that Pope's *Odyssey* is not Homer's suggests a skeptical attitude confirmed when in 1760 she detected with satisfaction an error in Pope's translation. Writing to Archbishop Secker, Carter objected to Pope's dependence on a Latin translation of a phrase in the *Iliad* that, given in the dative rather than the accusative case, changed the sense of the entire passage in which it occurred. "Mr. Pope has fallen into the trap of the Latin translation," she informed her correspondent (*Memoirs*, 447). Yet despite Carter's superior grasp of the Greek language, the stoic philosopher quotes Pope's Homer throughout her edition of *All the Works of Epictetus* (1752). For example, Epictetus reminds his interlocutor that death is only an apparent evil because it is a necessity. "For what can I do, or where can I fly from it? Let me suppose myself to be Sarpedon, the son of Jove, that I may speak in the same gallant way. 'Brave though we die, and honoured if we live; Or let us glory gain, or glory give'— *Pope*."[61] In fact, Pope's Sarpedon had said, "Brave tho' we fall" (7.395). Carter's frequent misquotations suggest that she was working from memory in many instances.

Carter's references to Pope's Homer in a work that demonstrates her own knowledge of Greek may be her homage to a preceding translator. Carter's allusions to the eighteenth century's premier version of Homer indicate her desire to participate in the same cultural movement that encouraged Pope to translate Homer for the unlearned. Her use of Pope also suggests that, although his epics were not Homer's, his stirring verses contrasted appropriately with the plain talk of Epictetus in what she called her "strange, wooden, blundering translation" (*Letters*, 2:38). Carter may not have considered Pope a classical scholar, but she acknowledged his superior poetical gifts. In her critical references and allusions, Elizabeth Carter offers an example of an eighteenth-century woman responding to Pope with confidence in her expertise, assessing the accomplishment of a fellow professional poet and translator.

Later in the century, Hester Lynch Thrale meditated on Pope's *Iliad* in her *Thraliana*, providing another candid female perception of the poet's translation. By the 1770's, Pope's work was being assessed more critically; chief among those reappraising the poet was Mrs. Thrale's mentor Samuel Johnson. Unlike Carter and Talbot, who had accepted the entire translation as, substantially, Pope's work, Thrale believed that "Pope translated but two of the Books [of the *Odyssey*] as Doctor Warburton himself told Mr. Johnson, when they met at Mrs. French's Rout, and grew quite fond of one another."[62] Warburton's lie encouraged Thrale's disillusionment with Pope, although her youthful couplet poems had been quite imitative of his manner and themes.[63] When, in December 1780, Johnson shared with her a manuscript while preparing his *Life of Pope*, Thrale compared Pope's creative process with her own.

> We have got a sort of literary Curiosity amongst us; the foul Copy of Pope's Homer, with all his old Intended Verses, Sketches, emendations &c. strange that a Man shd keep such Things!—stranger still that a Woman should write such a Book as this; put down every Occurence of her Life, every Emotion of her Heart, & call it a *Thraliana* forsooth—but then I mean to destroy it. (Piozzi, *Thraliana*, 1:464)

Thrale seems mystified by the vanity, or presumption, that would lead a man to preserve the drafts of his poetry. She equates Pope's impulse to save his foul copy with her creation of the *Thraliana*. A woman's insights, as she records daily events, resemble the ideas or attempts a male artist later shapes into poetry. Thrale's scorn at Pope's conservation of "such Things" reminds us that not until Virginia

Woolf's Mrs. Ramsay were a woman's nurturing duties commemorated as her distinctive art. Merely for keeping her journal, Thrale seems to accuse herself of presumption equal to Pope's, until she adds, "but then I mean to destroy it." Her attitude toward both "literary curiosities" is complex. Is her disclaimer simply female self-abnegation, or does she regard herself as morally superior to Pope because she will have the discrimination to destroy her journal?

Thrale claimed to find Pope guilty of poor judgment in saving his drafts for the perusal of later scholars. As she studied the manuscript, she detected

> All Wood & Wire behind the Scenes sure enough! one sees that Pope laboured as hard—
>
>> as if the Stagyrite o'erlooked each Line
>
> indeed: and how very little Effect those glorious Verses at the end of the 8th Book of the Iliad have upon one; when one sees 'em in all their Cradles & Clouts: and Light changed for bright—& then the whole altered again, and the Line must end with Night—& Oh Dear! thus—*tort'ring one poor Word a thousand Ways*. (Piozzi, *Thraliana*, 1:464)

That Pope had taken his own advice in the "Essay on Criticism," laboring to achieve classical refinement of expression, disappointed Thrale. Her concluding remark paraphrases Dryden's "MacFlecknoe" (208), suggesting that Pope's *Iliad* drafts display the kind of false wit Dryden had despised in his rival Shadwell's verse. The comparison is patently unfair; Dryden's insult referred to Shadwell's published poetry, not to his unpublished manuscripts. But Thrale defended her opinion.

> Johnson says 'tis pleasant to see the progress of such a Mind: true; but 'tis a malicious Pleasure, Such as Men feel when they watch a Woman at her Toilet &
>
>> see by *Degrees a purer Blush* arise. &c.
>
> Wood & Wire once more! Wood & Wire! (Piozzi, *Thraliana*, 1:464)

In this reflection, the poet with his rough drafts is metamorphosed from a privileged male arrogantly assuming that even his scraps have some literary value, to a Belinda unconsciously revealing the secrets behind her appearance. Thrale's comparisons of Pope's drafts to her *Thraliana*, to a baby's swaddling clothes, and finally to a belle's cosmetics suggest that to at least one late eighteenth-century woman, Pope was no longer a superior denizen of the patriarchal canon, but rather a feminine figure whose writing process resembled her own.

Thrale's remark on Pope's manuscript, equating his creative process with a woman's domestic activities, ironically recalls Pope's assumptions about women's interests in his *Iliad* commentary. Her reflection partly confirms Felicity Nussbaum's impression of Thrale as a woman who simultaneously resisted and reproduced contemporary constructions of femininity.[64] Her invidious comment almost certainly masked personal insecurity about her creativity. Thrale acknowledged that her writing process resembled Pope's: both recorded their first attempts at expression, his in drafts and hers in journals; and both concluded with revised public versions of this material—Thrale published, as Mrs. Piozzi, *Anecdotes of Dr. Johnson* and *Observations and Reflections*, among other works originating in the private journals. But her unfavorable comparison of the drafting process to a woman's cosmetic preparations questions the importance of creative activity. It also suggests agreement with cultural assumptions about women and the relative value of their activities. The drafting process may be similar for both male and female writers, but two of the metaphors used to trivialize Pope's endeavor, baby clothes and cosmetics, are traditionally feminine.

Thrale's disapproval also reflects late eighteenth-century identification of Pope with "smooth" or "sweet" verse, epithets whose gendered associations were leading some critics to demote Pope from his status as a "great" English poet.[65] In the preface to his translation of Madame Dacier's *Iliad*, John Ozell had discussed his ambition to produce an English verse translation: "By Verse I do not mean Rhyme; for I always thought That too Effeminate to express the Masculine Spirit of Homer." Throughout Pope's career, his enemies suggested that his sweet-sounding verse had made "Tuneful Alexis . . . The Ladies' Play-Thing." Until after midcentury, however, general critical opinion concurred with Pope's claim that "if he pleas'd, he pleas'd by manly ways" ("Epistle to Dr. Arbuthnot," 337). Thrale's metaphors reflect a revised estimate of Pope's poetry. Not only the verse itself but his method of composition is imaged as feminine. The poetry is consequently further devalued. "Those glorious Verses at the end of the 8th Book of the Iliad" have "very little Effect" after the "Wood & Wire" behind their polished surfaces have been exposed. The theatrical metaphor, as if Pope's published poems were a special effect made possible by mechanical ingenuity, leads inexorably to Thrale's ultimate image of a woman applying her cosmetics in view of her male suitors. The verses, the theatrical scenery, and the belle are artificial productions.

Hester Lynch Thrale, like Elizabeth Carter, recognized in Pope a fellow writer, but evidence of his limitations led her not to recognize his achievement as distinguished from her own but to denigrate both her own and Pope's creative processes. Given her ambivalence, it may seem surprising that when Thrale reflected in 1784 on the books she had selected for her daughters' education, the list included "The English & Roman Histories, the Bible . . . Milton, Shakespeare, Pope's Iliad, Odyssey & other Works, some Travels . . . some elegant Novels . . . & Young and Addison's Works" (Piozzi, *Thraliana*, 1:591). In the context of the canon she constructed for her daughters, Thrale's private estimate of Pope suggests the rebellious urge of an unrecognized female writer, revelling in the "malicious Pleasure" of catching an established male writer "undressed." Perhaps, in these reflections, Pope becomes a surrogate for such men as Henry Thrale and Samuel Johnson, gaining public applause during the years when Thrale herself, who nurtured them and knew their weaknesses, was largely confined to her journals for creative expression.

Such women as Catherine Talbot and Hester Lynch Thrale confided their responses to Pope's translations in letters and journals. In 1728, however, an anonymous enemy, speaking of Pope's Homer, had claimed that "some will observe that Ladies have admir'd / His Epic Strain, and been like P—— inspir'd." Although primarily concerned with the number of women subscribers to the epics ("When *Homer* was the Fashion, who I pray / To be first in't had more Pretense then they?"), this critic raises the issue of whether any women were inspired to emulate the poet's enterprise.[66]

At least one woman poet praised Pope's translations in print, although anonymously, as early as 1724.[67] Elizabeth Tollet's *Poems on Several Occasions. With Anne Boleyn to King Henry VIII* contained two epigrammatic tributes. Tollet, whose volume also included verses "On a Poem of the Right Honourable Lady Mary Wortley Montagu in Mr. Hammond's Miscellany," contended in "On Mr. Pope's Homer" that

The *Samian* Sage, whose venerable Breast
   Euphorbus' transmigrating Soul possest,
Cou'd he revive again, wou'd joy to see
That *Homer's* Spirit is transfus'd to thee.[68]

Tollet's playful reference to Pythagoras reflects her education and deflates Pope's enemy's fear that ignorant belles would follow his example.[69]

Tollet read French, Italian, and Latin, but not Greek.[70] Like many educated women, she no doubt rejoiced in the increasing opportunity to share classical literature through translations. Her other brief tribute, "The Triumvirate of Poets" (*Poems*, 1st ed., 53) ponders the resemblance of living "Augustan" male poets to their classical predecessors.

> Britain with *Greece* and *Rome* contended long
> For lofty Genius and poetic Song:
> Till this *Augustan* Age with Three was blest,
> To fix the Prize, and finish the Contest.
> In *Addison* immortal *Virgil* reigns;
> So pure his Numbers, so refin'd his Strains:
> Of Nature full, with more impetuous Heat,
> In *Prior Horace* shines, sublimely great.
> Thy Country, *Homer*! we dispute no more,
> For Pope has fix'd it to his native Shore.

Tollet's suggestion that Britain has won the contest between ancient and modern writers mirrors contemporary pride in refined morals, manners, and writing. She values Addison for the purity and refinement of his verse; Prior's impetuosity replicates the classical sublime. Tollet reserves her ultimate praise for Pope, whose translation has evidently "finish[ed] the Contest," even as her lines on Pope's Homer finish the epigram. Tollet's clever allusion to the scholarly dispute over Homer's birthplace suggests, at least, an attentive reading of Thomas Parnell's "Essay on Homer," which prefaced Pope's translation. Again, there is no suggestion of frivolity in Tollet's elegant compliment, but rather an appraisal at once balanced, discriminating, and witty, rather like the critical ideal Pope had established in his "Essay on Criticism."

Toward the end of the century, Phillis Wheatley, an American poet, found in Pope's Homer her chief model.[71] Perhaps because she was so often requested to compose elegiac verse, Wheatley was particularly drawn to Pope's descriptions of warriors' confrontations and deaths. Two of her poems recast a biblical and a mythical tale in couplets reminiscent of the *Iliad*. "Goliath of Gath" invokes "Ye martial pow'rs, and all ye tuneful nine" (1) to recall Israel's conquest of Philistia. Israel's fear of Goliath resembles the Greek's retreat before the Trojan onslaught; David, one of Homer's pastoral princes drawn to battle. Instead of Achilles' divine armor, David bears no protection but Jehovah's favor. But his slingshot produces the same kind of vivid, highly individualized death found in Pope's translation.

> And now the youth the forceful pebble flung,
> *Philistia* trembled as it whizz'd along:
> In his dread forehead, where the helmet ends,
> Just o'er the brows the well-aim'd stone descends,
> It pierc'd the skull, and shatter'd all the brain,
> Prone on his face he tumbled to the plain.
>
> 　　　　　　　　　　　　　　　　(174–79)

Wheatley condenses the myriad deaths of gigantic warriors in the *Iliad* into this single confrontation. Her focus on Goliath's thunderous fall magnifies Israel's swift victory compared with the Greeks' ten-year siege. Virtually unarmed, David represents a divine power far more powerful than Homer's gods. Wheatley appropriates Pope's Homeric style to the service of her deeply felt religious tradition.

But in "Niobe in Distress for her Children Slain by Apollo," Wheatley simply seems interested in staging and describing a series of heroic deaths in the manner of Pope's *Iliad*. Pope himself had marveled at the "*Diversity* in the *Deaths* of [Homer's] *Warriors*, which he has supply'd by the vastest Fertility of Invention" ("Essay on Homer's Battles," *Poems*, 7:252). Wheatley evidently challenged herself to invent the deaths of Niobe's fourteen children. The princes particularly recall Homeric warriors as Phoebus's arrows pursue them on the Theban plain. The poem concludes abruptly after the youngest princess's death. Wheatley may have lost interest in the poem, which was later concluded by "another Hand" (Wheatley, 104). If so, she may have chosen her subject for its potential as an exercise in Pope's Homeric style.

Few women poets emulated Pope's epic example. In 1786, Helen Maria Williams published her *Poems* in two volumes, featuring such fashionable contemporary genres as the hymn, ode, and gothic tale. Her most ambitious poem was a six-canto saga narrating the Spanish conquest of Peru.[72] Written in heroic couplets, *Peru* seems more indebted to Restoration heroic drama, with its love-honor debates, than to Pope's translations. The parting of Indian warrior Manco-Capac and his wife Cora in canto 4, however, echoes Pope's version of the parting of Hector and Andromache. The *Iliad* episode most admired by eighteenth-century readers, modeled by Pope to appeal to women, apparently seemed to Williams an indispensible part of her exotic, historical poem. Williams even improved on Homer's concept by providing a second, more anguished, parting in canto 6, in which Cora expires in Capac's arms after seeking him on the battlefield (*Poems*, 2:156–60).

Perhaps the most poignant evidence of Pope's inspiration, however, is found in Sir Walter Scott's "Biographical Preface" to *The Poetical Works of Anna Seward*.[73] The "Swan of Lichfield" had been a stout defender of Pope throughout her career: from 1789 to 1790 she engaged in a lively debate in *Gentleman's Magazine* with Joseph Weston and others, maintaining Pope's poetic preeminence against the claims of Dryden. The conclusion of her sixth and final contribution to that controversy—which proceeded until April 1791—indicates Seward's fondness for Pope's Homer.

> If with a single being, *but* Mr. Weston, it can *yet* remain a doubt, whether Dryden's style of versification in the heroic couplet, or Pope's, be the most happy, let him compare *Dryden's* Translation of the first book of Homer's Iliad and *Pope's*. He will find the latter conveying, with brilliant strength and harmonious sweetness, the same sense in a *less* number of lines than Dryden, with his feeble Alexandrines in the middle of sentences, and botching triplets; the superior conciseness is in a proportion of about eight to twelve. (16 June 1790; Foster, 103)

Seward based her arguments throughout these editorial letters on Pope's refined and melodious style, while her opponents retorted that Dryden had intended his occasional lapses of sound or meter to break the heroic couplet's monotony. As poets struggled at the end of the century to establish new models, Seward upheld Popeian concision and harmony as her unquestioned ideals.

While editing her poems and literary correspondence for publication the year after her death, Sir Walter Scott included Seward's instructions to him about placing a youthful effort—

> the first three books of an epic poem raised on the basis of Fenelon's Telemachus, but in very excursive paraphrase, harmonizing, as I

flattered myself, with the style of Pope's Homer. I once hoped to have compleated the poem, and that, in such a completion, it might have formed no unacceptable conclusion to the adventures of the young and royal hero left unfinished in the Odyssey. (*Works*, 1:xxxiv)

From her instructions, it is clear that Seward hoped her oeuvre would be viewed in relation to Pope's, somewhat as Pope had patterned his career after Horace's or Virgil's. After detailing her preferred disposition of the early poems, Seward added, "To these metrical volumes, I wish the juvenile letters may be added, succeeding the poetic volumes as in Warburton's edition of Pope's works" (1:xxxiv). Scott disagreed not only with Seward's estimate of her juvenile writings but with her professed taste. In his preface, he seems baffled that she had preferred "the flowing numbers and expanded descriptions of Pope's Iliad to Cowper's translation, which approaches nearer the simple dignity of Homer." Although impressed by her youthful "Defense of Pope's Odyssey against Spence, in which she displays much critical acumen, and has decidedly the better of the Professor," Scott declined to publish either that manuscript or the fragmentary epic, judging neither piece worthy of inclusion with Seward's mature writings (1:xxvi). Thus Scott's "romantic" taste, and his protective regard for a woman writer's reputation, kept from the public a glimpse of Anna Seward's intended sequel to the *Odyssey*.

It is perhaps more surprising that Seward herself never completed her epic translation, although she was pondering how to proceed beyond book 3 as late as 1798.[74] Defending and emulating Pope throughout her career, she would have produced a text that was at least an intriguing response to her predecessor's. Perhaps her cultural milieu intervened, making any straightforward imitation of Pope's work impossible in an era dominated by the sentimental and the Gothic. Or perhaps, to speculate in Harold Bloom's terms, the time had not yet arrived when a strong writer, such as Jane Austen, could rewrite Pope on her terms. Anna Seward, born just three years after Pope's death, was not destined to be considered Pope's female successor. Yet her desire to continue Pope's epic translations bespeaks an enormous ambition. And to the extent that his epics did not daunt women readers but stimulated their reading and response, Pope himself might be said to have fostered their ambition through his translations.

Pope published his Homeric translations in an era when the cultural horizon of expectations seemed—to a young poet anxious to attract a broad, upwardly mobile readership of both genders—to dictate an appeal to women reminiscent of the condescending banter in the *Tatler* and the *Spectator*. Such an approach, as we have seen, masked Pope's personal trepidation about addressing women, while assimilating women into the audience for classical literature in a manner nonthreatening to the male guardians of patriachal tradition (including Pope himself). But Pope's gesture toward women was derided by some contemporaries, who found the poet's efforts to engage women readers inappropriate. Pope's male critics were no more able than he to conceive of women as their intellectual peers. This state of affairs placed a terrific burden on Pope's eighteenth-century women readers. His translation and commentary anticipated, even dictated, certain female responses. Women were to find battles, bloodshed, and conventional scholarship tedious, and they were to seek refreshment in domestic interludes or notes about cookery and fashions.

The range of recorded responses by women to Pope's Homer reminds us how false and constricting were the feminine configurations of his time. No two women responded in the same manner, or even according to Pope's "script." Madame Dacier's and Lady Mary Wortley Montagu's ironies reveal their awareness that even noted intellectual women could not permit themselves masculine freedom to criticize. Yet they managed to convey their opinions to the poet. Catherine Talbot's delight in Pope's refined poetry was shared by such male contemporaries as William Melmoth, while Elizabeth Carter, confident in her superior knowledge of Greek, distinguished between Pope's gifts as poet and translator. Elizabeth Tollet's occasional epigrams suggest that Pope's translation complemented her knowledge of classical Latin works. And Anna Seward's youthful desire to continue Pope's *Odyssey* with her own *Telemachiad* proves that at least one eighteenth-century woman reader had "admir'd his epick strain, / And been like Pope inspir'd" (*Popeiana: The Dunciad I*, 33).

With one exception, all these women's responses to Pope were magnanimous. In the case of Hester Lynch Thrale, her hostile reflections on Pope's manuscript suggest not only the influence of Samuel Johnson but her self-abnegating identification with the poet and her subdued aggression toward the distinguished men in her life. The most negative recorded response, Thrale's is also the most complex. Given the restrictive nature of Pope's conception of women in his translations, the generosity of these female responses is striking. Because they had a tiny niche in his commentary, his women readers apparently took Pope's condescending addresses—hardly granting them "separate but equal" status—as an invitation to share classical culture with the growing numbers of genteel but unlettered men. Pope's idealizations of marriage and parenthood and his general attempts to evoke sentimental responses made his translations seem far more cognizant of women readers than his scattered appeals to the ladies warranted. Women either ignored the insulting implications of Pope's commentary while enjoying his feminine details or adopted an expanded focus in which the feminine commentary was merely one aspect of an epic refined to conform to modern taste. In either case, women readers expanded the boundaries of their experience by ignoring the boundaries Pope, or the conventions he adopted, set for them as readers.

The relegation of Pope's poetry, especially his translations, to the realm of the feminine in the late eighteenth century becomes paradoxically understandable and tragic for women readers. Anna Seward and other women who cherished the harmonious sweetness of Pope's verse found themselves on the wrong side of the movement toward "manly simplicity," a movement exemplified in the diction embraced by William Wordsworth in his preface to the *Lyrical Ballads*. Pope's translations had, perhaps unwittingly, invited women to take part in a broad cultural movement. The epic virtues of refinement, simplicity, and companionate marriage, in addition to such traditional values as strength and valor, implied that women could take part in shaping a culture superior even to Homer's. The women who responded to Pope in their letters and poems were eager to sanction his cultural vision, which included them if only in a subordinate role. Elizabeth Tollet, for example, also wrote "Hypatia," a 195-line poem defending female learning (65–72). Surely Tollet did not include Pope among those men who, like "barb'rous Tyrants, to secure their Sway, / Conclude that Ignorance will best obey" (48–49). For such women as Tollet, Catherine Talbot, and even Hester Lynch Thrale (who mourned that she could recite Pope's Homer by heart but did not understand Greek; Piozzi, *Thraliana*, 1:460–61), Pope's translations opened classical Greek literature to them at a time when England boasted a rival "neoclassical" culture. By the end of the century, the neoclassical ideal had been exchanged for a celebration of Gothic Britain, and women too were being assigned roles and expectations more consonant with Gothic models. Ironically, their horizon of expectations shrunk, or dimmed, at the same time that Pope's writings lost cultural esteem.

2

Women's Prose Responses
to Pope's Writings

By the end of the eighteenth century, women were alluding to
Pope's *Iliad* in a wide variety of texts. Novelists as disparate as Fanny
Burney and Ann Radcliffe recurred to Pope's epic imagery. In Burney's
Evelina (1778), the heroine describes her flight after rescuing Mr. Macartney from possible suicide: "Pale, and motionless, he suffered me
to pass, without changing his posture, or uttering a syllable; and
indeed, 'He looked a bloodless image of despair!' "[1] Evelina recalls
Idomeneus's personification of cowardice as he vindicates Meriones
in *Iliad* 13.

> No Force, no Firmness, the pale Coward shows;
> . . . .
> With chatt'ring Teeth he stands, and stiff'ning Hair,
> And looks a bloodless Image of Despair!
> (13.359, 364–65; Pope's trans.)

What at first appears merely a vivid, if borrowed, description is a key
to Burney's characterization of Macartney. Although jealous Lord
Orville suspects him of romantic rivalry, Evelina could never consider
Macartney a candidate for her hand. She recognizes the fundamental
cowardice of Macartney's apparent recourse to suicide to ameliorate
his misfortune. Her instinctive choice of allusion—she recounts the
incident while still "shocked to death" in its aftermath (181)—suggests
that while Evelina may pity Mr. Macartney, she could never sufficiently esteem a man who had nearly succumbed to despair. Macartney's potential as a tragic figure is undermined, already foreshadow-
ing his rather ignominious marriage with Polly Green at the novel's
conclusion.

Ann Radcliffe alludes to the *Iliad* in a very different but equally appropriate context in *The Mysteries of Udolpho* (1794). Chapter 13 of book 3 marks the nadir of Emily St. Aubert's adventures. After many harrowing episodes, the heroine is finally reunited with her beloved Valancourt, only to learn that he has apparently forfeited her esteem. For her epigraph to the chapter, Radcliffe chose an epic simile from *Iliad* 15, in which the Trojan army

> Bursts as a Wave, that from the Clouds impends,
> And swell'd with Tempests on the Ship descends;
> White are the Decks with Foam; the Winds aloud
> Howl o'er the Masts, and sing thro'ev'ry Shroud:
> Pale, trembling, tir'd, the Sailors freeze with Fears;
> And instant Death on ev'ry Wave appears.
> (15.752–57; Pope's trans.)[2]

Count de Villefort's revelation of Valancourt's debauchery bursts like a wave over Emily's consciousness. While Homer's storm threatens sailors with physical death, Valancourt's reputed misconduct seems the death of Emily's sustaining hope for their united future. Moreover, the Trojan incursion, like Valancourt's lost reputation, is only a temporary reversal, leading ultimately to the Greeks' triumph. The Trojan threat elicits Patroclus's assault and death, and thus the return of Achilles and the defeat of Hector. Emily diverts herself from thoughts of Valancourt by listening to old Dorothy's tale of the duchess de Villeroi. The tragic story proves the clue to both Emily's identity and the resolution of the novel's plot. Radcliffe's Homeric epigraph is therefore both thematically and structurally relevant.

Neither Burney nor Radcliffe merely plucks a memorable image from Pope's *Iliad*, although recent scholarship on eighteenth-century reading habits suggests that many contemporaries were familiar only with the "beauties" of longer poems found in anthologies of extracts.[3] Burney's and Radcliffe's allusions reveal their familiarity with Pope's translation and studious attention to the functions of his Homeric imagery. They also suggest the appeal of Pope's *Iliad* to women of very different gifts and tastes. Burney's allusion to Idomeneus's speech is subtly satirical, intimating the weakness of a sympathetic character. After reading Pope's *Iliad*, the sixteen-year-old Burney confided in her journal that "I never was so charm'd with a poem in my life."[4] In her novels, however, she usually alluded to Pope's satirical poems; *Evelina* elsewhere refers to *The Dunciad* and the "Epistle to Burlington."[5] Burney's gift for ironic observation led her to select even from Homer a satirical passage. Radcliffe was celebrated for what Rhoda Flaxman has called "cinematic word-painting."[6] When most inspired, Radcliffe evoked through her sublime landscape descriptions not only the passions of her characters but the significance of their activities. She was appropriately drawn to Homer's turbulent seascape, a vignette that mirrors both Emily's despair and the fact that Emily's dilemma marks the turning point of the novel's plot.

Burney's and Radcliffe's Popeian allusions resemble many eighteenth-century women's references to Pope. Though Pope was the greatest contemporary influence on women's poetry, women frequently alluded to or criticized his texts in their prose writings as well. Eighteenth-century women produced significant critical analyses of Pope, although many of these have virtually disappeared because they occurred in letters, journals, editorial notes, and other rarely reproduced sources. Because their opinions have not been sufficiently represented as part of Pope's critical history,[7] contemporary women seem to have received passively even work that sought a female audience. Recalling some of their responses not only will restore to Pope a more balanced critical heritage but will help to reconstruct a portion of women's intellectual history.

Women inherit a tradition of prose writing that, as Margaret Ezell has observed in *The Patriarch's Wife*, is obscured by recent emphasis on women poets and playwrights. Questioning current assumptions about the dearth of seventeenth-century women writers, Ezell contends that few scholars acknowledge the manuscript sources or the epistolary networks in which much of women's (and men's) writing appeared in an era still ambivalent about publishing. She further notes that women who published often remain unacknowledged because their religious, political, or philosophical polemics are now considered "unreadable."[8] Ezell concludes that women's participation in seventeenth-century intellectual life has been badly underestimated (162). Eighteenth-century women inherited many literary traditions from their seventeenth-century foremothers, similarly complicating assessments of their cultural participation and influence.

While men struggled to achieve professional status as writers, with only partial success throughout the eighteenth century,[9] women proceeded even more slowly because their maternal and domestic roles remained paramount. By midcentury, women were taking advantage of subscriptions, publishing their works for profit while limiting their audiences in compliance with feminine decorum. Such writers as Sarah Fielding, Charlotte Lennox, and Sarah Scott gradually built respect for women as professional novelists, and Fanny Burney and such great novelists of the 1790s as Charlotte Smith and Anne Radcliffe confirmed women's preeminence in that genre. But throughout the century, manuscripts and letters also remained vital means of circulating women's opinions, and much astute criticism of contemporary events and publications appeared first in writings intended for a select circle of readers.

Moreover, Ezell's complaint that seventeenth-century women's published prose has been ignored is equally applicable to the eighteenth century. Though less engaged in the polemics characteristic of the previous century, women wrote in such genres as the moral tract and the educational guide, which, popular at the time, attract little attention today.[10] Yet the criticism expressed by women in their letters and published prose is often astute, always forthright; many women's opinions were formed by wide reading. Their responses to Pope constitute a rich slice of literary history, spiced by occasional gossip or celebrity adulation. That women confidently expressed their literary preferences and opinions may owe something to their foremothers' expertise in argumentative prose. We should not ignore this heritage and perpetuate the myth that eighteenth-century women were tongue-tied by convention. In prose ranging from journals to novels, travel guides to critical essays, women confronted and assessed Pope's ideology and techniques.

Women's religious and political allegiances influenced their opinions of Pope's poetry, evoking tart critiques when his ideology diverged from theirs. Elizabeth Rowe and Frances Seymour, countess of Hertford, admired and quoted Pope's early poetry throughout their lives, but they heartily disapproved of most of his later satire. Rowe, the daughter of a Presbyterian preacher, was a religious enthusiast; Lady Hertford served Queen Caroline as Lady of the Bedchamber. Pope's Opposition poetry offended their religious and political sensibilities.

An example of vivid, if not particularly fair, criticism occurs in a letter from Lady Hertford to the countess of Pomfret in 1739.

> Mr. Pope has thought fit to publish a new volume of poems. It contains his Sober Advice, Seventeen Hundred and Thirty-eight, his Epistle to Augustus, and several things which he had sold singly

before. There are also an epitaph . . . and two or three epigrams. As a specimen, I send you one, which is prefaced with the pompous title: "Engraved on the collar of a dog which I gave to his royal highness:"

"I am his highness' dog at Kew:—
"Pray tell me, sir, whose dog are you?"

Does it not remind you of one of a more ancient date, which I believe is repeated in all the nurseries in England?

Bow, wow, wow, wow!
Whose dog art thou? &c.

I do not infer from hence that Mr. Pope finds himself returning into childhood, and therefore imitates the venerable author of the last, in order to shine amongst the innocent inhabitants of the apartments where his works are most in vogue; but I presume it is to prove that he can descend into the Bathos, with the same alacrity that he has formerly soared to the summit of Parnassus.[11]

The countess must have recoiled from the harsh satire of such poems as "Sober Advice" and the "Epilogue to the Satires." As we shall observe of the countess of Winchelsea and Lady Mary Wortley Montagu, Lady Hertford capitalized on Pope's lower social rank to reduce the value of his poems. Her remarks first portray Pope as an avaricious merchant, seeking additional profit on poems he has already "sold singly before." Her choice of epigram reveals her political and class bias; Pope's "pompous" insinuation of familiarity with the Prince of Wales was bound to offend an adherent of the king. Like many of Pope's politically inspired critics, the countess refuses to find any humor or irony in the resemblance between Pope's epigram and the traditional nursery rhyme. By ignoring his wit, she is free to intimate that Pope's works are "in the most vogue" in nurseries, and that the epigram, by her account a failed attempt at pomposity, is bathetic.

Despite her contempt for many of Pope's late works, Lady Hertford remained charmed by the "Epistle from Eloisa to Abelard." When her son passed the Paraclete in 1743 while on his grand tour, Lady Hertford eagerly inquired whether it was "the same where the convent stands which was founded by Abelard, and which is so well known here by Mr. Pope's *Letter from Eloisa?*"[12] Lady Hertford's "An Epistle from Yarico to Inkle" (1738) was among the century's better imitations of Pope's poem. In the poem and in her references, Lady Hertford refined Pope's eroticism to suit her genteel, Christian context. In 1748, still mourning her son's death while on his tour, she apologized to Lady Luxborough for her continuing distress: "But two lines of Mr. Pope's must plead my excuse: 'Of all Affliction taught a Suff'rer yet / 'Tis sure the hardest Science to forget' " (Hughes, 386). Lady Hertford's appropriation of Eloisa's passionate cry, substituting "suff'rer" for "lover," corroborates our modern impression that maternal love was among the few strong passions acknowledged by eighteenth-century ladies. It also testifies to Lady Hertford's conviction that in his early poems, before his plunge into political controversy, Pope had "soared to the summit of Parnassus."

Elizabeth Singer Rowe shared Lady Hertford's estimates of Pope's early and mature poems. In a 1735 letter to Lady Hertford, Rowe observes that the "Epistle to Dr. Arbuthnot" "seems to be writ with a malice more than human, and has surely something infernal in it. It is surprising, that a man can divest himself of the tender sentiments of nature so far, as deliberately to give anguish and confusion to beings of his own kind."[13] Rowe's political sympathies certainly influenced this response. She ignores Pope's "Advertisement" (*Poems*, 4:95), which explained the poem's origin as a reply to Lord Hervey's and Lady Mary Wortley Montagu's "Verses to the Imitator of Horace." The degrading imagery of that poem explains, if it does not justify, the violence of Pope's satire; Pope himself had been the victim of a poem intended "to give anguish and confusion." Like Lady Hertford, Rowe artfully ignores an obvious aspect of the text to reach her conclusion. Their critical dismissals result not from ignorance but from strong opinions and rhetorical agility.

Also like Lady Hertford, Rowe discriminated between Pope's poems directed to women readers, as well as his poems with Christian significance, and his political satire. After its appearance in Lewis's 1730 *Miscellany*, she copied "The Dying Christian to His Soul" into a letter, remarking, "I wish I may be in the happy disposition to repeat these lines at that final period."[14] Elsewhere, she applies Pope's description of Olympus (*Odyssey* 6.49–54) to heaven, observing to a female correspondent that "this gay scheme is I believe suited to your taste, tho' I am afraid it would not be at all agreeable to the reverend Mr.——'s sagacity" (*Works*, 2:227). Aware that Pope's baroque evocations of paradise were more sensual than orthodox, Rowe quotes from memory a pastiche of lines from "Eloisa to Abelard" to describe the moral pleasures of retirement, adding, "I am afraid these thoughts are rather flights of poetry, than devotion" (*Works*, 2:238).

Pope's tempting images nevertheless influenced Rowe's descriptions of heaven in her celebrated *Letters from the Dead to the Living* (1728) and *Letters Moral and Entertaining* (1728–32), which reconcile readers to mortality by promising an elysium rich in sensual delight and fulfilled love. Letter 10 of *Letters Moral and Entertaining,* for example, is a fantasia apparently derived from Pope's characterization of Ariel in *The Rape of the Lock.*[15] In "To Lady ——, from a Sylph," Ariel assures his mortal beloved that "was I permitted to appear in the rosy bloom of celestial youth, with my golden zone, my purple wings, and glittering Tiara, I should outshine the most splendid birth-night beau." Unlike Pope's rather insidious sylph, however, Rowe's Ariel has no amorous pretensions to the lady "'till your date of mortal life is expired; and then if you continue stedfast to the rules of virtue, you shall be mine by all the engagements of celestial love" (*Friendship*, 181). The sylph then offers his protégée a 16-line verse description of heaven, where youthful lovers

> . . . wander through Elysian Groves,
> Or banquet in the gay alcoves;
> And oft in Amaranthine bow'rs,
> Repose on fragrant beds of flow'rs.
>
> (9–12, *Friendship*, 182)

Pope's alluring sylph, shorn of the illicit erotic connotations of his Rosicrucian model, has become a moral agent, reminding a belle distinguished by vivacity and innocent wit of the immortal world. Rowe has revised Pope's "machinery," adapting the fanciful imagery she evidently found appealing to her didactic purpose in the *Letters*.

Lady Hertford's and Rowe's outright rejections of Pope's political satire and gentle revisions of the poems they approved indicate that, although a contemporary with whom each battled and from whom each swerved, he was not the chief precursor of these writers. Lady Hertford's horizon of awareness included a strong tradition of aristocratic patronesses of letters, a role she emulated even though such patronage declined during her lifetime. Rowe could look back to Katherine Philips as a precursor of her mystical compositions. More protracted struggles, in which Pope stood in relation to eighteenth-century women writers as the "Great Original," with all the imaginable complications of gender difference, awaited a younger generation.[16]

Such political prejudices as Lady Hertford's characterize the responses of Pope's whiggish aristocratic contemporaries. Baroness Mary Lepel Hervey, although Pope's friend before her marriage, disparaged the poet in her mature correspondence. Attributing his polished style to Lord Bolingbroke's influence, she declared in 1748 that Pope "would certainly never have wrote so elegantly, but that, as he bragged, *envy must own he lived among the great*".[17] Like Lady Hertford, Lady Hervey countered Pope's assumption of (Opposition) poetic preeminence with her own version of his indebtedness.

Later in the century, literary competition replaced personal antagonism. Moralist and educational writer Hester Mulso Chapone distrusted fanciful poetry "when gay description holds the place of sense."[18] Suspicious of rhetoric, she revised the opening couplet of Pope's "Sixth Epistle of the First Book of Horace Imitated."

> I have always thought that the very contrary of that maxim, which Pope gives us in "the very words of Creech," is true, and that, "To admire, is all the art I know, / To make men happy and to keep them so." When use and experience prevent our being surprised at any thing, and when, by comparing new things with old, we become difficult to be pleased, we seem to have lost the chief means of being happy. (2:190)

Pope's poem discourages extremes of fear and desire, not pleasant "surprise" at "new things." Chapone misread Horace's maxim, approved by Creech and Pope, to privilege her experience and wisdom over that of a triumvirate of forefathers.

Some women invoked Pope's sanction for their opinions or intellectual activities. Charlotte Lennox barely mentions Pope (or any previous scholar) in *Shakespear Illustrated* (1753), preferring to clear a space for her effort by stressing previous scholars' "unaccountable Neglect" of Shakespeare's sources.[19] Elizabeth Montagu, however, concurs with Pope's critical judgments throughout her *Essay on the Writings and Genius of Shakespear* (1769), disarming potential objections to her feminine criticism. She fights Voltaire under Pope's banner, quoting the prologue to *Cato*, "Eloisa to Abelard," "Epistle to Dr. Arbuthnot," and "Essay on Criticism" to substantiate her opinions.[20] She begins her introduction by recalling a Popeian comment, in his preface to *The Works of Shakespear* (1725). Montagu agrees that "of all English poets, this tragedian offers the fullest and fairest subject for criticism" (1). Disclaiming any competition with former learned editors, she nevertheless construes Pope's remark as an invitation for her contribu-

tion to Shakespeare scholarship. Warming to her defense, she paraphrases another of Pope's contentions, observing that "to form a
judgment of Shakespear's works, we are not to apply to the rules of
Aristotle, which would be like trying a man by the laws of one country,
who lived under those of another" (7). Shakespeare demands critical
deference.

> Great indulgence is due to the errors of original writers, who, quitting
> the beaten track which others have travelled, make daring incursions
> into unexplored regions of invention, and boldly strike into the path-
> less sublime. . . . Genius is of a bold enterprizing nature, ill adapted
> to the formal restraints of critic institutions, or indeed to lay down
> to itself rules of nice discretion. (8)

Montagu invokes the classical sublime, a concept most recently extolled by Edmund Burke in his *Philosophical Inquiry* (1757). But her
terms could serve as a prose gloss of Pope's defense of sublimity in
the "Essay on Criticism."

> Thus *Pegasus*, a nearer way to take,
> May boldly deviate from the common Track.
> Great Wits may sometimes *gloriously offend*,
> And *rise* to *Faults* true Criticks *dare not mend*.
>
> (150–53)

Montagu's allusions to Pope throughout her essay demonstrate familiarity with his canon. She proves adept at drawing or illustrating
critical precepts from a disparate selection of Pope's poems. She avoids
the impression of dependence on Pope's "Preface" while incorporating his authority into her defense.

Other women spurned Pope's authority, resisting his influence
in truly Bloomian fashion. In a fine literary biography, William McCarthy has analyzed Hester Thrale Piozzi's relation to Pope, the first of
her male precursors.[21] McCarthy argues that Piozzi's decisions to write
in such genres as the travel book, the synonymy, and history left her
virtually bereft of foremothers. As we observed of *Thraliana* in chapter
1, Piozzi's responses to Pope's translations suggest a covert rebellion
against the oppressive men in her life. A lengthy example from Piozzi's
later prose demonstrates her continuing engagement with Pope, even
at a point in her career when McCarthy feels she was "essentially
finished with him" (78) as poetic precursor. *British Synonymy* (1794)

contains about three dozen references to Pope—more than to any other eighteenth-century writer except Johnson. McCarthy observes that Piozzi swerved from Johnson in the *Synonymy* partly by refusing to use any of the illustrative quotations in his *Dictionary* (186). *Synonymy*'s illustrations represent Piozzi's breadth of reading, particularly her familiarity with Shakespeare, Milton, and a host of eighteenth-century writers.

Piozzi intended *Synonymy* to help foreigners discriminate among English words. Each entry constitutes an essay discussing and illustrating a list of potentially confusing words. When referring to Pope or to Johnson, she frequently corrects their usage as well, displaying what McCarthy has described as her combative instinct. Of "Dull, Stupid, Heavy," Piozzi observes, "Of the first upon this flat and insipid list Mr. Pope has greatly enlarged the signification, and taught us to call everything *Dull* that was not immediately and positively witty. This is too much, surely; and indeed one finds it received so only in the Dunciad or Essay upon Criticism."[22] This confident but patently unfair generalization about the poems enables Thrale to assert her authority over the language ("Information may be *Heavy* sometimes without being *Stupid* or *Dull*, I think," *Synonymy*, 1:176), and therefore over Pope.

In her entry for "Fluency, Smoothness, Volubility," Piozzi subverts a memorable aphorism in Pope's "Essay on Criticism":

These words if applied to conversation . . . seem to imply not only a copiousness with regard to words, but an idea as if eloquence were put in the place of instruction, and that there was more verbosity than matter concerned—Such was Pope's notion certainly, . . .

> Words are like leaves, and where they most abound,
> Much fruit of sense beneath is rarely found,

. . . yet one is never gratified by a sight of cherries nailed to a wall as I have sometimes seen them very bare of foliage in particular years; one likes rather to observe the fruit glowing through the leaves' delightful green. Pope and Swift had small conversation powers; their talent was in writing: but bullion is not current till 'tis coined; and the sea itself would stagnate with its quantity of solid contents, did not the tides toss it into active motion; while the stream whose *fluency* preserves the clearness of its bottom, carries some grains of gold into that ocean, when like a stream of sweet *volubility* in talk, it takes up the whole valuable part of every land through which it

flows—yet by its *smoothness* leaves to none a reason for complaint.
(*Synonymy,* 1:241–42)

Piozzi's strategy involves lifting Pope's simile out of context to demolish its usefulness. In Pope's "Essay on Criticism," lines 309–10 refer explicitly to written eloquence. The verse paragraph opens, "Others for *Language* all their Care express, / And value *Books*, as Women *Men*, for *Dress*" (305–6). Piozzi's response, however, is not merely a false quarrel, but an appropriately eloquent defense of "dress," the ornament of language that Pope (here) found offensively feminine. By casting Pope's epigram in terms of conversation, she shifts the grounds of the argument to a defense of volubility, traditionally used pejoratively, often to describe feminine speech. She complicates her defense by equating volubility with eloquence, a word synonymous with oratory and hence usually applied to masculine speech.[23] Piozzi's maneuver disrupts the boundaries between masculine and feminine conversation maintained by such etymologists as Johnson, exposes the supposed inadequacy that motivated Pope's opinion (he had "small conversation powers"), and usurps the authority of both forefathers.[24]

Piozzi wishes to assert that eloquence does not necessarily replace instruction—that verbosity does not obviate matter. Her first move opposes her vividly particular image to Pope's witty generalization. Pope suggested an agricultural analogy: eloquence deflects attention from inadequate sense just as abundant leaves disguise paltry fruit. The observation is as unadorned as the sensible rhetoric Pope recommends. There is no appeal to the senses through particularization (What kind of fruit?), no evocation of a personal experience. Pope intends a universal truism independent of climate, season, or individual. To Pope's general truth, Piozzi opposes her personal repugnance to "a sight of cherries nailed to a wall as I have sometimes seen them very bare of foliage." Pope's abstracted fruit and leaves become a specific image—cherries nailed to a wall. The appeal to the reader's imagination, as we visualize the wall and the leafless cherries, is rhetorically effective: Piozzi not only assumes her reader's assent to her argument ("one is never gratified" by such a sight) but makes that argument through the "dress" of language Pope affects to despise. To reinforce her opinion, Piozzi piles up metaphors, developed into an epic simile comparing "sweet *volubility*" to a cleansing tidal stream. She concludes by reengaging Pope's imagery, explaining that the most "unhappy talkers" are "copious without . . . smoothness." These "remind one of the brown wintry foliage sticking close to an old oak in January, or sullen beech tree, stiff in stale prejudice that yields with difficulty to new and brilliant thoughts, than of that verdant and luxurious leafy labyrinth which Pope's remark brings to our observation" (*Synonymy*, 1:242–43). Pope's simile is too general to create such an impression, but Piozzi's play with his image makes her point. Her appeal to the senses, to particular trees and leaves and fruits and seasons, subverts both his aphorism and his authority. Feminine volubility, dressing language in copious imagery, conveys both delight and, through its specificity, wisdom.

Piozzi literally gives Pope the last word in *Synonymy*. Lines 629–56 of *Dunciad* 4 (beginning with "She comes, she comes! the sable throne behold / Of Night primeval and of Chaos old!") conclude her final, gloomy discussion of current disdain for political limits or boundaries. McCarthy observes that she here permits Pope to voice the "counterapocalyptic" cry of which she felt incapable (*Piozzi*, 237). Yet elsewhere in *Synonymy*, through various rebukes and revisions, Piozzi disarms Pope, her first creative antagonist, to an extent she never achieved as poet. Perhaps the medium of prose, in which she felt most comfortable, enabled these repeated confrontations.

A cluster of allusions drawn from novels illustrates the extent to which women writers assumed readers' familiarity with Pope's poetry. In *The Adventures of David Simple* (1744), Sarah Fielding generally confines her allusions to Shakespeare, Milton, Congreve's and Addison's plays, *The Tatler*, and *The Spectator*.[25] Pope, however, figures in the conversation of Cynthia, a lovely young woman with an ill-fated reputation for wit. Cynthia quotes at length from the "Essay on Criticism" (lines 494–507) to illustrate how "those Persons who have Wit" are unjustly persecuted (*Adventures*, 102). Fielding here either indulges popular taste for Pope, or perhaps jogs the reader's memory. But later, she evidently expects the reader to recall the context of Cynthia's description of "a Man, who has such strong Sensations of every thing, that he is, as Mr. *Pope* finely says, 'tremblingly alive all o'er.' His Inclinations hurry him away, and his Resolution is too weak ever to resist them" (262). Pope's phrase, in *Essay on Man* (1.197), rebukes the stupidity of wishing for finer senses than God granted human beings. Cynthia's allusion carries a suggestion of moral condemnation, for those readers familiar with Pope's poem.

Sarah Scott's *A Description of Millenium Hall* (1762) and its sequel *The History of Sir George Ellison* (1766) are permeated with Popeian echoes, particularly of Pope's *Essay on Man* and his epistles on the use of riches.[26] Late in *Millenium Hall*, the ladies describe for Sir George the history of a mansion they are renovating. The former owner, a miser, had turned away all of his servants but one old woman; "Night and day growled before his inhospitable door a furious Dutch mastiff, whose natural ferocity was so increased by continual hunger, for his master fed him most sparingly, that no stranger could have entered the yard with impunity" (175). After the miser's death, his house was inherited by a profligate nephew, who "in one year . . . circulated through the kingdom the ready money which his uncle had been half his life starving himself and his family to accumulate" (177). Rescued from these versions of Old and Young Cotta (see "Epistle to Bathurst," 179–218), the house has now been "purchased to be the seat of charity and benevolence. How directly were we led to admire the superior sense, as well as the transcendent virtue of these ladies, when we compared the use they made of money with that to which the two late possessors had appropriated it!" (177).

The ladies of Millenium Hall fulfill Pope's ideal of the golden mean, combining "the sense to value Riches, with the Art / T'enjoy them, and the virtue to impart" ("Epistle to Bathurst," 219–20). Of the renovations, Sir George recalls, "It was pleasing to see numbers at work to repair the building and cultivate the garden and to observe that at length from this inhospitable mansion 'health to himself, and to his children bread, the labourer bears' " (178). In Pope's "Epistle to Burlington" (lines 170–71), the phrase recalls the natural cycle of poverty and plenty as consolation for the stupid magnificence of Timon. Scott's allusions to the epistles impart the sanction of a conservative ideology to her novel's moderate feminism. She places female characters in the places of Lords Bathurst and Burlington, suggesting that a coalition of pious women could equal, if not excel, these aristocratic men's attempts to adjust the cycle of poverty and plenty more equitably.

Sir George absorbs the ladies' Popeian philosophy. Back home, in *The History of Sir George Ellison*, he defends his modest way of life by echoing Pope's description of Timon's mansion ("Epistle to Burlington," 107–8, 127–32). He refuses to furnish a suite of rooms merely to impress visitors.

> If I have any inherent dignity, I presume it will accompany me in all places; if I have not, the grandeur of my apartments will not

bestow it. So much ceremony to bring us into the presence of an insignificant Being, in my opinion, wears an air of ridicule; and if during so long a progress, any ideas of greatness have entered our minds, they only serve to make the master of the house appear still more mean. (1:220)

Refuting his cousin Sir William's suggestion that he keep more than one footman, Sir George argues that moral damage is caused by superfluous servants' idleness. "Every man of moderate age, and tolerable health, is able to gain a subsistence, and that by means useful to the community, and beneficial to himself; *health to himself, and to his children bread, the labourer bears*" (1:223–24). Fired by the example of Millenium Hall, Sir George establishes a renowned course of charities. Although his own good works are extensive, he continues to regard Millenium Hall as his pattern; after revisiting Millenium Hall, he adopts the ladies' new plan for girls' schools. To follow the ladies' program is, Scott suggests, to fulfill Pope's vision of "the use of riches." Although Sir George is a model patriarch, the shared Popeian allusions of the two novels reinforce our recognition that Sir George's patriarchal program was first implemented by a benevolent matriarchy.

Frances Brooke's *The History of Emily Montague* (1769) palpably alludes to Pope through one of its heroines, Arabella Fermor.[27] Brooke's Arabella pays homage to Pope's creation of the ultimate coquette, and the novel elaborates assumptions about women implicit in *The Rape of the Lock* and "Epistle to a Lady." *Emily Montague* sympathizes with women; its principal theme is that couples should wed for love. But the notion that women should have more freedom in choosing husbands is modified by Brooke's advocacy, through her heroes, of a specialized education that will make women pleasing mates. Edward Rivers, the novel's sentimental hero, extols women's "lovely prattle beyond all the sense and learning in the world" (3:47). Arabella herself praises Lucy Temple for smiling even when her husband hurts her feelings (4:152). Arabella resembles Pope's Arabella/Belinda fallen into unexceptionable male hands. While Belinda endured the Baron's treachery at a Hampton Court card party, Arabella meets her forbearing suitor, Captain Fitzgerald, in the wilds of Canada. While Belinda endured a mock-rape in retaliation for her coquetry, Arabella merely believes she manipulates the Captain. But Captain Fitzgerald cooperates with Arabella's father to save her from herself; the men, and not Arabella, are completely in control. Brooke's characters frequently quote passages from Pope's canon, from the *Iliad* to

"Eloisa to Abelard" to his Horatian imitations. These quotations not only confirm the Belinda/Arabella allusion but establish *Emily Montague* as a refined development of Pope's ideas about women. Like *The Rape*, *Emily Montague* discourages feminine independence. Emily and Lucy, like Martha Blount in "Epistle to a Lady," are happiest when swaying through submission on retired estates. By the novel's conclusion, Arabella progresses toward this ideal. She is chastened by Fitzgerald's tenderness, a conclusion by which Brooke suggests that a proper (Rousseauian) feminine education would have ameliorated Belinda's difficulties. *Emily Montague* outlines Brooke's notion of the educational philosophy Pope might have sanctioned, but neglected to elaborate.

Although Charlotte Smith rarely alludes to Pope in her novels, her witty references to *The Rape of the Lock* suggest her fondness for the poem. In *Emmeline* (1788), the self-taught heroine rummages through the library at Mowbray Castle for a few books spared by mold: "Among them, were Spencer and Milton, two or three volumes of the Spectator, an old edition of Shakespeare, and an odd volume or two of Pope."[28] Later, her favored suitor Godolphin pleads with Emmeline to acknowledge her love, but she fears to break her engagement with the spoiled and hot-tempered Delamere: "She therefore candidly told him how great was her compassion for Lord Delamere, and how severe her apprehension of his rage, resentment, and despair" (479). Smith's allusion to Pope's description of "Cynthia when her manteau's pinn'd awry" (*Rape*, 4.8–10) suggests both disapproval of the young man's passionate tantrums and Emmeline's inability to take his attachment seriously. In *The Old Manor House* (1793), Mrs. Rayland's tyrannical but aging companion mourns her lost ability to dance the rigadoon: "Yet, with the true spirit of perseverance, Mrs. Lennard, though she danced no more, loved to overlook the dancers."[29] By paraphrasing Ariel's description of a dead coquette who "tho' she plays no more, o'erlooks the cards" (*Rape*, 1.54), Smith colors her mockery of Lennard's pride with a hint of pathos.

Much later in *The Old Manor House*, Orlando returns from the American War of Independence to an apparently deserted Rayland Hall. Seeking inhabitants, "he walked toward the kitchen. This was a room quite in the old-fashioned English style; and such as gave an immediate conviction, by the size of every utensil, of old English hospitality. It was such as Pope describes in his letter to the Duke of Buckingham, where the peasantry suppose the infernal spirits hold their sabbath; but upon a still larger scale" (399–400; see Pope, *Corr.*, 1:510). This allusion reminds us of the popularity and familiarity of Pope's correspondence throughout the century; women from Catherine Talbot to Fanny Burney debated its literary and ethical merits.[30] From this passage we can also observe that, like Ann Radcliffe, Smith found in Pope material compatible with a gothic setting. Women were slow to repudiate Pope when the dominant literary taste changed from neoclassical to romantic. In such poems as "Eloisa to Abelard" and "Elegy to the Memory of an Unfortunate Lady," and in his epistolary descriptions of favorite gothic sites, the poet seemed to anticipate current taste.[31] As the century waned and a new horizon of expectations emerged, Pope no longer dominated their literary models, but women continued responding to the poet. Whether enabling authority or covering cherub, Pope influenced the literary development of most eighteenth-century women prose writers.

Eighteenth-Century Women's Responses to Pope's Essay on Man

On 16 March 1752, Samuel Richardson wrote to Thomas Edwards,

What think you of the following criticism of a lady, on these lines of Pope?

He sees, with equal eye, as God of all,
A hero perish, or a sparrow fall;
Atoms or systems into ruin hurl'd;
And now a bubble burst, and now a world.

"This thought," says the lady, "appears to me far from a just one, and rather a poetical flight than sound reasoning. It is true, that in the Sight of the Supreme Being the greatest of his works may be very inconsiderable, as there must be an infinite distance between the Creator and the Creature: but still, as he has made unalterable differences between his creatures, and we must suppose, from our notions of his attributes, wisdom, justice, &c. that as by one he knows exactly these differences, so he will by the other act according to them. We cannot think an atom and a system, a hero and a sparrow, to be of equal value in his sight. Besides, we are told the contrary in Scripture, Matthew X.31. To us finite creatures objects appear greatly lessened, and confounded, by distance; which I take to proceed from some imperfections in our organs. But it cannot be so with God; and we should take care, when we presume to speak of him, and to describe his attributes, not to borrow resemblances from our own imperfect nature, and impute to God the defects of man.[32]

To this reflection, Edwards replied on 20 March:

The lady's remark . . . on those lines of Pope, is, I think, very just. I own I always looked upon that passage in the same light; and there is in my opinion as great an objection against another line in the Essay, where speaking of the angels, he says they may

—show a Newton as we show an ape.

For what pains soever his commentator may take to cover or disguise the real meaning of the words, the thought I think is false; since none, no not the highest order of beings, can look upon a fellow creature, who has improved the faculties of human reason, and exerted them in the noblest manner,—the pursuit and discovery of truth,—otherwise than with honor and approbation, not in a ridiculous and contemptible light; which is the obvious meaning of the image given us above. (Richardson, 3:47–48)

The two men's exchange indicates the seriousness with which Richardson and his circle received women's literary criticism. Richardson's question to Edwards—"What think you of the following criticism of a lady?"—might be construed as a condescending invitation to view a performance much like that of a dog walking on its hind legs, were it not for Richardson's earnest pursuit of women's responses to his own novels. The lady remains decorously anonymous, probably at her request, perhaps because her analysis pits her "sound reasoning" against Pope's "poetical flight" in an obvious inversion of gender conventions. The lady argues from orthodox theological speculations: "We must suppose, from our notions of [God's] attributes . . . that as . . . he knows exactly these differences, so he will . . . act according to them." She cites Scripture to refute Pope's assertion, subtly confirming contemporary suspicions of the poem's deism. Finally, the lady suggests that Pope has based these verses on a logical fallacy: she argues that God's is not the human perspective. Pope had opened his poem with the question, "What can we reason but from what we know?" (1:18). The lady's rebuttal reflects one of orthodox Christians' primary objections to the *Essay on Man*. Pope seemed to argue in places from the enlightened position that God can be known through human reason.[33] Edwards's reply to Richardson grants the justness of the lady's reasoning, although his own objections are open to the same criticism: he assumes that the angels must share human reverence for human reason. Of the two, only the lady has grasped what was for contemporary Christians a major philosophical flaw in Pope's *Essay*, while granting that all assumptions about God's attributes must be suppositious.

By midcentury, women were participating on both sides of the debate over the merits of Pope's *Essay on Man*, but their opinions are rarely considered today. Regarding Pope's relation to women readers, scholars have concentrated almost exclusively on the constructions of femininity in such poems as "Eloisa to Abelard," *The Rape of the Lock*, and the "Epistle to a Lady." As a result, Pope's contemporary women readers all but disappear, fading into an image of victimization, and only occasionally surfacing to register a protest, such as Lady Irwin's "An Epistle to Mr. Pope. Occasioned by his Characters of Women." But the women who read the poems Pope intended for women readers proceeded to read and comment on his entire canon. They evidently did not believe that Pope intended to limit their reading to poems that specified a female audience. Pope's *Essay* attracted as many responses by women as did "Eloisa" or the "Epistle to a Lady," for several reasons. As Margaret Ezell has demonstrated, tradition sanctioned women's participation in religious and philosophical argument. The *Essay on Man* was therefore a more appropriate subject for women's criticism than we might at first suppose, given our current preoccupation with the era's configurations of femininity. The *Essay* was vulnerable to Christian objections of the kind raised by Richardson's correspondent. An orthodox reply to the *Essay on Man* virtually constituted an act of piety. But the poem's rapid assumption of "classic" status also made it apt for quotation by unlearned readers for whom its alleged heterodoxy was irrelevant. Toward the end of the century, women exploring Rousseau's notion of a passionate female nature were citing the *Essay* in conjunction with "Eloisa," a fate Pope could never have imagined for his philosophical masterpiece.

During Pope's lifetime, women began to appear in the literary marketplace without forfeiting their reputations. Women of unimpeachable character, such as Elizabeth Rowe and Elizabeth Carter, published volumes distinguished for piety, exploding the traditional canard that any woman who offered her works for sale would probably, given sufficient temptation, offer her body as well. Elizabeth Carter first attracted a following as the pious and learned poetess

"Eliza" in Edward Cave's *Gentleman's Magazine*. She then made her prose debut in 1738 with a translation of Jean Pierre de Crousaz's *Examination* of Pope's *Essay on Man*, undertaken at Cave's request. Although the *Examination* was a philosophical inquiry, it may seem puzzling that a young lady (Carter was twenty-one at the time) would agree to translate it. Cave hoped to rush Crousaz's critiques into print because they were sure to generate controversy over Pope's principles and those of his masterpiece. Carter risked inclusion in the next edition of the *Dunciad* if her participation angered the Wasp of Twickenham. When the *Examination* appeared in 1738, it rivaled Edmund Curll's edition of the first epistle of Crousaz's *Commentaire*.[34] Scattered throughout the translation, however, were Carter's notes diminishing the force of Crousaz's attack. For example, Crousaz objected to *Essay* 1.77–90: "Since I give myself leave to kill a Sparrow, why should I make any difficulty to assassinate or poison a Hero, whenever Interest should prompt me to it, and I can commit the fact with security? God sees the Fall of the one, and the Fall of the other with an *equal eye*." To this, Carter replied, "Had the ingenious Author of the Examination regarded the Whole of this Passage, which he so much objects to, and not only a Part of it, he would perhaps have given a more favorable Interpretation."[35]

For her endeavor, Carter was lavishly praised by her father, Samuel Johnson, and Thomas Birch, in Latin epigrams that, for example, compared her to Pallas and Crousaz to Cyclops. Their compliments acknowledged her observations of Crousaz's willful misinterpretations and of his reliance on a flawed French translation of Pope's poem. Carter's notes probably accounted for her father's assumption that she might even win Pope's friendship. But beyond so much undoubted male approbation, Carter may have engaged in the translation to satisfy her curiosity, or even to explore her own misgivings about Pope's masterpiece.

Carter shared Mrs. Rowe's and Lady Hertford's distaste for Pope's Opposition politics. She probably found the *Essay*'s praise of Lord Bolingbroke particularly offensive. She wrote in 1751 to Catherine Talbot:

It is less difficult, perhaps, to excuse [Pope's] satires than his panegyrics; and indeed, when one compares the magnificent declamations which he and many other authors make about virtue, with the encomiums they bestow upon the most worthless and even profligate of the human race, one is absolutely at a loss to know what they mean by a man of virtue, unless it be one who has never been hanged (*Letters*, 2:49)—

or one who espoused Opposition principles, which Carter, author of the poems "On the Death of Her Sacred Majesty Queen Caroline" and "To Mr. Duck, Occasioned by a Present of His Poems," deplored. Several of Carter's poems (examined in chapter 5) reflect her uneasiness with Pope's choice of mentor and his self-confident, worldly philosophy.

Elizabeth Carter was not the only eighteenth-century woman of letters to begin her career by translating a French response to the *Essay*. By 1760, Hester Salusbury (Thrale Piozzi) had translated Louis Racine's *Épitre I sur l'Homme*, or rather she had mistranslated the poem so that Racine's attack on Spinozism became her attack on Pope's *Essay on Man*.[36] Although Racine had declared himself assured of Pope's orthodoxy before he wrote his poem, Salusbury incorporated Pope's phrases into her translation so that the *Épitre* appears to rebuke the *Essay*. According to her prefatory remarks, Salusbury translated Racine at the request of Rev. Bernard Wilson and her tutors Dr. Arthur Collier and Dr. William Parker (McCarthy, "A Verse 'Essay,' " 383). Like Carter's, her project obliged her male mentors.

Another prefatory remark may better illuminate why Salusbury chose Pope to be her lifelong antagonist. Salusbury complains that the principles expressed in Pope's *Essay* constitute "too tacit a submission to the direction of his Guide Philosopher and Friend . . . in whose vile Hand he was no other than an Instrument to convey & versifie those thoughts which Ld Boling^e was himself unable to express with the same Delicacy" (McCarthy, "A Verse 'Essay,' " 384). This belief suggests one source of Pope's attractiveness as both model and target of his female critics. Salusbury's remark transforms Pope into the passive victim of a wicked aristocrat, like the heroine of a tragic romance. The frail, socially subordinate Pope is cast in a feminine role relative to an infamous seducer. Salusbury's interpretation of the relationship resembles the snobbish dismissals of Pope by Lady Mary Wortley Montagu, Lady Hertford, and Lady Hervey. But her emphasis on the poet's passivity and victimization might help explain why so many contemporary women writers identified with Pope. Like him, they were comparatively frail outsiders seeking recognition in a culture dominated by aristocratic men. Paradoxically, Salusbury's configuration also demystifies the self-confidence with which even such youthful women as Carter and she attacked Pope's acknowledged masterpiece. Instead of regarding Pope as a patriarch expounding rigorous moral philosophy, Salusbury—and later Hannah More and Catherine Macaulay—imagined him the dupe or "Instrument" of his powerful friend. A misconception popular until the late twentieth century, the notion of Pope as a victim led women to either infatuation with or competition with a male writer brought down to their level.[37]

Salusbury, by then Piozzi, reserved her final comment on the *Essay on Man* until she wrote her *Synonymy* in 1794. Under "Knowledge, Science, Wisdom, Scholarship, Study, Learning, Erudition," she animadverts on Locke's advice "to fill the mind with useful reflections, rather than load it with a weight of *erudition*" (*Synonymy*, 1:337). Piozzi retorts that useful reflections are virtually impossible unless the mind is first stored with basic knowledge.

> That even moral philosophy, or ethics, must come to the grammarian for elucidation, as chronology must descend to the computist for proofs—might be shown from a couplet in the Essay on Man, where Mr. Pope asserts pretty roundly—I hope without understanding himself—that
>
>> For modes of faith let graceless zealots fight,
>> *His* can't be wrong, whose life is in the right.
>
> Now surely the Mahometan paradise is no truer, and the Mahometan faith no purer, for the good lives of some individual Musselmen. . . . Had then Mr. Pope only put the *personal* pronoun in place of the *possessive* one, as nominative case to the verb, and said,
>
>> *He* can't be wrong whose life is in the right,
>
> it had been *quite* sufficient, and explained his own meaning clearly; which doubtless went no further than to say how a virtuous Musselman was as valuable in the sight of his impartial Creator, as a virtuous Christian. . . . So much for the influence of grammar on a branch of *study* that has often enough professed a lofty contempt of it. (1:341–43)

Piozzi thus rewrites Pope in a digression from her quarrel with Locke, itself a digression from her primary intention to discriminate among synonyms for *knowledge*.

Piozzi's use of digression is a clever rhetorical tactic. Her interpretation of Pope's couplet claims merely to illustrate the importance of grammar to poetry. This assertion necessarily implies either that Pope was incapable of adequately expressing his meaning or that he did not completely understand what he intended to say. Piozzi claims both. She hopes Pope wrote "without understanding himself," which probably returns to her early theory of his submission to "his Guide Philosopher & Friend." In those early remarks, Piozzi had declared that the poem would probably remain suspected of Spinozism had not "He whose Fame will be extensive as his Learning . . . Immortal Warburton appear'd, to dispel those Phantoms which hover'd over Pope's Essay" (McCarthy, "A Verse'Essay,' " 384). Having bowed to William Warburton and his defense, she then proceeded to attack Pope in her "Essay on Man" as if his critics' charges had never been answered. Here, Piozzi appropriates the role of him "whose Fame will be extensive as His Learning," undertaking to rescue Pope from himself much as the officious Warburton had done in the *History of the Works of the Learned* in 1739 (see Pope, *Poems*, 3i:xxi). In her "Book of Knowledge," however, she goes Warburton one better (McCarthy, *Piozzi*, 196). She not only clarifies Pope's meaning but rewrites his couplet to better represent its orthodox signification. Piozzi again disguises the audacity of her gesture by containing it in a digression.

The disputed couplet occurs in *Essay* 3, concluding Pope's account of the evolution of mixed government. Although such a government is Pope's ideal, he cautions,

> For Forms of Government let fools contest;
> Whate'er is best administer'd is best:
> For Modes of Faith, let graceless zealots fight;
> His can't be wrong whose life is in the right:
> In Faith and Hope the world will disagree,
> But all Mankind's concern is Charity.

> (3.303–8)

Pope's argument in *Essay* 3 concerns "God and Nature" (line 317), the universal rather than a particular culture. As Maynard Mack observes in his notes to the Twickenham edition of the poem, Pope's apparent relativism resembles that of the Cambridge Platonists (Pope, *Poems*, 3i:124 n. 305–10). The statement was neither illogical nor foreign to Christian theologians. Far from not comprehending his own meaning, Pope had reiterated this position in letters to friends throughout his adulthood. For example, Mack quotes Pope's statement to Edward Blount that "it was not improbable but God might be delighted with the various methods of worshipping him which divided the whole world" (*Poems*, 3i:125 n. 307–8).[38] Piozzi's gesture therefore seems misguided and officious, until we consider her commitment throughout the *Synonymy* to reinforce what she perceives as endangered western values. Pope's couplet states not that the Muslim faith is as valid as the Christian faith but that no charitable person will be damned, contrary to the belief of "graceless zealots." His point about religion is similar to his point about government: human intention and behavior are more important than dogma. Piozzi's revision ignores the couplet's context and fits it to her own preference for western Christianity. By condescending to other religions, the revised statement no longer parallels the preceding couplet or functions as the climax to Pope's account of human social evolution. Moreover, just as in her quarrel with the "Essay on Criticism" under "Fluency, Smoothness, Volubility" (*Synonymy*, 1:241–43), Piozzi ignores context to choose her own grounds for attack. If Pope is guilty of a grammatical error, his reader not only can correct him but can rescue him from himself and from "those Phantoms which . . . w^d have defaced [the *Essay*] to all Generations" (McCarthy, "A Verse 'Essay,' " 384). Hostile and recuperative intentions compete as Piozzi, at fifty-three, attempts once more to resolve her earliest dispute with Pope.

In 1790, Catherine Macaulay Graham also questioned the logic of the *Essay on Man* in book 1 of her *Letters on Education*. Macaulay's purpose for attacking the *Essay* becomes clear in book 3, where she devotes letters 4–9 to exploding Lord Bolingbroke's *Reflections Concerning Innate Moral Principles* (written in 1724; published in 1752). Describing Bolingbroke as "foremost" among "injudicious defenders of the ways of Providence," Macaulay complains that his artfulness "is sufficient to impose on all those who, for want of literary sagacity, do not apply themselves to trace out all his numerous contradictions."[39] She proceeds to accomplish this task, demonstrating, for example, the dangers of "tracing God upwards by an attention to his works" (Macaulay Graham, 363), the method which Pope also recommends in *Essay* 1. Letters 7 and 8 take up the notion that self-love leads to social love, arguing that this belief is compatible with atheism and could be construed as exonerating even wicked behavior pursued from self-interest (409).[40] Macaulay's pains to discredit the *Essay on Man* precede these remarks but derive from her quarrel with Bolingbroke's *Reflections*. Pope's indebtedness to Bolingbroke for such ideas as the relation between self-love and social love rendered his poem, in Macaulay's opinion, dangerous to young readers with insufficient "literary sagacity."

Book 1, letter 14 of Macaulay's *Letters on Education* concerns the "Literary Education of young Persons." At sixteen, the student should read the "moral lectures" of Cicero, Plutarch, Epictetus, and Seneca, as well as Fénelon's *Telemachus* and Rollin's *Belle Lettres*. Some plays of Terence, Martial's epigrams, and Virgil's *Aeneid* and *Georgics* are permitted in Latin, while in French, Boileau's poetry and the plays of Corneille, Racine, Molière, and Voltaire are recommended. Of English literature, the student may read only selected plays of Shakespeare, Addison's *Cato*, Steele's *The Conscious Lovers*, and poems by Milton and Pope.

Macaulay is deeply suspicious of poetry. She cautions instructors to monitor the adolescent's reading of Pope: "His Abelard and Eloisa is only fit for the autumnal season of life; and . . . it would have been better if his imitations of Chaucer had been committed to the flames" (Macaulay Graham, 131). The chief danger of poetry, however, is neither eroticism nor bawdiness but "the potent power of numbers." She warns the tutor to accompany the student's reading with lectures on this danger, which might be illustrated

> by turning into plain prose some of the most striking parts of Pope's Essay on Man. The following brilliant passage will be found to be quite nonsense when stripped of the pomp of verse.
>
> > From Nature's Chain, whatever link you strike,
> > Tenth, or ten thousandth breaks the chain alike.
> >
> > . . . .
> >
> > The least confusion but in one, not all
> > That system only, but the whole must fall.
> >
> > . . . .
> >
> > Heaven's whole foundations to their center nod,
> > And Nature tremble to the throne of God.
> >
> > [*Essay on Man*, 1.245–46, 249–50, 255–56]

If a man in plain prose was to say, that were one of the minutest tribes of the minuter beings to be put out of existence, it would cause such confusion as to . . . make Nature tremble to the throne of God, we should either think him a bigot to the doctrine of a plenum, or regard him as a madman or a blockhead. Yet such are the charms of poetry, that most readers of this famous essay think they have gained a great many solid ideas from the most exceptionable passages; and even the philosopher gives way to the pleasures of sense, and suffers himself to be captivated by the power of harmony. (131–32)

Macaulay concludes that "with proper strictures on this and on other passages of Pope's works," a student "will be taught to admire without intoxication; and at the same time that he sets a just value on an art which can give to reason and to truth an irresistible strength, he will be ever on his guard against the delusive power of sound" (132).

Macaulay fears that adolescents will mistake the *Essay* for profound philosophy. Macaulay is not—as a modern reader might object—confusing poetry with philosophy. Pope himself presented the poem as a philosophical exercise. Pope hoped the poem contained "a *short* yet not *imperfect* system of ethics." In his prefatory remarks, Pope defended his decision to argue his system in verse because "principles, maxims, or precepts so written, both strike the reader more strongly at first, and are more easily retained by him afterwards" (*Poems*, 3i:7). Macaulay's worry about the "charms of poetry" to vulnerable adolescents (comparable to modern adult fear of films and television) grants Pope the power of his medium. But she finds the *Essay* a most imperfect system of ethics.

Macaulay's objection to the poem is also ideological. The passage she selects for ridicule is a straightforward representation of the great chain of being, the "doctrine of a plenum" long assumed by many who were neither mad nor blockheads. The notion of creation as a great chain "composed of an immense, or . . . infinite, number of links ranging in hierarchical order from the meagerest kind of existents . . . through 'every possible' grade up to the *ens perfectissimum*" had justified traditional, hierarchical western culture for centuries.[41] Pope's poem is often described as one of the last statements of this venerable concept, becoming archaic even as he wrote. Macaulay espoused another, radical political philosophy. In her *History of England from the Accession of James I to that of the Brunswick Line* (1763 83), she declared her intention to restore the founders of the Commonwealth to the heroic status they deserved.[42] Concerned throughout her writings to preserve the liberties of English citizens by limiting the power of government, she was necessarily unsympathetic to Pope's celebration of a philosophy that warned against attempts by "inferior" creatures to "press" on "superior pow'rs" (*Essay on Man*, 1.241–42). Pope's system apparently required humble acceptance of one's place in a providential scheme and regarded any attempt to disturb the given hierarchy as "Madness, Pride, Impiety!" (1.257–58). Read carefully, Pope's poem does permit discreet movement to reach one's proper place, but the passage Macaulay excerpted for analysis (1.245–56) seems to sanction a static state of affairs she regarded as intolerable. Her strictures on the *Essay* provide a discreet lesson in republican philosophy disguised as an objective lecture on the dangers of poetry.

Like Macaulay, Hannah More found both the religion and politics of the *Essay on Man* offensive. It is perhaps difficult to imagine a subject on which Macaulay and More would agree: while Macaulay had argued for extended suffrage during the restless period from 1765 to 1775, More composed pamphlets from 1790 to 1817 urging the poor to work harder and to accept their social place. While Macaulay's objections to Pope's theology complemented her republican political philosophy, More's evangelical religious sentiments accompanied conservative political opinions. However, women of widely varying ideologies approved certain of Pope's poems. The pious and whiggish Elizabeth Rowe had found "Mr. *Pope's Satire on Women* . . . more mild than I expected; and if well us'd, may reform the sex" (*Works*, 2:240). In her *Letters on Education*, Macaulay complained that women's "levity and influence have proved so hostile to the existence, or permanence of rational manners, that it fully justifies the keeness [*sic*] of Mr. Pope's satire on the sex" (Macaulay Graham, 213). In her *Strictures on the Modern System of Female Education* (1799), More quoted the "Epistle" to turn back on Mary Wollstonecraft not only her critique of Pope but her argument for women's rights.

> The beauty vindicates her rights, the wit the rights of women; the beauty fights for herself, the wit for a party; and while the more selfish though more moderate beauty "would be queen for life," the public spirited wit struggles to abrogate the Salique law of intellect, and to enthrone "a whole sex of queens."[43]

None of these women disputed the justice of Pope's portrait of modern female decadence. The "Epistle" became the focus of arguments over the extent of corruption, its source in nature or nurture, and its possible remedies. The *Essay on Man* served a similar function. Women as dissimilar as Carter, Piozzi, Macaulay, and More agreed to disagree with its system of ethics, each tracing the poem's flaws to its divergence with her own philosophy.

By 1811, More had long established her beliefs in submission to authority and in the efficacy of Christian charity. *Practical Piety, or the influence of the Religion of the Heart on the Conduct of the Life* contains her most sustained critique of Pope. In chapter 13, More ruminates on self-love.

> Self-love is the center of the unrenewed heart. This stirring principle, as has been observed, serves indeed
>
>> The virtuous mind to wake;
>
> but it disturbs it from its slumbers to ends and purposes directly opposite to those assigned to it by our incomparable bard. Self-love is by no means "the small pebble which stirs the peaceful lake." It is rather the pent-up wind within, which causes the earthquake; it is the tempest which agitates the sleeping ocean. Had the image been as just as its clothing is beautiful; or rather had *Mr. Pope* been as sound a theologian as he was an exquisite poet, the allusion in his hands might have conveyed a sounder meaning without losing a particle of its elegance. This might have been effected by only substituting the effect for the cause; that is, by making benevolence the principle instead of the consequence, and by discarding self-love from its central situation in the construction of the metaphor. (*Works*, 1:461)

In her *Synonymy*, Hester Thrale Piozzi had responded to Pope's disparaging remarks about women's admiration for dress by dressing up a rather abstract simile in the "Essay on Criticism." More ironically accuses Pope of over-dressing an image. His praise of self-love is equivalent to "arraying a beggarly idea in princely robes" (1:461).

More's objection refers to a climactic passage in *Essay on Man.*

> Self-love but serves the virtuous mind to wake,
> As the small pebble stirs the peaceful lake;
> The centre mov'd, a circle strait succeeds,
> Another still, and still another spreads,
> Friend, parent, neighbour, first it will embrace,
> His country next, and next all human race.
>
> (4.363–68)

Like Piozzi and Macaulay, More censures as untenable an idea far from peculiar to Pope. As Mack observes in his notes to the poem, the concept of self-love begetting social love had been expressed earlier by Seneca and St. Thomas Aquinas and had been developed more recently in the *Several Discourses* (1684) of Rev. Hezekiah Burton (Pope,

Poems, 3i:162 n. 353). Sounder theologians than Pope had approved the notion imaged by the exquisite poet. But while Macaulay had rejected the static hierarchy implicit in Pope's celebration of the great chain of being, More deplores the insubordination suggested by his panegyric on self-love. Once again, Lord Bolingbroke proves the real villain.

> Had [Pope] not blindly adopted the misleading system of the noble sceptic, "his guide, philosopher, and friend," he might have transferred the shining attributes of the base-born thing which he has dressed out with so many graces, to the legitimate claimant—benevolence;—of which self-love is so far from being, as he represents, the moving spring, that they are both working in a course of incessant counteraction, the spirit striving against the flesh, and the flesh against the spirit. (1:461)

Politically speaking, the aristocratic Bolingbroke would never have approved a baseborn claimant's usurpation of legitimate rank. More's analysis suggests, however, that Bolingbroke's (and Pope's) espousal of self-love paradoxically encourages an equivalent confusion in the human spiritual hierarchy.

More refutes Pope through the mouth of St. James. The apostle, she observes,

> appears to have been of a different opinion from the ethic bard; he speaks as if he suspected that the pebble stirred the lake a little too roughly. He traces this mischievous principle from its birth to the largest extent of its malign influence.—The question, "whence come wars and fightings among you," he answers by another question;— "Come they not hence, even of your lusts that war in your members?" (1:461)

Pope's concept of self-love waking the virtuous mind becomes in More's version a political agitator inciting a mob, a potent image during the Napoleonic era. Her reference to St. James intersects with Macaulay's objection to the same concept (see n. 40), but with reverse political implications. Macaulay had feared the potential of Bolingbroke's esoteric rhetoric to lead astray those with less "literary sagacity." Pope had assisted Bolingbroke in an abuse of aristocratic responsibility. More's reading casts Pope as a sort of rabble-rouser, dressing a "base-born thing" in the robes of "the legitimate claimant." Her solution, much like Piozzi's, is a revision of Pope's language, as if the poet had mistaken his diction: "It was only to dislodge the idol and make the love of God the centre, and the poet's delightful numbers might have conveyed truths worthy of so perfect a vehicle" (1:461). More argues that Pope should have written "Christian benevolence" instead of "self-love": "'This centre moved,' does indeed extend its pervading influence in the very manner ascribed to the opposite principle; does indeed spread from its throne in the individual breast, to all those successive circles, 'wide and more wide,' of which the poet makes self-love the first mover" (1:461).

More's revision, like Piozzi's, wrests from Pope the meaning of his poem, adapting the *Essay* to the service of More's conservative evangelism. Because only the "unrenewed heart" exalts self-love, More decides that Pope's poem must be rewritten "for the sake of her more youthful readers" (1:461). Like Piozzi and Macaulay, More first transfers Pope's authority to Bolingbroke, as if to avoid direct confrontation with the poet who, more than any writer before Samuel Johnson, embodied eighteenth-century cultural authority. Nevertheless, More's analysis, like the other women's, originates in religious and political philosophies deeply felt and long considered. Each woman's apparently oblique—even obtuse—approach to Pope's *Essay* arises from, and reinforces, her cultural critique.

While Carter, Piozzi, Macaulay, and More criticized the *Essay on Man* for ideological reasons, other women took advantage of the poem's aphoristic qualities. Such writers, rather than question the poem's philosophical basis, extracted maxims of unimpeachable morality to authenticate their own arguments or sentiments. Eliza Haywood had no reason to approve or flatter Pope, but she cited the *Essay* in her *Female Spectator*.[44] A periodical directed to the genteel readership of Steele and Addison's publications, the *Female Spectator* customarily alluded to Milton, Cowley, Dryden, and other established writers of the preceding century. Yet Pope's *Essay* took its place among the canon in a meditation on human discontent: "How fond soever we may be of the writings of the late celebrated Mr. Pope, it is but rarely we remember this maxim of his, and acknowledge with him, that '—Whatever is, is right' " (1:128). Even Laetitia Pilkington, whose *Memoirs* attempt to diminish Pope's reputation, quotes the *Essay* to allay readers' fears that they, too, may find themselves exposed: "I threaten not any, nor did I ever do it; but Characters are my Game, who '*Eye Nature's Walks, shoot Folly as it flies, /And catch the Manners living as they rise.*' "[45] Pope ironically appears to sanction Pilkington's attacks on his character. His own rubric renders him fair game for her metaphorical hunt.

The *Essay on Man* served women's purposes in several other ways. Mary Deverell apologized for publishing her sermons (1774), disclaiming in a preface her pretensions to scholarly theological debate.

> Perhaps those deep controversial subjects would have been as little pleasing, or improving, to the generality of my sex, as they are to her whose soul, as *Pope* describes his *Indians*,
>
> > "Proud Science never taught to stray,
> > 'Far as the Solar Walk, or Milky-Way.' "[46]

Ann Murry used the *Essay* in *Mentoria; or, the young ladies instructor* to inculcate imperialist and capitalist ideology in her charges. For example, she cites Pope's verses on the relativity of vice ("But where th'extreme of vice was ne'er agreed, / Ask where's the North? At York, 'tis on the Tweed"), changing the word *vice* to *cold* to explain how people adapt to extreme climates: "What happier natures shrink at with affright, / The hard inhabitant contends is right" (*Essay on Man*, 2.221–30).[47] Mentoria then compares "poverty" to the "frigid zone," to which Lady Mary responds, "But are these people happy, my dear Mentoria?" Mentoria replies, "The Beautiful lines, I have just recited from Pope, clearly indicate, the inhabitants of the frigid zone are not dissatisfied with their situation. It appears equally clear to me, that poverty is not incompatible with happiness, as by industry all the necessaries of life may be acquired, which is all our state requires" (132). Pope's passage, a metaphor for the difficulty of eradicating vice, has first been transformed into a literal geography lesson, and finally into a new metaphor apologizing for the economic injustices of emergent capitalism.

Most frequently, what Antonia Forster has described in a different context as "Mr. Pope's Maxims"[48] appear in women's novels, journals, and letters, functioning like the Greek and Latin quotations that adorned the prose of Pope and his privileged contemporaries. Sarah Scott's *Millenium Hall* and Hester Thrale Piozzi's *Observations and Reflections* allude to the *Essay* in this manner.[49] Elizabeth Montagu exemplifies this practise in the numerous Popeian allusions of her letters. In fact, Pope is quoted more frequently than any author not of Mrs. Montagu's extensive literary acquaintance, attesting to his assumption of classic status while he was still living. For example, in a letter of 9 May 1741, she ruminates to the Reverend Mr. Freind:

While to the smallest creature in the creation a large portion of happiness is allotted, shall the most favoured and dignified of its works be clouded with fear and distrust? We have great reason, as first in happiness, to be first in thanks; but of all creatures we only are repining for our safety. Let us be satisfied that we

Are in the hand of one disposing power,
Or in the natal or the mortal hour.

[*Essay on Man*, 2.287–88]

And for our particular circumstances of fortune, that we know this truth, enough for man to know,

Virtue alone is happiness below.

[*Essay on Man*, 4.310]

Much praise should be given to Mr. Pope for making morality speak by the voice divine of poetry.[50]

Ironically, Mrs. Montagu's fondness for the *Essay* later led her to quote the poem in letters to Elizabeth Carter. She assured her friend that "It is a noble privilege in a London life that one can never be too long in the same temper; whether willingly or unwillingly, one must steer 'from grave to gay, from lively to severe' " (*Letters*, 4:220–21). How did Carter respond to this application of Pope's encomium of Boling-broke? On another occasion, Montagu voiced concern over Carter's depression after her stepmother's death, arguing that Carter's health was "a public concern": "God has blessed you with talents which will be useful to thousands; to ordinary persons in this world 'Their time's a moment, and a point their space,' but you are qualified to spread a lasting influence" (4:244). Given Carter's diffidence and humility, the modern reader wonders how she responded to a reflection so well-intended but uncongenial to her philosophy.

Toward the end of the century, women novelists appropriated Pope's *Essay on Man*. In *Laura and Augustus* (1784), one of Eliza Brom-ley's heroines ponders the difference between rustic and town life early in the epistolary novel: "O happiness! our being's end and aim! / . . . Say in what mortal soil thou deign'st to grow?"[51] The quotation later assumes significance as a justification of the heiress Laura Leve-son's clandestine marriage with the irresistible but penniless Lt. Au-gustus Montague. Augustus quotes "Eloisa to Abelard" when sepa-rated from his beloved, but Laura recurs to the *Essay* as the couple sinks into poverty: "Indeed I almost now begin to agree with my favourite author Pope, 'That whatever is, is right;' had not your poor

Laura been driven through the tyranny of her father into such embarrassed circumstances, her darling child would never have been thrown
into that line of life, which may be the means of drawing forth [her]
virtues and talents" (3:10–11). Both hero and heroine of this sentimental novel die, amidst a plethora of allusions to various writers, but
Bromley's choice of "Eloisa" and the *Essay on Man* to justify their
pursuit of a marriage based on passion is echoed in at least one other
late-century novel.

In Mary Hays's *Memoirs of Emma Courtney* (1796), Emma is raised
by an aunt and uncle who encourage her when only six to read Pope
and Thomson aloud before company.[52] Her tragic turning point occurs
when she reads Rousseau's *Héloïse* as a teenager (25), but she uses
the terms of Pope's *Essay on Man* to justify the impassioned pursuit
of Augustus Harley that consumes her life. At one point, she invokes
Popeian logic to rationalize her obsession with Augustus.

> If, as we are taught to believe, the benevolent Author of nature be,
> indeed, benevolent . . . he surely must have intended the *happiness*
> of his creatures. . . . Individual happiness constitutes the general
> good:—*happiness* is the only true *end* of existence;—all notions of
> morals, founded on any other principle, involve in themselves a
> contradiction, and must be erroneous. Man does right, when pursu-
> ing interest and pleasure—it argues no depravity—this is the fable
> of superstition: he ought only to be careful, that, in seeking his own
> good, he does not render it incompatible with the good of others.
> . . . I feel in myself the capacities for increasing the happiness . . .
> of a few individuals—and this circle, spreading wider and wider,
> would operate towards the grand end of life—*general utility*. (118–
> 19)

Emma convinces herself that her pursuit fulfills a moral imperative:
chasing Augustus is her being's end and aim.

Heedless of Augustus's wishes, Emma plunges forward. She borrows Pope's image of the pebble tossed into the lake, claiming that
her obsession will ultimately serve the general good. Later, when
Augustus shuns her, Emma imagines herself a second Eloisa and
persists in her passion. The novel ends tragically after Emma discovers
that Augustus has long been secretly married. Augustus dies, the
husband Emma married in despair kills himself, her daughter dies,
and Emma is bereft of all but Augustus's son. Hays's attitude toward
Emma is ambiguous. A friend of Mary Wollstonecraft, Hays appar-

ently intended Emma's story as a warning against narrowing women's characters by excessive emphasis on sensibility and romantic love (60–61). Her deprecation of "Eloisa to Abelard" follows from this premise, but her allusions to the *Essay on Man* remain puzzling. Emma is a compelling heroine, despite her unfortunate obsession. Her twisted appeals to the *Essay* are clever and almost persuasive. Emma's appeals to reason to justify her pursuit make the novel appear at times a feminist defense of women's passion. Her final isolation, however, confirms that Emma's allusions to the *Essay* are perverse. They represent the crippling effect of Rousseauian sensibility on a woman's capacity to reason. They also render Pope's poetry, not just the passionate "Eloisa to Abelard," suspect, consigning Pope to a catagory of writers potentially dangerous to women.[53]

For all its sentimental passion, *Memoirs of Emma Courtney* dramatizes a warning similar to those of Macaulay's *Letters on Education* and More's *Practical Piety*. Macaulay had insisted that a tutor accompany adolescent readings of poetry, lest the student become "captivated by the power of harmony." Like Odysseus and the siren, youthful readers must "guard against the delusive power of sound" (Macaulay Graham, 132). More admitted her own former susceptibility as excuse for the harshness of her strictures: "She has not forgotten the time when, in the admiration of youthful enthusiasm, she never suspected that the principle of these finished verses was less excellent than the poetry" (1:461). Emma's tragedy occurs partly because her earliest guardians encouraged her to relish the sounds of poetry she did not understand. She recalls that at six, she "read aloud before company, with great applause . . . Pope's Homer, and Thomson's Seasons, little comprehending either. Emulation was roused, and vanity fostered: I learned to recite verses, to modulate my tones of voice, and began to think myself a wonderful scholar" (Hays, 12). At fourteen, Emma's father entrusts her with the keys of his library, but fails to supervise her reading. By the time he interrupts her absorption in Rousseau's *Héloïse*, the damage has been done: "The impression made on my mind was never to be effaced—it was even productive of a long chain of consequences, that will continue to operate till the day of my death" (25). Emma's reliance on the *Essay on Man* to rationalize her obsession illustrates Macaulay's and More's claims of the danger of poetry. She ironically invokes Pope's commendation of self-love, the very passage that both Macaulay and More warned against as a license for self-indulgence. In adolescent hands, even Pope's "not *imperfect* system of ethics" is easily twisted into a manifesto of Emma's right to passion.

Hays's didactic purpose resembles those of the education writers. Although Hays, unlike Macaulay and More, focuses on poetry's threat to young women, her feminist misgivings parallel Hannah More's evangelical warnings of the *Essay*'s potential danger. Perhaps Piozzi's, Macaulay's, More's, and Hays's fin-de-siècle struggles with Pope are symptomatic of a culture seeking to overthrow its precursors and proceed in new directions. If so, the price of women's increasing participation in print culture seems to have included their adherence to conservative ideology. Even when women found in the *Essay* a sanction for their intellectual activities, they chose passages intimating humility and submissiveness. For women seeking to exercise their traditional right to engage in prose polemic, however, the *Essay on Man* offered an opportunity for discreet iconoclasm. Pope's masterpiece could be condemned as an invitation to hedonism rather than to philosophical resignation. Pope's attraction for such critics may have been his apparent vulnerability, as a Catholic poet composing a system of ethics, or as the alleged dupe of Lord Bolingbroke. Pope appeared a man whom ladies might contradict because of their pious orthodoxy and educational responsibilities. While Pope declared that "[women's] Virtues open fairest in the Shade" ("Epistle to a Lady," 202), some of his readers claimed an earlier feminine tradition, the privilege to defend virtue in print. Women's willingness to grapple with the poet ironically confirms Pope's importance to women, as well as women's growing strength as writers challenging their predecessors.

From "Moral Guide and Director" to "Wicked Wit": Pope as Women's Precursor

The selection of letters in Mary Jones's *Miscellanies in Prose and Verse* (1750) confirms her choice, manifest in her poems, of Pope as her chief model.[54] Although praised by Margaret Doody for the wit and honesty of her Swiftian poems "Holt Waters" and "Epistle from Fern-Hill,"[55] Jones most often appropriated the style of Pope's Horatian epistles. Perhaps Jones's social status among her friends explains her attraction to Pope's Horatian persona. Proficient in French and Italian— Roger Lonsdale speculates that she may have met her aristocratic acquaintances while serving as a governess—Mary Jones lived with her brother Rev. Oliver Jones, Chanter, then Senior Chaplain, of Christ Church Cathedral in Oxford.[56] However she met them, Jones was a regular visitor to the estates of her friends and to Maid of Honour Martha Lovelace's apartments at Windsor Castle. She appreciated their hospitality, and her friends cherished her literary ability. Lady Bowyer initiated the publication of her *Miscellanies*, in which Jones acknowledged that her letters were included because "the ladies to whom they are address'd . . . thought proper to preserve them" (vi). In her published letters, Jones often alludes to her modest income and inferior social status. Her determination to live contented with her means while enjoying the companionship of aristocrats explains her affinity to Pope in his role of friend to the great.

In a letter of August 1734 to Martha Lovelace, Jones ponders her comfortable but rather nondescript ancestors (excepting "the famous Sir *William Penn* the Quaker, and his Father the Vice Admiral," 305): "Our real Worth must depend on Our selves. . . . For, after all our blust'ring and strutting, Mr. *Pope* will still be in the right, '*Nought can ennoble Sots, and Slaves, and Cowards, / Alas! not all the blood of all the Howards*'" (307–8). The bravado of Jones's reference to the *Essay on Man* (4.215–16) belies her situation as a clergyman's dependent sister. Perhaps Pope's staunch claims for individual value enabled Jones, who in 1734 had no prospect of literary reputation, to tolerate her circumstances. A year later, she extols the Horatian simplicity of her life: although Fortune has granted her only "the Cottage, the Mutton, and the Feather-bed" (318), she has no cause for self-reproach.

> Such Retrospections as these have been able to make the worst, that Fortune has done for me, sit easy upon my Memory and tho' (I thank her) she has never shewn me any severe Reverse; yet I can truly say, I never was indebted to her for a single Blessing I've enjoyed. Even now she's playing me a Trick ———But "*Welcome, for thee, fair Virtue! all that's past; / For thee, fair Virtue! welcome ev'n the last.*" You see, I can quote no-body but Mr. *Pope.* (319)

Pope's impassioned submission, in "Epistle to Dr. Arbuthnot" (358–59), to even "the Whisper that . . . / Perhaps, yet vibrates in his Sovereign's Ear" seems a disproportionate response to Jones's modest way of life. Yet she evidently associated Pope's defense of his integrity with her sense of having earned her privileged friendships, a state of affairs onlookers may have attributed to mere good fortune.

Jones enjoyed casting her own friendships in the mold of Pope's relationships with literary and aristocratic friends. In a letter to Miss Lovelace after her commencement as maid of honor (1737), Jones wishes for a visit: "I do assure you, if ever such an event should happen . . . I wou'd leave ev'n *Pope* himself to speak to you. This perhaps you . . . may think no great Compliment; yet nevertheless, 'tis the greatest I can pay you, and what, I assure you, I never offer to any thing below crown'd Heads" (364–65). Not long after, she assures her friend that "I do firmly believe there are a matter of four or five Women of Honour left in the World, who have receiv'd a smile from the Queen, and pretty near as many Men, who hope for one from the King—notwithstanding all Mr. Pope, my moral Guide and Director, has said upon the case" (377–78). Despite her friend's employment at court, Jones compares their friendship with that between Pope and Lord Bolingbroke. Of her search for happiness, she concludes, "'Tis every where, and no where, unless 'tis where You are at the present Writing—'And fled from Monarchs, dwells at length with Thee' " (382; see *Essay on Man*, 4.16–18). Although Lovelace could hardly have been said to have "fled from Monarchs," and despite Jones's acquaintance with the Princess of Orange, Jones evidently liked to imagine herself a Popeian recluse from the court, preferring Miss Lovelace to her royal employers.

Jones also appropriated Pope's persona among literary acquaintances. In a letter of August 1741, she addresses an anonymous lady who was apparently a potential patron. "You take one into your Dressing-room, seat one in one of *Rabelais'* easy Chairs, unlock your Treasures of Science, and (tho' one has never spoke to you before) lead one thro' all Subjects with so much ease, and so little reserve, that 'tis not above five Minutes that one can possible fancy one's self a Stranger" (193). Although patent flattery, the remark is typical of Jones, who may seriously have wished to attribute both Rabelais's wide-ranging knowledge and his insistent earthiness to an admired friend. Casting herself as Pope in *The Dunciad*, addressing her new mentor as Swift, who might "laugh and shake in Rab'lais' easy chair" (*Dunciad*, 1.22), Jones suggests her independence and literary abilities even as she duly flatters her new correspondent.

Jones particularly admired Pope's letters. In August 1735, not long after the publication of *Letters of Mr. Pope and Several Eminent Persons*, she wrote Martha Lovelace that

> I've at last had the inexpressible Pleasure of reading Mr. *Pope*'s Letters; and am so well satisfied with 'em, that I shall read all future Letters (except Miss *Lovelace*'s) with a great deal less Pleasure for their sake. In his other Productions I have always admir'd the Author, but now I love the Man. There is, throughout, such a spirit of Benevolence, such noble strains of Generosity . . . that the Breast must be a stranger to all the tenderness, all the dignities of human Nature, that can read him without being warm'd with the same Affections. (313–14)

Jones compares the letters to "the most finish'd Piece . . . in the Beauty-room at *Hampton-Court*," and to the "regular wildness" of Kensington Gardens, then confesses the inadequacy of both similes. "'Twill be doing him more Justice to say—he is inimitable like Nature, in all his Works" (314).

Sixteen months later, Jones attempted a more critical response, but her adulation of Pope problematized analysis. Facetiously extolling her own epistolary style, Jones boasts that

> I've often thought there never was a Letter wrote well, but what was wrote easily. . . . And in this Easiness of Writing . . . methinks I excel even Mr. *Pope* himself; who is often too elaborate and ornamental, even in some of his best Letters; tho' it must be confess'd he outdoes me in some few Trifles of another sort, such as Spirit, Taste, and Sense. But let me tell Mr. *Pope* that Letters, like Beauties, may be over-drest. There is a becoming Negligence in both; and if Mr. *Pope* could only contrive to write *without* a Genius, I don't know any one so likely to hit off *my* Manner as himself. (341)

Jones's ambivalence is manifest as she struggles to criticize Pope's "elaborate and ornamental" style. She can only claim superior simplicity and "ease" while simultaneously deriding her "Spirit, Taste, and Sense," paraphrasing Pope's mockery of critics in the "Epistle to Dr. Arbuthnot" (163). Her comment seesaws between criticism ("Letters, like Beauties, may be over-drest") and self-abnegation ("if Mr. *Pope* could only contrive to write without a Genius, I don't know any one so likely to hit off *my* Manner"). Evidently overwhelmed by her reading of Pope's correspondence, Jones could not bring herself to express her critical differences even in a letter.

In later letters, Jones appropriated some of Pope's epistolary strategies. For example, in April 1740, she compares her literary creativity with Lovelace's (now Lady Beauclerk's) maternity: "Your ladyship . . . certainly has the prettiest Conceptions . . . and the easiest Delivery of any Lady upon Earth. In short, I always admire your Ladyship's Quickness and Vivacity, but as I take this last Production to be your *Chef-d'oeuvre*, am fill'd with Impatience to peruse it" (388–89). Jones borrowed her metaphor from an early, courtly letter of Pope's to an anonymous lady. Pope had compared the lady's daughter to a painting "done with abundance of spirit and life: and wants nothing but time to be an admirable piece. . . . 'tis certain you have a strange happiness, in making fine things of a sudden and at a stroke, with incredible ease and pleasure" (*Corr.*, 1:4). Jones's choice of Pope's crude metaphor recalls her attraction to Swift's earthy poems, the quality that Doody maintains is still fresh and shocking in Jones's poetry. Pope's metaphor becomes doubly suggestive, its comparison of literary invention and maternity even more appropriate when applied to a woman writer. Jones's appropriation of this image anticipates what Gilbert and Gubar have described as a nineteenth-century phenomenon, women's contention that the pen/penis is not the only metaphor for creativity.[57] In another letter, Jones echoes Pope's frequent assurances to friends that his letters constitute epistolary conversations.[58] "Your Ladyship talks of coming to Town," she writes Lady Beauclerk in June 1742; "I wish you may come soon; for I've been talking to you this half hour in my Imagination" (397).

Although incapable of direct confrontation with her "moral Guide and Director," Jones nevertheless borrowed his phrases and images to suit her context. Genteel but confined to modest circumstances, Jones found Pope's Horatian persona convenient in defining her relations with aristocratic friends. In her Popeian guise, Jones could express proud contentment with "the Cottage, the Mutton, and the Feather-bed," while accepting her wealthy friends' hospitality and patronage. Pope figured not only as her mentor but as guarantor of her integrity. Jones never thoroughly swerved from Pope, never achieved the repudiation Bloom describes as crucial in the development of strong poets. In her poems as in her letters, Jones remains Pope's (and sometimes Swift's) disciple. The letters suggest that her Popeian role-playing facilitated her creativity. Harriet Guest has astutely inferred that Jones's claim, in the final letter of *Miscellanies*, that "Gold" is her "sole End and Aim" in publication was a pose assumed by many women for whom pursuit of literary fame was somehow less admissable than the quest for money.[59] Jones's self-presentation as a Popeian recluse likewise appears to be her strategy for seeking a literary reputation while advocating an appropriately ladylike retirement. After *Miscellanies*, Jones eventually stopped writing for publication, refusing an invitation in 1761 to contribute to the *Monthly Review*.[60] Her reputation established by *Miscellanies*, she seems to have lost her need to publish poetry to maintain her pose as retired poet; she simply seems to have enjoyed her circle of literary acquaintances.

A far different situation compelled Laetitia Pilkington (ca. 1708–50) to compose her *Memoirs* and to record an impression of Pope opposite to Jones's. Near the end of her life, Pilkington intended the *Memoirs* to retrieve her reputation and the full record of her writings, both sadly lost during a precarious career. To lure readers and justify her behavior, Pilkington included anecdotes of her celebrated acquaintances Jonathan Swift and Alexander Pope. While Swift, her first mentor, appears eccentric but honorable in the *Memoirs*, Pilkington questions Pope's integrity throughout. Her motivation for reducing Pope to an envious hypocrite emerges from her autobiography. Like the imaginary Emma Courtney's, Pilkington's first literary aspirations were associated with Pope. At five, Laetitia Van Lewen taught herself to read, despite her mother's discouragement. When, in her mother's absence, her father discovered her reading, he kissed her and promised her a shilling when she memorized a poem, "which he put into my Hand, and proved to be Mr. Pope's sacred Eclogue, which Task I performed before my Mother returned Home" (1:15). Impressed, her parents then permitted her to read as much as she liked. She especially loved poetry, "and, from a Reader, I quickly became a Writer; I may truly say with Mr. *Pope*, 'I lisp'd in Numbers, for the Numbers came' " (1:16).

This childhood idyll belied Pilkington's tragic career. Her father's approval encouraged the little girl to identify with another child prodigy and to expect reward for her ambition. As an adult, however, Pilkington was betrayed by her husband, whose early admiration of her literary ability turned to envy. Male approval led not to reward but to treachery, as the man invested with her father's authority deserted her. Pilkington soon discovered that while a girl might be caressed for precocity resembling Pope's, a woman had little chance of emulating his career. Her patriarchal culture refused to sanction the career Pilkington's father had apparently encouraged.

Laetitia Van Lewen assimilated these bitter facts soon after her marriage to Rev. Matthew Pilkington in 1725. Jonathan Swift patronized the young couple, particularly delighted with Laetitia's pert wit. Perhaps she imagined herself retracing Pope's career as she impressed Swift with her literary facility and won his confidence. She seems to have, perhaps unconsciously, begun insinuating herself into Pope's place in the dean's affection, or at least contrasting her ingenuity with Pope's hypocrisy. She recalls an occasion when Swift requested her help binding his letters. After reading a number of Pope's letters,

> I could not avoid remarking to the Dean, that notwithstanding the Friendship Mr. *Pope* professed for Mr. *Gay*, he could not forbear a great many satirical, or, if I may be allowed to say so, envious Remarks on the Success of the *Beggar's Opera*. The Dean very frankly owned, he did not think Mr. *Pope* was so candid to the Merits of other Writers, as he ought to be. I then ventured to ask the Dean, whether he thought the Lines Mr. *Pope* addresses him with, in the Beginning of the *Dunciad*, were any Compliment to him? . . . "I believe, says he, they were meant as such; but they are very stiff;"— Indeed, Sir, said I, he is so perfectly a Master of harmonious Number, that had his Heart been in the least affected with his Subject, he must have writ better. (1:75–76)

Pilkington's reconstruction of the conversation sets her own irrepressible honesty ("I could not avoid remarking") against Pope's hypocritical praises of Gay and Swift. She and the dean speak the same language; Swift "very frankly owned" Pope's lack of candor and criticized his encomium in the *Dunciad*. Pilkington and Swift appear kindred "plain-dealers" exposing Pope's invidious underside. Pilkington's final expression of dismay reiterates her sympathy and intimates Pope's incapacity for sincere friendship. Though admittedly fabricated from memory, the exchange suggests Pilkington's youthful desire to supplant Pope as object of the dean's approval and to do so by demonstrating her superior affinity with Swift.

Although some readers agreed with Pilkington's suspicious estimate, many more found Pope's letters the monument of friendship he intended. Nineteen-year-old Fanny Burney, reading them in 1771, found Pope's expressions of friendship particularly moving (*Journals*, 1:177–80). Pope's reputation for integrity remained largely intact throughout his life, despite detractors' persistent efforts. Laetitia Pilkington experienced the opposite phenomenon. Her husband's successful divorce suit, following her reputed "scandalous" behavior while attempting to retrieve their marriage in London (where Pilkington was involved with an actress), injured her reputation beyond recall.[61] She lost custody of her children and was reduced for the rest of her life to subsist by marginal writing assignments and projects, such as her failed book and print shop, sponsored by patrons. For the child who had "lisp'd in numbers," or even for the young woman befriended by Swift, this fate must have seemed bitter indeed.

Throughout the *Memoirs*, Pilkington attempts to illuminate this injustice by contrasting her frankness with the dishonesty or inaccuracy of her successful model/rival. For example, Pilkington compares her husband's account of his fine reception by Pope at Twickenham and Pope's subsequent letter to the dean in which Pope complained of Rev. Pilkington's impertinence. When she complained that Pope "was highly ungenerous to caress and abuse [Pilkington] at the same time," Swift "flew into . . . a Rage . . . [and] asked me, 'Why I did not swear that my Husband was six Foot high?' " (1:130–32). Although Pilkington includes the episode to record her first suspicion of Matthew Pilkington's poor character, the anecdote also reiterates Pope's hypocrisy.

Pilkington quotes Pope frequently throughout her *Memoirs*, applying his couplets to observations ranging from her low estimate of a gentleman who propositions her (2:176) to her opinion of Delarivière Manley's and Eliza Haywood's novels (2:293). But she sometimes qualifies Pope's authority, as when she claims amazement that Swift has memorized *Hudibras*: "I say, it surprized me, because I had been misled by Mr. *Pope*'s Remark, *'That where Beams of warm Imagination play, / The Memory's soft Figures melt away,'* To think Wit and Memory incompatible things" (1:136). Demonstrating the inaccuracy of Pope's assertion in the "Essay on Criticism" that "one *Science* only will one *Genius* fit" (56–61), Pilkington concludes, "Indeed, I know not how any Person can be witty without a good Memory." As in Piozzi's *British Synonymy*, empirical evidence defies Pope's confident generalization. On another occasion, Pilkington robs Pope of authority by misattributing an allusion. She excuses her own vanity as merely

> the ruling and darling Passion of our Sex Tho' I shall never carry it
> to such an unnatural Height, as Dr. *Young* makes a Lady do, when
> she is dying,

> Odious, in Woolen! 'twould a Saint provoke! . . .
> And—Betty, give my Cheeks a little red.
>
> I must beg my Reader's Pardon for these numerous Quotations; but, as *Swift* says, 'those anticipating Rascals the Ancients, have left nothing for us poor Moderns to say:' But still to shew my Vanity, let it stand as some sort of Praise, that I have stolen wisely. (1:229)

Pilkington grants Pope's classical status even though she assigns the couplet from Pope's "Epistle to Cobham" (lines 242–43) to Edward Young. Her confusion of the two satirists is plausible, but the ambivalent tribute appears a Freudian slip because of the abundance and accuracy of her allusions to Pope elsewhere.

Late in her second volume, Pilkington replies to a pamphlet that made a parallel comparison between her first volume and the memoirs of Teresia Constantia Phillips, the notorious courtesan. Incensed by the comparison, Pilkington takes the anonymous author (an "Oxford Scholar") to task, rebutting his accusations.

> Then you ask me, how I dare mention Mr. *Pope*? Why truly, like *Drawcansir*, all this I can do, because I dare.—I never refused doing Justice to his poetical Merits; but all your Art can never persuade the World, that he was not an envious Defamer of other Men's good Parts, and intolerably vain of his own. How does he boast of his Acquaintance with the Great, even to childish Folly? The late Earl of *Peterborough* could not divert himself with pruning a Tree in his Garden, but presently we are told of it in these high-sounding unharmonious Words:
>
>> And he, whose Thunder storm'd th'Iberian Lines,
>> Now forms my Quincunx, and now prunes my Vines.
>
> Why, one would have thought he had hired the Earl for a Gardener. (2:351)

Pilkington next berates Pope for his satire on Timon's villa, arguing that Pope showed unwarranted ingratitude to the duke of Chandos. She concludes that Pope ridiculed Chandos's library "because he did not find his own Works there. Shall I proceed, or have I said enough . . . ?" (2:352).

Pilkington's anger with Pope seethes with disappointment in her own career. An outcast while Pope is venerated, Pilkington has nothing left to lose and can adopt Drawcansir's quixotic boast. Even more than Drawcansir, Pilkington seems to imagine herself a female David, aiming her slingshot at Pope's apparently unassailable reputation. Although she patently exploits her friendships with Swift, Colley Cibber, and Lord Kingsborough in the *Memoirs*, Pilkington accuses Pope of even more vulgar exploitation ("one would have thought he had hired the Earl for a Gardener"). The reader infers that Pope's self-glorification is worse than Pilkington's; at least she professes gratitude to her patrons. But Pilkington must have realized that her claims of damning evidence ("have I said enough?") would never lessen the distance between herself and the man she orginally dreamed of emulating. Defeated at the outset of her career by circumstances from which her more culpable husband eventually emerged unscathed, Pilkington had little to plead but her frankness. At least, she boasts, "I have stolen wisely," later reminding readers that "while [Pope] is insulting *his* Betters, his Ethic Epistles are little more than Lord *Shaftsbury*'s Rhapsody berym'd; *his Windsor Forest* stollen from *Cooper's-Hill*; and his *Eloisa* and *Abelard*, the most beautiful Lines in it, taken from *Milton*'s *Il Penseroso*" (3:10). Pilkington's *Memoirs* constitute the tragic record of a thwarted female attempt to compete with a male predecessor.

Far different is the record of Anna Seward's relation to Pope, whom the "Swan of Lichfield" hailed as the "Sweet Swan of Twickenham" (*Letters*, 2:208 and *passim*). Nationally respected for both her poetry and her critical opinions, Seward (1747–1809) avowed Pope as her model and defended his reputation. Pope's was not the sole influence on Seward's mature poetry. She composed in fashionable late-century modes, such as the ode, song, elegy, and sonnet. Seward used couplets for occasional poems, prologues, and epistles, but she seems to have imitated Pope most closely in juvenile poems. Her early ambition was to continue Pope's *Odyssey* with her *Telemachiad*. A note in her *Poetical Works* explains that the "Love Elegies and Epistles" between Evander and Emillia "were written in the early youth of the author" and bear the same relation to a genuine "correspondence between that unhappy pair . . . as the real letters between Abelard and Eloisa bear to Pope's Love-Epistle" (1:25n). Indeed, Evander's plaints echo Eloisa's; in one epistle, he exclaims, "Tender and ardent is that heart of thine, / But ah! not pierced,—not rapt,—not lost as mine" (*Works*, 28; cf. "Eloisa," line 196). Seward described *Louisa, A Poetical Novel* (1784) as an attempt "to unite the impassioned fondness of Pope's *Eloisa*, with the chaster tenderness of Prior's *Emma*" (*Works*, 2:219). Seward matured into a poet with the tastes and techniques typical of her generation, but in such details as attention to assonance and to internal and imperfect rhyme, she remained indebted to Pope, for to such techniques she attributed the sweet sound of his verse. The voluminous criticism preserved in her correspondence, even as revised for publication, reflects Seward's complex response to the poet whom she revered and emulated, but whom she finally classed below Shakespeare, Milton, and Southey (*Letters*, 6:376).

Introducing his edition of Seward's correspondence in 1936, Hesketh Pearson claimed that "it is impossible not to laugh at Anna nowadays." But, he continues, the "sincerity and fidelity to fact" of Seward's descriptions of customs and people warrant a selection of her letters, "rigidly excluding those tedious critical disquisitions on the literature of past ages that take up the greater part of her private correspondence."[62] Over half a century later, Pearson's condescension to Seward seems sexist and inappropriate. Her critical "disquisitions" chronicle the encounters between a well-read, self-confident woman and her past and present literary competitors.

Seward's critical opinions are mocked today because she equated such contemporaries as William Hayley and Robert Southey with Dryden, Pope, Shakespeare, and Milton.[63] Perhaps Seward's enthusiasm for her contemporaries seems contemptible because we expect poets living in what Bertrand Bronson has called "the trough of the wave" to be aware of occupying the lull between the age of Dryden and Pope and the Romantic age.[64] As Bronson observes, later eighteenth-century poets were likely to feel themselves inspired more than depressed by their Augustan predecessors. Seward argued that hers was as great an age of poetry as Queen Anne's. She writes that "all sort of fine writing is in much greater abundance. Perhaps that very abundance forms the chief reason why genius is so much less distinguished [by patrons] than it was in those days." Far from being intimidated by the age of Pope, Seward contended that "the times of Swift and Pope had no lyric poet. Ours have four very resplendent ones, Collins, Gray, Mason, and Warton. . . . Surely Mr. Hayley's verse breathes a more creative and original genius, than even the brilliant Pope, who excels him in nothing but in the high and laboured polish of his enchanting numbers" (*Letters*, 2:86–87). Seward's support for her contemporaries may have been more healthy than foolish. Her belief that Hayley had improved Pope's style, even as Pope had refined Dryden's techniques, enabled her to contend with Pope more effectively than could, for example, Mary Jones.

Seward, like most eighteenth-century women poets, taught herself to write by imitating native models. When Rev. Richard Sykes requested her guidance for Miss F. Cayley in 1793, she observed that "a young poet should compose as a student in painting paints, from the best models, not with servile minuteness, but with generous emulation and critical attention" (*Letters*, 3:324). She recommends close attention to technique.

> I advise our young friend to get by heart, at every leisure interval when she reads or walks alone, a portion of poetic writing from our best authors, observing what are those life-strokes which bring its pictures to our eyes, and what the arrangement of those accents which give smoothness, and of those which energize the numbers: that the iambics give perfect melody, while the trochaics gain in spirit and picturesque effect, what they may lose in smoothness—and that to use them both, in judicious variation, completes the perfection of verse, whether blank or in rhyme. (3:321)

Seward illustrates these observations with examples from Pope's *Homer*, Darwin, and Gray. She recommends active verbs and present tense and warns against tense shifts. She asks her student "to remark, that pleasing effects are often produced by judicious discords in poetry, as well as in music," and to "feel the frequent happiness of transposition" (*Letters*, 3:323). These precise instructions remind us that although women poets were usually self-taught, they were not ignorant of literary terms and techniques.

Seward's letter permits us to glimpse a woman writer's preparation, snatched during precious "leisure interval[s] when she reads or walks alone." Her training was not necessarily less rigorous for being informal and solitary. Seward scoffed at a male contemporary who claimed never to have read or studied poetry. "If Shakespeare's talents were miracles of uncultured intuition, we feel, that neither Milton's, Pope's, Akenside's, Gray's, or Darwin's were such, but that poetic investigation, and long familiarity with the best writers in that line, cooperated to produce their excellence. What folly, then, of the wise, is a disingenuousness so glaring!" (*Letters*, 3:325). Seward's later skepticism about Wordsworth's and Coleridge's claims to originality resulted not from lack of discernment, or from an obstinate refusal to hail the Romantic age, but from conviction that poets learn by studying chosen precursors (*Letters*, 5:55–62). In this instance, her response coincides with twentieth-century opinion.

Seward's technical familiarity rendered her a formidable opponent in poetic disputes. We have glanced at her participation in the Dryden versus Pope controversy (1789–91) in *Gentleman's Magazine*, one of several periodical literary debates to which Seward contributed. "Truth is elicited in such kind of disquisition; prejudices are brought to her test, and the perplexities of thought disentangle by developement," she assures Thomas Park in 1801, reminiscing about her defense of the "sweet swan of Twickenham" (*Letters*, 5:384). Seward deduced "truth" from empirical evidence, defeating her opponents with a barrage of counterexamples. In an exchange of criticism with a "Dr. S——" in 1785, she repudiates his aversion to imperfect rhyme: "Pope, the most musical of all our bards, gives us the imperfect rhymes very lavishly in all his verses, and equally in his picturesque as in his pathetic passages" (*Letters*, 1:72). She produces three couplets from *The Rape of the Lock* and one each from "The Temple of Fame" and "Windsor Forest" to illustrate her point.

Pope authorized many of Seward's technical preferences, particularly throughout her exchanges with George Hardinge. Hardinge seems often to have baited Seward with criticism of her own and her friends' writings. He persisted even after she declined to continue a correspondence so little congenial to her taste and temperament. Seward was nettled by Hardinge's pedantry. "Now, seeming to allow the privilege of mutilating the vowel *e* in blank verse, you assert that it ought never to be done in rhyme," she acknowledges in 1786. But "the musical Pope, in the most exquisitely polished of all his ever-highly-polished verse, the Eloisa to Abelard, curtails it twice in one line" (*Letters*, 1:202). The "Temple of Fame" and "Essay on Criticism" further defy Hardinge's maxim. Pope enabled Seward to counter Hardinge's objections to her diction (*Letters*, 1:332, 2:11) and to her use of ellipsis. She lectures Hardinge:

> That, and which, and whom, are words poets ought always, upon established privilege, to omit, wherever their omission does not produce obscurity. . . . Not to leave such things to be supplied by the reader's imagination is to suppose it dull indeed. Pope would have stared had a poetic reader told him, that the following couplet was obscure for want of the word *whom*,

> O Death! all eloquent, you only prove
> What dust we doat on when 'tis man (whom) we love.

Surely inelegance results from the insertion, not from the omission of such feeble expletives! (*Letters*, 2:12)

Seward repeatedly wondered at contemporary estimates of Pope. To Joseph Weston, her adversary in the *Gentleman's Magazine* debate, she exclaims in 1789:

> What a strange power has prejudice, since it can strike such a mind as yours so blind, as to make you fancy Pope little more than a brilliant versifier, because he successfully endeavoured to polish his numbers high. If ingenious allusions, striking and graceful imagery, sound, perspicuous, and pointed good sense were not, in happy succession, to be found throughout his writings, their beautiful harmonies would be of trivial import to me. (*Letters*, 2:210)

To Weston's ally, poet John Morfitt, she retorts: "It is not true of Pope, that he polished everything high. His Satires, his Ethic Epistles, the glorious Dunciad, and even several parts of the Essay on Man, frequently present passages in a plain unornamented style, though not, it is true, with the *says he's*, and *says she's*, and the *belikes* of Dryden" (*Letters*, 2:239). When Erasmus Darwin espouses the late-century opinion "that poetry admits of few abstract terms," Seward replies, "Poetry that is merely imaginative and picturesque may not. If we find few abstract terms in the Rape of the Lock, we find a profusion of them in the sublimer Essay on Man. Their nervous and condensing power seems to me peculiarly adapted to serious poetry, to that species of the art which addresses at once the understanding and the fancy" (*Letters*, 2:267). Seward championed Pope, not with Mary Jones's ecstacy ("he is inimitable, like Nature," Jones, 314), but with examples gleaned from her intense study and imitation of his poems.

However, perhaps because she found his work imitable, Seward classed Pope beneath Shakespeare and Milton in her private canon. She disagreed with certain of Pope's practises, admitting to Joseph Weston that "Pope's indiscriminate aversion to the Alexandrine verse is as ill-judged as Dryden's licentious use of it." She also preferred "the sense to overflow the couplet . . . oftener than it ever does in Pope and Johnson" (*Letters*, 2:210). Her tastes were certainly influenced by those of her generation. In 1807, she flatters Robert Southey while denouncing the opinions of "Don Manuel Espriella," whose translated letters "pronounce[d] Dryden and Pope the best English poets": "No foreigner ever did . . . attain that perfect knowledge of our language which might enable him to comprehend the dignity and beauty of our noblest blank-verse; consequently they will never perceive the superiority of Shakespeare, Milton, and Southey, to any writer that ever gemm'd the runic fetters" (6:376). Seward's estimate of Pope enabled her to accept serenely comparisons of herself with her favorite "swan." In March 1785, she thanks William Hayley, who had intended to put Romney's portrait of Seward in his library and flank it with busts of Pope and Prior, "That on each side of Seward who rivals 'em both, / They might properly honor that Queen of the Lyre." The sculptor, unfortunately, sent a bust of Newton instead of Pope, inspiring a whimsical but flattering poem ("The fond Student of Light may well wait upon her, / Whose Fancy has all the rich hues of the Sun"; see *Letters*, 1:23).

Long familiarity taught Seward Pope's manner. In 1788, she describes for George Hardinge a poem she would have written on the slavery issue, given adequate leisure.

> I would call upon the Genius of England . . . and conjure him, by casting away the galling, and hitherto indissoluble chain, from the naked savage, toiling for him beneath torrid suns, to open a prospect of golden days to come,
>
> > Where the swart negroes, 'mid the palmy groves,
> > Might quaff the citron juice, and woo their sable loves.
>
> (*Letters*, 2:112)

Her paraphrase of "Windsor Forest," lines 409–10, suggests that the poem was never composed because Pope had, in effect, already written it. A humorous example of Seward's assimilation of Pope's style occurs in a 1794 letter to Mrs. Hayley, where she claims that if Pope had described an eagle's nest, "it would probably have been in these kind of numbers—"

> Thus, on the cedar top, the eagle builds
> His dancing eyrie in etherial fields;
> It scorns the winter's wind, and beating rain,
> And summer suns shoot vertical in vain. (*Letters*, 4:26)

Seward's assonance and alliteration parody Pope's subtle technique. But the caricature suggests that, after years of analysis, Seward achieved a greater degree of objectivity in her relation to Pope's style than did many of her female (or male) contemporaries.

Three years before her death, Seward revised a Popeian dictum. Like Piozzi's and More's, Seward's revision arose from settled convictions; her voracious critical reading suggested the inaccuracy of previous definitions of wit. She first expresses this opinion to Eleanor Ponsonby in May 1799, objecting that the dictum "True wit is nature to advantage dress'd, / What oft was thought, but ne'er so well expressed'd" ("Essay on Criticism," 297–98) "applies better to eloquence" than to wit (*Letters*, 5:232–33). Seward's criticism echoes Samuel Johnson's statement in the *Life of Cowley* (1779) that Pope's couplet "reduces [wit] from strength of thought to happiness of language" (*Lives*, 1:19). But Seward granted imaginative originality a more prominent role in constituting wit than Johnson was willing to concede.

Returning to the topic in 1806, Seward describes wit to Dr. Mansel as if it had been the Odyssean bow of her Augustan predecessors. She points out the inadequacies of Dryden's, Locke's, and Addison's discussions, finding Pope's couplet "equally . . . indeterminate."

> Wit has certainly more to do with art than with nature. Nature is simple, but wit is combined. The couplet does not even apply to any species of excellent writing, since, if the thoughts be commonplace, no grace of expression, no harmony of numbers, can render them justly admirable.
>
> Least of all do Pope's lines apply to wit, since if the attempt do not strike and surprise, it is not wit. Ideas which are familiar to every mind, that is in any degree capable of reflection, cannot either strike or surprise, with whatever verbal elegance they may be given. New thoughts, or at least new combination of thoughts, are the very essence of wit. (*Letters*, 6:306–8)

Seward's quarrel constitutes an act of poetic misprision. Her assertion that "nature is simple, but wit is combined" returns to Locke's definition equating wit with imagination, which she then privileges in a manner familiar to Seward's generation but foreign to Pope's. Taken out of context, Pope's couplet, a delicate attempt to reconcile the competing claims of fancy and judgment, appears to extol commonplace observations rather than "new combination of thoughts." But Seward's swerve from Pope's intended meaning enables her to restring the bow abandoned by her precursors. Though she admits her presumption, she encloses for Dr. Mansel her attempt to define "that subtle effervescence," multiplying Pope's single couplet into five. Her poem contends that wit is vigorous but never coarse.

> Sprung from strange images in contact brought,
> The bright collision of an agile thought;
> And when together struck like flint and fire,
> We start delighted, ponder, and admire;
> While by the union charm'd, we laugh, and wonder,
> How things so like so long were kept asunder.
>
> (*Letters*, 6:308)

Seward's conception of wit is Augustan, but her delight in the charming union of strange ideas is Romantic.

Seward's poem remains obscure, but Pope's aphorism lingers in our cultural consciousness. The "bright collision" of Augustan and contemporary influences in her work probably accounts for our modern estimate of its failure. But Seward's attempt to succeed precisely where her patriarchal elders failed conveys a strength that many eighteenth-century women poets lacked in their relation to Pope. More often than other women, Seward eschewed self-effacing imitation for confident analysis. She invoked Pope's authority for her poetic decisions and continued to compose Popeian couplets, but she also crafted her own style. That neither her poetry nor her opinions are much regarded today matters less than her example as a sturdy thinker, a woman for whom Pope was a fellow "swan" as well as an august precursor.

3

Women's Poetic Addresses to Pope

Women apparently felt themselves addressed by Pope with greater immediacy and sympathy than by any previous canonical male poet. Although he worked within traditions of verse intended either to reform or to compliment women, Pope moderated these inherited genres. Like his letters, Pope's complimentary verse could be facetious or could convey sympathy with women's limitations. Either strategy undermines conventional gallantry. Consequently, such poems as "Epistle to Miss Blount, with the Works of Voiture" or even *The Rape of the Lock* appear to be about real women rather than idealized nymphs, addressed by an individual rather than by a conventional persona. And though Pope participated in the tradition of satires against women, many women readers welcomed his comparatively gentle treatment of female inconsistency and his celebration of a modest, good-humored woman friend.[1]

Pope was not the first poet to address women in a manner they found particularly sympathetic. In *Feminist Milton*, Joseph Wittreich documents women's reliance throughout the century on Milton as an advocate of their rights. John Dryden acknowledged the daily circumstances of women's lives in certain poems and granted them legitimate power as his patronesses in others.[2] But Pope's language was less extravagant than either Milton's or Dryden's. Moreover, he idealized neither the mother of the human race, the British queen, nor titled ladies, although he occasionally penned playful verse for the maids of honor. He domesticated Helen and Andromache and claimed sympathy for such victims of passion as Eloisa and the Unfortunate Lady. But chiefly, women recognized familiar aspects of female experience in Miss [Teresa] Blount, kneed by a boorish suitor; in Belinda, primping for her afternoon excursion; and in Pope's friend Martha Blount in "Epistle to A Lady," serene despite falling china and an irate husband. Such evocations invited not only a female readership but women's responses in kind.

Other circumstances encouraged women's poetic responses to Pope. Their culture actively encouraged women's familiarity with Pope, unlike some other writers' works intended for women readers. Lydia Languish frantically hides her sentimental novels, not her *Works of Pope*. Women throughout the century knew Pope through manuscript and published miscellanies, educational tracts, conduct books, periodicals, and extracts,[3] not to mention numerous reprints of his collected *Works*. By midcentury, Pope's *Works* were as acceptable a gift to a young lady as had once been Belinda's Bibles. A future lord chancellor, Charles Yorke, accompanied his present of Pope's *Works* with verses recalling Pope's "Epistle to Miss Blount, with the Works of Voiture":

> These strains no idle suit to thee commend,
> On whom gay Loves with chaste Desires attend;
> Nor fancied excellence, nor amorous care,
> Prompts to rash praise, or fills with fond despair;
> Enough, if the fair volume find access;
> Thee the great poet's lay shall best express;
> Thy beauteous image there thou may'st regard,
> Which strikes with modest awe the meaner bard.[4]

Yorke concludes that if the poet had known his addressee, Pope would have neglected Belinda and refrained from satirizing women. This slight poem suggests that Pope's poems were considered safe reading for women, at least until 1780, because they did not teach women to indulge fantasies of power or to expect extreme emotional responses, such as "rash praise" and "fond despair." Yorke commends his friend for her beauty, but also for "the blush of honour, and the grace of truth" (14). She is superior to Belinda, and so may read "the fair volume" complacently, finding mirrored her "beauteous image" but no recognizable foibles. Yorke's compliment presupposes his addressee's acquiescence in both his and Pope's notion of female excellence. Partly because their culture sanctioned Pope's feminine configurations, women were not only permitted but encouraged to read his verse.

Because of this state of affairs, women with access to little other literature read Pope throughout the century. Immersion in Pope's writings began early and included his entire canon. We have observed

Mentoria's schoolroom use of *The Essay on Man* and Laetitia Pilkington's childhood encounters with her precursor. Such testimony helps explain Macaulay's, More's, and Hays's consternation when, late in the century, they expostulated against girls' unmediated reading of poems long deemed unexceptionable. Many women's educations probably resembled that of Charlotte Smith's Emmeline: unsupervised gleanings from a few volumes, invariably including the works of Pope. Though meager, such an education strengthened women's proprietary sense of Pope as their poet, a consensus strengthened by Pope's marginal status as a Catholic (which limited his formal education), as an Opposition sympathizer, and as a crippled hunchback.

While men addressed Pope throughout the century in a flood of poems—emulating, flattering, correcting, or reviling—a remarkable number of women also chose to address Pope as poets. Poetry had long been a gentleman's prerogative; Pope followed Jonson and Dryden in considering it his profession. Men who answered Pope in verse were engaging in man-to-man debate and often expected to gain some professional advantage. Pope's male emulators might view their attempts as competitive tests of skill, an attitude acceptable among men. For women, despite the precedent of Aphra Behn, engaging in similar contests required courageous willingness to ignore a cultural taboo. That a number of women poets did so suggests that for various reasons they viewed Pope not as an intimidating "other" but as an eligible competitor. By inviting women to read, Pope encouraged women to participate in their culture. He made accessible to them images and ideas that had inspired men for centuries. In such poems as *The Rape of the Lock* and "Eloisa to Abelard," he also gave women images and phrases illuminating their own experiences. The more ambitious among his female readers responded to his version of their psychology or used his images in contexts better suited to the lives of genteel women. Some disputed his philosophical or political principles.

Many eighteenth-century women poets considered invoking, rebuking, or emulating Pope a female as well as a male prerogative. That prerogative, however, was never lightly exercised. Pope's female contemporaries defied or circumvented disapproval of ladies' publishing. Apprehension of Pope's satirical replies was exacerbated by his near-mythic status, first as prodigy, then as Horatian poet in his grotto. Few women chose to risk public opprobrium by attacking such a figure. Two writers illustrate both the range of women's poetic responses and the cultural rewards and pitfalls that conditioned them. Both were early friends of Pope whose relationships with the poet were eventually curtailed. Their poetic addresses were poles apart, epitomizing different gifts, temperaments, and accomodation to their culture.

Lady Mary Wortley Montagu and
Judith Cowper Madan: New Myths for Old

Robert Halsband, Maynard Mack, and Valerie Rumbold have traced in biographical studies the rise and fall of Pope's friendship with Lady Mary Wortley Montagu.[5] All agree that the precise reason for their vendetta will never be recovered and that opposing politics and a mutual propensity for satire made their quarrel inevitable. Rumbold observes the roots of future discord in the letters Pope and Lady Mary exchanged during her Turkish embassy (135–41). Lady Mary's surviving letters were rewritten as if for publication, leaving few traces of the encouragement, however noncommital, Halsband supposes Pope found in her originals (*Life*, 63). All complacency expunged, Lady Mary's compilations record her maneuvers to distance herself from Pope's fervent gallantry. While Mack suggests the "wry pathos" of Pope's letters (*Pope*, 306), and James Winn has discussed Pope's epistolary fantasies as tortuous admissions of love (*Window*, 111–18), Lady Mary might have felt somewhat persecuted by his indecorous rhetoric. Like many harrassed women, she coped by ignoring Pope's suggestive language rather than rebuking and potentially estranging him. Lady Mary wished to retain Pope's friendship while resisting his manipulation. Their letters consequently resemble a tug-of-war between the impetuous, idealistic poet and his determinedly sensible, worldly correspondent. Their final exchange includes poems that foreshadow eventual rupture.

As Rumbold notes, Pope's letter to Lady Mary of 1 September 1718 was a final attempt to elicit tenderness before she arrived home (140–41). After his usual effusion of compliments and oriental fantasy, he narrated the recent deaths of two laborers struck by lightning at Stanton Harcourt (*Corr.*, 1:493–96). Elaborately producing the event as a pastoral tragedy, Pope described the victims as betrothed lovers, "as constant as ever were found in Romance" (494). John Hewet and Sarah Drew died while sheltering from the storm under a haycock, John's arm protectively shielding his fiancée. Pope was moved by their fate, perhaps because he construed his own relationship with Lady Mary as a romance tale resembling the doomed love of a princess for her dwarf (*Corr.*, 1:365). He included two epitaphs. The first suggested his preoccupation with Lady Mary's "Oriental Self"; he compared the pair to "Eastern Lovers" burning on a pyre with "their faithful Fair." His second attempt represented the lovers as spotless victims of divine sacrifice, types of the exemplary death: "When God calls Virtue to the grave, / Alike 'tis Justice, soon, or late." He begged that Lady Mary supply a better epitaph, or at least "a Tear from the finest eyes in the world. I know you have Tenderness; you must have it" (*Corr.*, 1:496). The account was calculated to evoke sentiment, as if Pope were trying to engineer at least a moment of shared empathy.

His attempt failed miserably. Lady Mary's response from Dover began by stripping his "pastoral lovers (vulgarly called Haymakers)" of their romance pretensions. She failed to see anything "marvellous" about the couple or their attachment and found Pope's epitaph rather impious ("Time and chance happen to all men"). She nevertheless obliged Pope with her own epitaph, "more just, tho' not so poetical" (Pope, *Corr.*, 1:522–24). The 20-line poem is a masterpiece of cynicism, from her deliberate misstatement of one lover's (John Hewet's) name—"Here lies John Hughes and Sarah Drew; / Perhaps you'll say, What's that to you?" (1–2)—to her concluding flattery—"Now they are happy in their doom, / *For Pope Has Wrote Upon Their Tomb*" (19–20). As Pope had attempted to manipulate her sympathy, Lady Mary enlisted Pope's pride to assuage his disappointment. On one level, the epitaph is an exercise in telling the truth. Lady Mary vigorously rejects Pope's constructions of her as the vulnerable heroine of a romance. She presents herself as an aristocrat with little interest in peasants. She also intimates her impatience with Pope's idealization of marriage: "For had they seen the next year's sun, / A beaten wife and cuckold swain / Had jointly curs'd the marriage chain" (17–18).

Her own marriage had apparently left Lady Mary disillusioned, but these lines also reject utopian fantasies about the childlike innocence of "primitive" people. Pope had plagued her with such notions throughout his letters, imagining a Lady Mary liberated from European decorum by her Turkish sojourn. Embarking for home, Lady Mary subtly countered Pope's presumptuous suggestion that she would return "so much nearer Innocence (that is, Truth) & Infancy (that is, Openness)" (*Corr.*, 1:494). Her travels, moreover, had convinced her that "primitive" people were neither more virtuous nor more decadent than others. Pope's dream of pastoral innocence was an ill-judged appeal to the woman who observed, "'Tis just as 'tis with you, . . . the Turkish Ladys don't commit one Sin the less for not being Christians."[6] Lady Mary's epitaph is a resolutely hard-hearted response to Pope's. Its relentless antiromanticism is even more striking in the context of her letters to other correspondents. As Cynthia Lowenthal has observed, Lady Mary often viewed Turkish culture through the medium of romance. She was particularly adept at idealizing or minimizing foreign culture "to argue for the autonomy and freedom the female heroic promises."[7] In the parodic epitaph, she turned with equal facility to harsh satire, to avoid being trapped in Pope's version of romance. Lady Mary evidently refused to enter into romantic fantasy on any but her terms. The epitaph intimates her rejection of Pope's wistful courtship. Sensing the wish fulfillment lurking in his narrative, she refused to play his game: "I . . . had rather continue to be your stupid, *living*, humble servant, than be *celebrated* by all the pens in Europe" (Pope, *Corr.*, 1:524). As Rumbold concludes, Pope refused to heed Lady Mary's implicit warning (141). Perhaps he persisted until a later, explicit rejection. More likely, the relationship finally snapped when they could no longer reconcile such manifestly different perspectives.

Valerie Rumbold has traced Pope's progressive transformation of Lady Mary into Sappho, the monstrous rhetorical incarnation that still affects discussions of her character.[8] Rumbold observes that Pope's earliest complaints, with some basis in personal knowledge, rapidly gave way to "a rhetoric with a life of its own" (156), incorporating Lady Mary into the tradition associating learned women with "filth, meanness and lewdness" (159). Lady Mary's rhetorical transformation of Pope into a moral and political pariah kept pace with his degenerating constructions. The correspondence has been less observed, however, because two of Lady Mary's three satirical replies remained in manuscript until 1803.[9] No matter which of the pair started their public quarrel, Lady Mary soon faced an unequal contest. Pope's opening salvo, "The Capon's Tale: To a Lady who father'd her Lampoons upon her Acquaintance" (1726; *Poems*, 6:256–57) accused Lady Mary of implying his or Swift's authorship of her libelous occasional pieces. Lady Mary's poems were usually intended to remain in manuscript, genteel women's traditional method of restricting readership. Like Pope, Lady Mary suffered some witty pieces to be published while denying authorship; other verses were published without her consent.

She probably equivocated about the authorship of some scandalous poems to protect her reputation. At any rate, Lady Mary could not openly indulge in a public literary feud as could Pope. While Pope had to be somewhat circumspect to preserve the credibility of his satiric persona, Lady Mary's reputation was jeopardized by each publication.

By adopting Lord Hervey as her literary ally, Lady Mary could publicly combat Pope in at least one instance. But the greater challenge remained his absorption of her personality and activities into the myth of Sappho, traditionally the archetype of the slatternly literary lady. Elizabeth Rowe, among others, was beginning to combat this convention in her *Letters from the Dead to the Living* (1728), but Pope took full advantage of its remaining vitality. In Lady Mary's poetic responses to Pope, she sought an equally powerful and painful mythic construction with which to oppose his. "Her Palace placed beneath a muddy road" (1729; *Essays*, 247–51) is comparable to Pope's earliest, most personal references in *Dunciad* (1728), where he alluded to her entanglement with Nicolas-François Rémond (2.125–28).

In Lady Mary's anti-*Dunciad* set in Pope's Grotto, the Goddess Dulness seeks her heir among the competing Scriblerians. Warned that Addison, following Milton, will have soon vanquished ignorance and coarseness, her ministers propose candidates for leadership. Prophanation champions Swift; Obscenity, Gay; a third courtier, Arbuthnot. But Dulness seeks an heir with the gifts of all three, who "Shall sing of Worms in great Arbuthnott's strain, / In Lewd Burlesque the Sacred Psalms prophane, / To maids of Honour bawdy Songs address" (108–10). Lady Mary's account caricatures Pope's early career, capitalizing on her knowledge of the bawdy ephemera Pope publicly disclaimed. Her reflections on his Catholicism ("His early Youth in Superstition bred," 114) and preference for the rhymed couplet (117–19) are reductive but recognizable aspects of Pope's life and art. Lady Mary concocts a prophecy based on Pope's career: patronized by Lords Lansdowne and Bolingbroke, Dulness's now-penniless heir will rise to prominence and return Britain to her sway (120–31).

A companion poem, "Now with fresh vigour Morn her Light displays," continues the tale (*Essays*, 251–55). Dulness, disguised as mutual friend "Duke" Disney,[10] awakens a debauched Bolingbroke and demands he patronize Pope or risk the ruin of her kingdom (lines 52–72). When Bolingbroke demurs (he would rather attempt converting Addison to their cause), Dulness reveals herself and demands compliance: "Tis I, your Tropes, and Florid Style, bestow. /

After such wreaths bestow'd, such service done, / Dare you refuse protection to my Son?" (100–102). Lady Mary's poems comprise a riposte to the *Dunciad* at least as amusing as most published Whig opposition to Pope's poem. Lady Mary's attempt to construct Pope as the true heir of Dulness, her own mythic account of his career, demonstrates a use of her ability to structure reality different from the use observed by Lowenthal in the Turkish embassy letters. But Lady Mary probably realized that a full-blown response to the *Dunciad*, no matter how politically motivated, would be interpreted as an acknowledgment of Pope's scandalous insinuations. Trapped—as Pope knew she was—by decorum, she withheld her reply. Thus she missed an opportunity to publish a myth countering Pope's version of himself as the heir of Dryden and champion of refined, nonpartisan poetry.

Even Robert Halsband admits that Lady Mary's "Verses Address'd to the Imitator of the First Satire of the Second Book of Horace" (1733) is "as crude and bludgeoning a lampoon as appeared in the pamphlet wars of the time" (*Life*, 142). The poem's cruelty is perhaps mitigated when seen as the second step in a campaign that Lady Mary perceived as correspondingly escalated on Pope's side. Confederacy with Lord Hervey provided some shelter for her; although the "Verses" were printed as by "A Lady of Quality," Pope believed Hervey responsible for their publication (Halsband, *Life*, 143). The poem's accusations that Pope was a poor translator and inept satirist were far from novel but retailed with energetic scorn. Its ugliest feature, the cruel allusions to Pope's deformity, was also typical of contemporary Pope-bashing satire. Even the poem's identification of Pope with Cain was anticipated in a pamphlet by John Ozell (Lady Montagu, *Essays*, 270 n. 111). But the poem's persistence in identifying Pope with the Genesis myth, first with the snake (lines 54–59), then with Cain (lines 100–12), suggests a fresh attempt by Lady Mary to contain Pope in a damning structure.

Although Lady Mary's precise contribution will never be known (the poem's opening derision of Pope's "inaccurate" translation may derive from Pope's substitution of "Sappho" for "Cervius" in his imitation), "Verses" logically follows the comparatively benign trivializion of Pope in her previous poem. Wounded by his potent and damaging references to Sappho, she turned to stronger satire, attempting to identify Pope with the embodiment of evil. Unfortunately, the poem's characterization is inconsistent. Lady Mary and Lord Hervey probably felt that to identify Pope with Satan granted him too much power. So in the midst of God's curse on the poet "as to *the Snake of Eve*" (54), Pope metamorphoses into a porcupine, provoking but impotent (73–78). The "Verses" then rise to exhort Pope as Cain.

> Like the first bold Assassin's be thy Lot,
> Ne'er be thy Guilt forgiven, or forgot;
> But as thou hate'st, be hated by Mankind,
> And with the Emblem of thy crooked Mind,
> Mark'd on thy Back, like *Cain*, by God's own Hand;
> Wander like him, accursed through the Land.
>
> (107–12)

Though grand, the peroration's equation of character assassination with the first murder is disproportionate enough to be anticlimactic, an effect worsened by the poem's penultimate image of Pope as a porcupine. The poem indicates intense struggle, but Lady Mary had yet to fit Pope to a myth that would begin to affect his reputation as his references to Sappho injured hers.

"P—— to Bolingbroke" (1734–35; *Essays*, 279–84), Lady Mary's final poetic response, was her most successful, although it was read only in manuscript by select acquaintances. The poem constitutes her replies to both the *Essay on Man* and Pope's imitation of the "Second Satire of the Second Book of Horace." Lady Mary abandons her attempt to assimilate Pope to a structure, such as the Biblical fall into sin or Dulness's choice of heir. Instead, Lady Mary grants Pope's myth of himself as Horatian recluse, suggesting very different motives for his behavior than those he proclaimed through his persona. Her poem is unfair but quite comical, particularly when juxtaposed with the earnest, dignified version of himself Pope cultivated throughout his mature career. Lady Mary impersonates Pope, twisting his conservative principles into hypocritical cant.

Lady Mary commences by mimicking Pope's final address to Bolingbroke in his *Essay*.

> While with Contempt you view poor human-kind
> Weak, willful, Sensual, Passionate and blind;
> Amidst these Errours thou art faultless found,
> (The Moon takes Lustre from the Darkness round)
> Permit me, too, a small attendant Star,
> To twinkle, tho' in a more distant Sphere.
>
> (5–10)

To a woman of Lady Mary's firm Whig sympathies, Lord Bolingbroke's failures resulted precisely from weakness, willfulness, sensuality, and passion. Pope never claimed Bolingbroke's faultlessness in the *Essay*, but by exaggerating Pope's tribute to his mentor's politeness and eloquence (*Essay*, 4.381–82), Lady Mary suggests a more unequal relationship than he portrays. Long familiarity with Pope's verse may have suggested her substitution of moon and star for Pope's description of himself as a little bark attending Bolingbroke's fame (*Essay*, 4.385–86). Pope habitually described women he admired as mild moons. In his manuscript verses to Judith Cowper (1722; *Poems*, 6:306), Erinna's moonlight shines while Sappho's "glaring sun declines" (7). Lady Mary had most likely seen the generalized version of this metaphor published in Pope's "Epistle to a Lady" (February 1735; lines 253–56). Her appropriation of this characteristic metaphor suggests Pope's obsequiousness and—in the context of his characteristic application of the metaphor to women—emasculates both Pope and his patron.

Lady Mary's "Pope" proceeds to lavish on Bolingbroke ironic praise reminiscent of the "Epistle to Augustus." Lamenting his own inconsequence, he recalls Bolingbroke's early career in Queen Anne's cabinet: "Let *Oxford* own, let *Catalonia* tell, / What various victims to your wisdom fell" (19–20). The seeming panegyric refers to Bolingbroke's treacherous machinations as Secretary of State. "Pope" admiringly recalls the embarrassing episode of Bolingbroke's self-exile, during which he first served, then deserted, the Pretender. While others lucky enough to obtain pardon for such activities would happily retire, Bolingbroke continues to seek power. "Oh, was your Pow'r like your Intention good, / Your native Land would stream with civil blood" (42–43). "Pope" confesses his envy of Bolingbroke's capacity for mischief; Lady Mary rehearses her version of his career as fraudulent translator and ungrateful friend (51–62). "Pope" justifies his and Bolingbroke's conduct according to the *Essay*'s philosophy.

> We, who with piercing Eyes look Nature through,
> We know that all is right in all we do.
> Reason's erroneous, honest Instinct right.
> Monkeys were made to grin, and Fleas to bite.
>
> (65–68)

Lady Mary's observation that Pope's defense of providence rationalizes sedition and libel anticipates moralists' uneasiness with his declaration that "Whatever is, is Right."

Lady Mary reserves her final stroke for Pope's Horatian boast of abstemiousness in the "Second Satire of the Second Book."

> When I see smoaking on a Booby's board
> Fat Ortalans, and Pies of Perigord,
> My self am moved to high poetick rage
> (The Homer, and the Horace of the Age).
> Puppies! who have the insolence to dine
> With smiling beauties, and with sparkling wine,
> While I retire, plagu'd with an Empty Purse,
> Eat Brocoli, and kiss my antient Nurse.
>
> (76–83)

Among the charms of Pope's Horatian imitations is their specificity, Pope's substitution of a detailed image of eighteenth-century life for Horace's Roman targets. In Lady Mary's parody, Pope's evocation of modern gourmet excess becomes finicky, the misplaced outrage of an envious hermit. Her aristocratic sympathy with convivial consumption recoils from Pope's "middle-class" advocacy of moderation. She detects behind Pope's sermon on gluttony not moral outrage over the cultural decadence such behavior signifies but poverty and loneliness. The image of Pope kissing his nurse, derived from happier times, reiterates Lady Mary's desire to wound Pope as he had abused her confidence to slander her (in the instance of Rémond, for example). At the poem's conclusion, "Pope" congratulates Bolingbroke on their birth in an age that permits such infamous behavior: "Yet this remains our more peculiar boast, / You scape the Block, and I the Whipping-Post" (97–98).

Maynard Mack describes "P—— to Bolingbroke" as an "anemic effort" (*Pope*, 561), a judgment understandable from his perspectives as Pope's biographer and as the premier student of Pope's Horatian persona in *The Garden and the City*. But Lady Mary's sophistic deconstruction of Pope's Horatian pose remains her most successful attempt to counter his attacks. Her image of the Homer and the Horace of his age stooping to rail at meat pies undermines Pope's satiric pretensions, however perverse her account of his motives. Lady Mary was no more interested in fairness than was Pope when he repeatedly invoked Sappho. But Pope was safe from Lady Mary's satire, spared by the very imperatives of reputation that rendered his attacks on her so injurious. Because Lady Mary dared not exacerbate her identification with Sappho, two of her three responses remained in manuscript.

Lady Mary's association with "Verses Address'd to the Imitator" drew insulting replies even from women readers.[11] In "Advice to Sappho" (1733), "a Gentlewoman" infers Lady Mary's guilt from her angry invective.[12] "Retrieve lost Fame; nor is it yet too late / The Beauties of [Pope's] mind to emulate," she admonished (16–17). If she read this pamphlet, Lady Mary might have been particularly offended by its erotic portrait of Pope, contrasted with her poem's image of the poet as a hated outcast.

> Nay, *Pope* can love; for great and gen'rous Hearts
> Are always touch'd with *Cupid's* keenest Darts:
> The Poet and the Painter quickly feel
> Th'Effects of Love, 'cause they in Beauty deal.
> The happy She that does his Love controul,
> May boast a Conquest o'er a mighty Soul.
>
> (48–53)

The gentlewoman concludes her awkward praise of Pope's charisma by admitting, "I'm at home, be sure, to Master *Pope*" (71), testifying to the established power of his persona against Lady Mary's claim of misrepresentation.

About two months after "Verses" appeared, "a Lady" dedicated *The Neuter: or, a Modest Satire on the Poets of the Age* to Lady Mary.[13] The author chose Lady Mary as patron of her 71-line poem because "a Person less celebrated for their Wit and Writings, must consequently be less concern'd for the visible decay of a noble Art, which has of late, been miserably abused by a set of bad Poetasters" (3). Perhaps she thought that by appealing to Lady Mary she recommended her poem to both Whigs and Tories. The poem, however, is a roll call of Whig party writers who attacked Pope for including them in the *Dunciad*. After denouncing each, she concludes, "When *Dunciad* Heroes can with railing harm, / . . . Or when they write with Harmony and Fire; / Then ever pleasing *Pope* shall quit the Lyre" (66–69). Either the lady was oblivious to Lady Mary's participation in the anti-Pope pamphlet war, or she intended to coerce acquiescence that could only be disowned by admitting authorship of the "Verses." Both alternatives exposed Lady Mary to insult, discouraging further attempts to counter Pope's slander by publishing her own.

Throughout her poetic duel with Pope, Lady Mary perceived herself as his equal in wit. Far from acknowledging his literary preeminence, her poems challenge his themes, characterizations, and structures. Like his other aristocratic female critics, Lady Mary never felt compelled to defer to Pope, her social inferior.[14] Obliged by her culture to forgo acknowledged publications, she stood her ground throughout their correspondence and, later, in manuscript verse. But cultural conventions inevitably reduced Pope's and Lady Mary's quarrel to a duel manqué, a series of public affronts to which one of the principals responded ineffectually. Lady Mary's letters and poems suggest the difficulty of challenging slander without descending to equal cruelty and further blasting her reputation. They also reveal her powerful, but thwarted, desire to contest Pope's harrassment, a dilemma that still haunts women today.

Pope must have turned with relief to Judith Cowper, by youth and temperament eligible to soothe the irascible poet. Valerie Rumbold has analyzed Cowper's charms for Pope: her admiration and her willingness to play the moon to his Apollonian sun (145–50). My interest is in Cowper's constructions of herself as Pope's acolyte, present in each of her poetic responses to him. Her earliest, "To Mr. Pope—Written in his Works," probably initiated their correspondence. She composed the poem, honoring his 1717 *Works*, in 1720. A mutual friend, probably Mary Caesar or Henrietta Howard (later Lady Suffolk), shared it with Pope in 1722.[15] The 78-line tribute pays homage to both his poems and the recently completed *Iliad*, complimenting Pope for fulfilling the ideal of his "Essay on Criticism": "Throughout the whole with blended power is found / The weight of sense and elegance of sound" (15–16). Cowper particularly distinguishes "Windsor Forest" in lines 19–32, and she refers to *The Rape of the Lock* when she invites Pope to sit "in judgment o'er our fav'rite follies . . . / And soften wisdom's harsh reproofs to wit" (37–38).

The *Iliad* rouses Cowper's emulation as well as her praise: "Oh for a muse like thine, while I rehearse / Th'immortal beauties of thy various verse!" ("To Mr. Pope," 45–46). Her description of the epic suggests attentive study of Pope's technique; her praise of his synthesis of sense and sound was not mere compliment. Her portrait of Achilles follows Pope's example in the "Essay on Criticism" (365–73).

> But when *Achilles*, panting for the war,
> Joins the fleet coursers to the whirling car;
>
> . . . .
> In rough hoarse verse we see th'embattled foes,
> In each loud strain the fiery onset glows:

With strength redoubled here *Achilles* shines,
And all the battle thunders in thy lines.

                                        (51–52, 57–60)

Cowper's juxtaposition of high-register and low-register vowel sounds in line 52 mimics the tense yoking of spirited horse to chariot; line 56 appropriates Pope's model for conveying surging, roaring sound ("Essay on Criticism," 368–69). If, as Rumbold suggests, Pope's *Works* were crucial to Cowper's creative development (145), they functioned not as mere inspiration but as practical instruction. In "To Mr. Pope," Cowper literally and figuratively aspires to "a muse like [Pope's]," evolving her style by imitating his. Her final lines allude to another poem in the 1717 volume, Pope's "Epistle to Mr. Jervas" on their dedication to sister arts. Just as Pope modulates from pastoral landscape description to epic battle narrative, she implies, "so the bright magick of the painter's hand / Can cities, streams, or far-stretch'd plains command" (60–61), switching at will to "a work . . . / Where bolder rage informs each breathing line" (69–70). She concludes that when a painter captures Caesar on canvas (as well, by implication, as Pope has depicted Achilles), "we own the mighty master's skill, as boundless, as complete" (78). Pope had warned, in the "Essay on Criticism," against ending poems with "needless" alexandrines (356). But Cowper evidently intended hers to dignify "To Mr. Pope" with a resonant conclusion.

"To Mr. Pope" is the work of a beginner, but a beginner determined to learn from this poet who welcomed women readers. Pope returned her compliment by including "To Mr. Pope," albeit anonymously, in his *Miscellany Poems* (1736), a reprint of the 1717 *Works*. Perhaps Cowper's permission to print the poem was hard-won; she probably insisted on anonymity. But that Pope thought highly enough of Cowper's commendation to include it among his dedicatory poems suggests his pride in the young woman's enthusiastic response.

Because "To Mr. Pope" so plainly acknowledges Pope as her model, Cowper must have been delighted by the opportunity to correspond with the poet himself. But Pope resisted the role of mentor. Carol Virginia Pohli has observed the deliberate opacity of Pope's remarks on Cowper's writings, his denial of genuine criticism.[16] "I would, with as much readiness, play the Apothecary or the Nurse, to mend your Headakes, as I would play the Critick to improve your verses," he assured her on 30 September 1722 (*Corr.*, 2:137). While overtly disavowing his professional competence to improve Cowper's poems, Pope's metaphor covertly suggests that mentoring a young woman was beneath his dignity as a gentleman poet.[17] As Pope would not associate himself professionally with apothecaries or, even more ludicrously, with nursemaids, so he would not consult with young Miss Cowper about her verses. "I sincerely tell you I can mend 'em very little, & only in Triffles, not worth writing about, but will tell you every tittle when I have the happiness to see you," he added. Pope and Cowper may never have met, so this deferral effectively excused him from critical guidance. In Pope's defense, we must recall that he had lost William Wycherley's friendship in 1710 for too zealously revising some poems (*Corr.*, 1:84–87). If Cowper's friendship compensated for his lost intimacy with Lady Mary, then Pope probably avoided rigorous consultation about her poems to insure a mutually pleasant correspondence. He preferred greeting Cowper's verses as "Tokens of heav'nly favour" (*Corr.*, 2:198) rather than subjecting them to his professional critique. Both Cowper's elder and the superior writer, Pope manipulated their epistolary friendship to serve his needs without alienating his young female neighbor on Parnassus (*Corr.*, 2:141).

Cultural influences beyond Pope impeded Cowper's poetic development. She, like Lady Mary, hesitated to publish. Only a handful of her poems were printed during her life. One poem, however, was reprinted frequently enough to establish her reputation. In contrast to Pope's subtle disparagement of her verse, Thornton and Colman, the editors of *Poems by Eminent Ladies* (1755), found Cowper's "Abelard to Eloisa" "certainly much superior to all those pieces that have appeared on the same subject: and indeed this Lady's *Abelard* is no mean companion to *Pope's Eloisa.*"[18] Cowper's is the first known reply to Pope's heroic epistle, probably inspired, like "To Mr. Pope," by his *Works* (1717). Contemporaries seem to have agreed with Thornton and Colman's estimate of "Abelard to Eloisa," paired with Pope's throughout the century in such pamphlets as *The Unfortunate Lovers* (1756).[19] In their introduction to the poem in *Eminent Ladies*, Thornton and Colman observed "it as an odd accident, that *Eloisa*'s Letter should have been put into metre by a man, and that *Abelard*'s should at length come to us in elegant verse from the hands of a Lady" (136). "Abelard to Eloisa" warranted its place beside "Eloisa" as a contemporary woman's response to Pope's poem. Rumbold finds the poem disappointing because of its conventional and "somewhat unconvincing resolution"

(147)... But Cowper's typically "feminine" attempt to resolve the tensions of Pope's epistle particularly pleased contemporaries, who found her poem a satisfying denouement to Pope's ambiguous conclusion.[20]

Cowper had most difficulty constructing consistent characters. Unlike Pope's Eloisa, who speaks throughout in the heightened language of the heroic epistle, Cowper's Abelard shifts from feminine to masculine concerns, from a heroic to a conventional point of view. Cowper structures her "Abelard to Eloisa" as the monk's reply to Eloisa's epistle. Like "To Mr. Pope," the 178-line poem is both an homage to Pope's poem and a close study of his techniques, echoing the previous poem throughout. Contrary to Eloisa's assumption that her castrated lover has "no pulse that riots, and no blood that glows" ("Eloisa," 251), Cowper's Abelard has glowed with "guilty transport" as he read her letter, "and streaming torrents from my eyes fast flow'd" (5–6). Enraptured to discover that she has not forgotten him, he cries, "O *Eloisa*! art thou still the same?" (7). But his joy is soon chastened by the recollection that theirs is a forbidden love, endangering their salvation (13–19). Like Pope's heroine, Abelard confesses that years of penitence have not broken his passion. As she admitted her capacity to "hope, despair, resent, regret, / Conceal, disdain—do all things but forget" (199–200), so Abelard reveals "I hope, despair, repent— yet still I love" (26). Unlike Eloisa, however, Abelard regrets his loss of youthful beauty, imagining his lover's disgust to find "*Abelard* the young, the gay, remov'd, / And in the hermit sunk the man you lov'd" (45–46). Cowper projects onto her male protagonist conventional feminine concern with youthful appearance.

Abelard's account of his sufferings, although not as explicitly sexual, parallels Eloisa's. He struggles to obliterate her "melting phantom" (60) from his reveries. Failing, he begs God to "change the temper of this lab'ring breast" (69), only to realize his hypocrisy: "Would I this touch'd, this glowing heart refine / To the cold substance of this marble shrine?" (77–78). Cowper alludes to Eloisa's defiant address to the Paraclete's statues: "I have not yet forgot my self to stone" (24). She develops the image in Abelard's reciprocal plea to the saints: "A holier rage in your pure bosoms dwelt, / Nor can you pity what you never felt" (91–92). In this passage, simultaneously desperate and resentful, Cowper most nearly approaches the tension of Pope's epistle. As if acknowledging her fleeting success, Lady Mary chose to echo these lines when satirizing Cowper in 1723.[21]

But after this momentary empathy with Pope's creation, Cowper proceeds more conventionally. Her poem's unevenness resulted inevitably from her youthful inexperience and feminine education, compounded by her reliance on Pope. According to Cowper's recapitulation, Eloisa was a twelfth-century Belinda. "Abelard" compares her to rays of sunshine: "Bright as their beams thy eyes a mind disclose, / Whilst on thy lips gay blush'd the fragrant rose" (105–6). Pope's description of seductive feminine appeal (*Rape*, 2.9) seems at first inapplicable to the scholarly young Eloisa. But the allusion, together with Cowper's reluctance to make Abelard fully responsible, reminds us that contemporary sources trained young women to avoid seduction partly by blaming its victims. Cowper's Abelard falls victim to Eloisa's charms: "Prest by my fate, I gaz'd—and was undone" (108). His diction suggests a reciprocal seduction. Eloisa's beauty "prest" Abelard much as he importuned his mistress. Although merely the object of his gaze, she was responsible for his attempt. Abelard admits he seduced Eloisa, but he regrets she was "Too fond, alas! too fatally inclin'd" to capitulate (118). Pope's Eloisa had conceived of her passion as uniquely heroic, but Cowper relates it to contemporary warnings about women's easily roused sexuality. Likewise, Abelard's account of his sufferings resembles a scholarly version of the love versus honor debates in seventeenth-century drama. While Pope's Eloisa mourned the demise of a grand affair ("There dy'd the best of passions, Love and Fame," 40), Abelard regrets his wasted career: "There dy'd the gen'rous fire, whose vig'rous flame / Enlarg'd my soul, and urg'd me on to fame" (109–10). He wishes Eloisa would at least fulfill her feminine responsibility to inspire his spiritual regeneration.

> But if unhappy, wretched, lost, in vain,
> Faintly th'unequal combat you sustain;
> If not to heav'n you feel your bosom rise,
> Nor tears refin'd fall contrite from your eyes;
> If still your heart its wonted passions move,
> If still, to speak all pains in one—you love;
> Deaf to the weak essays of living breath,
> Attend the stronger eloquence of death.

> (145–51)

Cowper's final evocation of Pope's heroine rings true. Her Abelard recognizes that Eloisa has yet to, and may never, achieve pious resignation. Responding to that ambiguity, Abelard pleads with Eloisa to repent after his death. Like Pope's Eloisa, he invites his lover to view his corpse: "See all my wild, tumultuous passion o'er, / And thou, amazing change! belov'd no more" (163–64). Abelard's interjection ("amazing change!") admits defeat. He cannot conceive of overcoming his passion. But unlike Pope's Eloisa, who wished for Abelard a death ecstatic as physical love, Cowper's Abelard exhorts Eloisa to repent: "Let love divine frail mortal love dethrone / And to your mind immortal joys make known" (172–73). The sentiments are Eloisa's drained of sexual connotation. Cowper avoided such imagery, either because it was unladylike or because Pope's prophane diction (e.g., "And Saints embrace thee with a love like mine," 342) created the ambiguity her poem meant to resolve. Rumbold implies "Abelard to Eloisa" ends weakly because Cowper herself had no faith in her poem's simple reduction of passion to crimes resolved by the spectacle of death. But by casting the lovers in rather conventional gender roles throughout, Cowper inevitably reached a conclusion simpler than Pope's. Her contemporaries may have appreciated her poem precisely for the "feminine" conventionality that enabled its resolution. Cowper comforted readers with the promise that Abelard would eventually hush Eloisa's racked soul to peace (line 178).

Cowper's early poems frequently invoke Pope as fabled bard or privileged friend. Her final sustained homage to Pope occurs in her most ambitious poem, "The Progress of Poetry" (1721; revised in 1731).[22] Falconer Madan has commented that Cowper "was not, and at her age could not be, equipped for a survey of all literature in verse" (266). His remark is certainly true; Cowper omitted Shakespeare from her first version of the poem. Even in its early form, however, the poem bespeaks Cowper's longing to participate in, if only by celebrating, a tradition of literary genius beginning with Homer and culminating in Pope. The poem's structure is parabolic. After her modest invocation to the muses (lines 1–12), Cowper defines her criteria. She will celebrate genius, not correctness; Addison and Pope, rather than Dennis (13–28). Her priorities are those of Pope's "Essay on Criticism," confirmed by her initial praise of Homer as the wellspring of all poetry (29–56). Cowper's descriptive eulogy reminds us that she owed her familiarity with Homer to Pope. The ever-growing number of translations made possible this young woman's tribute to ancient poets. Pindar, Sappho, Anacreon, Virgil, and Horace each claim her notice before her muse leaves its "foreign task," impatient "to exalt her Country's fame" (106–7).

Cowper sings of liberty as the inspiration of Britain's literature, a conventional claim but poignant in its suggestion of her yearning to participate in the making of a national canon. Chaucer and Cowley open her list of British bards, but Waller and Milton merit her lengthiest praises ("Progress of Poetry," 135–74), a tribute to the twin merits of refinement and sublimity redolent of Pope's "Essay on Criticism." Dryden, Denham, Addison, and Garth continue her British worthies, heralding her champion, the fulfillment of national literary promise.

> High on the radiant list great *Pope* appears,
> With all the fire of youth, and strength of years;
> Where'er supreme he points the nervous line,
> Nature and Art in bright conjunction shine.
> How just the turns! how regular the draught!
> How smooth the language! how refin'd the thought!
> Secure, beneath the shade of early rays,
> He dar'd the thunder of great Homer's lays,
> A sacred heat inform'd his heaving breast,
> And Homer, in his genius, stood confest;
> To heights sublime he rous'd the pond'rous lyre,
> And our cold isle grew warm with Grecian fire.
>
> (205–16)

After enumerating a handful of contemporaries—for example, Prior, Granville, and Rowe—as further confirmation that Britain has achieved an Augustan epoch, Cowper refuses to choose a preeminent bard (229). She excuses herself, claiming that modern poets are as numerous and dazzling as stars, and consequently indistinguishable.

Cowper's conclusion in "Progress of Poetry" was the only plausible course for a modest young woman, and we may detect the conciliatory strategy of a woman arbitrating among a host of competing male poets. Her refusal to name "th'excelling Bard" (229) effaces her role in this cavalcade. She refuses to exercise her judgment or dominate a sequence more indicative of convention than of personal choice (reminded later that she omitted Shakespeare, she obligingly added him). Her self-effacing conclusion thus lacks the ambition implied in Pope's conclusion to the "Essay on Criticism," where his diction inexorably reminds us that he is himself the great sublime he has drawn. The structure of "Progress of Poetry" confirms Pope's self-estimate in the "Essay." The poem swings, bowl-shaped, from praise of Homer to praise of Pope as Homer's embodiment. After her opening reference to Homer's immortality and the *Iliad*'s "full perfection" (36),

Cowper's climactic description of Pope as Homer reborn virtually grants him the laurel.

Cowper celebrates Pope in terms established by his "Essay on Criticism." Pope urged the cooperation of Art and Nature, or imagination and reason. Cowper likewise finds in Pope "the fire of youth, and strength of years"—youthful fancy blended with mature judgment. Pope warned that very few poets could neglect the classical rules of composition. Cowper extols Pope's correctness, the decorous regularity of his verse: "How smooth the language! How refin'd the thought!" (210). Pope regarded Homer as the source of all poetic greatness: "Be *Homer's* Works your *Study*, and *Delight*, / Read them by Day, and Meditate by Night" (124–25). Cowper's apotheosis of Pope as Homer confirms her partiality. Homer literally "inspires" Pope with his own breath: "A sacred heat inform'd his heaving breast, / And Homer, in his genius, stood confest" (213–14). Her concluding enumeration of subordinate British poets enthrones Pope as Homer among his fellow neoclassicists. Although Cowper forbears naming the bard "who most labours with th'inspiring God" (232), her reticence seems mostly a display of appropriate feminine deference. According to her "Progress," Pope's poetry weds Homer's fire with modern refinement. In Pope's "Essay on Criticism," refinement (or "Art") remained poetry's greatest challenge after Homer encompassed nature in his work. "The Progress of Poetry" thus resolves and completes the "Essay on Criticism" much as "Abelard to Eloisa" completed Pope's "Eloisa to Abelard." Cowper achieves this by creating a new myth, Pope as the reincarnation of Homer, a myth latent in his "Essay" but never articulated. Her poem's conclusion reflects Pope's dominance over her imagination. Modern poetry appears a blur of "undistinguish'd brightness," further "progress" unthinkable after Pope's triumphant reconciliation of art with nature. That Cowper was dazzled by Pope's technical mastery is understandable. Samuel Johnson expressed a similar opinion in his "Pope" (*Lives*, 3:251).

To progress further with her poetry, Cowper had to extricate herself from Pope's influence. After her marriage to Captain Martin Madan in 1723, she composed mostly lyrics praising her husband and family. Later, she converted to Methodism and wrote religious verse. Although some of her poems achieved a tender, pleasingly individual voice, during her lifetime she was best known for "Abelard to Eloisa" and "The Progress of Poetry."[23] Publishers sought these formal, conventional poems, not her domestic, occasional verse.

Although, or because, her early poems were so indebted to Pope, Cowper was praised for them as enthusiastically as Lady Mary was later denounced for her anti-Pope "Verses." *The Flower-Piece* (1731), for example, featured both the expanded "Progress of Poetry" and Cowper's elegy "To the Memory of Mr. Hughes."[24] An anonymous poem in the same volume, "To the ingenious Lady, Author of the Poem entitled, *The Progress of Poetry*," praised her discriminating canon:

> Such judgment in thy noble choice appears,
> As fame shall echo thro' revolving years:
> If *Hughes* and *Pope* had labour'd both to show,
> How much to *British* bards the world does owe,
> They cou'd not have display'd their boundless praise
> In strains more strong than thy immortal lays.
>
> (15–20)

The author declares Cowper the "brightest genius" (23), despite her modesty, and finds her achievements (along with those of Boadicea, Elizabeth I, Anne Stuart, and Queen Caroline) sufficient to discredit misogyny. The poem finally proclaims beauty a mere moon, fading beside the refulgent sun of female intelligence (93–98). As Rumbold might observe, this was a dangerous compliment to a woman who sought Pope's approval. Hardly appropriate for the deferential Cowper, such extravagant tributes may have embarrassed more than they pleased. Cowper attracted such gallantry, however, because her poems reflected public consensus. We may not assume that Cowper would have been ignored if her "Progress" had displayed more independent judgment, or if she had exercised her "female wit" otherwise than in the "softest numbers" ("To the ingenious lady," 147). But her verse attests that she had no wish to be consigned, with Lady Mary, to the realm of glaring female suns.

One other, rather peculiar eulogy typified contemporary association of Cowper with Pope. Preserved among the British Library's Birch manuscripts, the anonymous 42-line poem appears to have been copied between 1725 and 1731.[25] If Thomas Birch wrote the poem in his early twenties, he was probably unaware of Cowper's marriage in 1723 and may have been responding to a reprint pairing Pope's and Cowper's heroic epistles. The poem first addresses Pope as non-partisan, despite his evolving persona as virtue's champion: "Thy

Pen, Great Pope! the wonder of the Age, / Nor Wealth, nor Power cou'd ever yet Engage / To varnish Crimes, or join in Party-Rage" (1–3). Pope's known probity guarantees "immortal Fame" to his chosen friends (9–12), a distinction particularly deserved by one "Sprightly Nymph" (13): "'Tis lovely Cowper! that Inspired Fair! / Apollo's Darling, & the Muses care" (14–15). The poet extols her shapely form and bright eyes, before adding that she has a "perfect Mind."

> Her tender Song, & Sweet Harmonious Strains,
> Like Orpheus' musick, softens all our Pains.
> But when she Paints Great Abelard's sad State,
> With Sympathizing Grief we Mourn his Fate.
> Those strugling Passions raging in his Heart,
> None but that Nymph cou'd with such force impart.
> Who reads the work, but dwells on ev'ry line?
> Like thine, Her tow'ring thoughts are all sublime.
>
> (25–32)

The poet commands Pope to sing Cowper's praises; Pope alone "can keep her flight in view" (35). Finally, the poet warns Pope to "shun" Cowper. "Admire, like us, the Beauties of her Mind, / . . . But don't approach—or fatally you'll Prove, / No Heart's secure against the Force of Love" (39–42). This writer could evidently conceive of no way to praise Cowper except by imagining her the object of romantic love.

The poem describes both Pope and Cowper according to gender conventions. Pope is the aggressive author of ethical satire, "boldly adher[ing]" to truth (line 5) as he praises and blames. Cowper, an "Inspired Fair" whose beauty enhances her "tender Song," "softens all our Pains" in true feminine style. Although the poem claims that "Abelard to Eloisa" rivals Pope's epistle in effect, the reward for her towering thoughts and sublime skill must be, not Pope's respect or even rivalry, but his love. This admittedly clumsy poem exemplifies the obstacles facing eighteenth-century women poets in their quest for literary reputation. If they remained in Pope's shadow, as did the young Cowper, they were rewarded by accolades to their beauty or by compliments as meaningless as they were extravagant. When Lady Mary dared to compete with Pope, her reputation was questioned even by other women. Between these poles moved other poets, negotiating their responses to "Great *Pope*."

Women's Poems Addressed to Alexander Pope

Besides Lady Mary and Cowper, other women among Pope's first generation of readers conversed with or corresponded with Pope. Not all of these ladies were poets or even professed interest in literature.[26] But several of Pope's female acquaintances addressed Pope in poems, anticipating response. Anne Finch, countess of Winchilsea, was an early friend. A pioneer among women writers, Lady Winchilsea published her *Miscellany Poems* in 1713 and patronized the youthful Pope. She invited him to dine and to hear a play read (Pope, *Corr.*, 1:203), and she contributed dedicatory verses to his 1717 *Works*. Taking advantage of her age (she was fifty-two; Pope, twenty-five) and superior status, Lady Winchilsea chided Pope, perhaps at the recorded dinner, for those couplets in *The Rape of the Lock* that denigrate women writers. In canto 4, Umbriel addresses the Goddess of Spleen as "Parent of Vapours and of Female Wit, / Who give th'*Hysteric* or *Poetic* Fit," and "make some take Physic, others scribble Plays" (59–60, 62). The countess, author of two plays and a poem on "The Spleen," refrained from personal application of the verses, citing the tradition of great female poets to prove the injustice of Pope's insult. More willing to flatter than to quarrel, Pope replied, in an "Impromptu, To Lady Winchilsea," that her efforts to defend women writers were futile: "Ev'n while you write, you take that Praise away: / Light to the Stars the Sun does thus restore, / But shines himself till they are seen no more" (10–12).

The editors of the *Norton Anthology of Literature by Women* describe Finch's response as "correspondingly deferential," while Rumbold finds Finch's "The Answer" as complimentary as it is critical.[27] In her reply, a 36-line poem in ballad rhythm, Lady Winchilsea reminds Pope not only of her aristocratic status but of the consequences he might suffer professionally if he persists in insulting women writers. She begins by conceding victory in their argument to Pope, but not because she admits the truth of his insinuation: "Disarmed with so genteel an air, / The contest I give o'er."[28] Despite his gallantry, however, Lady Winchilsea puts Pope in his place by addressing him familiarly and warning him not to repeat his offense: "Yet, Alexander, have a care, / And shock the sex no more" (3–4). Lady Winchilsea's use of Pope's Christian name establishes their intimacy and thus her right to debate informally with him on this issue. Her tone and form of address remind Mr. Pope of his inferior status and comparative youth; she metaphorically wags at him a threatening forefinger. She next reminds Pope that although spleen may rule women, women "rule the world" through their acknowledged power over men (5–8). Frivolous today, her threat was plausible when Richard Steele and Joseph Addison were arguing for women's education because of their influence over husbands and children. Thus far in her response, Lady Winchilsea has matched Pope in his vein of conventional compliment, her insults masked as playful admonition.

Finch next illustrates an instance of women's literal power over men by recalling the tale of Orpheus, "who would like you have writ, / Had he in London town been bred, / And polished too his wit" (10–12). This travesty of a great poetic precursor undercuts his heir's pretensions. Lady Winchilsea mocks misogynists as she recalls Orpheus's naive complacency.

> But he poor soul thought all was well,
>   And great should be his fame,
> When he had left his wife in hell,
>   And birds and beasts could tame.
>
> (13–16)

The couplets suggest Orpheus's relief at discarding a partner less tractable than the wild animals he charmed with his lyre, as well as the folly of his assumption. The rollicking ballad rhythm of the poem so far suggests its light-hearted spirit. Even Lady Winchilsea's address of Pope as "Alexander" might be interpreted as an endearment. Nothing prepares the reader for the violent imagery of its next eight lines.

> Yet venturing then with scoffing rhymes
>   The women to incense,
> Resenting heroines of those times
>   Soon punished his offense.
> And as the Hebrus rolled his skull
>   And harp bemeared with blood,
> They clashing as the waves grew full
>   Still harmonized the flood.
>
> (17–24)

Lady Winchilsea quickly reassures Pope that such could never be his fate ("The lock won't cost the head," 28), but her grisly evocation of Orpheus's severed head and bloody lyre rolling downriver was perhaps her revenge for the pain inflicted by Pope's unwarranted insult.

Her immediate promise that a similarly dreadful punishment will not befall Pope seems as prescriptive as it is descriptive, given the occasion of her poem: "But you our follies gently treat, / And spin so fine the thread, / You need not fear his awkward fate" (25–27). An invisible "if" seems to follow that initial "But."

Lady Winchilsea concludes by reiterating her expectation that Pope's future poems will not only sustain but raise women's admiration of his work, and she appears to acknowledge Pope's right to chastise "Female Wit."

> Yet sooth the ladies I advise
>   (As me too pride has wrought),
> We're born to wit, but to be wise
>   By admonitions taught.

(33–36)

She has humbled herself to accept the kernel of truth in Pope's strictures, and she bids other women to do likewise. But in the context of the entire poem, that final couplet seems to advise the witty male poet as well as her female readers. Pope, too, must learn to temper his native wit by heeding the admonitions of his older, wiser, titled female contemporary, if he expects to maintain the female readership his poem was designed to attract.

Lady Winchilsea's poems frequently suggest her ambivalence toward the challenges facing contemporary women writers. That such a fine poet retained many of her poems in manuscript rather than risk public censure by publishing them reveals at least her painful awareness of an unpropitious historical moment. In this little poem, nevertheless, Lady Winchilsea displays genuine verve in her response to a rising male literary star. Rather than capitulate, overwhelmed by his art and opinion, she crafts a response at once more vigorous than his fulsome "Impromptu" and quite subtle in its manipulation of tone and image, to mock and upbraid, as well as flatter, Pope. The "genteel . . . air" of Lady Winchilsea's conclusion disarms Pope at his favorite game of double-edged compliment. Though Pope failed to abide by Lady Winchilsea's advice, he appreciated the poem enough to print an anonymous modified version of it (omitting the use of his christian name, "Alexander"!), along with seven other poems by Lady Winchilsea, in his miscellany *Poems on Several Occasions* (1717).[29] The poem's insidious mockery apparently escaped Pope as completely as it has evaded the detection of Gilbert, Gubar, and Rumbold. Or perhaps Pope (who, in a far different context, once called himself "that little Alexander the women laugh at," *Corr.*, 1:114), appreciated the artfulness with which Lady Winchilsea countered his unanswerable gallantry.

Lady Winchilsea desired to instruct and chasten as well as flatter in her other poems addressed to Pope. When *The Works of Mr. Alexander Pope* appeared in 1717, Lady Winchilsea's "To Mr. *Pope*" was second among its seven dedicatory poems, reflecting her rank below John Sheffield, duke of Buckingham, but above the untitled male dedicators.[30] Pope may have intended the gesture to silence rumors that he had travestied Lady Winchilsea as Phoebe Clinket in *Three Hours After Marriage*. The inclusion of Lady Winchilsea's poem suggests public acknowledgement of the countess as a female patron.

Lady Winchilsea's 43-line poem is fairly conventional, rehearsing the contents of the volume and praising Pope's accomplishment. Her first eight couplets assert poets' inevitable desire for praise "whatever they pretend" (5) and enjoin judicious praise from Pope's dedicators, "who strive for you as *Greece* for *Homer* strove" (14). While the comparison flatters, Lady Winchilsea's injunction heralds her own advice to the poet. Disclaiming mere compliment ("Me Panegyrick verse does not inspire," 17), the countess chooses rather to "counsel" Pope (20): "Go on, to gain applauses by desert, / Inform the head, whilst you dissolve the heart" (21–22). She advises Pope to "inflame the soldier," "elate the young," "warm the sage," and allure females with "tender verse" (23–25). He should continue to describe Windsor Forest in its vernal sweetness and to recount tales "easy, natural, and gay" (27–29). Pope is to proceed in the style of his early poems, "and for the future charm as in the past" (34). If he does so, "every artful hand" will contribute poems to his volumes.

> In you no vanity could thence be shown,
> Unless, since short in beauty of your own,
> Some envious scribler might in spight declare,
> That for comparison you plac'd 'em there.
> But envy could not against you succeed,
> 'Tis not from friends that write, or foes that read;
> Censure or Praise must from our selves proceed.
>
> (37–43)

The conclusion apparently compliments Pope for poems that merit self-approbation, the most valuable praise. Her reference to "envious scribler[s]" suggests a motive for those who claimed Pope's "ingratitude" following *Three Hours After Marriage*.[31] Yet even these lines intimate a veiled threat. After praising Pope's youthful verse, Lady Winchilsea reminds him that enemies may continue to insult his deformity. If so, the consciousness of having written harmless, charming verse should maintain the poet's self-approbation. But what if Pope's future poems were neither as harmless nor as charming as these early pieces? Lady Winchilsea hints that Pope should refrain from developing his poetic gifts in any but her prescribed modes. Perhaps she intended to discourage the satiric tendency she deplored in the *Rape*, maintaining that if Pope continued to insult his readers, he would be left without even self-approbation to cushion the blows of "envious scribler[s]." The countess certainly realized that no serious artist can, or should, resist creative development. Her own poems often deplore the limitations imposed on women writers. Her wish that Pope confine himself to tales, to love verse, and to pastoral was futile, but it accurately predicted the critical barrage that greeted Pope's mature satiric verse.

Lady Winchilsea's advice in "To Mr. *Pope*" was consistent with her personal practice. She suppressed such verse as the bitter "Introduction" during her lifetime, preferring to avoid controversy rather than to publish her resentment of women's narrow opportunities. Perhaps the countess recognized that she, by her gender, and Pope, by his background and deformity, were similarly handicapped. By counseling Pope to avoid rousing "envious scribler[s]," she shared her wisdom with another vulnerable initiate to the literary marketplace. In any event, Pope chose not to heed Lady Winchilsea's advice, asserting "manly" independence over "feminine" concern for public reception.

In her final poem addressed to Pope, Lady Winchilsea recognized the young poet's aggressiveness and admitted the inevitability of critical attacks. "The *Mastif* and *Curs*, A Fable inscrib'd to Mr. Pope" describes a stately "Masty" harrassed by a mob of lapdogs and "butchers curs" (13). A "gen'rous man," baffled by the mastiff's failure to defend himself, attempts to "rouze his anger" (31–32). The mastiff replies that he intends his passive disdain to illustrate

. . . the diff'rence . . .
Between this bawling troop, and me.

Comparison your observation stirs,
I were no masty if there were no curs.

(51–54)

As Rumbold observed, Pope evidently appreciated the compliment implicit in Lady Winchilsea's representation of the poet as a large, strong dog (154–55). He included the beast fable among his selection of her poems in the 1717 miscellany (Ault, *Miscellany*, 131–33). But the poem is surely as cautionary as complimentary, the advice consistent with that in her other poems to Pope. The countess's praise is, as usual, double-edged, the flattering portrait of Pope as huge mastiff offset by her image of competing poets as so many dogs in the marketplace. Pope chose to acknowledge her compliment rather than her caution, and he returned the flattery by generously representing her poetry in *Poems on Several Occasions* (of other women's writing, he included only Elizabeth Rowe's "Upon the Death of her Husband"). But Lady Winchilsea's poetic addresses to Pope, traditionally dismissed as conventional praise, seem instead to be a gifted poet's subtle attempts to assume the role of Pope's sole female mentor.

Among Pope's other female acquaintances, several addressed purposeful verses to the poet, their expectations raised by specific poems. Mary Barber included in her *Poems on Several Occasions* (1734) a request "To Mr. *Pope*: Intreating him to write Verses to the Memory of *Thomas*, late Earl of Thanet."[32] Barber alludes to the "Epistle to Bathurst," complaining, "Shall for the *Man of Ross* thy Lyre be strung, / And sleeps illustrious *Thanet* yet unsung?" (1–2). Barber claims inability to eulogize Thanet, hoping to inspire Pope: "Let me, unequal to the Task, excite / Thy matchless Muse, to do his Merit Right" (5–6). Despite the disclaimer, however, Barber's 106-line poem is a dignified tribute to Lord Thanet, portrayed less as Pope's John Kyrle than as his Bathurst, whom Pope commanded, "To Want or Worth well-weighed, be Bounty giv'n / And ease, or emulate, the care of Heav'n" ("To Bathurst," 229–30). Unlike the Man of Ross, who hired the poor to build public works, Thanet gave away large amounts of money: "With God like Pity ev'ry Pray'r receives, / Each Wish fulfills, and ev'ry Want relieves" ("To Mr. *Pope*," 17–18). Kyrle sponsored the construction of a new church steeple, which Pope regarded as a characteristic expression of his virtue ("To Bathurst," 285–86). Thanet's worship was more conventional: "The hallow'd Altar, grateful, he survey'd, / And there his lowly Adoration paid" ("To Mr. *Pope*," 35–36). Barber links Thanet to Pope's evocation of the aristocratic golden mean by contrasting him with Old and Young Cotta-like figures of avarice and profusion (37–46). "To Mr. *Pope*" restores aristocratic paternalism to the central position from which Pope had nudged it by celebrating Kyrle, who managed his benevolence with an estate of just five hundred pounds a year. Barber's address to Pope is not, finally, the confession of incompetence she initially claims. Her poem creatively misreads Pope's "Epistle to Bathurst," rewriting Pope's advice on the use of riches as her own tribute to Thanet.

Pope may never have met Mary Barber, although he subscribed to her volume, probably at the request of their mutual friend Swift.[33] He was certainly acquainted with Viscountess Anne Ingram Irwin, whose "Epistle to Mr. Pope. Occasioned by his Characters of Women" is perhaps the best-known woman's response to Pope's "Epistle to a Lady."[34] First published in *Gentleman's Magazine* (December 1736), the 120-line poem demands that Pope "instruct as well as please" women, instead of merely criticizing them. But the "Epistle" also borrows themes and techniques from Pope's *Essay on Man* and all four "Moral Essays," to modify Pope's theory of the ruling passion. Unlike the anonymous male correspondent who, a few months earlier, had expressed his hope in *London Magazine* that British women would be inspired by Pope's *Iliad* to take up spinning,[35] Lady Irwin challenged Pope to encourage "reason and reflection" in his women readers. Her poem opens with a bold denial of Pope's theory of radically different male and female natures: "But would the satyrist confess the truth, / Nothing so like as male and female youth; / Nothing so like as man and woman old" (3–5). Answering Pope's assertion in "To a Lady" that, while men may be compelled by many different passions, women are inevitably driven by "the Love of Pleasure, and the Love of Sway" (210), Lady Irwin retorts that "in either sex the appetite's the same, / For love of power is still the love of fame" (21–22).

Lines 9–24 of Lady Irwin's "Epistle" employ the authoritative tone and aggressive commands Pope used to prove his opinions in the *Essay on Man*. Just as Pope had gestured toward general examples to evoke agreement based on observation (e.g., "Behold the Child," "Look round our World," "See Falkland dies"), Lady Irwin also commands her reader to "view daring man stung with ambition's fire" (9). Her examples of a "conquering hero, or the youthful 'squire" (10) invite agreement that both are animated by desire for reputation, although "one murthers man, the other murthers game" (12). This notion resembles Pope's contention in the "Epistle to Cobham" that "the same adust complexion has impell'd / Charles to the Convent, Phillip to the Field" (59–60). Having made a similar point, however, Lady Irwin next commands us to "view a fair nymph blest with superior charms . . . / No eastern monarch more despotick reigns / Than this fair tyrant" (13–16). By gender-balancing her examples, Lady Irwin reveals the gap in Pope's vision of human nature. Had Pope included more female examples in his "Epistle to Cobham" or males in his "Epistle to a Lady," he would have revealed that "women must in a narrow orbit move, / But power alike both males and females love" (24–25). The difference between soldier and squire is no greater than the difference between either and a belle.

Like Pope in his epistles and especially in the *Essay*, Lady Irwin opens her third verse paragraph with a rhetorical question: "What makes the difference then, you may inquire, / Between the hero, and the rural 'squire," between the pampered belle and the housemaid? (25–28). All strive as hard as they can for fame, but "in education all the difference lies; / Women if taught, would be as bold and wise / As haughty man, improv'd by art and rules" (33–35). Alluding to Pope's observation, in the "Essay on Criticism," that "some [men] are bewilder'd in the Maze of Schools, / And some made Coxcombs Nature meant but Fools" ("Essay," 26–27), Lady Irwin mourns an even greater loss due to women's lack of education: "Where God made one, neglect makes twenty fools" ("Epistle," 36). She nevertheless refuses to concede that there are more foolish females than males; alluding now to Pope's famous characterization, in *The Rape of the Lock*, of women's hearts as "moving toyshops," she contends that "flutt'ring *Nugators* equally abound; / Such heads are toyshops . . . / And can each folly with each female share" (38–40). Ostensibly replying specifically to the "Epistle to a Lady," Lady Irwin responded to Pope's failure throughout his career to admit fundamental similarities between the sexes.

Her next two verse paragraphs recall the epistles to Bathurst and to Burlington on the use of riches. In those poems, Pope compares his friends' tasteful, responsible, and charitable investments of their wealth with the miserly or profligate abuses of the Cottas, Sir Balaam, and Timon. He suggests that his friends' beautiful estates mirror their moral and intellectual superiority: "'Tis Use alone that sanctifies Expense, / And Splendor borrows all her rays from Sense" ("To Burlington," 179–80). Lady Irwin's fourth verse paragraph develops an agricultural analogy between uncultivated fields and women's minds. A reader of Pope's "Essays," convinced that a well-organized estate proclaimed its master's refinement, might agree that if "a female mind like a rude fallow lies; / . . . As well might we expect, in winter, spring, / As land untill'd a fruitful crop shou'd bring" ("Epistle," 41, 43–44). The following verse paragraph employs anaphora to convince the reader that no man is expected to understand processes he has never been taught: "Ask the philosopher the price of stocks, / Ask the gay courtier how to manage flocks" (51–52). She assumes the reader's acceptance of her claim, and of Pope's economic analogy, applied to men: "Reason's not reason, if not exercis'd; / Use, not possession, real good affords; / No miser's rich that dares not touch his hoards" (64–66).

Verse paragraph six demonstrates that the same principle both Pope and Lady Irwin have proved true of men applies equally to women. If no one expects men to have mastered knowledge outside their disciplines, how much less likely are women to practice virtue or pursue learning, despite Pope's complaints?

> Bred to deceive even from their earliest youth;
> Unus'd to books, nor virtue taught to prize;
> Whose mind a savage waste unpeopled lies;
> Which to supply, trifles fill up the void,
> And idly busy, to no end employ'd:
> Can these, from such a school, more virtue show,
> Or tempting vice treat like a common foe?
>
> (78–84)

Pope himself, in the "Epistle to Cobham," had claimed, "'Tis Education forms the common mind, / Just as the Twig is bent, the Tree's inclin'd" (101–2). Throughout the *Essay on Man* and the "Moral Essays," Pope suggested the importance of education to channel the ruling passion. In the "Epistle to a Lady," however, Pope offered no healthy channel for a woman's innate ambition. Sublimating her drives meant sublimating herself: accepting, submitting, disdaining losses. Lady Irwin questions whether women, left "strangers to reason and reflection" (75), can be expected to follow Pope's ideal. Pope's model is self-negating. Women desperately need positive ways to develop "the savage waste" of their minds, to employ themselves for useful purposes. Only women taught more than to dress and to dance—taught, for example, history and philosophy—will attain the moral stature necessary to combat the self-indulgent vices Pope catalogs in his "Epistle." Though she does not deny the truth of Pope's strictures, Lady Irwin suggests that his antiheroines are cultural victims, with the same capacity for moral and intellectual instruction Pope repeatedly recommended for men.

Lady Irwin's penultimate verse paragraph contrasts the Roman heroine Portia with "the gay moderns of the female race" (106). While Pope gestured toward Martha Blount as a living exemplar, Lady Irwin resorts to ancient history for a few women "taught by philosophy all moral good" (97). Her description of Portia, like Pope's construction of Martha, stresses the heroism of self-denial. Portia learned "how to repel in youth th'impetuous blood, / How her most favorite passions to subdue" (98–99). But Lady Irwin stresses that Portia was taught how to behave nobly, unlike Pope's version of Martha, who he claimed was endowed with sense and good humor by Apollo. Moreover, Portia pursued "fame through virtue's avenues" (100). Martha shines soberly, but Portia, "to *Cato* born, to noble *Brutus* join'd, / . . . shines invincible in form and mind" (103–4). Lady Irwin's ideal is finally more powerful, if still bound by her culture's notions of femininity.

Having countered Pope's female psychology and exposed his failure to suggest a positive program to ameliorate women's vapid minds and lives, Lady Irwin concludes by requesting Pope's help. Recalling the *Essay on Man*, his "Moral Essays," and his Horatian imitations, Lady Irwin asks,

> Wou'd you, who can instruct as well as please,
> Bestow some moments of your darling ease,
> To rescue woman from this *Gothic* state . . .
> For who stands unconvinc'd by generous Pope?
>
> (111–18)

Appealing to the "Essay on Criticism's" definition of the critic "pleas'd to teach" ("Essay," 632), Lady Irwin recalls Pope to his own ideal. She grants Pope's understanding of the human mind but asks him to exert his wisdom on behalf of women, a task that her poem demonstrates he has failed to perform. Her suggestion that Pope relinquish some of his "darling ease" in Twickenham "to rescue woman" rouses the poet to the vigorous virtue-in-use concept found in his epistles and to her own classical ideal; "Then would the *British* fair perpetual bloom, / And vie in fame with ancient Greece and Rome" (119–20).

Having exploded his theory of women's alien nature, Lady Irwin slyly asks "generous Pope" to do better—to elaborate her superior concept. Her poem, permeated with allusions to themes and techniques spanning Pope's career, offers another early example of poetic misprision. Lady Irwin suggests that Pope's "Epistle to a Lady" failed, in its conclusion, to offer an adequate countervision of the good woman. Lady Irwin applies what she takes to be the universally true aspects of Pope's moral and intellectual theories and rewrites a more positive conclusion to his poem on women.

Though Lady Irwin's "Epistle" strikes Valerie Rumbold as deferential and constrained by contemporary definitions of femininity (265), I am impressed with her attempt to expand current notions of female psychology. Pope's "Epistle to a Lady" assumes gender distinctions long since popularized by such writers as Richard Steele, who maintained in *The Tatler* 172 that "there is a Sort of Sex in Souls" (Steele et al., *Tatler*, 2:444). Among women of Lady Irwin's generation, even Lady Mary Wortley Montagu had once agreed that women were a lower part of the creation (*Letters*, 1:45). Pope's "Epistle" appealed to many women readers because his assumptions were part of their horizon of expectations. Such readers as Lady Hertford, disenchanted with Pope's ethics or politics, nevertheless welcomed his attention to women's characters as if these constituted a sphere distinct from his other concerns. To craft her response, Lady Irwin appropriated concepts that appeared unexceptionable to her contemporaries and rhetorical techniques that had gained Pope general assent. She turned Pope's language back on itself, using the very words and manner of canonical discourse to argue against Pope's—and their culture's—gender distinctions. Her "Epistle," addressed to a living contemporary, presumed an exchange. Lady Irwin spoke to Pope in his language, hoping to modify his opinions. That her imagination was limited by contemporary expectations does not cancel her accomplishment, because she anticipated less gender-bound definitions of male and female psychology.

Lady Irwin's response to Pope's "Epistle to a Lady" was far less conventional than Sarah Dixon's, who addressed the poet in "On the Loss of Stella's Friendship."

> Ingenious *Pope*! whose better skill
> Can dive into a Woman's Will,
> How truly have thy Numbers told

'Her Soul is of too soft a Mould,
'A lasting *Character* to hold.'
Her Inclination's fickle Side,
The varying Gust[s] of *Passion* guide;
And her Affection['s] shifting Stream,
Flows and reflows as mov'd by them.[36]

Although the speaker does not associate herself with feminine inconstancy, she invokes conventional assumptions about women throughout the poem. Loss of friendship is as irrevocable as a woman's lost reputation (lines 29–32); women prefer flattery to truth (57–64). Dixon resolves the poem humorously, expecting that Stella will once again change her mind and renew their friendship. The lighthearted poem hails Pope's grasp of female psychology, finding consolation in his doctrine of fickleness: Stella will not even be able to sustain her inconstancy. That Dixon admired Pope is evident throughout her book, to which he subscribed. "The Strong Box," for example, echoes his epistles on the use of riches (Dixon, 10). In "To the Muse," Dixon's speaker compares her muse to a lover she feared might betray her: "I then at once grew peevish, sullen, wise, / Cou'd even *Pope* and *Addison* despise, / And call'd their Inspirations—Fooleries" (lines 25–27). Her rejection of the muse resembles Stella's fickleness; neither change of heart is justified. At the poem's conclusion, the muse returns to the speaker, who greets with relief "my lov'd Companion to my Wishes Kind" (69). Dixon's conception of the muse as a male lover in this poem is intriguing, but she constructs her speaker, a woman writer, as a conventional jealous female. The speaker's impatience with Pope and Addison, outrageous in the context of Dixon's other poems, equates her brief defection from the muse with a "feminine" foible. Elsewhere in *Poems on Several Occasions*, light satires on women's love of trinkets and quadrille confirm Dixon's homage to the "Epistle to a Lady." The volume suggests two possible conclusions. Women poets who hoped for Pope's patronage echoed his manner and opinions, as did their male counterparts. Furthermore, for women poets less concerned than Lady Irwin with the causes of female levity, Pope's constructions authorized their own generalizations about women's behavior.

Although the extent of their acquaintance is unknown, Dixon at least won Pope's support through his subscription. If he read her poems in manuscript, he may have been flattered by her dependence on his satiric precedent. There is no record of Pope's response to

Elizabeth Boyd, who addressed to him in 1739 her prologue to *Don Sancho: or, the Students Whim*.[37] Boyd was an uneven poet, whose *Variety* (1727) and "Truth" (1740) are marred by doubtful control of syntax and parts of speech and by her fondness for triplets.[38] That Pope would have sponsored such a protégée is doubtful. Boyd wrote to support her family, hoping for reward from the public figures her poems celebrated, such as Lord Harrington and Admiral Haddock.[39] The same motive probably explains her recourse to Pope, whether or not she anticipated the poet's approval of her "windmill Farce" ("Prologue," 30). In "Prologue," Boyd defends her choice of patron.

> But where, oh where shall we a Critick gain!
> A Friend sincere of the all-hallow'd Strain,
> Who frankly will his Sentiments declare,
> Or make an untaught Female Toy his Care,
> Great Faults revise, and little Errors spare.
>
> (12–16)

Boyd addresses the Pope of "Essay on Criticism," not the irritable bard of "Epistle to Dr. Arbuthnot." Rather like Lady Irwin, Boyd reminds Pope of his youthful ideal, the man "still *pleas'd* to *teach*, and yet not *proud* to *know*," who could "to a *Friend* his *Faults* . . . freely show" ("Essay on Criticism," 632, 637). Assuming his desire to teach women, she offers her "untaught Female Toy" for his correction: "Of thee, great Pope, the Nation's darling Theme / We beg Perusal of this *Medley-Whim*" (17–18). Unfortunately, Pope had dismissed in the *Dunciad* such "operas" as *Don Sancho*, whose sole redeeming attraction might have been the apotheosis of Shakespeare and Dryden after their ghosts are raised by a trio of curious Oxford students. Boyd's plea for Pope's revision of the opera's "great faults," moreover, recalls his disdain in "Epistle to Dr. Arbuthnot" for the hack who begs, "The Piece you think is incorrect: why take it, / I'm all submission, what you'd have it, make it" (45–46). Her wish for Pope's approval may have been quixotic, but Elizabeth Boyd's prologue reiterates contemporary women's impression of his interest in their education.

Mary Leapor composed three poignant poems to Pope shortly after his death. She invoked Pope as her mentor in "On Mr. Pope's Universal Prayer," alluding to early verses Pope had revised to supplement his *Essay on Man* in 1738. Pope may have published his prayer, an expression of Christian tolerance and submission, to counter rumors of

the *Essay's* skepticism. "On Mr. Pope's Universal Prayer" hails Pope
with an innocent faith similar to that of his hymnlike poem.

> Ah thou! whom Nature and thy Stars design'd,
> At once the Joy and Envy of Mankind.
> To thy lov'd Memory this Sigh I send;
> To thee a Stranger, to thy Lines a Friend:
> How blest the Muse cou'd she like thine aspire,
> So smooth her Accent, and sublime her Fire;
> With bright Description make the Bosom glow,
> Charm like thy Sense, and like thy Numbers flow:
> O teach my Soul to reach the Seats divine,
> And praise her Maker in a Strain like thine.[40]

Leapor's homage embraces Pope's canon while ostensibly praising
one poem. Her couplets echo Pope's lament in the "Essay on Criticism" that he might never reach the poetic heights scaled by his late
mentor, the Earl of Roscommon (725–38). But she also recalls Pope's
boast of forsaking verse "where pure Description held the place of
Sense" ("Epistle to Dr. Arbuthnot," 148). According to Leapor, the
simple "Universal Prayer" fuses sensual and intellectual appeal. Her
plea to Pope for instruction likewise fuses, perhaps to conceal, dual
purposes. Although the poem requests spiritual inspiration, Leapor
regarded Pope as her poetic precursor, a choice manifest throughout
her writings. The "Seats divine" to which Pope will lead are as much
the heights of Parnassus as those of the Christian afterlife. Beneath
the former cook-maid's prayer that Pope inspire devotional verse lurks
a more audacious invocation of his poetic power. During her brief
career, Leapor declined waiting for a muse's assistance. She endowed
herself with a portion of Pope's expertise through study and imitation.
    "On Mr. Pope's Universal Prayer" is an apprentice poem, Leapor's
miniature equivalent of an "Essay on Criticism" inspired by the *Essay
on Man*. In "Essay on Criticism," Pope had demonstrated mastery
of critical and technical skills while professing appropriate humility.
Leapor defers to Pope as a devotional writer ("Read [Pope's] grand
Verse, then tremble and adore," 12), but she supplements his poem
with an explanatory context. Leapor invents a myth, tracing contemporary skepticism to self-serving repudiation of religious persecution
(lines 25–44). Leapor's myth justifies Pope's ecumenical expression
of devotion: "Virtue and Grace are not to Sects confined; / They blend
with all, and spread amongst the kind" (21–22). Her use of myth to

defend religious tolerance resembles *Essay on Man* 3, where Pope's myth of social and political evolution bolsters the doctrine of self-love leading to social love. Leapor's description of virtue and grace blending and spreading echoes Pope's famous image of self-love as a pebble dropped into a lake, gradually expanding to universal charity.

In her conclusion, Leapor recalls Pope's appeal to Bolingbroke in *Essay* 4. A "little bark" attending his mentor's reputation "along the stream of Time," he asked Bolingbroke to help him achieve equanimity: "Form'd by thy converse, happily to steer / From grave to gay, from lively to severe" (373–86). In turn, Leapor requests,

> But thou whose Name (immortal as thy Rhymes)
> Shall live and brighten through succeeding Times . . .
> Teach me between the two Extremes to glide,
> Not brave the Stream, nor swim with ev'ry Tide:
> But more with Charity than Zeal possesst,
> Keep my own Faith, yet not condemn the rest.
>
> (45–52)

Applying to Pope, as Pope had once turned to Bolingbroke, Leapor similarly appropriates her mentor's rhetoric. Written when Leapor was about the same age as Pope when he wrote the "Essay on Criticism," "On Mr. Pope's Universal Prayer" emulates Pope's "Essay" by modestly intimating Leapor's ambition. Still an apprentice, she had not broken or even swerved from his "lov'd memory." But by this poem's conclusion, she invokes Pope himself rather than a Popeian muse. If she had lived longer, Leapor may eventually have outgrown such dependence on her precursor.

Mary Leapor's devotion to Pope originated in her underprivileged childhood. A nurseryman's daughter, "her whole library consisted of sixteen or seventeen odd volumes, among which were part of the works of Mr. *Pope*, her greatest favourite."[41] Betty Rizzo has described Leapor's strange posthumous career as a "natural poet" patronized by Samuel Richardson and his circle.[42] Leapor's gifts blossomed during the last fifteen months of her life, encouraged by her first patron, Bridget Freemantle. But Rizzo suggests that Freemantle's subscription for Leapor's first volume succeeded mostly because of "the fortuitous removal from the scene of the one greatest obstacle to success—Leapor's unprepossessing person" (251). Skinny, homely, insufficiently humble in life, Leapor was resurrected as "Mira," poet of untaught genius akin to Chaucer's, Shakespeare's, and Richardson's.

Rizzo's sympathetic account exposes the self-aggrandizing motives of Leapor's posthumous patrons. But her study also suggests two reasons for Leapor's intense attachment to Pope, "the Author she most admired . . . [and] whom she chiefly endeavoured to imitate" ("To the Reader," in Leapor, *Poems*).[43] Among her contemporaries, the extent of Leapor's imitation of Pope is equaled only by Mary Jones's.[44] Jones emulated Pope's dignified attitude toward aristocratic friends. Leapor also modeled her poetic persona on Pope's. From a similar satiric vantage point, the cook surveyed and ridiculed the fine ladies and pompous gentlemen of her neighborhood. But descriptions of Pope's appearance probably strengthened Leapor's attachment. If her person was so repulsive as to retard subscription efforts in her behalf, Leapor may have been comforted by Pope's triumph over greater deformity.

For these or other reasons, Leapor composed two poems recording her response to Pope's death. Both mourned the loss of a potential friend even more than the death of a favorite celebrity. "On the Death of a justly admir'd Author" (Leapor, 252–54), a 46-line pastoral elegy, laments "Sylvius' " springtime demise.

> The verdant Groves their wonted Charms regain,
> And laughing Nature paints the gaudy Plain;
>
> . . . .
>
> But Man once blasted takes a long Farewel.
>
> (9–10, 14)

Leapor regrets the death of an incomparable poet ("Ev'n *Homer* shines with Beauties not his own," 24) and moralist. But her sense of loss extends to personal deprivation. She envies those privileged mourners "whom once he honour'd with the Name of Friend," compared with those "condemn'd at distance to admire" (32, 35). The "hopes that with our Guide expire" (36) seem to include not merely poetic example but personal acquaintance. As the poet turns from the "sylvan Scenes" and "Fair Nymphs" Pope immortalized, she admonishes herself: "Hence sigh in secret, and his Loss deplore, / Who ne'er, O ne'er, shall grace our Regions more" (45–46). Leapor's persona of pining shepherdess recalls the appeal of Pope's early translations and poems to many contemporary women, and it is complicated because Leapor belonged to the rural working class. But "On the Death of a justly admir'd Author" ignores this irony, probably because only in pastoral fantasy could Leapor imagine herself sharing Pope's poetic landscape.

Leapor also composed a more ambitious tribute, "Celadon to Mira" (Leapor, 136–42). Internal evidence suggests that the poem's ghostly speaker, who dispels "Mira's" fear of death, is Pope. "Celadon" ostensibly composed this 123-line epistle to comfort Leapor/Mira, moved by her grief "at Night when, lonely by the Taper's Flame, / In a still Whisper thou hast breath'd my Name" (5–6). The image endows Leapor's nocturnal study of Pope with a sense of personal loss. Unlike living beaux, Celadon reassures the homely young woman in terms that recall Clarissa's speech in *The Rape of the Lock* (5.33–34): "Bright Eyes in vain may roll, / I read no Charms but in the purer Soul" (17–18). He suspects Mira of insufficient resignation.

> Canst thou presume thy little Bark may steer
> From Griefs black Eddy and the Gulphs of Fear?
>
> . . . .
>
> Sound Judgment, Learning, Wisdom, too was mine,
> And piercing Wit superior far to thine;
> Yet gaping Rage stood ready to devour,
> And Dulness rain'd on me a Leaden Shower:
> Now stung with Scoffs, and now with Flatt'ry tir'd,
> Defam'd, applauded, envy'd, and admir'd:
> This Fate was mine—to hope canst thou presume
> A milder Passage and more easy Doom?
> Deluded Girl!
>
> (31–32, 39–47)

Celadon's challenge is drawn from the *Essay on Man*, his career from *The Dunciad* and "Epistle to Dr. Arbuthnot." Leapor transforms those poems into private instruction, wresting personal comfort from public texts. Poems originally addressed to distinguished gentlemen become exhortations to a "Deluded girl." Celadon advises Mira to rectify her ambition: "Ask not for what will make thy Pray'r offend, / But ask Content, a Parent and a Friend; / Ask Bread and Peace, 'tis all that Nature craves" (51–53). His counsel, redolent of "Epistle to Dr. Arbuthnot" and the "Universal Prayer," preaches humility while paradoxically granting Leapor the special bond denied by her gender and obscurity during Pope's lifetime.

Celadon/Pope, like the spirits in Elizabeth Rowe's *Letters from the Dead to the Living*, intends his letter to resolve a spiritual conflict. He pities Mira's warring attitudes toward death, exclaiming, "Ah, what so various as a Woman's Soul!" (66), an aside worthy of the "Epistle to a Lady." Celadon devotes twenty-nine lines to generalized character portraits in the classical manner, illustrating the propriety of resignation. He suggests the vanity of Mira's reluctance.

> Might'st thou with us unbodied Spirits fly,
> From Sphere to Sphere and trace the boundless Sky?
> Then wou'd the Lives of little Mortals shew,
> Like empty Bubbles rais'd of Morning Dew:
> All seem as Trifles, whether we behold
> A Monarch banish'd, or a Sparrow sold.
>
> (74–79)

Leapor rather whimsically permits the dead poet himself to vindicate his account of divine perspective in *Essay on Man*. From that vantage, Iphenia's, Clodius's, and Pero's youthful deaths were merciful, while Laura's long life merely increased her doubts and fears. Mira should accept her mortality; after all, "I bore the same, whose Life was more desir'd, / More lov'd, more known, and justly more admir'd" (116–17). Celadon admits that her "grand Fear is wove with Nature's Laws" to inspire repentance (118). Mira can cure her "Vapours" by mending her life, with proper assistance: "Still look to Heav'n and its Laws attend, / And next the Lines of thy aerial Friend" (122–23).

Whether Leapor intended to comfort herself with Pope's lines or Celadon's is debatable. Barred from the living poet's acknowledgment, perhaps she enjoyed fantasizing about Pope as a secret "aerial Friend." Or she may have found more solace in her ability to mimic Pope, to rewrite his poems as private messages. Leapor might eventually have found her development hampered by the need to ventriloquize her dead mentor. Or she may have liberated herself and embarked on more ambitious revisions. Dead at twenty-four, her promise remained unfulfilled.

Mary Leapor's poems, in effect love letters to the deceased Pope, are among the most poignant addresses to the poet. Later in the century, another laboring-class woman poet saw Pope as an overwhelming obstacle. "To praise thy sense and judgement, heav'nly Bard! / It is for my poor pen a task too hard," protested Elizabeth Bentley in "On Reading Mr. Pope's Poems. 1786."[45] Donna Landry has observed the eroticism characteristic of working women's poetic responses to Pope, suggested here by Bentley's representation of herself prostrate before the semidivine bard.[46] Superior social status enabled such women as Lady Irwin to assume toward Pope the traditional pose of satiric adversaries, but such a relation was unthinkable for Leapor or Bentley. Lacking other possibilities, these women adopted the conventional erotic relation of weak female to strong male in their addresses to Pope, ravishing his texts in turn as they appropriated his discourse (Landry, 46). Class certainly influenced these wistful poems, although neither Sarah Dixon's nor Elizabeth Boyd's poems are more erotic than those of supplicating male contemporaries. But assumption of an erotic relation seems to have liberated Leapor. In "Celadon to Mira," she ironically acquires the poet's pen while fantasizing his personal attention. Bentley, however, admits defeat in "On Reading Mr. Pope's Poems," exaggerating Pope's reputation ("Did ever genius so conspicuous shine?," 2) in comparison with her own insignificance. Later in her volume, in "Lines, Addressed as a Tribute of Gratitude to the Subscribers in General" (p. 67), Bentley wishes for "*Pope's* or *Gray's* harmonious lyre" (17), or a spark of Thomson's, Shakespeare's, or Milton's genius. But she concludes that "since unerring Fate's divine decree / Has fix'd my lot to sing in humbler strain, / I'll sound the simplest shell" (29–31). For Bentley, anxious to reassure subscribers of her humility, deference to male models was a marketing strategy as well as a self-imposed curb to ambition.

Although each of these women hovered closer to Judith Cowper's complimentarity than to Lady Mary's satirical vein, their poetic addresses (with the exception of Bentley's) are not characterized by undue deference. Lady Winchilsea's poems, both formal and occasional, subtly mingle advice and criticism in a blend Pope found pleasing enough to publish. Her poems express affection for the young poet she hoped to guide and sponsor. Lady Irwin's epistle, published for the readers of *Gentleman's Magazine*, was nevertheless constructed as a debate with Pope. Rather than rail at the poet, Lady Irwin used his ideas and images, evidently hoping to persuade Pope, or at least Pope's readers, that his grasp of female psychology was inadequate. Her description of Pope as "gen'rous" seems less a rhetorical ploy than a genuine appeal to a man capable of reflecting and changing his mind. Both Mary Barber and Sarah Dixon deferred to Pope advisedly, hoping for patronage—expectations that the poet rewarded by subscribing to their volumes. Elizabeth Boyd supplicated with impunity on behalf of her "windmill Farce." Her hope for acknowledgement of an "untaught Female Toy" suggests Pope encouraged rather than intimidated some nonaristocratic female contemporaries. Boyd's wish for Pope's personal interest in her opera anticipates Mary Leapor's yearning for relationship with the poet. Leapor's verses to her dead mentor are poignant but assert her intention to commune with Pope by pursuing the same vocation. Only Bentley's poem, written long after Pope's demise, is truly abject, but she evidently constructed an abject persona for the consumption of subscribers.

Women writing during Pope's lifetime (or in Leapor's case, shortly after his death) approached the poet cautiously but assumed that, duly complimented, the Wasp of Twickenham would prove an ally. Encouraged by his interest, some attempted to correct his attitudes. Others seized the notion of Pope as potential mentor of women entering the literary marketplace. Each of these writers believed Pope took women seriously enough to consider their advice, engage them in debate, or encourage them professionally. Other women throughout the century, while not directly addressing Pope, imitated, appropriated, corrected, supplemented, and even mocked his verse.[47] Each poet's ambition and point of view were influenced by gender, class, and historical proximity to Pope.

4

Eighteenth-Century Women and Pope's Early Poetry

Alexander Pope asked Dr. Arbuthnot, "Why did I write? What sin to me unknown / Dipt me in Ink, my Parents', or my own?" ("Epistle to Dr. Arbuthnot," 126–27). This plaintive query prefaced Pope's apology for his career. Goaded by slander, Pope defended his pursuit of an "idle trade" (129). Raised a gentleman, he had published to please distinguished mentors, not for money or popular acclaim. The phrase "idle trade" captures Pope's ambivalence about writing and publishing. He wished to appear both the leisured gentleman and the professional entitled to wield the "sacred Weapon! left for Truth's defence" ("Epilogue to the Satires: Dialogue II," 212). Rhetorical aptness aside, such conflicting phrases characterize Pope's relation to his art. During his lifetime, literature hovered between avocation and profession, traditional patronage and the marketplace. Pope helped establish the profession but suffered attacks on his qualifications as a man of letters. Accusations that his status and irregular education should have barred him from writing poetry still hounded Pope in 1735.

Women throughout the century faced greater discouragement. From such public issues as women's participation in the literary marketplace to psychological conflict over their entitlement to write, an array of barriers opposed women writers. But increased leisure, literacy, and publishing opportunities beckoned women to write and to publish. Like Pope, many women expressed understandable ambivalence toward a situation seemingly hospitable but mined with deterrents. Inevitably, Alexander Pope figured in women's responses to their dilemma. "That little fellow Pope," as Janet Little called him,[1] had defeated famous obstacles before conquering Parnassus. Simultaneously mentor and unattainable standard, hero of the marginalized and embodiment of high culture, Pope represented both the lure and the snare in their literary environment. In their poems, some women struggled with Pope's complex significance; others endeavored to assimilate his opinions, themes, and techniques. In either case, Pope proved the strongest influence on eighteenth-century women's poetry.

Fairly early in his career, Pope figured in one woman's rationale for writing. In an anonymous British Library manuscript, a lady excuses her authorship of an epithalamium, explaining that Pope had too much poetic business on his hands to compose it himself. She reminds Phoebus that Prior and Addison are dead.

> Pope only of thy favrite tribe remains
> To sing th'Adventures of Brittania's plains
> Alas but one—The God of Love does bring
> More dayly conquests than one bard can sing
> Lewis Lucinda weds, Oh Teach my Tongue
> In Numbers just to sing the Nuptial song.[2]

Phoebus replies that he has already assigned the wedding song to "Harriot," whom he has blessed with "a double Spirit" for the task (38). The poet thus effaces herself, but not before sanctioning another female poet and introducing a novel rationale for women's poetry. Perhaps this undated poem was written during the brief interval between Prior's death (1721) and Young's and Thomson's initial publications (1725–26), when Pope appeared to some the only great living poet. If so, this anonymous woman considered the moment propitious for female aspirants. His chief male competitors dead, she thinks Pope might even welcome women writers, who could at least take some occasional poems off his hands.

This lighthearted vision never materialized. Mary Deverell's ambivalence, surfacing in her *Miscellanies in Prose and Verse* (1781) was more typical of women's attitudes toward poetry and Pope.[3] Contemporaries observed her uneasiness with poetry, although her sermons and letters were well received.[4] In "An Epistle to a Physical Divine, who requested the author to write poetry" (*Miscellanies*, 2:208–13), Deverell blames Pope for alternately inspiring and discouraging her poetic compositions. Confessing her addiction to the *Iliad*, which "lure[s] my mind from humble prose" (line 73), she blames Pope's translation.

With tuneful trumpet *Pope* hands down,
The ten years siege of *Troy*'s famed town;
Makes all their glitt'ring armour shine,
With burnished glory in his line.
In youth,—he sung with past'ral ease,
And made his *Windsor-Forest* please,
When he describ'd the lawns, and glades,
With all th'enamour'd lover's shades,
That might a *Galen*'s bosom fire,
And the cold *hermit*'s breast inspire,
With all the mighty pains of love!
Whene'er he trod the Arcadian grove.

Thus *Pope* has led my soul astray,
By list'ning to his tuneful lay.

(83–96)

Pope's early verse roused Deverell's ambition. She describes Pope's intoxicating power to rouse martial or amorous passions. Deverell admires Pope's control as he modulates from descriptions of battle to "past'ral ease," manipulating readers to feel "all the mighty pains of love!" For Deverell, writing poetry evidently meant aspiring to the power that had "led [her] soul astray." But, as she explains in her poem, Pope himself seemed to forbid her attempt. She paraphrases his advice in the "Essay on Criticism" to "drink deep, or taste not the Pierian spring" ("Essay," 216), interpreted as a warning not to write "unless on wings sublime we mount" ("Epistle," 105), well-fortified with classical learning. Deverell describes a typical female predicament. Lacking the prerequisite classical education, most women approached writing with trepidation. Deverell counters with an alternative theory, that excellence results from repeated attempts: "And those who soar in *Pindar's* clime, / First try'd their flight in simple rhyme" (113–14). Although she illustrates her opinion with the example of a boy learning to swim (116–18), Deverell was clearly defending her right as a self-educated female to compose poetry, to cultivate the enchanting power she had first encountered in Pope's *Iliad* and *Works*.

Deverell's poem exemplifies women's ambivalence toward themselves as writers and toward poetry, both encapsulated in her response to Pope. As if to avoid a serious challenge, she confines her complaint to hudibrastic couplets. Elsewhere in her volume, she composes in heroic couplets. "Letter II: To a Young Lady" (*Miscellanies*, 2:207–9) enlists the "Essay on Criticism" and "Epistle to a Lady," recommending that modern belles adopt ancient virtue and accomplishments. Deverell assumes Pope's authoritative tone, and even his words, to exhort her correspondent.

> Great share of beauty to thy form is giv'n,
> Thy mind's an emblem of all-bounteous heav'n!
> With these endowments let good sense conspire,
> "To teach the world with reason to admire."
>
> (65–68)

Deverell evidently felt more comfortable speaking authoritatively when recommending Penelope and Lucretia as models for modern women than when defending her poetic aspirations. In "Letter II" she reinforced classical models of feminine submission; in "Letter to a Physical Divine" she intimated her literary will to power. The latter poem's awkwardness, contrasted with her smooth mimicry of Pope's satirical voice in "Letter II," suggests Deverell's longing, and hesitation, to assume poetic authority.

Contradictions throughout Deverell's miscellany reveal gender as the source of discomfort. Deverell champions women's learning in two letters "on learned and good Ladies" (*Miscellanies*, 2:47–90) and describes her pleasure in poems by Anne Finch (2:174–76) and Phillis Wheatley (2:268). But elsewhere, she disclaims women's intellectual pretensions. "I . . . wish for *man* to fill the throne, but to admit woman to the footstool," she writes of literary assemblies (1:114). Uncertain of women's claim to write, let alone to speak their minds in the cultural forum (recall her adaptation of Pope's couplet about Indian primitivism to excuse the "feminine" lack of learning in her sermons), Deverell never developed a consistent poetic style. To Mary Deverell, Pope represented both inspiration and a masculine culture forbidden to women. Deverell never mastered the longed-for art of poetry. Her responses to Pope manifest the ambivalence that dogged her poetic attempts.

Deverell was not the only woman poet who found Pope's influence both baleful and inspiring. Esther Lewis confessed her anxiety by including in her *Poems Moral and Entertaining* (1789) "A Resolution."

> When Pope I read, good God! I cry,
> Was ever such a fool as I?
> To torture thus my stupid brain,

Waste paper, pens and ink, in vain:
For tho' I think with all my might,
What wretched stuff I still indite,
Nor have I prudence to conceal
My folly, but must it reveal:
Farewel my paper, ink and pen,
I vow I'll never write again.[5]

Taken at face value, this is the cri de coeur of a woman stifled by Pope's model. Her own poems appear a wretched waste of time and paper compared with his verse. Worse still, she defers to Pope by abjuring further publication of her poems. "A Resolution" suggests that Pope's influence was potentially pernicious if women felt bullied into abandoning their poetic aspirations. However, Lewis's hudibrastic meter and comically informal diction undermine her complaint's seriousness. The deliberate repetition and tortured syntax deny Lewis's pretense that, having failed to duplicate Pope's sublimity, she must cease writing. No reader is surprised when Lewis proclaims "Woman's Frailty" six pages later.

I lately quarreled with my pen,
And vow'd I'd never write agen,
But women's vows, alas! how frail,
I cannot stop 'till paper fail.

("Woman's Frailty," 1–4, *Poems*, 152)

Behind the blithe reference to feminine inconstancy, the embarrassing self-deprecation (she calls herself "stupid as . . . an owl," 7–8), lurks Lewis's determination not to be intimidated. Lewis blames her "stubborn quill" but keeps writing (10).

Esther Lewis seems an unlikely sufferer from female ambivalence toward writing. She was championed first by Dr. Samuel Bowden, then by her husband, Robert Clark.[6] Secure of male approval, she nevertheless accused men in "Slander Delineated" of denigrating women's literary performances and encouraging female suspicion of women writers (*Poems*, 162–69). "A Resolution" and "Woman's Frailty" paradoxically reiterate cultural scorn of female "wit," as Lewis heaps on herself the kind of criticism she imagines from others in "Slander Delineated." In her mock resolution and retraction, however, Lewis repeats such criticism to disarm it. She acknowledges Pope's potential to depress the woman writer but invokes her femininity to elude his power. The poems' slightness absolves her from competition with the master, while the self-abuse in them atones for her continued writing. The poems dramatize Lewis's feelings of unworthiness and her resentment of Pope for inflicting it, but they also portray her persistence. They suggest that despite her fortunate relations with male patrons, Lewis suffered from cultural disapproval of women's writing. "A Resolution," "Woman's Frailty," and "Slander Delineated" recognize a complex situation, in which Lewis experimented with feminism and self-mockery as alternative strategies to justify women's writing in a hostile culture.

Elsewhere in her volume, Lewis demonstrates ways women learned to craft their poems by studying Pope's. "The Heart Unfathomable" (*Poems*, 110–12) originates in the *Essay on Man*.

> By reason led, by heav'n-born wisdom taught,
> Athirst for knowledge man with pains has sought;
> The ways of nature, thro' her windings trod,
> And in all nature seen all nature's God.
>
>   (1–4)

Although Lewis's subject is "that mazy labyrinth, the human heart" (14), Pope's *Essay* provides her rationale, her structure, and even, as in line 4, her choice of words. "Man more happy than Brutes" (*Poems*, 99–105) is even more dependent on the *Essay*. It is unclear whether that poem appropriates the *Essay* to refute skeptical poems leveling humans and beasts, or, more likely, is a drastic misreading intended to refute Pope. In either case, Pope spurred Lewis's philosophical argument, suggesting such strategies as rhetorical questions, anaphora, chiasmus, and parallelism. Lewis learned a powerful argumentative structure from Pope that belies her capitulation in "A Resolution." While "A Resolution" disclaims any pretensions, both "A Heart Unfathomable" and "Man more happy than Beasts" attest to Lewis's ambitious, even competitive, reading of Pope. The awkward hudibrastics of "A Resolution" by no means disclose Pope's full significance to Esther Lewis. Her *Poems Moral and Entertaining* reveals how women's struggle to accept themselves, and to be accepted, as professional writers competed with their determination to imitate, and even challenge, the century's dominant poet.

Ambivalence was only one of myriad ways women greeted Pope's influence. Some gratefully borrowed his authority for their opinions.

Pope's famous argument in the *Essay on Man* for resignation to providence was particularly useful when claiming an appropriate feminine submission to vicissitude. In her *Poems on Several Occasions* (1770), Priscilla Pointon admonished a well-wisher who had commiserated her blindness: "*Pope* wisely tells us, to obey is best."[7] Catherine Upton concluded a poem describing the economic necessity that forced her to pursue a career as author and governess.

> Whether in London doom'd to lead my life,
> A hapless maid, or more important wife;
> Whether condemn'd in cities large to roam,
> Far from my kindred, friends, and native home;
>
> . . . .
>
> My mind shall still enjoy it's wonted rest,
> And think, with Pope, 'Whatever is, is best.'[8]

In an era when women feared that publishing appeared an unfeminine attempt to dictate the circumstances of their lives, Upton's allusion placed her career under the aegis of her culture's chief exponent of resignation.

Other women longed to be not merely influenced by but literally possessed by Pope's gifts. Mary Masters appealed to Pope in 1733 when addressing their mutual patron, the earl of Burlington: "Would thy vast Genius lend me half its Fire, / And one short Hour my panting Breast inspire . . . / In one short Hour a lasting Fame I'd raise."[9] The heightened diction of panegyric ("Fire," "panting Breast") seems erotic from a woman's pen and hints undue submission. But a later poem suggests a different interpretation of Masters's rhetoric. "Souls have no Sex, nor Male, nor Female there, / A manly Mind informs the well-taught Fair," she declared in her 1755 volume.[10] Masters complained bitterly of a meager education in her 1733 preface, an education feminine rather than manly. In the poem to Burlington, she wishes for a "vast Genius"—specifically, Pope's—to inform her verse. From that perspective, Masters's invocation of Pope seems more bold than passive. Given her choice of poetic minds, she would take Pope's. Her conventional wish for inspiration implies Masters's longing for intellectual power more than her passive submission to Pope's influence.

While Mary Masters, like Mary Leapor and Elizabeth Bentley, avowed her wish for Pope's poetic genius, many women poets simply appropriated his style for their own poems. Most recorded no feelings of unworthiness or incompetence relative to the great bard, no struggle to reconcile Pope's inspiration with his intimidation. As Anna Seward advised, they taught themselves poetic techniques by studying and applying available English models. Encouraged by Pope himself, by social consensus, and by the sheer availability of Pope's writings, women inevitably chose Pope as their chief model. As the century progressed, women's poetry reflected the influence of successive fashionable male poets: Young, Thomson, Collins, Gray, Percy, Macpherson, and Burns. But Popeian couplets and phrases abound in women's poetry throughout the century. His style may dominate an entire volume or may merely echo in ballads and odes. Even when women adopted the lyric forms popular in each decade, they included versions of "Eloisa to Abelard" or satiric epistles in their collections. Eighteenth-century women poets chose Pope as their precursor as often as the Romantics chose Milton. That few women emerged as strong poets from Pope's influence reflects cultural circumstances beyond Pope's or his women readers' control. But women poets kept trying, kept honing poetic skills despite crippling restraints on their education and experience. As we look more closely at Pope's influence on women's poetry, we may admire women's ingenuity in adapting his verse for appropriately feminine purposes and in cloaking less appropriate passions and ambition in Popeian rhetoric.

"Devoirs to the Rural Muse": Women and Pope's **Pastorals**

Eighteenth-century women's fondness for Pope's early verse appears throughout their prose, from Lady Hertford's letters to Hannah More's essays. A number of women were drawn to his earliest publications, the *Pastorals*, as models for their verse. Their attraction, seemingly explicable in terms of many women's predominately rural lives, belies the long history of pastoral as a male genre. In *Literature and the Pastoral*, Andrew V. Ettin has explained the relative scarcity of women's pastoral poetry despite the tradition's emphasis on "'feminine' functions, emotions, and values."[11] He argues that the very adaptability of traditional pastoral themes to women's lives made the pastoral an unattractive vehicle for pre-eighteenth-century women who were "sufficiently unconventional to present themselves as writers" (146). For Lady Mary Wroth or Aphra Behn, pastoral was feasible only when subverted or parodied (146–47). Ettin traces pastoral's artificiality to its function of incorporating feminine values and emotions into men's experience, which soon reduced it to an exercise for young poets rather than a serious expression of adult ideas (149).

Curiously, the very conventionality and unimportance to which pastoral had been reduced by the eighteenth century recommended it to many women poets. Unlike William Cowper or Wordsworth, who breathed new life into the tradition by departing from its established forms and idiom, women sheltered themselves in pastoral's artificiality. A genre patently removed from experience required little of the experience women were told they needed before they could write.[12] Pastoral was inoffensive because it was unimportant. Pope had remarked of his own early poetry, "Soft were my Numbers, / who could take offense / While pure Description held the place of Sense?" ("Epistle to Dr. Arbuthnot," 147–48). That hacks had assailed his flowery themes and purling streams outraged him in retrospect. Women poets, too, regularly propitiated critics by announcing the pastoral nature of their verse. Mary Whateley hoped certain poems' amorousness would be excused as the unavoidable consequence of "pay[ing] one's Devoirs to the Rural Muse."[13] Ann Curtis, dedicating her book to the duchess of Devonshire in 1783, explained she had "endeavoured to preserve simplicity of Style, and delicacy of Sentiment, which the celebrated Pope says, are the chief Beauties of Pastoral Poetry."[14] And Ann Francis, in "The Sylph," endowed herself with a poetic guide who prescibes her genres: "the lyric smooth, and roundelay, / Pastorella's easy strain." The sylph warns Francis not "to tempt the daring heights of song"; she is to be no Pindar, but a "rural Muse."[15] For these women, pastoral was a safe alternative to more ambitious genres that critics would consequently judge more harshly.

Pastoral, as Ettin describes it, traditionally offered men a way to express "feminine" feelings, such as love, and it also sanctioned late-century women poets' explorations of the same emotions. Bound by decorum, how was the unmarried Mary Whateley to describe "what fine Sensations move / The Female Heart to *hope, despair,* or *love*" ("Delia, A Pastoral," 11–12, *Poems,* 50)? Whateley admitted in "The Power of Destiny" that if she had been a man, she would have fled her profession

> And in some Cot, retir'd from Crowd and Noise,
> Have sought serene Delights and rural Joys;
>
> . . . .

My most exalted Wish, and only Aim,
Had been to eternize the fav'rite Dame.

                                        (45–46, 51–52, *Poems*, 3–5)

As a pastoral poet, Whateley could appropriately concentrate on emotions ranging from friendship to despair over lost love without jeopardizing her reputation.

Pope's *Pastorals* and "Windsor Forest" surface repeatedly in Whateley's poems, placing her celebrations of love and friendship firmly in the classical pastoral tradition. For example, Whateley borrows Hylas's amorous complaint in Pope's "Autumn" for her "Elegy on a much lamented Friend" (Whateley, *Poems*, 12–14). Hylas's claim that "Thro' Rocks and Caves the Name of *Delia* sounds, / *Delia*, each Cave and ecchoing Rock rebounds" ("Autumn," 49–50) becomes Whateley's description of mourning Nymphs: "*Fidelia's* dead!" they cry, and all around— / "*Fidelia's* dead!" the cavern'd Rocks rebound" (21–22). Whateley chastens Hylas's cry into the ritual chant of a nymphs' chorus mourning a female friend. That Pope deliberately transformed his classical prototype, Virgil's second eclogue, to avoid suggestions of homosexual love (see *Poems*, 1:80 nn. 3–4) adds piquance to Whateley's redirection of his lament into an affirmation of female friendship. But by the late eighteenth century, women's mutual expressions of passionate friendship were more acceptable than such claims between men and women. The same convention that required Pope's Hylas to burn for Delia and his Lycidas to mourn Daphne encouraged Whateley to adapt a couplet from Pope's most passionate pastoral for her portrayal of one woman's funeral lament over another.

In "Delia, a Pastoral," Whateley echoes Pope's "Summer," "Autumn," and "Winter" in Delia's confession of love for Cynthio. This poem probably inspired Whateley's dedicatory warning lest her poems' amorousness be attributed to personal experience. Many readers, however, would have recognized not personal but Popeian constructions of passion in this pastoral. In Pope's "Autumn," for example, the shepherds sit "beneath the Shade a spreading Beech displays" (1). In Whateley's "Delia," Delia and Monimia rest "beneath a spreading Osier's friendly Shade" (1). While Alexis mourned his departed lover in Pope's "Summer," "the Streams forgot to flow" (5). In "Delia," "the Winds forgot to blow, / And Streams to murmur, as [Delia] breath'd her woe" (3–4). Pope/Alexis dedicates "Summer" to Dr. Garth, punning on the notion of love as an incurable disease. Delia confides her predicament to Monimia (the Miss M—— of Whateley's inscription), who understands "what fine Sensations move / The Female Heart to *hope, despair,* or *love*" (11–12). Women's empathy replaces Garth's metaphorical healing ability in Whateley's sole distinctly feminine adaptation of Pope's material. Delia's complaint is a pastiche of shepherds' laments from "Autumn" and "Winter," with even a hint of "Windsor Forest" (cf. "Ah! what avails it what the Shepherds sing," in "Delia," line 19, with Pope's dying pheasant in "Windsor Forest," line 115: "Ah! what avail his glossie, varying Dyes"). Delia even wishes she could sigh like the "Numbers . . . / As tell the slighted *Lesbian*'s deathless Woe" (35–36). The allusion in this context seems not to Sappho's verse but to Pope's "Sapho to Phaon," included with the *Pastorals* in his *Works* (1717).

Whateley's conclusion echoes Hylas's plea in "Autumn." "Come, *Delia,* come; ah why this long Delay?" ("Autumn," 48) becomes "Come, *Cynthio* come, and bless thy *Delia*'s Eyes" ("Delia," 39). In Pope's poem, Delia finally returns to her ecstatic Hylas: "Ye Pow'rs, what pleasing Frensie sooths my Mind! / Do Lovers dream, or is my *Delia* kind? / She comes, my *Delia* comes!" (51–53). Whateley's Delia greets her swain with equal delight: "Heav'ns! do I dream?—or is it *Cynthio*'s Voice? / He comes, he comes" (51–52). Whateley's allusion to "Sapho to Phaon" suggests that as she modeled a deserted shepherdess's lament, she turned to Pope, author not only of her favorite *Pastorals* but of impassioned heroic epistles, to supply sentiments avowedly missing from her experience. Not only pastoral convention but the Ovidian heroic tradition sanctioned Delia's passionate exclamations.

Whateley's pastorals do not always merely plunder Pope's. In "Rural Happiness. To a Friend" (*Poems,* 18–22), she orchestrates passages from "Spring" and "Windsor Forest" to create an appealing description of the autumn countryside near Birmingham. Behind Whateley's "And bright-ey'd *Ceres* crown'd with *Plenty* reigns; / With blushing Fruit the bending Branches shine" (14–15) we glimpse Pope's "Here blushing *Flora* paints th'enamel'd Ground, / Here *Ceres*' Gifts in waving Prospect stand" ("Windsor Forest," 38–39). Whateley flattens Pope's gestures toward his scene, but she recovers them as she evokes a pastoral landscape: "Here, white with bleating Flocks the Uplands rise, / There, Hills whose azure Summits pierce the Skies" ("Rural Happiness," 17–18). The latter image recalls Pope's "There wrapt in Clouds the blueish Hills ascend" ("Windsor Forest," 24), evidence that Pope's painterly description influenced the way Whateley viewed her own surroundings.

In "Rural Happiness," Whateley's opening verses on the Birmingham countryside owe more to Pope's idealized "Windsor Forest" than to reality. She even incorporates Strephon's claim "O'er Golden Sands let rich *Pactolus* flow, / . . . / Blest *Thames*'s Shores the brightest Beauties yield" (Pope, "Spring," 61–63) into her description. "No more let Poets . . . / . . . paint the Treasure that *Pactolus* yields" ("Rural Happiness," 21–22) she boasts of her retirement, where

> . . . 'mid the tufted Trees, the rural Cell,
> Where *Health*, and sweet *Content*, and *Virtue* dwell,
> Displays its straw-crown'd Roof, and smiles secure
> From all those Cares the guilty Great endure.
>
> (25–28)

But the rest of Whateley's poem diverges sharply from "Windsor Forest." Pope's poem envisions warfare, political injustice, and rape, rendering precious an interim of Stuart "Peace and Plenty" among the tufted trees. Whateley has no such political agenda. The second half of "Rural Happiness" is more accurate than the first in that she introduces some local detail, rejoicing that the midlands escape coastal plunder (33–35), and praising a local estate, Bardsley Hall (37–38).

Whateley's "Rural Happiness" is relentlessly optimistic about rural life (see line 69), as suggested by her earlier assumption that the poor in their one-room thatched cottages are more secure than the conscious-stricken rich (lines 25–28). Any reader of social history, not to mention of Goldsmith's "The Deserted Village" or Wordsworth's "The Ruined Cottage," will question Whateley's choice of the cottage as an emblem of security. Whateley's metaphor suggests her inexperience and her impulse, as a poetic apprentice, to experiment with phrases and themes of favorite models. "Rural Happiness" detours through Pope's "Ode on Solitude" (49–54) en route to a "lonely Cot" (69) where Whateley imagines herself living amidst Health, Pleasure, Truth, Contemplation, and Freedom (81–85). This vision derives from Collins, who—along with Thomson, Young, and Burns—influenced the poems of her second volume.[16] But Pope's pastoral poems were Whateley's first inspiration, sanctioning her explorations of passion set in a benign landscape. Among her eighteenth-century women contemporaries, Mary Whateley was the most indebted to Pope's *Pastorals*.

Other eighteenth-century women poets also responded to Pope's earliest poems. In "To Mira," Charlotte Ramsay (later Lennox) invited a friend to "range the Plains, / Amongst the rustick Nymphs and Swains; / In rural Dress, devoid of Care."[17] The young ladies will sit beneath the trees when tired of strolling, and "our Thoughts to heavenly Numbers raise, / Repeating *Pope*'s harmonious Lays, / Now *Homer*'s awful Leaves turn o'er" (37–39)—in Pope's translation. Ramsay's invitation grants adolescent girls the healthful routine of "Study and Ease" attributed to rural gentlemen in Pope's "Ode on Solitude" (line 13). Her description of two carefree young ladies reading and discussing Pope suggests why so many eighteenth-century women retained fond memories of Pope's early poems throughout their lives. Many of them, like Ramsay, probably read Pope with friends, nurturing the kind of platonic attachment she celebrates in this poem. Her association of Pope with an idealized pastoral landscape also surfaces in "A Pastoral from the Song of Solomon" (*Poems*, 1–6). Ramsay renders the ancient lyric in heroic couplets: "Arise, My Love, the dear Enslaver cries, / My beauteous Maid, my lovely Fair, arise" (30–31). Her version exhorts the beloved, "See where you tread, fresh blooming Flowers arise, / New Charms appear where'er you turn your Eyes" (45–46), a distinct allusion to the most musical lines of Pope's "Summer" (73–76). Ramsay's couplet acknowledges the sublimity of Pope's famous passage in a graceful tribute to her favorite poet.

Other women poets capitalized on the juvenile appeal of Pope's *Pastorals* that had so delighted the teenaged Charlotte Ramsay (about eighteen when she published *Poems on Several Occasions* in 1747). Reversing the notion of pastoral as a young writers' genre, women poets adapted it as a didactic vehicle for young readers. For example, Anne Penny included "Amyntas" as the last of three pastorals in her *Poems* (1771).[18] The two preceding pastorals have epigraphs from Thomson, and "Amyntas" is not particularly Popeian. But the poem's epigraph is a well-known couplet from Pope's *Essay on Man*: "Self-love thus push'd to social, to divine, / Gives thee to make thy neighbour's blessing thine" (*Essay*, 4.353–54). "Amyntas" illustrates Pope's principle through the tale of a shepherd who rescues a tree uprooted by a stream. In return, the "Syren Dryad of the oak" (34) grants him a wish, offering India's wealth in return for his care of her tree. The virtuous swain requests only the restoration of his friend's health, prompting the "wond'ring Dryad" (56) to bless both shepherds. Palemon regains his health, while the gods shower Amyntas with wealth and "unnumber'd" benefits (61). Penny's poem reduces Pope's philosophy to its simplest terms in a pastoral fairy tale suitable for the children of a burgeoning capitalist society. The dryad offers wealth as a suitable reward for Amyntas' charity, and even greater wealth blesses his persevering altruism. Set in the pastoral community, Penny's fable teaches young readers a modern economic motivation for old-fashioned paternalism.

Ann Murry—who dispensed capitalist philosophy in *Mentoria* via the *Essay on Man*—also recognized the didactic potential of pastoral verse. Her *Poems on Various Subjects* (1779) features "Damon and Thyrsis," "designed to express the sanguine hopes of a Person launching into Life; to which are opposed the different sentiments occasioned by long intercourse with the World."[19] Unmistakeable echoes connect Murry's poem with Pope's series. Young Thyrsis implores Damon "Oh! deign to listen to my Delia's praise" (9), recalling Alexis's plea "Oh deign to visit our forsaken Seats" in Pope's "Summer" (71). When Damon warns him of women's inconstancy, Thyrsis retorts that love does not invariably entail sorrow.

> If Delia would but deign to smile on me,
> From its dominion, I should then be free.
> Ye painted meadows, and ye murm'ring rills!
> Ye gentle zephyrs, and ye lofty hills!
> Without my Delia ye no pleasures give,
> For 'tis in her, superior beauties live.
>
> ("Damon and Thyrsis," 39–44)

Thyrsis's claim derives from the singing contest in Pope's "Spring." In "Spring," Strephon boasts that even when "Nature Mourns," "if *Delia* smile, the Flow'rs begin to spring" (69, 71), a more metaphorical expression of her power to prevent sorrow. Strephon admits that in Delia's absence, the fields and hills cease to please (78–80). And Daphnis replies that "ev'n Spring displeases, when [Sylvia] shines not here, / But blest with her, 'tis Spring throughout the Year" (81–84). Murry's Thyrsis conflates both shepherds' claims, granting Delia's transforming power over the landscape.

Her allusions suggest that Murry adapted her structure, the shepherds' contention and reconciliation, from Pope's "Spring," although she could have found numerous precedents. Murry used the structure for a distinctive moral purpose. Her younger shepherd, not her elder, seems drawn from Pope's "Spring," although Thyrsis praises not only

Delia's beauty but her "moral rectitude, and grace" (46). Damon's replies—for example, "In Nature's works, what lessons are we taught. . . . The more we read, the more our feelings glow / To seek the cause from whence such blessings flow" (55, 57–58)—seem drawn more from the *Essay on Man*. Convinced at last, Thyrsis seeks Damon's advice: "Say, Happiness, art thou an empty sound?" (78). He receives a Johnsonian answer: "Hope leads us on, thro' Life's progressive stage" toward eternal life (79). Capitalizing on pastoral's association with youthful attitudes, Murry portrays Thyrsis's growth toward a mature, unpastoral point of view. She invokes, then gently repudiates, Pope's *Pastorals*, while transforming the love debate of classical pastoral into a Christian sermon.

Women's Imitations of "Eloisa to Abelard," from A(zor) to Z(elida)

Although less useful for didactic purposes, Pope's "Eloisa to Abelard" inspired women throughout the century. Pope's adaptation of Ovidian and Miltonic material created a vogue for passionate heroines trapped in gloomy retreats.[20] Heroic epistles had been composed in the sixteenth and seventeenth centuries by such poets as Drayton, Donne, and Behn (Pope, *Poems*, 2:275–79), but Pope's epistle most fully captured contemporary imaginations. Women were particularly drawn to this genre, perhaps because it sanctioned exploration of feminine passion. Like Mary Whateley's pastorals, women's heroic epistles contained dangerous passions in a traditional structure. And while women wrote heroic epistles unrelated to Pope's (Charlotte Ramsay's "Shallum to Hilpah" and Anne Francis's "Leah to Jacob," for example), many relied on "Eloisa to Abelard" for structure and sentiments. Perhaps the recognizable form added an extra margin of safety to their impersonations of deserted lovers. More likely, Pope's readers despaired of surpassing his depiction of frustrated yearning.

Geoffrey Tillotson observed that modern readers are rarely moved by the poem's rhetoric (Pope, *Poems*, 2:288), but contemporaries thought "Eloisa to Abelard" epitomized poignant suffering. Charlotte Smith ended the first of her *Elegiac Sonnets* (1784) by paraphrasing Pope's conclusion: "Ah! then, how dear the Muse's favors cost, / *If those paint sorrow best—who feel it most!*"[21] Roger Lonsdale notes that Smith's reviewers greeted as genuine, and wondered about, her sonnets' pervasive melancholy (365–66). Smith was suffering financial and marital reverses, but a chief source of this particular sonnet's effect is its final, enigmatic paraphrase. Deliberately obscure, Pope's phrase linked him with Eloisa's romantic suffering in a suggestive manner, fully intelligible only to Lady Mary Wortley Montagu. By importing this teasing reference into her poem, Smith associated herself with Pope's suffering heroine and with his own unspecified grief. For Charlotte Smith and her readers, and for many women, Eloisa's lament appeared not mere rhetoric but a moving expression of anguish.

Women responded immediately to what Tillotson characterized as Pope's refinements to the heroic epistle (Pope, *Poems*, 2:288). Though he did not invent either, Pope heightened the heroine's spiritual conflict and her gothic surroundings. These aspects distinguish Elizabeth Tollet's "Anne Boleyn to King Henry VIII," first published in 1724 in her anonymous *Poems on Several Occasions* (85–99). Trapped in a "gothick tower" (269), Anne endures a debate between her physical shame and fear and her need for spiritual resolve. After terrible "presaging Dreams" (287), she gradually resigns herself to martyrdom, renouncing even her hope for Henry's pity. While the poem is not precisely indebted to Pope for style, Anne's prison and the structure of her internal debate were inspired by Tollet's favorite author.

Helen Sard Hughes characterized another example, Lady Hertford's "An Epistle from Yarrico to Inkle," as "in style and mood a palpable imitation of Pope's 'Eloisa to Abelard.' "[22] Having versified "The Story of Inkle and Yarrico" from *Spectator* 11, Lady Hertford was evidently tempted to complete the tale of Inkle's perfidy in the manner of a cherished poem. Her dependence on Pope was not really as "palpable" as Hughes claims. Nevertheless, "Eloisa" lurks behind Yarrico's confession that "close in the deep recesses of my breast, / [Inkle's] lovely image still remains imprest" ("Epistle," 9–10). Pope's Eloisa asks, "Canst thou forget that sad, that solemn day, / When victims at yon' altar's foot we lay?" ("Eloisa," 107–8). "I well remember that unhappy day, / In which I gaz'd my liberty away," muses Yarrico of her first glimpse of Inkle ("Epistle," 13–15). Eloisa feels imprisoned in her convent: "Yet here for ever, ever must I stay" ("Eloisa," 171). Yarrico endures literal slavery, complaining, "Yet still I must my hated life sustain, / Still linger on my anxious years in pain" ("Epistle," 39–40). Yarrico endures spiritual conflict. She contemplates but resists suicide on the advice of a "hoary Christian priest" ("Epistle," 41) reminiscent of the "sad sister" who consoles Eloisa ("Eloisa," 310).

Unlike Eloisa, however, Yarrico finally warns her faithless lover that he risks hell. Though she admired Pope's poem, Lady Hertford preferred a heroine whose repentance was unambiguous, a model of Christian virtue.

Eighteenth-century women who imitated "Eloisa to Abelard" invariably cleared their heroines of deliberate immorality. While Eloisa proclaimed a "curse on all laws but those which love has made!" (74), ladies' epistolary heroines were victims of unjust circumstances. Charlotte Ramsay apparently found Eloisa's amorality unappealing and her fate unbearably harsh. In Ramsay's "An Epistle to Moneses. In Imitation of Ovid" (*Poems*, 73–80), Ardelia never explains why she fled her adored swain. But the first line of her epistle reminds him that she was "urg'd by Honour" to banish herself. Moneses evidently made dishonorable proposals. Ardelia's wish that "some happy Chance to us unknown" might "without a Crime confirm me all thy own" (108–9) suggests that he is married.[23] The "pleasing Hope" Ardelia cherishes may be the death of Moneses' spouse (112). Nevertheless, Ardelia has removed herself from temptation and intends to remain secluded until an honorable relationship becomes possible. She is thus distinguished from Eloisa, the unrepentant mistress torn from her lover. Because a slender hope of fulfillment remains, Ardelia's dilemma is likewise less extreme than Eloisa's. Eloisa vacillates between heaven and Abelard, finally settling for a vision of Abelard in heaven. Ardelia compares the possibility of renewed relationship with Moneses to "suff'ring Martyrs['] . . . future Heaven" (114–15). Ramsay's adjustments attempt to incorporate Eloisa's passion and eloquence in a less problematic, less doomed, heroine. "An Epistle to Moneses" seems altogether representative of young women readers' response to "Eloisa." Ramsay declined subjecting her heroine to Eloisa's despair, perhaps reflecting her own adolescent optimism. Further, Ardelia's self-exile is a disillusioned response to lost, first love, but her very ability to tear herself from Moneses suggests she may eventually heal. Ramsay may not have intended the latter reflection, but Ardelia is far from Eloisa's death wish.

Given these distinctions, Ramsay incorporates a surprising number of Popeian allusions into "Epistle to Moneses." Moneses has written Ardelia complaining of her desertion, unlike Eloisa, who reads Abelard's letter by chance. She assures him of her indescribable sorrow, which "equal Misery alone can paint" ("Epistle," 12). Like Eloisa, Ardelia feels her lover's griefs as her own (21–22). She blames herself for fleeing, commanding Moneses, "O rather hate me, drive me from your Breast, / By scorn and hate be all thy Soul possest" (47–48). Her wish recalls Eloisa's "Fly me, fly me!" ("Eloisa," 289), but the earlier heroine's plea represents a final, hard-won spiritual resolve. Ardelia's resolution occurs earlier, after a momentary vacillation. She never seriously contemplates returning to Moneses. Her account of their relationship, however, follows Eloisa's; Moneses nearly seduced her with "prevailing Eloquence" ("Epistle," 58). Ardelia softens, begging Moneses to "come once more . . . and renew / Those tender Vows, and I'll believe them true: / Let me once more behold those melting Eyes" (59–61; see "Eloisa," 119, 122). As Eloisa spurned empires in comparison with passion, Ardelia invites "Love [to] claim all his Empire in my Soul" ("Epistle," 65). Then, horrified to realize she is "still . . . enslav'd by guilty Love" (66), much as Eloisa was "confess'd within the slave of love and man" ("Eloisa," 178), Ardelia recoils. She vows to "drive [Moneses] from my Breast" but finds that even the "lonely Shades" give no ease ("Epistle," 70, 75). She hears Moneses' name in the "whisp'ring Winds" and wastes the night pining for him (77). As in Pope's poem, night restores Moneses, who appears in Ardelia's dreams as a "charming Phantom" eluding her "clasping Arms" (84–85; see "Eloisa," 225–34). Ardelia wonders whether Moneses dreams of her, and she asks, "O why is it a Crime to love?" ("Epistle," 85), a gentle variation of Eloisa's "Curse on all laws but those which love has made!" ("Eloisa," 74). Ardelia confesses the same dilemma: "My tortur'd Breast conflicting Passions tear, / And Love and Virtue wage unequal War" ("Epistle," 98–99). But her very self-consciousness distinguishes her from Eloisa, whose rhetoric rationalized her lingering passion. Ardelia echoes Eloisa once more as she defines her problem: "Seas roll between us, but the active Mind / Still springs to thee" (106–7). She resolves to wait, however, for an honorable reconciliation. Ramsay used Pope's phrases as building blocks, rearranging Eloisa's debate in a more wholesome context. While Eloisa seems addicted to Abelard's "delicious poison" ("Eloisa," 123), Ardelia escaped Moneses' "subtle Poison" ("Epistle," 55) before losing her honor. Ramsay endowed her chaste heroine with Eloisa-like passion but spared her its worst consequences.

A later imitation justifies the heroine's passion as matronly love. Jael Henrietta Pye based "Elgiva to Edwy" on a tenth-century royal marriage declared illegal by the archbishop of Canterbury because the pair "were too near a-kin."[24] The same story later inspired Fanny

Burney's first attempt at tragedy. Margaret Doody finds Burney's play a subtle protest against contemporary repression of women.[25] Pye emphasized a different political aspect of Elgiva's plight. Elgiva and Edwy are equally victims of Archbishop Odo's ambition. "Ah! little think the herd that envy kings, / The train of ills that purple greatness brings," laments Elgiva (83–84). Her philosophical speculation eliminates the guilt that attended Pope's lovers because they were driven by personal passion. In Pye's poem, personal choice of spouse distinguishes "sweet Mediocrity" from wretched greatness (89). Nevertheless, Elgiva resembles Eloisa throughout her plea. Her opening lines paraphrase Pope's conclusion as she contemplates her miserable fate, "condemned in ceaseless absence to deplore" (5; cf. "Eloisa," 361). Like Eloisa, she cannot forget "that sad day, that ever fatal hour" when Odo dissolved her marriage ("Elgiva," 7). She now wastes her days recalling her husband: "E'en now I see thee, gaze on all thy charms, / And court the phantom to my longing arms," she admits (15–16), another close paraphrase of "Eloisa" (233–34). Elgiva longs to hear Edwy's "soft voice [that] in sounds persuasive flows" ("Elgiva," 26).

Elgiva's account of courtship, however, is quite distinct from Eloisa's. The lovers knew "no sensual, low, inelegant desire" ("Elgiva," 31). Married by her father's command, Elgiva had little wish to be queen—a chaste variant of Eloisa's ambition to be a mistress. Pye's chronicle includes a mutilation, but the victim is Elgiva, branded an adulteress. Banished to Ireland, she wonders, "Throbs there a heart with hopeless love like mine . . . ? / She, only she, by kindred pangs can tell, / The death-like anguish of our last farewell" (51, 53–54). She calls on Religion and Reason to "snatch the rod, / And vindicate the injured laws of God" (62), anticipating Pope's *Essay on Man* by eight centuries. Elgiva struggles to wish Edwy happily remarried, but she is forced to confess herself the jealous "slave of love" (80). She wishes she and Edwy had been born into the middle class and permitted to enjoy "unenvied happiness" (100). She spends near-sleepless nights tormented by horrible visions. The dreams portend her escape from Ireland and subsequent murder, foreseen in terms similar to Abelard's castration: "Sudden I'm seized; a ruffian band appears, / Deaf to my cries, regardless of my tears: / Their savage hands my trembling limbs disgrace" (111–13). Elgiva defies these prophetic dreams and prepares to seek her husband.

The story of Elgiva and Edwy must have been irresistible to both

Pye and Burney. As an authentic, native gothic tragedy, it seemed bound to please contemporary readers. The chaste, suffering queen resembled such popular heroines as Lady Randolph in John Home's *Douglas* (1757).[26] Pye cleverly perceived the story's potential as a heroic epistle. But her choice to filter the pure Elgiva's story through Eloisa's is curious; only the barbaric Odo could brand Elgiva's connubial love infamous. Pye's decision reveals the structural and technical appeal of Pope's poem. Women evidently admired his depiction of Eloisa's tortured thought process. Like Ramsay's Ardelia, Elgiva follows Eloisa's pattern of memory and reflection. The memories themselves are similar in each case, as if Pope had discovered the archetypal pattern of this particular feminine plot. His phrases begin to resemble Vladimir Propp's "functions": indispensible segments of the epistolary heroine's interior quest.[27] Each heroine recalls her lover's eloquence, pursues in dreams his phantom, and wishes for a kindred sufferer to tell her story. Propp concluded that his functions suggest a common psychological basis for all fairy tales, regardless of culture or historical period (106). Several eighteenth-century women writers apparently found "Eloisa to Abelard" a similarly generic record of female response to passion and to loss.

Ann Curtis's "Zelida to Irena" continues the pattern (*Poems*, 30–35). Zelida writes to her friend from Europe, where the Spaniards abducted her after conquering Peru. Her initial lament parallels Eloisa's: "What means this bursting sigh, these falling tears? / Why swells my soul within its fix'd retreat? / Why glows my bosom with unusual heat?" ("Zelida," 4–6; cf. "Eloisa," 4–6). Her love, however, is a "chaste . . . fire" ("Zelida," 31); Spanish soldiers dragged her from the altar on her wedding day. Zelida curses the Spaniards' ambition (19–22), another variant of Eloisa's disclaimer. Her recollection of the abortive wedding ceremony recalls Eloisa's religious profession: "The never-dying lamps were burning round, / When lo! the temple shook—the altar groan'd!" (23–24). Eloisa, too, observed that "the shrines all trembled, and the lamps grew pale" when she took the veil ("Eloisa," 112). "Their swords still reeking with [Zelida's] country's blood," the Spaniards kidnap Azor and take Zelida to Europe ("Zelida," 40). The context recalls Abelard's mutilation, another violent cause of involuntary separation. According to Zelida, Azor was brainwashed by the Spaniards and disowned his culture. She worries that he may already have married a European woman, but she conjures herself to "hear, that he never more shall bless my sight, / And calmly own—'whatever is, is right' " (65–66). Her anachronistic quotation of the *Essay on Man* may deliberately acknowledge Curtis's Popeian source or may suggest Pope's philosophy as the proper antidote to women's passionate outbursts. Zelida admits she mourns incessantly, wandering at night through a grove where her sighs accompany the wind. She finally prepares to inhabit a hermit's cave, like Eloisa's cell, until death; "Then will each care, and ev'ry grief be o'er, / And faithless Azor be belov'd no more" (96). Curtis's insistent allusions beg recognition of her poem's model. "Eloisa to Abelard" shapes this tale of an abducted sixteenth-century Peruvian bride, yet another acknowledgment of the universal validity some women ascribed to Eloisa's experience and response.

Curtis's quotation of the *Essay on Man* reiterates her belief in universal human nature—or rather, universal male and female natures—a popular point of view throughout the century. The modern reader, aware that culture modifies behavior and, if a feminist, convinced that nurture rather than nature is the root of much "feminine" behavior, may laugh at the notion of an Arcadian shepherdess, a tenth-century Saxon queen, and a sixteenth-century Peruvian maiden lamenting lost love in the same manner as a scandalous twelfth-century French nun. But eighteenth-century women's adoption of Eloisa's monologue for their chaste heroines did more than assert that passion, even overwhelming passion, was a universal feminine experience. By placing Eloisa's cries in the mouths of virginal brides and martyred queens, they vindicated feminine passion while protecting their own reputations. Pope's poem became the vehicle through which these writers claimed "good" women's right to love passionately. Their heroines suffered as much as any deserted mistress in the *Heroides*, but women's heroic epistles grope toward nonpejorative acknowledgment of women's sexuality.

The quest for this acknowledgment of women's passion was admittedly a slow process, as suggested by yet another variant on Pope's epistle. Buried in Maria Falconer's "Alfred and Ethelinda" (1788) are the lineaments of a lurid, sentimental, gothicized "Eloisa to Abelard."[28] The lengthy ballad repeats the story of a maiden seduced by her tutor. Desperate to escape a forced marriage, Ethelinda agrees to elope with her tutor, Alfred. When she learns that Alfred has already married, she stabs his bride Celimene, only to discover that Celimene was Alfred's sister, living with him to assist his courtship. Edmund, Ethelinda's fiancé, arrives, fresh from killing "the traitor Alfred" (295). Horrified, Ethelinda urges his flight to a cloister, while she seeks a retreat so that each, "in gloomy state," can spend their lives in solitary mourning for "the sad vicissitudes of fate" (325, 327–28). Despite the uncharacteristic violence, Falconer introduces her heroine in an "Eloisa"-like setting.

> Within a convent's lonely wall
>   Immers'd in death-like gloom,
> Whilst hollow echoes seem'd to call
>   From each surrounding tomb:
>
> From each terrestrial joy confin'd,
>   A lovely sainted maid,
> The beauteous weeping Ethelind,
>   With fair Matilda stray'd.
>
> (1–8)

Falconer's awkward epithet "sainted maid" suggests that her lurid, gothic poem is really a sixteen-year-old's plea for eighteenth-century parents to honor their daughters' choice of spouses. "Eloisa," filtered through other women's interpretations, lingers behind the young poet's warning not to thwart women's passion.

Because women evidently relied on Pope's style and structure to sanction their heroic epistles, few of these poems possess a distinctive voice. One late exception is Susanna Blamire's "The Nun's Return to the World, by the Decree of the National Assembly of France, February, 1790."[29] Blamire's long narrative poem weaves bits of "Eloisa" into a defense of women's affections. The opening paragraph evokes the Paraclete as Sister St. Agnes prepares to leave her forced retirement.

> Farewell ye walls, where solitude has thrown
> Her long dark shadow on each silent stone,
> Where the slow pulse but feebly dares to creep,
> Or give the wretched the sad leave to weep;
> Where struggling sighs break forth from every breast,
> And wasting sorrow wears a holy vest;
> Where pure religion seldom ventures nigh,
> Or owns the tear that hangs within the eye,
> Which trembling long, at last in secret falls,
> The heart-wrung offering to relentless walls.
>
> (1–10)

Blamire borrows the rhyme sounds of "Eloisa," lines 21–24—Pope's description of cold shrines, pale-eyed virgins, and weeping stone—for her first four lines. The "relentless walls" are also indebted to Eloisa's description of convent walls as an "eternal bound" (141).

As an Englishwoman, Blamire probably had little idea what an actual convent was like. She turned to Pope's fictional Paraclete to convey the imagined horrors of Catholic religious life. While Eloisa dreamed of Abelard "now warm in love, now with'ring in thy bloom" ("Eloisa," 37), St. Agnes describes even contented nuns "warm with life, yet hover[ing] o'er the tomb" ("Return," 18). St. Agnes, her convent disbanded by the National Assembly's decree, rejoices that she will soon be restored to normal activities and relationships. St. Agnes explains that, even with the best intentions, religious withdrawal is misguided. "When the slow organ swells the lengthen'd note" (23; the same music that encourages Eloisa's lascivious reveries in "Eloisa," line 271), some nuns fervently join in prayer: "When Conscience dictates the prompt will obeys" ("Return," 33; cf. "Eloisa," line 16, where Eloisa's heart dictates and her hand obeys). Blamire's inversions of Pope's lines suggest nuns delude themselves, a suspicion St. Agnes confirms. She knows that women's happiness depends on family relationships, "when father's, mother's, sister's, voice was heard" ("Return," 43). She sighs for her domestic youth, "when useful life was held a female part, / And 'twas no sin to feel I had a heart" (47–48). St. Agnes transforms Eloisa's love for Abelard ("Eloisa," 68, 151–52) into conventional feminine expectations. She recalls a visit to a pastoral cottage, an image of the domestic bliss cruel parents forbid her. Although many years have passed, she looks forward to nurturing others after her release.

The final third of "The Nun's Return" records a less happy outcome. St. Agnes regrets leaving behind one friend, "sweet Cecilia," who refuses to depart (205). Cecilia was forced by friends to take the veil. Her "pure and ardent" suitor died of "frantic rage" (195–96). Had he lived, "to the world I might again have flown, / And not, as now, 'forget myself to stone!' " (197–98). The quotation establishes Cecilia as yet another chaste incarnation of Eloisa. Blamire suggests, through both nuns, that Eloisa was not so much guilty as thwarted in her choice of mate. Cecilia indulges in Eloisa's activities, pondering her lover's "idea" (218), indulging her grief at twilight in the chapel. There, mourning her lover's "reliques" (227), she intends to stay until death, when she hopes "for my countless tears and sighs, to be forgiven" (240). She exhorts St. Agnes to work for the end of "cloister'd misery" (248), and blesses the National Assembly for promoting revolution: "All Nature sees, and hails the hour with me, / That gives to man the Mountain-Liberty" (267–68). Blamire joins such women as Mary Wollstonecraft and Helen Maria Williams in linking women's rights with the early French Revolution. In "The Nun's Return," Pope's gothic convent has become not a reflection of Eloisa's guilt but a symbol of repressed womanhood. Seventy-three years later, Blamire appropriated Pope's embodiment of unruly passion to defend women's right to fulfilled affection.

Not all women detected recuperative potential in Pope's heroic epistle. In "On reading Pope's Eloiza to Abelard" (1789), Elizabeth Hands repudiated Eloisa's apology for illicit love.[30] "No passions soft, or sadly-pleasing pain, / But rage and madness in thy bosom reign" (11–12), she admonishes Pope's heroine. Donna Landry detects veiled protofeminist sentiment behind Hands's repudiation of Eloisa's contempt for marriage. By calling Eloisa's attitude "vain" (17), Hands suggests the impossibility of any woman's triumph over that institution (Landry, 209). On the surface, however, Hands declares her preference for constraints on women's behavior. Hands writes that Eloisa forfeited her right to pity by boasting of her "tainted virtue, and [her] honour lost" (8); only when she "lament[s] at once [her] honour and [her] love" (22) will Hands compassionate. Perhaps Hands's status as a domestic servant, uncertain of her poetry's reception by genteel patrons, discouraged empathy with Eloisa or recognition of the poem's rhetoric as a potential expression of chaste feminine passion.[31] Hands's favorite genre also influenced her attitude. An able satirist, she voiced conservative values and opinions similar to those of the mature Pope, of Lady Mary Wortley Montagu, and of many satirical writers. But Hands's dismissal of Eloisa also reflects the powerful late-century cultural conservatism that eventually canceled what progress had been made toward acceptance of women's sexuality. Hands's disgust with Eloisa's "rage and madness"—reconstructed as acceptable feminine passion by so many earlier women writers—leads to denunciation: "And while thy bosom glows with guilty fire, / Let every hope of happiness expire" (19–20). Hands refuses to share Pope's empathy or to entertain the notion that Eloisa's love is anything but a "guilty fire" to be combated rather than nurtured.

At least two other women, one genteel, one aristocratic, shared Hands's misgivings about Pope's construction of passion, but they revised rather than rejected the poem that all three found compelling. One of Anna Seward's earliest and most popular publications, *Louisa, A Poetical Novel* (1784), exemplifies her desire to refine Pope's poetry.[32] In the preface, Seward declared her intention "to unite the impassioned fondness of Pope's *Eloisa*, with the chaster tenderness of Prior's *Emma*; avoiding the voluptuousness of the first, and the too conceding softness of the second" (*Works*, 2:219).[33] Seward's first epistle, "Louisa to Emma," is the most dependent on Pope's, perhaps because Seward began composing it when she was only nineteen (*Works*, 2:221). Instead of a passionate nun, Seward's heroine is a virtuous young lady whose fiancé married a wealthier woman. Louisa has not really been deserted. She anticipates her brother's return from his grand tour to avenge Eugenio's betrayal.

Seward was evidently most impressed with Pope's use of scenery to mirror Eloisa's emotional state. In "Louisa to Emma," Louisa inhabits a vale, once the springtime scene of romance, now the late-autumn setting of her tortured musings. As in "Eloisa," where melancholy "breathes a browner horror on the woods" (170), Louisa's grove exacerbates her plight.

> Loud, and more loud the blast of evening raves,
> And strips the oaks of their last, lingering leaves;
> The eddying foliage in the tempest flies,
> And fills with duskier gloom the thick'ning skies.
>
> ("Louisa," 207–10)

Louisa imagines her brother's vengeance but recoils from the thought of "Eugenio, pale and bleeding, on the plain" (346). She compares Eugenio to a fallen angel or to a deserted chapel when "horrors gather round the darken'd fane; . . . Through the dim aisles pale spectres seem to flit, / And hollow groans the whispering walls repeat" (394, 397–98).

Having imported into her poem the Paraclete's gothic ambience, Seward concludes by supplying Louisa with a "guardian spirit" (415), somewhat like the "sainted maid" who consoles Pope's heroine by promising that "grief forgets to groan, and love to weep" after death ("Eloisa," 307–16). Louisa's apparition lures her from suicide by promising "the soft exemption and the long repose" of imminent death (411–28). But unlike Eloisa, who wishes Abelard an ecstatic death where "saints embrace thee with a love like mine" ("Eloisa," 342),

Louisa asks Emma to imagine her arrival in heaven: "By kindred seraphs see thy friend embraced, / Nor one slight thought on false Eugenio waste!" ("Louisa," 415–16). If, to late twentieth-century taste, "Louisa to Emma" is "Eloisa to Abelard" purged pallid, grateful contemporaries valued Seward's poetical novel precisely for its refinement of Pope's voluptuousness.

A final response to Pope's "Eloisa to Abelard," previously unobserved, completes the canon of replies to Pope's heroic epistle. Although Lawrence Wright claimed in 1934 to discuss all known replies to "Eloisa," he omitted Lady Sophia Burrell's "Abelard to Eloisa," published in her collected *Poems* (1793).[34] Wright was probably unaware of Lady Burrell's poem, but his reluctance to include women's replies in this subgenre (he misattributed Judith Cowper's "Abelard" to William Pattison) is compatible with his argument that poets implicitly challenged Pope by composing their own versions of his epistle. That two women joined the contest, stringing Odysseus's bow among a dozen male competitors, may have seemed unlikely to Wright, who records the harsh critical treatment usually meted the contenders. Nevertheless, Lady Burrell contributed to the tradition a 166-line companion to Pope's "Eloisa."

Although most of her poems reflect fashionable tastes for Ossian and for the gothic, Lady Burrell described Pope in "To Mrs. L——. On her making me a present of Mr. *Pope*'s Portrait" (*Poems*, 2:83) as "that bard . . . / Whom, of all poets, I admire the most" (11–12). She dedicated her book to lord chancellor William Murray, earl of Mansfield, whom Pope had addressed as a young barrister in his Horatian imitations. She recalled the relationship in "On the Anniversary of the Earl of Mansfield's Birth-Day" (*Poems*, 2:204–5) and on her title page. Lady Burrell, like many late eighteenth-century readers, particularly cherished the early poems in which Pope anticipated the gothic trend. She hailed Pope's role as Lord Mansfield's philosophical mentor, and she paid him more substantial homage as her gothic precursor. "Abelard to Eloisa" employs the Augustan practice of imitation as free translation and modernization of a classical, foreign, or archaic text. Pope had clothed Horace and Donne in contemporary dress, and Lady Burrell complimented Pope in turn by veiling his "Eloisa" in the delicate sentiments preferred by her generation.

Lady Burrell's "Abelard to Eloisa" opens, like Pope's, with a series of exclamations, as the monk addresses "ye gloomy horrors! ye religious cells!" of his confinement (1). Like Eloisa, he complains to the walls and to the saints in his loneliness, and he regrets the religious ban on suicide (2–10). Also like Pope's heroine, the monk is unable to sleep because of his longing for his beloved (11–20). Unlike Eloisa, however, who confesses sexual longing ("Fancy restores what vengeance snatch'd away. . . . All my loose soul unbounded springs to thee," 225, 228), Abelard describes only nocturnal meditation and weeping (16). Daring to imagine she still shares his grief, he decides to send Eloisa this tearstained letter. This premise distinguishes "Abelard to Eloisa" from most other versions, framed as replies to the original epistle. Lady Burrell structures her poem as if it preceded Pope's. Eloisa's statements now appear to answer Abelard's desperate questions.

> Say then, my love! Shall Abelard complain,
> And thou not bear a portion of his pain?
> Have rigid nuns and pious legends taught
> Thy soul, to stifle every tender thought?
> Art thou afraid, where sculptured saints appear,
> To give at least one sympathetic tear?
> Or have those walls wherein thou art enshrin'd,
> Harden'd that heart, which was for love design'd?
>
> (37–44)

The reader already knows that Eloisa has not yet forgot herself to stone ("Eloisa," 24), and that she keeps vigil among "pitying saints, whose statues learn to weep" (22). We know that she longs for Abelard to more than share, to give her all his grief (50). But Lady Burrell's Abelard has little counsel to offer Eloisa, his heart consumed with an identical passion.

In Lady Burrell's poem, Abelard describes his affair with Eloisa, but—typical of late eighteenth-century decorum in general, and of restraints on ladies' expression in particular—he omits its sexual dimension. Again inverting Pope's story, Abelard recalls being "beguiled" by Eloisa's "soft eloquence" and transported by her "intelligent, . . . active mind" (46, 66). Unlike the historical tutor who seduced his pupil, this Abelard implies that he was seduced by Eloisa's bewitching conversation. As the lovers strolled, "I only listen'd to thy tuneful tongue; / The beauties of the scene were lost on me, / For all my looks were fondly fix'd on thee" (70–72). Pope's Eloisa recalled a more conventional situation. Her Abelard's learned eloquence "Too soon . . . taught me 'twas no sin to love" ("Eloisa," 68). Lady Burrell's Abelard never accuses Eloisa of deliberately testing his vows, but his hapless account of their affair (less intellectually inclined than Pope's lovers, the couple sang, walked in the woods, and exchanged vows) absolves both from the guilt that paradoxically enhanced the tragic stature of Pope's heroine. Abelard, like Pope's Eloisa, dreams of his lover, but the dream merges with Eloisa's vision of a "sad sister" beckoning her to death ("Abelard," 95–110; cf. "Eloisa," 307–10). His only consolation is that "perhaps in Paraclete's white walls confin'd, / My Eloisa's soul delights to rove, / Beyond her cell, and greatly soars above" (116–18). But "a thousand agonizing griefs return" (125). Abelard rages through the monastery, throwing himself "on some tomb" to "talk of love to those who sleep below" (131–32). Lady Burrell's conclusion is less ambiguous than Pope's. Abelard despairs of any pious solution, resigning himself to "woes which my heart is destined to endure, / Since ev'n religion fails to work my cure" (149–50). He concludes where Pope's Eloisa begins, with the recognition that "to write his woes, and to record his love, / Is all the comfort Abelard can prove" (155–56).

The poems thus comprise a hopeless cycle in which neither lover will conceivably strengthen the other's spiritual resolve. As if to emphasize Abelard's futility, Lady Burrell echoes a phrase in "Eloisa" that Pope had repeated in "Elegy to the Memory of an Unfortunate Lady." Eloisa anticipates her death, when "ev'n my *Abelard* [will] be lov'd no more" ("Eloisa," 334). In the "Elegy," the speaker grieves that at his death, his "Muse [will be] forgot, and thou belov'd no more!" (82). Lady Burrell's Abelard begs his lover, "When all my follies and my griefs are o'er, / And Eloisa is belov'd no more, / Forget me not" ("Abelard," 163–65). Pope's Eloisa appends her hope for Abelard's "extatic" reception in heaven, their interment in a common grave, and eventual literary fame. Lady Burrell's "Abelard" follows the "Elegy" in giving the last word to oblivion; Abelard merely requests that Eloisa "chaunt a requiem" for his soul (166). While less rigorous about the lovers' culpability, Lady Burrell denies them hope of heavenly or fictional reunion. Lady Burrell's response to "Eloisa" is thus less generous than the poem she honors, which grants Eloisa tragic greatness, and the lovers literary immortality. Her poem is characteristically "ladylike" in that few genteel women writers portrayed sexual passion as explicitly yet sympathetically as Pope had conveyed Eloisa's torment. Lady Burrell's imitation appeals to her generation's notion of moral refinement. Historic milieu, gender, and social status guided her response.

Women Reading and Responding to Pope "as Women"

Since Jonathan Culler distilled ten years of debate over reading "as a Woman," scholars have continued exploring the implications of gendered reading practices.[35] Culler argued that feminist criticism's primary struggle is against the male point of view habitual not only to critical theory but to most men and women readers. Until recently, writers questioned whether, or to what extent, eighteenth-century women could read or write as women, from a point of view unique to women. Susan Schibanoff defines the problem in "Taking the Gold Out of Egypt: The Art of Reading as a Woman," an essay primarily about medieval women readers.[36] Schibanoff concludes that rather than liberating women, "literacy was and remains an effective and efficient means of indoctrination, of immasculation. When we ask why, between Christine [de Pisan] and the Wife of Bath's time and the sixteenth and seventeenth centuries, women's status declined and roles narrowed, increased female literacy may, in fact, provide part of the answer" (100). Sandra M. Gilbert and Susan Gubar have located the first concerted rebellion by women readers/writers against male constructions of femininity in the nineteenth century, despite isolated protests by such eighteenth-century writers as Aphra Behn, Anne Finch, and Mary Wollstonecraft (3–104). In *Women and Print Culture*, Kathryn Shevelow's analysis supports Gilbert and Gubar's by demonstrating how generations of eighteenth-century women read and contributed to periodicals that inculcated an ideal of silent, domestic femininity (146–90).

But eighteenth-century women's resistance to immasculation may have been more persistent than these analyses suggest. Ruth Salvaggio has devoted a chapter of *Enlightened Absence* to Anne Finch's persistent writing as a woman in an era notoriously devoted to "masculine" intellectual systems (105–26). According to Salvaggio, Finch writes "simultaneously in the historical predicament of an actual woman, and through the process of disruption that was suppressed in the discourse of Newton, Pope, and Swift" (107). Donna Landry finds in plebeian women's responses to Pope's texts their refusal to be silenced by either Pope's and other male writers' continued reproduction of contemporary commonplaces about women or their own consequent expulsion from the literary establishment. In spite of [their] rapturous praise of Pope's textuality . . . this production of supplements represents something of a quiet mutiny in the history of women's writing in Britain. (55)

Pope's prominence in both Salvaggio's and Landry's studies is not coincidence. Eighteenth-century women of all classes read Pope, their responses varying from rapturous praise to disgust. Salvaggio's conclusion about Finch and Landry's about laboring-class women poets applies to all of Pope's women readers: they persevered, despite harsh cultural obstacles, to read and write as women. Pope declared in "An Essay on Criticism" that "a perfect Judge will *read* each Work of Wit / With the same Spirit that its Author *writ*" (233–34). Pope's critical authority was uncontested until late in the century, and Milton, Dryden, Swift, Pope, and other prominent male authors constituted eighteenth-century women poets' chief models. Such influences could have insured women's reading—and writing—with a masculine "Spirit," from a man's point of view. That they did not partly results from their culture, which tirelessly reminded women of their difference from men, particularly of their incapacity for "masculine" intellectual application. By inviting them throughout his notes to read the *Iliad* as women, Pope himself subtly denied that women could be "perfect Judge[s]" of Homer.

Still other considerations rendered Pope the inevitable focus of women's quiet mutiny. Because of his physical and political disabilities and his middle-class status, Pope seemed accessible to female contemporaries, whether as sympathetic ally or vulnerable opponent. His writings were literally accessible to them throughout the century. And Pope's writings were attracting women readers while print technology was becoming more available to them as writers. Women poets entered the literary marketplace with skills partly learned from Pope's frequently reproduced texts. Their indebtedness and their eagerness to acknowledge this prominent aspect of an education too-often circumscribed resulted partly from the contiguity of women's Popeian reading with their incipient professional opportunities.

Eighteenth-century women read and wrote as women; that is, conscious of their culturally constructed femininity. That they also "wrote woman," in the French feminist sense of disrupting the dominant masculine system, is less obvious to twentieth-century observers.

But both activities characterize women's responses to Pope's early poems. Even their choice of models is revealing. In his dedication to Arabella Fermor, Pope claimed that *The Rape of the Lock* "was intended . . . to divert . . . young Ladies." Yet women rarely imitated that poem, though they frequently adapted the *Pastorals* and "Eloisa to Abelard." Admittedly, the sophisticated wit and technical virtuosity of *Rape* were not as imitable as the juvenile *Pastorals* or as "Eloisa," which Anne Finch described as giving "courtly grace" to the "darling passion" of "the Female race" (Finch, "To Mr. Pope," 25–26). But while women both imitated and criticized Pope's "Epistle to a Lady"— perhaps because it included and praised Martha Blount's attitude— they evidently found it nearly impossible to adapt *The Rape of the Lock* to a woman's point of view.

Women's few allusions to *The Rape of the Lock* tend to adapt Pope's sylphs to a feminine, often Christian, context. Elizabeth Carter's "On Hearing Miss Lynch Sing" (1740) exemplifies this practice (*Poems*, 9). In *The Rape of the Lock*, the sylphs are selfish creatures, guarding coquettes in hopes of enjoying the belles' favors themselves. In Carter's poem, Miss Lynch's sylphs are more like cupids or guardian angels. They assist a young lady whose voice, unlike Belinda's shriek after the rape, "beats Measure to the well-tun'd Mind within" (16).

> Ye guardian Sylphs, who listen while she sings,
> Bear the sweet accents on your rosy Wings:
> With studious Care the fading Notes retain,
> Nor let that tuneful Breath be spent in vain.
>
> (7–10)

While Pope's sylphs prevent lost necklaces and lost hearts, Carter's sylphs aid the virgin to inspire love "that gently steals the ravish'd Soul away" (4). Her sylphs' power to "retain" Miss Lynch's ephemeral breath to attract virtuous love contrasts with Pope's sylphs' inability to prevent Belinda's "rape" by the Baron. Carter and other women poets admired the sylphs but resisted Pope's double entendres at Belinda's expense. Extracting the sylphs from their misogynist context, such women writers as Carter and Elizabeth Rowe rewrote Pope's magical beings from a genteel woman's point of view. The result contradicts Pope's smug reduction of young women to "moving toy-shops" directed by perverse "machinery" (*Rape*, 100). Carter's Miss Lynch, like Belinda, is uncannily captivating, but her power reflects the care of gracious supernatural beings. Pope's structure is disrupted, if not, in the French feminist sense, shattered.

Women's versions of "Eloisa to Abelard" particularly suggest resistance to Pope's constructions of femininity. Elizabeth Hands's "On reading Pope's Eloiza to Abelard" describes her near seduction by Pope's rhetoric:

> Ah! Eloiza, ever exil'd maid,
> I read thy sorrows, sorrowing as I read:
> My sympathetic heart now shares thy grief,
> Repeats thy sighs, and wishes thy relief.
>
> (3–6)

Hands commences as Pope's ideal reader, reading from Eloisa's point of view in the spirit that Pope writ. She soon pulls back, however, realizing that Pope has in a sense tricked her into identifying herself with a woman of "tainted virtue." Hands distinguishes between an innocent tale of a "hapless Fair" or of "banish'd lovers" (1–2), a poem worthy of her empathy, and the "rage and madness" she actually encounters (12). Her disgust signals Hands's refusal to read "Eloisa to Abelard" from Pope's perspective. Eradicating any suspicion of complicity, Hands exhorts Pope's heroine to repent. According to Hands, an uncritical reader of "Eloisa to Abelard" risks mistaking "rage and madness" for the "passions soft, or sadly-pleasing pain" (11) concomitant to distressed but virtuous womanhood. Her poem informs potential readers that although a domestic servant, Hands's notion of feminine heroism is morally superior to Pope's. Her poem also defines women readers' chief problem with "Eloisa to Abelard": his brilliant rhetoric manipulated readers into identification with a dangerously flawed heroine. While Hands recoiled, angered by the poem's seductive appeal, other women who read as women revised the poem to reflect their point of view, incorporating Pope's powerful rhetoric in an acceptable context.

Charlotte Ramsay's "An Epistle to Moneses. In Imitation of Ovid" illuminates women's resistance to centuries of masculine images of women, a tradition of which Pope was merely the latest representative. Ramsay's epistle creates a heroic situation unlike any in the *Heroides*.[37] Her Ardelia is neither an abandoned mistress, a rejected or unjustly accused wife, or a hapless maiden. She has voluntarily fled temptation before succumbing to dishonor, a remedy she laments but steadfastly maintains. Ardelia is not a passive victim of masculine persuasion. She is a chaste young woman capable of self-defense. The epistle emanates from her chosen stronghold rather than from the site of banishment or desertion. Likewise, Moneses' name ("alone / delight," a plant with one blossom) suggests potential Ovidian transformation, but his story diverges from, for example, the story of Narcissus in the *Metamorphoses*.[38] Ramsay probably chose the name to suggest Moneses' masculine vanity, his indifference to the well-being of an affectionate woman, but Ardelia, unlike Echo, is not about to die for her lover. Ramsay's epistle reveals the misogyny latent in Ovid's repeated focus on helpless, ruined women and callous gods or men. Within the boundaries of cultural constraints (for example, Ardelia flees home rather than confront Moneses, and she cannot imagine a second lover), Ramsay imagines a new feminine response. Ardelia loves passionately but evades seduction; feminine will overcomes feminine weakness in defense of feminine honor. "An Epistle to Moneses" reveals Ovid's limited conception of femininity and sponsors a more admirable model of feminine heroism.

Ramsay's appropriations of "Eloisa to Abelard" in the service of Ovidian revision suggest an intermediate status for Pope's poem. Like other women imitators, Ramsay found Eloisa's expressions of grief plausible and moving. But while Elizabeth Hands rejected the poem after detecting Eloisa's "rage and madness," Ramsay reinstated Eloisa's expressions in an exemplary context. This conservative, but distinctly feminist, maneuver acknowledged Pope's achievement, his simulation of feminine passion, but it adjusted his creation to reflect feminine honor, dignity, and strength.

A similar impulse distinguishes Tollet's, Pye's, Curtis's, Blamire's, and Seward's rewritings of "Eloisa." Though all their heroines are victims—a predicament indispensable to the genre—each boasts her piety and her chastity. None of these versions finds feminine passion blameworthy. Feminine passion is distinctly good, the natural expression of chaste love for a husband or fiancé. Love enables Tollet's Anne Boleyn to achieve magnanimity and Pye's Elgiva to face death rather than accept exile from her husband. Zelida strives for philosophical calm, and St. Agnes anticipates a charitable life.

Modern readers may find these writers too compliant with the cultural demand for feminine piety and chastity. But each began as a skeptical reader of Pope, willing to explore the possibility of extending his model of passionate response to virtuous women. To a limited but vital extent, Pope's women readers inscribed their point of view on a popular cultural artifact each time they rewrote "Eloisa to Abelard." Ovid's myth of a femininity vulnerable to illicit passion may not have been shattered by these multiple revisions, but its foundations were shaken.

5

Pope and Women's Poems
"Something like Horace"

Despite the affection most women professed for Pope's early writings, they most often imitated his Horatian satires. Particularly in the early century and midcentury, women writers inhabited a literary culture addicted to satire. Yet Dryden had admitted in his "Discourse Concerning the Original and Progress of Satire" (1692) that "in English, to say Satire, is to mean Reflection, as we use that word in the worst Sense" (*Works*, 4:48). Invective was not an avocation for ladies. Horace, as described by Dryden, offered women writers a model of satire written with delicacy, intended "to correct the Vices and Follies of his Time, and to give the Rules of a Happy and Virtuous Life" (*Works*, 4:59). While declaring Horace the best instructor, Dryden confessed his preference for Juvenal's "vigorous and Masculine Wit" (*Works*, 4:63). But the tactful didacticism Dryden found insipid rendered Horace women's most appropriate model if they chose to write in what was, for at least half the century, the dominant poetic genre.

As bitter, solitary railers, neither Persius nor Juvenal were comfortable models for women, who risked being labeled scolds or disappointed old maids rather than disaffected philosophers. Horace was identified with praise of country retirement, an attitude easily applied to many women's circumstances. He was particularly associated with the satiric epistle, a form that supposed discourse between friends. The epistle generally concentrated on social follies rather than on vices, and conferred praise as well as blame.[1] All of these qualities attracted women writers. The familiar letter was the contemporary literary form most practiced by aristocratic and middle-class women alike.[2] The Horatian satirist's good-natured sociability also ideally characterized ladies, making the verse epistle's persona readily adapt-

able to the female speaker. Because Juvenal represented the satiric
sublime, Horace suited women's favorite pose of unambitious, often
pastoral, muse.

Howard Weinbrot has attributed the strength and richness of
Pope's satire to the poet's mingling of Persian, Horatian, and Juvenalian traditions (*Pope*, 276–330), but cultural forces impelled women
toward Horace as their sole truly practicable model. Weinbrot correctly
notes that most of Pope's imitators failed because they concentrated
on one rather than all three of the poet's influences (*Pope*, 364). But
in women's case, Pope's version of Horace enabled them to write in
what otherwise might have been judged an inappropriate genre for
women. At best, as in Mary Jones's epistles to distinguished friends,
their Horatian satires rise to moments of Juvenalian indignation inspired by Pope's example. Like Pope's, women's poetic essays and
epistles are—as he expressed it in the original title of his "Epilogue
to the Satires: Dialogue I"—"Something like Horace."

Although women had other available models, Pope's imitations
chiefly attracted them. Among many reasons, Pope's mature writings
constituted a broad range of Horatian models, from the epistolary
Essay on Man through the *Epistles to Several Persons* to the imitations.
Jane Brereton, whose first Horatian imitation appeared in 1716, defined Pope's satiric appeal in "On Mr. Nash's Picture at full Length,
between the Busts of Sir Isaac Newton, and Mr. Pope."

> *Pope* is the Emblem of true Wit,
>   The Sun-shine of the Mind;
> Read o'er his Works for Proof of it,
>   You'll endless Pleasure find.[3]

Brereton, like many women, preferred the genial sunshine of Pope's
Horatian pose to the more caustic wit of Juvenalian imitators.

Not only was Pope already an established favorite with women,
but his Horatian persona—including a number of biographical details—could be tailored to suit various women writers. Mary Chandler
provides an early example of such tailoring. Although Chandler's
correspondence has disappeared, enough evidence remains to suggest
some tantalizing parallels between her life and Pope's and to reinforce
the impression that she modeled her Horatian persona on his. Mary
Chandler was born at Malmesbury in 1687, but she spent most of her
life at Bath, where she died in 1745.[4] In her childhood, she, like Pope,

contracted a diseased spine that deformed her and stunted her growth. While Pope's father, a prosperous, retired merchant, privately educated his son to inherit a small fortune, Chandler's father, a Presbyterian minister with two sons, educated his daughter but permitted her to open a millinery shop near the Bath Pump Room when she was only eighteen. While young Pope was serving his poetic apprenticeship in the rarified literary circles of London, Mary Chandler was establishing a thriving business, selling lace to spa visitors. Her brother Samuel reported that she mourned her lack of a classical education but "endeavoured to repair [the loss] by diligently reading, and carefully studying the best modern writers, and as many as she could of the ancient ones, especially the poets, as far as the best translations could assist her. . . . Among these, Horace was her favorite" (Shiels, 5:345).

That Pope was among Chandler's favorite modern writers is beyond dispute. Her brother proudly reported that "Mr. Pope favoured her with [a visit]" (Shiels, 5:353), complimenting her on her poems, and she alludes to him throughout *A Description of Bath . . . With Several Other Poems*.[5] First published in 1733, her title poem pleased enough readers to merit eight editions by 1767. Although only the "Epistle to Dr. Arbuthnot" and two of Pope's Horatian imitations had appeared before the publication in 1736 of Chandler's third edition, which included her occasional poems, Pope's adaptation of Horace's self-characterization may well have influenced hers.

Chandler's "A Letter to the Right Honourable the Lady Russel," though it does not imitate a particular Horatian epistle, participates in the tradition of verse epistles celebrating the virtues of retirement (*Description*, 21–23). The 53-line poem opens "at my low Cottage, on a chearful Morn, / When slanting Beams did ev'ry Scene adorn" (1–2), a typically pastoral scene. Chandler's reference to her "low Cottage" contrasts with her dignified guests, Sir Harry and Lady Russel (the reader might think forward to Pope's description of his "little House, with Trees a-row, / and like its Master, very low," in "The Seventh Epistle of the First Book" [1737], lines 77–78). Chandler, in true Horatian style, has resisted the urge to provide extravagant fare for her guests. Like both Bethel and Pope in "Satire IIii," she explains, "My Treat was homely, and my Table small, / My Cloth and Dishes clean, and that was all: / For thus it suited to my low Estate" ("Letter to Russel," 5–7). Pope had described himself among his great visitors in "Satire IIi," when "*St. John* mingles with my friendly bowl" and Peterborough "forms my Quincunx" (127–30), and he had announced

in "Satire IIii" that "no Turbots dignify my boards" (141). A Horatian
recluse provides for his or her guests a retreat from more sophisticated
ways of life. Over breakfast, Chandler relates, "Hum'rous [was] our
Talk, and innocently gay" ("Letter to Russel," 9). So far, she describes
the traditional "Feast of Reason and . . . Flow of Soul" (Pope, "Sat.
IIi," 128), but the conversation soon turns toward a characteristically
feminine concern, the real topic of the poem.

   "Our Subjects [were] various," reports Chandler, "Manners, Men,
and Play" ("Letter to Russel," 10). Up to this point, the speaker could
be Pope. But Chandler adds, "And Love, and Wedlock: This our
fav'rite Theme" (11). While, in "Satire IIi," Pope ignored Fortescue's
suggestion that he cure his insomnia by marrying (15), Chandler's
failure to marry preoccupies her friends. She must endure their semi-
serious attempts to arrange her life.

> "Maid! *said Sir Harry*, come, 'tis Time to wed;
> "By Sympathy chuse C—— to be your Head.
> "Two Bodies so exactly paired! 'tis plain
> "Heav'n made the Match, and destin'd him the Man."
> My Lady offer'd me her Farmer's Son:
> Sir *Harry* positive for C—— alone.
> Soon I accepted: Either was my Choice.
>
>   ("Letter to Russel," 13–19)

It is difficult to imagine Pope, or any male Horatian, recounting a
friend's suggestion that he marry a woman because she is equally
crippled. Lady Russel's obliging condescension in offering Chandler
"her Farmer's Son" appears merely humorous until the poet informs
us that the young man was present as her guest. At that point, Lady
Russel's lighthearted suggestion appears a potential source of embar-
rassment. The spinster's status makes her appropriate sport even
among her guests.

   Chandler's response to her friends' raillery teases them in return
and reverses her position among them from object of laughter to moral
exemplar. She begins by appearing to accept Sir Harry's advice: "So
I may wed, I'm not exceeding nice" ("Letter to Russel," 21). But her
ensuing description of the qualities she demands of a husband ("True
to his Country, and Fair Virtue's Cause; / Unaw'd, unbrib'd, by Pow'r,
or by Applause," 26–27) reveals that she is "exceeding nice." Few
men could match Chandler's expectations, despite the deformity and
spinsterhood that have invited her companions' mirth. Three years

before, Pope had characterized himself, at the climax of "Satire IIi," as "to Virtue Only and Her Friends, A Friend" (121). In the "Epistle to Dr. Arbuthnot," he described the abuses he had suffered throughout his career, "Welcome for thee, fair Virtue!" (358). Joining Chandler's praise of C—— (who meets these requirements) with Sir Harry's description of C——'s body "so exactly pair'd" to hers, we suspect a veiled allusion to P——, or Pope, as her ideal man. At least she explicitly asserts that a Pope-like man is her ideal male counterpart, before she breaks the poem's tension with a lighthearted interlude. Perhaps Chandler believed it would be more ingratiating for the female speaker to declare her expectation of a spouse's righteousness than to proclaim her own. Pope functions as her alter ego. Chandler identifies herself with his professional and political integrity but protects her feminine identification with private life. The allusion to Pope's famous resistance to aristocratic corruption enables Chandler to parry her titled friends' well-meaning, but intrusive, suggestion.

In her second, brief verse paragraph, Chandler reveals the young farmer's presence but "fears" that a "young and fairer" rival, also present, might "win his Heart" ("Letter to Russel," 35–37). Her tone here is rather melodramatic and keeps her reader and companions in suspense: is she genuinely sorry that no worthy man is available? Her penultimate paragraph immediately removes all doubt and changes the tone, dramatically, to one of lofty apology, quite similar to Pope's technique in "Satire IIi," "Satire IIii," and the "Epistle to Dr. Arbuthnot."

> Thus far in Mirth.—But now for steady Truth;
> I'm climb'd above the Scale of fickle Youth.
> From Pain of Love I'm perfectly at Ease:
> My Person Nature never form'd to please.
> Friendship's the sweetest Joy in human Life;
> 'Tis *that* I wish—and not to be a Wife.
>
> ("Letter to Russel," 38–43)

Similar to his "Satires" and "Epistle," where Pope finally defends his character by proclaiming himself a good friend, Chandler defends her choice of a single life by claiming her preference for friendship. Her dispassionate assessment of her appearance reinforces her claim to sober maturity. Her choice of "the sweetest Joy in human Life," as she sits at ease among teasing but affectionate friends in her garden, seems judicious and authentic.

Chandler concludes by protesting that she has written these "artless lines" only at the command of Lady Russel ("Letter to Russel," 45). After her noble defense of friendship, she reverts to the pose of rural muse, disclaiming any pretense of artifice. Her verses are "rough as the Road on which I gave them Birth, / Dull as the clouded Moon, or barren Heath" (48–49). Returning to the insistent humility of her poem's opening lines, Chandler brings her poem back to its rustic compass and rests her tone several notches below that of her self-apology. Her artful artlessness is perfectly within the tradition of Horatian translation with which she was familiar, and it recalls Pope's mastery of rhetorical manipulation. Whether Chandler was deliberately recalling Pope's recent imitations of Horace (her poem ends by praising Lady Russel's "Virtue strong," 51) or simply demonstrating the possibility of adapting a popular genre to women's lives and concerns—naturally more private and often rural—will probably never be known. While Horace and his male imitators employ retirement as a vantage point for comment on public life, Chandler focuses her poem on a conversation private among relaxed friends but especially vital, as vital as any public scandal, to women. Yet her private concerns become an opportunity to compliment her better-known friends C—— and Lady Russel and to declare her devotion to friendship and virtue. A woman's experience may appear more limited, but it provides equal opportunity for the kinds of reflections appropriate to her chosen genre.

Chandler's image of herself as a sickly, ill-shaped, female Horatian recluse, who prefers her distinguished friendships and her muse to marriage, recalls Pope's frequent autobiographical references to his own stature, friendships, hospitality, and bachelor status. Mary Chandler seems to have felt the applicability of many of Pope's images to her own, distinctly feminine verse. Chandler seems moreover to have identified with Pope's characterization of himself, and she may have cast herself as a female version of his Horatian persona. In any case, she followed him in publishing a recognizable version of herself as heroine of her poem, a bolder stroke for an unmarried milliner than for a genteel male poet.

Mary Leapor also appropriated Pope's satiric persona, emphasizing at times her different gender and circumstances, but finally gaining authority as a Horatian speaker. The opening of Leapor's "An Epistle to a Lady" (*Poems*, 38–41) borrows from Pope its illusion of conversational exchange: "In vain, dear Madam, yes in vain you strive, / Alas!

to make your luckless *Mira* thrive" (1–2). Leapor has apparently been discussing her poverty with a patron (probably Bridget Freemantle), and the poem promises an economic discussion similar to Pope's epistles "On the Use of Riches." Instead, Leapor first concentrates on reversing Pope's metaphorical compliments to Martha Blount in his "Epistle to a Lady." In the conclusion of his poem, Pope designates Martha as Apollo's darling: "This Phoebus promised (I forget the year) / When those blue eyes first opened on the sphere; / Ascendant Phoebus watch'd that hour with care" (283–85). Pope construes Martha's modest circumstances as proof that Apollo "deny'd the Pelf / That buys your sex a Tyrant o'er itself" and granted instead "Sense, Good-humour, and a Poet" (287–88, 292). In Leapor's "Epistle," Mira, a Martha manqué, mourns that "no golden Planet bent its Rays on me" (4). She mimics Pope's coy refusal to specify Martha's age (with echoes of Swift's birthday poems to Stella): "'Tis twenty Winters, (if it is no more) / To speak the Truth it may be twenty-four . . . Since *Mira's* Eyes first open'd on the Sun" (ll.5–6, 8). But Mira's birth was no glamorous astrological event: "'Twas when the Flocks on slabby Hillocks lie, / And the cold Fishes rule the watry Sky" (9–10). Leapor's repulsive images contrast humorously with Pope's warm metaphor of Phoebus ripening gold and human spirits. A woman born amidst slabby hillocks under watery skies has little chance of becoming Apollo's darling or anyone else's. Mira, neglected by Sol, is simply poor. Leapor's self-description as Mira, the reverse of Pope's Martha, is both comical and, in the context of her wistful tributes to Pope in other poems, poignant. Mira, unlike Martha, has had no Apollo/Pope to waft her from the slabby hillocks.

But the influence of Pope's Horatian style is visible in the structure and resolution of Leapor's "An Epistle to a Lady." Mira achieves self-possession in the course of Leapor's epistle. After confessing that she foolishly dreams of wealth while her kitchen goes unswept and her clothes unmended, Mira confronts her fear of death that renders both fantasies and actual poverty inconsequential. As the 66-line poem concludes, she summons courage to "fall resign'd beneath the mighty Blow " (62), recalling that her fate will be shared that day with thousands (65–66). Mira's comical self-abuse throughout the first half of the poem makes her final serenity seem hard-won and touchingly precarious. Leapor insists that even obscure cookmaids yearn for wealth and recognition, and that they need as much courage as the more fortunate to face death. Leapor earns her poem's final tone of poignant resignation through preceding shifts, from humor to regret to earnest inquiry. Such shifts are crucial to Pope's technique in, for example, the "Epistle to Dr. Arbuthnot," which rises from world-weariness to moral indignation, then subsides to acceptance. Although Pope's images echo throughout Leapor's "An Epistle to a Lady," her poem is finally most indebted to her study of tonal modulations in Pope's Horatian poems.

Other poems in Leapor's volume follow Pope's imitations of Horatian characters. In "The Way of the World," Sir Wealthy, Sylvia, Alcidas, Courtine, and others illustrate the consequences of flattery (Leapor, 90–97). "The Way of the World" particularly suggests that Pope's example enabled Leapor's satiric comments on the gentry. Her characterization of Sir Wealthy, Sublimo, and Virginius probably owes as much to Pope's portrayal of Bubo, Timon, and Sir Balaam as to Leapor's experience with potential patrons. Pope's vignettes helped Leapor shape her perceptions into universal satiric types. In "The Way of the World," Leapor's final portrait of the good man ("Not sway'd by Int'rest, nor in Passion hurl'd, / But walks a calm Spectator through the World," 119–20) resembles Pope's description of his father in "Epistle to Dr. Arbuthnot." She probably found it impossible to construe her own father, a gardener, as the idealized inhabitant of a "fair Dome" blessed with "Peace and Plenty" ("Way of the World," 131–32); hence the secondhand type. Pope's Horatian style robbed such poems as "The Way of the World" of the conviction based on personal experience, but it gave Leapor a voice in which to assess her "betters." Behind her Horatian/Popeian mask, the Brackley cook-maid defined ideal men and condemned boorish patrons. Without such a persona, it is difficult to imagine Leapor assuming the cultural authority associated with satire.

In "Essay on Friendship," Leapor synthesizes allusions from several Horatian poems to adjust Pope's female psychology (*Poems*, 74–80). Addressed to Artemisia/Bridget Freemantle, this poem rebuts the assumption of "saucy Wits" "that Women's Friendships, like a certain Fly, / Are hatch'd i' th'Morning and at Ev'ning die (8–10). Pope had applied this image to Sappho in "Epistle to a Lady" (27–28), culminating his introductory assertion of feminine inconstancy. Leapor resents the fact that "our Sex has been from early Time / A constant Topick for satirick Rhyme" ("Friendship," 11–12). She admits that "we're often found, / Or lost in Passion, or in Pleasures drown'd" (13–14), but she asserts that there are some women "who keep the mod'rate

Way, / Can think an Hour, and be calm a Day" (17–18). So far, Leapor's opinions echo Pope's, granting the justice of his charges and idealizing feminine moderation. Leapor's ideal women resemble Pope's portrait of Martha. Such women

> . . . ne'er were known to start into a Flame,
> Turn pale or tremble at a losing Game.
> Run *Chloe's* shape or *Delia's* features down,
> Or change Complexion at *Celinda's* Gown:
> But still serene, compassionate and kind,
> Walk thro' Life's Circuit with an equal Mind.
>
> (19–24)

Although Leapor's tribute closely follows Pope's, she borrows from "Epistle to Dr. Arbuthnot" the image of the good man walking innoxious through his age (395).

Through the rest of Leapor's "Essay on Friendship," mingled images of masculine and feminine traits modify Pope's notion that a good woman is a softer man. For example, Pope had claimed that Calypso "charm'd" men with her "Strange graces" and "stranger flights" ("Epistle to a Lady," 46, 49). Leapor contends that "Good-Breeding, Wit, and Learning, all conspire / To charm Mankind, and make the World admire" ("Friendship," 33–34). Her notion that learning confers charm on a woman differs sharply from Pope's conventional opinion. Leapor cautions, however, that none of these qualities are essential to friendship: "The main Ingredient is an honest Heart" (36). Her statement recalls Pope's declaration in *Essay on Man* that "an honest man's the noblest work of God" (4.248). By attributing to women qualities Pope attributed to men, Leapor extends his claim that an ideal woman combines masculine and feminine traits.

Leapor's unconventional assignment of gendered traits extends to herself as the speaker of "Essay on Friendship." She invokes a potentially immortal Muse, a pose more reminiscent of Margaret Cavendish than of most eighteenth-century women poets.

> Now let the Muse (who takes no Courtier's Fee)
> Point to her Friend—and future Ages see
> (If this shall live till future Ages be)
> One line devoted to *Fidelia's* praise.
>
> (39–42)

Leapor imagines herself as Pope often presents himself in the satires: the sole poet left unbribed by patronage to craft memorials of pure friendship. Her tone seems indignant, like Pope's weary plea "Yet let this Verse . . . remain" in the "Epilogue to the Satires" (1.172–73).

Given her plea for immortality, readers might be disappointed by Leapor's description of Fidelia as a compound of Belinda and Martha Blount: her "harmless Thoughts are sprightly as her Eyes, / By Nature chearful, and by Nature wise" ("Friendship," 44–45). Leapor, deprived of Pope's national, political arena, applied his style to her celebration of women's friendship. Although his public mode jars with her private concerns in this poem, we see her straining for a pose other than domestic muse, trying to redefine assumptions about women as friends and as poets. Her aversion to dining with duchesses—"To sit with formal and assenting face" (52)—aligns Leapor with Pope as he sat with sad civility when dunces called and with Pope's Addison when he assented with a civil leer ("Epistle to Dr. Arbuthnot," 37, 201). The female satirist, by implication, suffers fools as impatiently as does the male. As for her chosen companion, Leapor describes Artemisia as a cross between Pope's Burlington and his Martha Blount. She has "a Taste . . . giv'n / By mighty Nature and the Stamp of Heav'n" and a "Soul unstain'd with Envy or with Pride," which "unmov'd, can see gilt Chariots whirling by, / Or view the Wretched with a melting Eye" ("Friendship," 64–65, 72–73). Leapor's characterization of Artemisia gives new meaning to Pope's concept of a softer man, incorporating taste and learning into the ideal feminine personality.

Leapor concludes her "Essay on Friendship" after a series of portraits of women patterned closely on those in Pope's "Epistle to a Lady." Her final paragraph returns to "Epistle to Bathurst" for its conversational image. Leapor concludes: "Grave Authors differ—Men of Sense incline / This way or that—Opinions rarely join. / Their Thoughts will vary. Why? Because they're free" (120–22). The only indisputable truth is that "our chief Task is seldom to offend" and that friendship is "life's great Blessing" (124, 125). In Pope's poem, as in the *Essay on Man* and several Horatian imitations, the illusion of philosophical dispute between cultured friends reinforces his authoritative tone. Leapor assigns the same authority to herself and Bridget Freemantle as they debate the essence of friendship. Her amalgamation of feminine topic with masculine authority is at times awkward, but by assimilating Pope's strategies, Leapor liberated herself from the self-deprecation that plagued many of the century's "untutored geniuses." The extent of her success remains a remarkable, if finally incomplete, accomplishment.[6]

Mary Jones also found a version of Pope's Horatian persona conducive to her relationships with aristocratic friends. In the "Advertisement" to her *Miscellanies in Prose and Verse* (1750), Jones insists she would never have undertaken such a "disagreeable . . . task" as publishing, except "for the sake of a relation, grown old and helpless thro' a series of misfortunes," whom the subscription would benefit (*Miscellanies*, v). She dismisses her poems, claiming it "quite accidental, that her thoughts ever rambled into rhyme" (vi). The first poem in her volume challenges this disclaimer. "An Epistle to Lady Bowyer" passionately defends Jones's right to compose verse on her own terms, a defense hardly worth making if her poems were nothing but accidental rambles.

Jones's 127-line epistle derives from Pope's "Epistle to Dr. Arbuthnot" and "Epistle to Burlington," suggesting she deliberately adopted Pope's tone of righteous indignation from those poems. Her poem opens with breathless exclamations similar to Pope's in "Epistle to Dr. Arbuthnot": "How much of paper's spoiled! what floods of ink! / And yet how few, how very few can think!" ("To Lady Bowyer," 1–2). Jones evokes the same horde of scribblers Pope deprecates. She admits, "The knack of writing is an easy trade" (3)—Pope called it "an idle trade" in "Epistle to Dr. Arbuthnot" (129)—but she complains that few have the brains to write well.

> Once in an age, one genius may arise,
> With wit well cultur'd, and with learning wise.
> Like some tall oak, behold his branches shoot!
> No tender scions springing at the root.
> Whilst lofty *Pope* erects his laurell'd head,
> No lays, like mine, can live beneath his shade.
> Nothing but weeds and moss, and shrubs are found.
> Cut, cut them down, why cumber they the ground?
>
> (5–12)

Pope, who defined genius in his "Essay on Criticism" as the marriage of wit and judgment, inevitably occurs to Jones as the fulfillment of his own ideal. Her rather unhappy comparison of Pope to a tall oak recalls Lady Winchilsea's choice of a large mastiff for a flattering metaphor. But the image of a lofty tree absorbing sun needed by vulnerable saplings aptly describes Pope's intimidating effect on such poets as Jones. Her very wish for obliteration ("Cut, cut them down") echoes Pope's "Shut, shut the door" ("Epistle to Dr. Arbuthnot," 1), as if Jones wished to demonstrate that she wrote in Pope's shadow—or worse, that dependence on Pope had obliterated her individual style.

Yet Jones exudes passion throughout "An Epistle to Lady Bowyer," the direct result of her Popeian mimicry. She cries: "And yet you'd have me write!—For what? for whom? / To curl a fav'rite in a dressing room?" (13–14). Her question parallels Pope's weary "Why did I write?" ("To Arbuthnot," 125), drawing from Jones a similar defense of her creativity. Lady Bowyer has urged her "to get a name" ("To Lady Bowyer," 18), an ambition with questionable associations for women in the middle of the eighteenth century. Yet Jones never considers the gendered implications of fame in this poem. She frames her apologia entirely in terms of Pope's.

> Alas! I'd live unknown, unenvy'd too;
> 'Tis more than *Pope* with all his wit can do.
>
> . . . .
>
> The world and I are no such cordial friends;
> I have my purpose, they their various ends.
> I say my pray'rs, and lead a sober life,
> Nor laugh at *Cornus*, or at *Cornus'* wife.
> What's fame to me, who pray, and pay my rent?
> If my friends know me honest, I'm content.
>
> (19–20, 23–28)

Pope had pleaded "O let me live my own," asserting "I was not born for Courts or great Affairs, / I pay my Debts, believe, and say my Pray'rs" ("To Arbuthnot," 261, 267–68). He had defended his right to privacy as the world's most famous poet, a claim Jones cannot make for herself. But Jones discerns a curious equivalency between herself, a woman urged to publish her privately circulated poems, and Pope, a man disowning ambition after a long public career. Her assimilation into Pope's Horatian pose is so complete that she overlooks its gendered nuances. For example, Pope joked, "Poor *Cornus* sees his frantic Wife elope, / And curses Wit, and Poetry, and *Pope*" ("To Arbuthnot," 25–26). Jones refuses to laugh at the couple, but she mentions Pope's indelicate anecdote. "What's fame to me . . . If my friends know me honest" strikes the pose of a Horatian recluse, but with ambiguous implications in an era obssessed with women's reputations. By fitting herself to Pope's Horatian role, Jones claims more freedoms than the license to write.

As "An Epistle to Lady Bowyer" continues, Jones departs somewhat from her Popeian model to defend herself from the indignities of turning "Auth'ress" (33). Unlike Pope, she is encouraged to flatter a Bubo-like patron. She protests "I've neither friend, nor interest at court" (41), except for her friend Martha Lovelace. Jones execrates "the tiny great" in terms worthy of Pope, as "patriots, who sell their country for a place" (50, 53). She imagines visiting a prospective patron and, while waiting for him to dress, being entertained with gossip about "what my lady eats, and how she rests: / How much she gave for such a birth-day gown" (63–64); "Sick at the news, impatient for my lord, / I'm forc'd to hear, nay smile at ev'ry word" (66–67). She echoes Pope's disgust when, "Sick of Fops, and Poetry, and Prate," he abjured the theater ("To Arbuthnot," 229). Her distress when the maid assumes her interest in such feminine inanities strips Jones for a second of her Popeian mask; to this servant she appears not an indignant Horatian poet but just another female supplicant. Jones turns the tables on her potential patron by casting him as Timon from the "Epistle to Burlington," from whom Pope had departed "sick of his civil pride" (166). Like Timon, "his lordship seldom reads" ("To Lady Bowyer," 72). His footman offers to critique and "recommend your poetry—and you" (79). Jones retreats, "Shock'd at his civil impudence" (80), as Pope had withdrawn from Timon's villa. She turns for relief to Nevil Lord Lovelace, embodiment of magnanimity. "Too honest to be great," he alone merits her praise ("To Lady Bowyer," 95).

Having commended Lovelace, Jones returns to her Popeian model: "Peace to the rest. I can be no man's slave; / I ask for nothing, tho' I nothing have" (98–99). This magisterial dismissal, similar to Pope's "Peace to all such!" ("To Arbuthnot," 193), suggests the difficulties Jones faced among her well-born friends because she was a clergyman's dependent sister. Her indignant refusal to be a slave certainly exaggerates her circumstances, but it probably reflects an interior struggle for dignity and intellectual independence. As Pope had concluded "To Arbuthnot" by defending his parentage, Jones concludes "To Lady Bowyer" by describing her parents.

> Of honest parents, not of great, I came;
> Not known to fortune, quite unknown to fame.

Frugal and plain, at no man's cost they eat,
Nor knew a baker's, or a butcher's, debt.
O be their precepts ever in my eye!
For one has learnt to live, and one to die.
Long may her widow'd age by heav'n be lent
Among my blessings! and I'm well content.

(106–13)

Jones's parents were a humbler version of Pope's. He had boasted "gentle Blood" and hereditary fortune ("To Arbuthnot," 388, 390). While Pope's father was "Healthy by Temp'rance and by Exercise" (401), Jones's parents were frugal and plain from economic necessity. Yet they were proudly independent, avoiding debt, and Jones lives according to their example.

Jones's heritage of proud independence explains why she construes her career as an imitation of Pope's as he presents it in "Epistle to Dr. Arbuthnot." It must have been difficult for Jones to avoid feeling dependent on the friends whose estates she visited, friends she may have met while working as a governess. Recalling parents who preferred abstaining to accumulating butcher's and baker's debts, Jones repudiates patronage as slavery and proudly proclaims, "I ask for nothing": "No household lord, for better or for worse. / No monstrous sums to tempt my soul to sin, / But just enough to keep me plain and clean" ("To Lady Bowyer," 119–21). Like Pope, whose muse "serv'd to ease some Friend, not Wife" ("To Arbuthnot," 131), Jones seeks only to amuse her friends: "And if sometimes . . . / *Charlot* should smile, or you approve my lay, / Enough for me" ("To Lady Bowyer," 122–24). With this final allusion (to *The Rape of the Lock*, line 6), Jones refuses the quest for literary fame, claiming instead her allegiance to Pope's Horatian ideal.

Jones's relationship to Pope in this poem is paradoxical. In her "Advertisement," she gave the classic feminine excuse for creative accomplishment: her poems were accidents published for altruistic reasons. "An Epistle to Lady Bowyer" offers a more plausible explanation. Jones's creativity enabled her to serve and amuse her wealthy friends—to reciprocate their hospitality. Through poetry, Jones satisfied her need to feel independent, despite the disparity between her own and her friends' incomes. This craving for independence drew her to Pope's Horatian self-defense in "Epistle to Dr. Arbuthnot." In her poem, she matched her persona to Pope's, even where his statements poorly suited a contemporary woman's biography. Her startling contempt for reputation in the poem reflects Jones's distress over the economic and social constraints on her activities. By claiming the Horatian recluse's self-possession, Jones avoided one obvious avenue to publication and critical favor, the potentially humiliating quest for patronage. She demanded the freedom to write for her purposes and no one else's.

But insisting on Pope's precedent ironically impeded Jones's quest for independence. Pope's persona in "Epistle to Dr. Arbuthnot" was the pose of a man who had pursued and attained success in the literary marketplace. He manipulated facts to defend himself from literary enemies made over a long, contentious career. Though equally a pose, Jones's persona denied her the option of pursuing a public literary career. Jones permitted herself the pride, the creative drive, the satiric impulses of a male writer, but she refused to entertain the ambition that would have driven an equally capable man to the marketplace. "An Epistle to Lady Bowyer" reveals that Jones took her poetry much more seriously than she claimed in her "Advertisement." But while enhancing her self-esteem, Jones's Horatian pose justified her ladylike determination to remain a literary amateur. Jones stopped publishing after the *Miscellanies* established her literary reputation. Apparently iconoclastic, "An Epistle to Lady Bowyer" finally confirms Jones's desire for conventionally feminine privacy.

Pope's Horatian style nevertheless endowed Jones's poems with passion and authority. She accompanied her most ambitious poem, "Of Patience: An Epistle to The Right Hon. Samuel Lord Masham," with a table of contents like that of the *Essay on Man* (Jones, 8–25). Throughout the 300-line poem, Jones borrows rhetorical tactics from Pope. "But granting nobler motives to the few" (16) hails from Pope's concession in "To Bathurst" that "useful, I grant, [gold] serves what life requires" (29). Her use of illustrative characters resembles Pope's. She generalizes Pope's "But touch me, and no Minister so sore" ("Satire IIi," 76) into "The man of wit in many parts is sore, / Touch but a genius, and he smarts all o'er" ("Patience," 36–37). Her balanced constructions, rhetorical questions, and commands ("Behold the man of luxury and wine!" 194) emulate Pope's brisk arguments in the *Essay on Man*. Jones directly takes her rationale for human suffering from Pope's *Essay*.

> Know, thankless man! that he who rules the ball,
> In goodness infinite permits it all.

For nat'ral evil, rightly understood,
Works but the grand design, our moral good.

(236–39)

Her Popeian style allows Jones to reason with Lord Masham "man
to man," the manner in which Pope had addressed Lords Bolingbroke
and Bathurst. Nothing in the poem hints Jones's gender, probably
because such allusions would not conform to her conception of the
appropriate style for her philosophical topic and distinguished addressee.

Jones's "Of Desire: An Epistle to The Honourable Miss Lovelace"
is similarly redolent of Popeian tactics and phrases (Jones, 26–35).
Jones's sole innovation in this 179-line poem is to gender-balance her
satiric examples. Fulvia, Elvira, and Dyctinna vie in folly with Cotta,
Courtine, and an avaricious cleric. In another of Jones's Popeian incar-
nations—"No ties forgot, no duties left unpaid, / No lays unfinish'd,
and no aching head" (165–66)—the examples illustrate that "hope
springs eternal in the human breast" (Pope, *Essay on Man*, 1.95).
Jones's characters are conventional: Fulvia dreams of a coach-and-six;
Cotta, of political office. But while Pope's illustrations of human traits
are usually masculine, Jones at least provides both masculine and
feminine examples. This slight adjustment indicates both the advantage and danger of Jones's Popeian impersonation. She speaks with
engaging confidence, but—unlike Chandler's and Leapor's versions—
her Horatian role leaves little room for a woman's distinct perspective.

Women's poems throughout the century also criticized or supplemented specific Horatian poems, such as the *Essay on Man*. When
John Nichols reprinted Elizabeth Tollet's 261-line "The Microcosm"
in his *Select Collection* (6:71–80), he observed it "may be considered as
a very judicious answer to what has been advanced on the same
subject by Bolingbroke and Pope, tending to depreciate human nature" (6:71).[7] Tollet herself intended the poem as a reply to Henry
Baker's "The Universe" (1734), a poem Baker "intended to restrain
the pride of man."[8] Published in the wake of the *Essay*, both poems
supported Pope's philosophy, although from opposing vantage
points. "The Microcosm," arguably more original than "The Universe"
because it is less dependent on Pope's evocations of cosmic order,
celebrates the human body and mind as God's most miraculous gift.
Tollet does not contradict the *Essay on Man*, although Pope's poem
cautions humans not to regard themselves as the sole important aspect

of creation. "The Microcosm" supplements the *Essay*, reminding humans that God granted their "superior excellence" to stimulate reverence for "the great Creator's mystic ways" (229, 238). At times, "The Microcosm" echoes the *Essay*, applying Pope's reasoning about the creation to the smaller world of the body. As in the great chain of being, human limbs were made "each for itself, and each for mutual aid" (36). Preeminence over the elephant and whale, tamed by human hands, was not granted to stimulate pride: "In these great gifts their greater Author own" (75). As for tiny creatures,

> Nor think thy Maker was in part unkind,
> And to minuter objects left thee blind,
> When in the microscope thou canst descry
> The gnat's sharp spear, the muscles of a fly.

> (144–47)

These verses do not challenge Pope—"Why has not Man a microscopic eye? / For this plain reason, Man is not a Fly" (*Essay*, 1.193–94)—but suggest the same truth from a different perspective: God gave man not microscopic eyes but microscopes, to encourage not pride but humility. Tollet encourages her reader to "acknowledge Him, who taught mankind to try / The curious use of that fictitious eye" (154–55).

The *Essay on Man* discourages curiosity, reflecting Pope's fear that modern intellectuals, armed with Newtonian physics and boundless confidence in reason, might attempt to transcend human limits: "All quit their sphere, and rush into the skies" (*Essay*, 1.124). "The Microcosm" welcomes scientific inquiry but equally cautions against prying into secrets of the universe: "Ambition! never weep for worlds unknown; / But learn to be contented with thy own" (182–83). The stars were given for "necessary use," not Icarus-like exploration. Tollet's conclusion urges pious use of God-given curiosity.

> Can thy small heart this ample world contain?
> Yet there has God infixed the keen desire;
> Excites, and not forbids thee to inquire:
> A pleasing task! though none can comprehend
> Its first beginning, or its latest end.
> How well was that advice, 'Thyself to know,'
> Ascribed to Heaven by sages long ago!

> (245–51)

Instead of contradicting Pope, Tollet echoes his advice. Only cursory readers could construe "The Microcosm" as an answer to Pope's rebuke of human complacency. Tollet urges readers to consider their limbs and faculties miraculous, and this appraisal properly leads to worship of the Creator. For Tollet, as for Pope, to "know thyself" is more humbling than self-aggrandizing. "The Microcosm" supplements Pope's survey of the "vast chain of being" (*Essay*, 1.237) with Tollet's inverse, but complementary, survey of the "universe in man" ("Microcosm," 6). Contrary to Nichols's impression, Tollet, whose education had been approved by Sir Isaac Newton, applied her learning to support Pope amidst the flurry of replies to his poem.

Elizabeth Carter also echoed the *Essay on Man* in her poems, but her attitude toward Pope's poem was critical rather than congenial. While Tollet supported Pope's attitude toward science, one of Carter's earliest published poems contains a passage that implicitly rebukes the *Essay*'s "system of ethics." As he concluded *Essay* 4, Pope summarized his argument that the good man, "slave to no Sect . . . / . . . looks thro' Nature up to Nature's God" (331–32). He reiterated that love for God results from "Self-love . . . push'd to social" (4.353), like the concentric circles radiating from a pebble tossed into a lake: "God loves from whole to parts: but human soul / Must rise from individual to the whole" (4.361–62).

One year after Pope published the *Essay on Man*, Carter composed a 62-line poem, "In Diem Natalem" (1735), before her eighteenth birthday.[9] Her second verse paragraph asks,

> Grant me, great God, a heart to Thee inclin'd:
> Increase my faith, and rectify my mind:
> Teach me betimes to tread thy sacred ways,
> And to thy service consecrate my days.
> Still as thro' life's perplexing maze I stray,
> Be thou the guiding star to mark my way.
> Conduct the steps of my unguarded youth,
> And point their motions to the paths of Truth.
>
> (25–32)

Pope had characterized life as "a mighty maze! but not without a plan," confident that with Bolingbroke's help he could "vindicate the ways of God to man" (*Essay*, 1.6, 16). The *Essay* opens with an image of the two men striding about Bolingbroke's estate in the morning, a metaphor for Pope's brisk, optimistic philosophy. Carter, however, suggests her own isolation and helplessness. Life is a "perplexing maze" in which she wanders at night, "unguarded"—a frightening situation for contemporary women. While Pope and Bolingbroke beat the fields for game, suggesting manly skill and proprietorship, Carter is simply lost, off the beaten track. Her supplication for a ray of light to guide her to the correct path contrasts with Pope's conviction that man will ultimately find his own way to God. "Teach me betimes," she prays; for Carter, the only way to God is through divine revelation. In Carter's poems, God must intercede and incline human hearts to devotion, a complete reversal of Pope's account. His good man, "slave to no Sect," was Carter's reprobate. When she prays, "Be my religion such as taught by thee" ("Diem," 41), this daughter of the rector of Deal clearly refers to Anglican Christianity.

"In Diem Natalem" suggests sufficient motivation for Carter's translation of Crousaz's *Examen*. But like most contemporary women of letters, she frequently alluded to Pope's works in her own poetry. In some poems, Carter merely adapted her allusion to a genteel, feminine, usually Christian context. Other poems by Carter are full-scale revisions of Pope's. "To Miss D'aeth" (1744; *Poems*, 22–25) opens with distinct echoes of Pope's "Epistle to a Lady." While Pope often portrayed himself and his friends at their country retreats, Carter's "Bethia" is in town for the winter season assumed dear to females:

> Say, dear *Bethia*, can thy gentle Mind,
> In hurrying Crowds a genuine Pleasure find?
> Amidst those Scenes the giddy World admires
> That Whim directs, and Levity inspires?
> Where *Folly* each revolving hour employs
> In one mad Circle of unsettled Joys:
> Her Bells she jingles and her Tinsel spreads,
> To please deluded Hearts, and flutt'ring Heads:
> With Baubles arm'd her trifling Race untaught,
> To kill that Foe to human Quiet, Thought.
> With Vanity's fantastic Colours gay
> In Youth's warm Sun the glitt'ring Insects play,
> Careless how soon the wintry Blast must come
> That sweeps their useless Beings to the Tomb.
>
> (1–14)

In "Epistle to a Lady," Pope and Martha Blount surveyed a gallery of ladies pursuing pleasure and sway through a whirl of social adven-

tures. Martha, gazing at these portraits, was further distanced from
the poem's frenzied activity by Pope's concluding tribute. She alone
understood that women's "virtues open fairest in the shade" (202).
Carter's Bethia has been plunged against her will into the "hurrying
Crowds" of the London season. Her "gentle Mind" recoils from the
"mad Circle of unsettled joys," unlike Pope's faded beauties who
glided "round and round" seeking distraction (241). The verse paragraph also alludes to Pope's description of Rufa and Sappho as "morning Insects that in muck begun, / Shine, buzz, and fly-blow in the
setting-sun" (27–28). Carter's metaphor not only rephrases Pope's
image in more decorous language but implies the moral reflection
that will dominate her poem.

Amidst the cacaphony suggested by the hurrying crowds, jingling
bells, tinsel, baubles, and fantastic colors of Carter's imagery, Bethia
sighs for her father's estate. As the poem continues, Bethia conjures
up the peaceful spring landscape of Knolton, questioning the "perverse . . . Fate / That draws [her] far from this congenial State" ("To
Miss D'aeth," 39–40). Carter acknowledges what Pope merely implies
in "Epistle to a Lady": ladies often had little control over their seasonal
locations or activities, and young ladies particularly were expected to
participate in the social rounds of the marriage market. Carter cannot
request that Bethia withdraw from the glittering scene inimical to her
peace, but she can suggest that her friend transform uneasiness into
moral exercise. Knolton's placidity represents no challenge to virtue,
which is only "wak'd to Action by alarming Woes" (52). The poem
ends with a reminder of the spiritual estate Miss D'aeth insures by
behaving virtuously in her London exile.

> Secur'd by Heav'n her fair Possession lies,
> Beyond the Gloom of sublunary Skies.
> . . . .
> And all my lov'd *Bethia* loses here,
> The blooming Walks of Eden shall repair.
>
> (63–64, 67–68)

Carter offers Bethia practical but demanding moral instruction of the
kind Lady Irwin had sought in vain in Pope's "Epistle to a Lady."

"To Miss D'aeth" is also unmistakeably feminine in its emphasis
on dispossession. Many of Pope's later poems refer to men's agricultural techniques, landscape designs, hospitality, even their purchase
or rental of estates, as metaphors for their virtue or vice. In this poem,

Knolton in bloom aptly signifies Bethia's mind, but she no more controls her presence or absence there than she does the seasons. Carter implies that piety comes more easily to women than to men, because women better understand the tenuousness of the human grasp on material possessions. She refutes Pope's assumption that most women (the Miss Blount of his epistle "On her leaving the town after the Coronation," Belinda, Rufa, Sappho, and others) love the town for its prospect of immediate gratification.

As Sylvia Harcstark Meyers has concluded, Carter's poems are interesting today not so much for their poetic merit but "as the work of a woman who wrote as a private person with deep religious feelings" (175). But several of Carter's poems were much admired by her contemporaries. Both Lady Hertford and Catherine Talbot praised her "Ode on Melancholy" (1739), and Samuel Richardson esteemed her "Ode to Wisdom" (1747) so highly that he printed it without her knowledge in *Clarissa*, as the work of his heroine. Carter herself was evidently proud of her elegy "On the Death of Mrs. Rowe" (*Poems*, 10–12). She published the poem twice in *Gentleman's Magazine*—after Elizabeth Rowe's death in 1737, and in 1739. She appended her name to the thoroughly revised 1739 version.

"On the Death of Mrs. Rowe" alludes to several of Pope's poems, invoking an alternative, pious, female poetic tradition. Carter begins by deploring old, misogynistic stereotypes: "Oft' did Intrigue its guilty arts unite, / To blacken the records of female wit" (1–2). Carter could have found many sources of such intrigue, but Pope, through his Sappho, Astraea, and Eliza, had contributed his share.[10] Carter claims a nobler purpose for women's writing:

> To raise the thoughts, and moralize the mind;
> The chaste delights of virtue to inspire,
> And warm the bosom with seraphic fire;
> Sublime the passions, lend devotion wings,
> And celebrate the first great *Cause* of things.
>
> (8–12)

Carter's description conflates two Popeian phrases. In "Epistle to a Lady," Pope urged Martha Blount "to raise the Thought" (250), while in "Epistle to Dr. Arbuthnot," he claimed to have "moralized his song" in his mature poetry (341). Carter typically enjoins women to active rather than passive virtue; they must write and publish poems that inspire principled behavior. Given Pope's repeated emphasis on "th'Eternal Cause" in the *Essay on Man* (for example, 1.130), Carter's demand that women "celebrate the first great *Cause* of things" implies a pious, feminine alternative to masculine heterodoxy.

This impression deepens as Carter describes Elizabeth Rowe, or "Philomela," as the paradigmatic female poet,

> Who charms the fancy, and who mends the heart.
> In her was ev'ry bright distinction join'd,
> Whate'er adorns, or dignifies the mind:
> Her's ev'ry happy elegance of thought,
> Refin'd by virtue, as by genius wrought.
> Each low-born care her pow'rful strains controul,
> And wake the nobler motions of the soul.
>
> (14–20)

Her image is both like and unlike Pope's description of his ideal woman, Martha Blount. In "Epistle to a Lady," Pope claimed that "Woman's at best a Contradiction still" (270), a blend of "feminine" and "masculine" characteristics, such as reserve and frankness, softness and courage. Because she can "raise the Thought and touch the Heart," her "Charm shall grow" even after youthful beauty fades (250, 251). Carter's Philomela not only touched but mended hearts. She, too, harmonized a paradoxical blend of gendered traits, such as adornment and dignity, virtuous refinement and highly wrought genius. But Pope honored Martha chiefly for her common sense and good humor, qualities that insured her personal happiness. Carter honors an artist, whose "pow'rful strains" could "wake the nobler motions of the soul."

Carter's praise for Rowe culminates in a conceit even more extravagant than the conclusion of Pope's "Ode for Musick, on St. Cecilia's Day" (1708). Pope, seeking to surpass Dryden's conclusion where Cecilia's music drew an angel down from heaven, claimed that while Orpheus's "Numbers rais'd a Shade from Hell, Hers lift the Soul to Heav'n" (133–34). In Carter's tribute, Philomela's "heav'nly accents" were so ravishing that angels hung earthward in attention.

> They, in the midnight hour, beheld her rise
> Beyond the verge of sublunary skies;
> Where, rapt in joys to mortal sense unknown,
> She felt a flame extatic as their own.
>
> ("Death of Rowe," 33–36)

Elizabeth Rowe was best known for her rapturous devotional verse. Dr. Carter had warned his daughter not to emulate Rowe's enthusiasm. The conceit is therefore an appropriate, and affectionate, allusion to Rowe's writings. But on a less traditional level, Carter's vision of the poet rising heavenward on the strength of her own song replaces the myth of Cecilia, celebrated by male wits since Dryden, with a powerful, female-created myth based on a contemporary woman's achievement.

Carter's Popeian allusions grow particularly resonant in her final verse paragraph, which echoes the conclusion of the *Essay on Man*.

> O while distinguish'd in the realms above,
> The blest abode of harmony and love,
> Thy happy spirit joins the heav'nly throng,
> Glows with their transports, and partakes their song;
> Fixt on my soul shall thy example grow,
> And be my genius and my guide below;
> To this I'll point my first, my noblest views,
> Thy spotless verse shall regulate my Muse.
>
> ("Death of Rowe," 37–44)

The contrast is almost comically pointed. Pope had hailed Bolingbroke, whom Carter considered a pernicious influence, as his "Genius," his "guide, philosopher, and friend" (*Essay*, 4.390). Carter asks a saint "to be my genius and my guide." Pope imagined future statesmen reading his verse after Bolingbroke's name had flown "along the stream of Time . . . / . . . and [gathered] all its fame" (4.383–84). From Carter's point of view, Pope's wish for fame in time suggested insufficient piety. She too wished "for fame, / That joins my own to Philomela's name" (47–48), and she reiterated her wish by signing her name to the poem. But Pope asked the worldly Bolingbroke to help him cope with temporal vicissitude: "happily to steer / From grave to gay, from lively to severe" (4.379–80). When Carter claimed to copy Philomela's "original" (46), she aspired to the "heav'nly throng," an eternal community of praise that finally supplanted individual fame. Finally, Pope's conclusion admitted Bolingbroke's controversial reputation. Carter's "genius" was a woman of undisputed piety, the author of "spotless verse." If "On the Death of Mrs. Rowe" announces a new, feminine poetic tradition, Carter defined that tradition partly by subverting the themes and images of the most prominent contemporary male poet.

Later in the century, Anna Seward responded directly to Pope's "Epistle to a Lady" in her "Epistle to Cornelia" (*Works*, 110–23). Unlike Lady Irwin, Seward did not rely principally on Pope's phrases or techniques, although she composed the 344-line verse epistle in heroic couplets. She seized the controlling image of Pope's epistle and turned it against him. As Seward's poem opens, the speaker, a version of Seward, has received a letter from Belinda extolling Cornelia's recent visit. Seward doubts Cornelia enjoyed the occasion and wonders why Belinda invited her studious friend to "join her modish crew" (6).

> Friend of my youth, what Cynic could upbraid
> The laugh of scorn, when in thy tints array'd,
> Those consecrated hours before us roll,
> Their feasts of reason, and their flow of soul?
> Thee, summon'd to adorn that festal board
> With all that Friendship, Science, Wit afford,
>
> . . . .
> While she in mystic rites consumes the morn,
> The fancied vestment studious to adorn.

(25–30, 35–36)

Seward's opening strategy casts herself and Cornelia as equivalents of Pope and his gentlemen friends. She recalls Pope's imitation of "The First Satire of the Second Book of Horace," where he describes his Twickenham entertainment of "Chiefs, out of War, and Statesmen, out of Place" as the "Feast of Reason and the Flow of Soul" (126–27). Seward's Belinda seems transplanted from *The Rape of the Lock*. She spends the morning enacting "mystic rites" before her mirror. She finally descends to dinner, but for a different object than the lavish French cuisine of her table: "Round for a dearer feast she looks the while, / With triumph's gay anticipating smile" (53–54). Like her namesake, Belinda concludes her entertainment at the card table, "to yield victorious Pam his wonted rites" (70). Meanwhile, Cornelia recoils, her wit wasted, her eloquence ignored. Seward appears to grant Pope's contention that sensible women are as rare as these two friends in a social world dominated by Belindas.

Seward compares Belinda's letter to a spider's flimsy web and her friendship with Belinda to tasteless juice spilling, disappointingly, from an inviting orange gourd (11–18, 103–12). Seward argues that Belinda does not represent most women, despite Pope's memorable claims.

> From such vain models spleen'd Museus drew
> The light camelion nymphs that meet our view,
> While in the immortal beauty of his lays
> Lives bold Injustice to remotest days.
>
> (135–38)

Seward seizes her authority as Horatian observer to question Pope's constructions of femininity.

> Ah! do the empty tribe his fancy paints,
> Dispassion'd Sinners, and voluptuous Saints,
> Coquets, that seize the Sage's clue, and spin it,
> With all the cloud-form'd Cynthias of the minute,
> Do these epitomize the female kind,
> Than man more virtuous, more than man refin'd?
>
> (141–46)

Seward's response is emphatically negative. She enumerates common examples of women caring for elderly parents, enduring their husbands' infidelity or alcoholism, or resigning their fortunes to profligate spouses. Gesturing toward these models of patient endurance, Seward demands "Creation's Lords, impartial own, / If right, or wrong, the spleenful Bard defin'd / The general texture of the female mind!" (174–76). She particularly questions Pope's narrow account of female psychology.

> Say, do two passions only sway our soul,
> The thirst of pleasure, and of proud controul?
> And, while the mortals masculine pursue
> The various object, seen in various view,
> As "some to business, some to pleasure take,"
> Is "every woman at her heart a Rake?"
>
> (177–82)

Given her examples of female martyrdom, Seward finds Pope's witty formula not merely trivializing but cruel. She turns for vindication to a rival male artist who, she contends, painted ordinary women's sufferings from life.

Seward devotes the next 101 lines of "Epistle to Cornelia" to a tour of William Hogarth's *The Rake's Progress*, focusing on its images of Sarah Young, the rake's betrayed but loving mistress. In the context of the first plate, Tom Rakewell's cruel seduction of Sarah, Seward imagines Sarah now "to keen reproach and taunting scorn consign'd" (208), yet "his fate more dreading, than she dreads her own" (212). Seward describes each print in the series, interpreting Hogarth's sympathetic portrayal of Sarah's fidelity to Tom. As Tom struggles against his chains in Bedlam, Sarah hovers over him, "shock'd, yet assiduous to assuage his woe" (289), fulfilling the destiny she feared in the opening plate. To Pope's gallery of society portraits, Seward opposes Hogarth's record of a humble woman's tragedy.

Through his characterizations in "Epistle to a Lady," Pope suggests that an apt metaphor for all women is privileged women's expensive, frivolous portraits of themselves as saints and shepherdesses. Seward's counterexamples suggest that Pope's metaphor is too exclusive to support such a generalization. Her choice of Hogarth's reproducible series suggests that good women, contrary to Pope's one exception, may be as numerous as Hogarth's prints. Moreover, Hogarth's Sarah renders most real women, virtue intact but equally patient and loving, even more admirable by comparison with his fallen heroine. While Pope's poem reduces even titled women to rakes at heart, Hogarth's series compassionates the seduced maiden and, by extension, ennobles her ordinary, but reputable, viewers. Jean Hagstrum observed the contemporary appeal of Sarah Young, unique among Hogarth's female characters, as an exemplar of "the power of sentimental love and bourgeois virtue" (177). Seward cleverly seized this appeal, conducting her reader through Hogarth's moving series instead of through Pope's gallery of "dispassion'd Sinners and voluptuous Saints" ("Epistle to Cornelia," 142).

Seward completes her argument in "Epistle to Cornelia" by asking the "satiric pupils of Museus' train" to compare Pope's notions with Hogarth's and choose the most accurate (293). She taunts Pope's disciples, "Which passion govern'd [Sarah Young] through each hapless hour, / The love of pleasure or the love of power!" (297–98). If still uncertain, they may observe Cornelia—educated, beautiful, and an exemplary wife and mother. She addresses men who instance Pope's satires as their excuse for avoiding matrimony.

> You, with the tetchy bard's invidious sneer,
> Will you asperse the sex you should revere?
> Resemble him, who felt each passion warm
> Check'd by the influence of his hapless form?
> Who, sore with disappointment's galling pain,

Hated the sex, to which he sued in vain.
Turn from the Railer! . . .

(321–27)

A wise man will avoid the "gaudy snare" set by such women as Belinda and will cherish such qualities as Sarah's enduring love and Cornelia's "brilliant wit with soberest wisdom join'd" (335, 341).

Seward's recourse to Pope's deformity, her argument that unrequited love resulted in misogyny, apparently contradicts the devotion to his poetic gifts we observed throughout her correspondence. But perhaps esteem for Pope's poetry led Seward to adopt this myth of emotional trauma. How came such a gifted poet to judge so unfairly? The "tetchy bard's . . . hapless form" provided a convenient explanation while completing the symmetry of her response. After opposing Hogarth's print series to Pope's portrait gallery, she advances Pope's aberrant psychology to challenge his critique of female psychology. The psychological theory also spared Seward from confronting the misogyny endemic in her culture, which she (as her idealization of female martyrdom attests) inherited and partly shared. The "Epistle to Cornelia" remains a strong attempt to challenge Pope's rhetoric, though the challenge is limited by Seward's acceptance of women's domestic destinies. Seward's assurance of her own gifts, her belief that Pope's skills could be learned and refined, stimulated her adamant reply.

Various other women imitated Pope's Horatian poems throughout the century, for pragmatic or philosophical reasons. In 1739, Elizabeth Boyd paraphrased the *Essay on Man* and the "Epilogues to the Satires" amidst Opposition clamor for war against Spain. "Admiral Haddock: or, The Progress of Spain" stirred patriot anger by comparing modern ambition with Elizabethan Spanish pretension. "What monstrous Evils and Disorders spring / From low Ambition, when it swells a King?" she asks, aligning her poem with Pope's and Bolingbroke's anti-Walpole campaign (51–52). She conjures a world void of justice, where "Truth seems hov'ring on the Verge of Law" (56), a direct allusion to Pope's "Dialogue II" (249), where Pope defied national corruption. Her description of the Spanish court resembles Pope's account of "Old *England's* Genius" dragged in the dust ("Dialogue I," 152–53).

Honour, the Emulation of the Great,
Abandons, in Disgrace, the royal Seat:

Deserts the Patriot, in his ample Trust,
Indignant crawls, and grov'ling licks the Dust.
                                ("Admiral Haddock," 57–60)

Boyd eschews subtlety for instant identification of her political opinions with Pope's. She appeals to readers with Opposition notions of England's monarchy, court, and ministry, readers convinced by *The Craftsman* and Pope's satires that justice, truth, and honour had fled the island.

Most women writers found it more convenient to ignore the political significance of Pope's diction. Particularly as the century waned and Pope's context faded, women construed his campaign for virtue in a more conventional moral sense. In her "Advice to a *Friend*, sent on *Valentine's* Day" (1787), Eliza Thompson boasts she "boldly dares espouse fair Virtue's cause."[11] Rallying a male friend from his dissipated life, Thompson ignored the obsolete political signification that had once given Pope's phrase subversive power.[12]

Other women adapted the *Essay on Man* to suit Christian didacticism. Ann Murry's *Poems on Various Subjects* (1779) features brief reflections on aspects of the *Essay*. "An Essay on Pride" addresses Pope's concern in *Essay* 1 with that chief human vice. Of changing fortune, she observes, "From hence vain Man, correct and know thyself, / Learn the true estimate of pow'r or pelf; / Disdain vain Pride" (29–31). For Murry, to "know thyself" means knowing that "a Christian's lively faith subverts" pride (37). Likewise, Murry's "Reflections on Life, and the Expectations of a Future State" recalls Pope's suspicion of modern science, but for specifically Christian ends: "The proud Philosopher, I hear exclaim, / 'What, no regard for Wisdom, and for Fame? / 'For Science, which can search great Nature's laws, / 'Trace the effect, to the efficient Cause?' " (31–34). Murry claims due respect for "scientific boasters" (38), but she reminds readers that their confidence is best placed in God and in Christian redemption. Murry, who drew geography lessons from the *Essay* for her *Mentoria*, evidently found the poem equally adaptable for moral instruction.

Esther Lewis's volume (1789) contains a poem, evidently written much earlier, that adapts Pope's *Essay* to prove "Man more happy than Brutes" (Lewis, *Poems*, 99–105). Lewis reacts indignantly to the possibility of animals' superior happiness, "and thus to vindicate her *God* aspires" (l.8). In *Essay* 1, Pope had considered the special gifts of each species, culminating in human reason (1.222–32). He affirmed

God's omnipresence, "as full, as perfect, in a hair as heart" (1.275), emphasizing divine power rather than the equal happiness of all creatures. Lewis, however, apparently accuses Pope of believing animals happier than humans, probably because his poem does not mention the Christian promise of immortality for humans. Her poem particularly recalls Pope's argument in *Essay* 1 that God withholds comprehension of His purposes from humans, just as humans withhold similar knowledge from horses and lambs (1.61–84). Of immortality, Pope cautions, "What future bliss, [God] gives not thee to know, / But gives that Hope to be thy blessing now" (1.93–94). Lewis evidently found Pope's analogy outrageous. She describes the comparatively greater suffering of animals, victims of human carelessness and greed (130–61).

> If to disease, or man, they yield their breath,
> They only see the gloomy side of death:
> No pleasing prospects of a blissful state;
> Dreadful annihilation is their fate.
> O then retract the ill consider'd lays,
> And merit, as before, esteem and praise.
>
> (162–67)

In her indignation, Lewis mistook part of Pope's argument for the whole. He never claims that animals are happier than, or even as happy as, humans. She has mistaken a limited analogy for an article of faith. Like Hester Piozzi, Hannah More, and other late-century women readers, Lewis found the *Essay's* lack of explicit Christianity offensive. Like Elizabeth Carter, Esther Lewis found it impossible to moralize Pope's song.

In *Poems on Subjects Chiefly Devotional* (1760), American poet Anne Steele objected to one of Pope's minor Horatian poems.[13] Although Pope claimed to have written his "Ode on Solitude" when he was twelve, he refined the poem throughout his career. The ode salutes the retired life of country gentlemen, "whose wish and care / A few paternal acres bound" (1–2). Pope praises the secluded routine of "study and ease" on a self-sufficient estate, compared with what he described in one unpublished revision as "The Business and the Noise of Towns" (*Poems*, 6:3). With no specific model, the "Ode" nevertheless belongs to the Horatian tradition of poems extolling country retirement, opposed to urban corruption, as the ideal human aspiration.

Steele, a fine devotional poet, questioned the validity of this classical tradition.

Steele's "Imitation of Mr. Pope's Ode on Solitude" views the poem not in its Horatian context but from her Christian point of view. She challenges Pope's recommendation of a solitary life endowed with "health of body, peace of mind" ("Ode on Solitude," 11).

> Some gentle spirit aid my flight
>   To this delightful, blissful spot,
> From human converse, human sight;
>   Blest, and forgot.
>
> Illusive dream! it fleets in air!
>   No paradise is found below,
> No solitude secludes from care,
>   Or shuts out woe.

("Imitation," 5–12)

Given the inevitable vicissitudes of a fallen world, the only happy man is he "whose soul aspires / To a fair paradise above" (25–26). Steele concludes by wishing for serene endurance, "till death's kind sleep shall close my eyes; / Then wake to bliss" (31–32). From misprision, Steele proceeds to an antithetical revision of Pope's image of earthly bliss. As Pope himself had adapted an ancient tradition to suit English country gentlemen, so Steele reinterpreted his adaptation for her New England protestant milieu. Her version reinstates the Christian piety missing from Pope's classical ode but crucial to her own vision.

At least one midcentury poet, Henrietta Knight, Lady Luxborough, simply borrowed Pope's landscape ideal in "Epistle to Burlington" for an occasional tribute. "Written at a *Ferme Ornée* near Birmingham, August 7th, 1749" praises William Shenstone's The Leasowes.[14] There, "modest art in silence lurks conceal'd: / While Nature shines, so gracefully reveal'd, / That she triumphant claims the total plan" (7–9). Lady Luxborough recalls Pope's advice to "treat the Goddess like a modest fair" (51), congratulating Shenstone for revealing the genius of his place.

As the century ended, echoes of Pope's Horatian style grew fainter, although lingering in women's verse epistles. In an essay "On the Classics," Anna Laetitia Barbauld observed, "It is amusing to follow an idea from century to century, and observe the gradual accession of thought and sentiment; to see the jewels of the ancients new set, and the wit of Horace sparkling with additional lustre in the lines of Pope.[15] In "The Invitation" (1773; *Memoir*, 2:1–8), Barbauld's description of the duke of Bridgewater's canal modernizes Pope's praise of Lord Burlington's landscape.

> The sons of toil with many a weary stroke
> Scoop the hard bosom of the solid rock;
> Resistless, through the stiff opposing clay
> With steady patience work their gradual way;
> Compel the genius of the unwilling flood
> Through the brown horrors of the aged wood. . . .
> . . . .
> The ductile streams obey the guiding hand,
> And social plenty circles round the land.
>
> (59–64, 77–78)

Though contemporary engineers now compel an unwilling version of what Pope had called the "Genius of the Place" ("Epistle to Burlington," 57), the resulting canal brings plenty. Barbauld's anticipation recalls Pope's promise that Timon's landscape will eventually disappear "and laughing Ceres re-assume the land" ("Epistle to Burlington," 176).

Other women's poems associate Pope's Horatian mode with literary and social trends. Janet Little was a disciple of Burns, but among her *Poetical Works* (1792) are several epistles in heroic couplets. The epistles appear among Little's ballads in Scottish dialect, but in "Given to a Lady who asked me to write a Poem," she praises Burns, her model, as successor to Pope, Swift, Thomson, Addison, and Young (Little, 113–15). In her epistles to and from Loudon Castle, Little adapts Pope's couplets to describe the site of her dairy as an ideal retreat. Popeian themes and images surface—Nell longs to visit "the sweetly, vari'd scene"—but in modern guise; Nell imagines flying to the castle in a hot-air balloon ("Nell's Answer," 11, 18, Little, 120–21)). In "Another Epistle to Nell" (Little, 122–24), Little exhorts her friend in terms reminiscent of Pope's challenge to Lord Burlington ("Epistle to Burlington," 191–204).

> Go on, dear Nell, the laureate-wreath pursue,
> In time perhaps you may receive your due.
> We'll beat the bushes for the rural muse,

Where ev'ry dunce her inspiration sues.
'Mongst the vast crowd, let you and I aspire
To share a little of Apollo's fire.

(23–28)

The Horatian poet who commanded his aristocratic patron to build public works has metamorphosed into a milkmaid encouraging her friend's literary aspirations. Pope might have confused these rural maids with the dunces they shun. But by imagining her life in the dairy at Loudon Castle as a kind of Horatian retreat, Janet Little aspired to the company of her admired Pope and Swift, Elizabeth Rowe and Lady Mary Wortley Montagu. In her epistles, characteristic of an era flirting with notions of greater social equality, Pope's celebrations of rural retirement underpin a milkmaid's literary pretensions.

Pope's Horatian style accomodated women throughout the century. Mary Chandler discovered that her life as a crippled, unmarried milliner whose poems had attracted titled acquaintances was readily adaptable to Pope's Horatian persona. Such women as Mary Leapor and Mary Jones, ruefully aware of their constrained status, nevertheless developed authoritative satiric voices. Both Elizabeth Carter and Anna Seward borrowed Pope's phrases to structure poems quarreling with his philosophy. Flexibility distinguished Pope's Horatian model. A range of laboring-class and middle-class women found his persona empowering. Even Lady Luxborough, the sole aristocrat represented in this chapter, cultivated a Horatian style while banished to an isolated estate, accused of adultery. She, like Pope's other women imitators, sought refuge in his modest but confident manner.

Speaking "something like Horace," Pope declared moral and aesthetic judgments to his betters, a privilege eighteenth-century women poets appropriated with enthusiasm. Their desire to imitate his manner countered most misgivings about Pope's possible hypocrisy (which had angered Lady Mary Wortley Montagu and Anna Seward) or impiety (which distressed Elizabeth Carter, Hannah More, and others). Most women found Pope's opinions sufficiently orthodox to merit adaptation. Even pious Catherine Talbot echoed the "Epistle to Dr. Arbuthnot" in one of the nine poems published in her posthumous *Works* (1772).[16] Her "Elegy" concludes:

Hence, far begone, ye fancy-folded pains,
    Peace, trembling heart, be ev'ry sigh supprest:

> Wisdom supreme, eternal goodness reigns,
>   Thus far is sure: to Heav'n resign the rest.

(21–24)

Pope's poem, as Talbot's editor notes, concluded "Thus far was right; the rest belongs to Heav'n" ("To Arbuthnot," 419). Talbot's paraphrase suggests that women mined Pope's poems for such aphorisms. Pope's debatable moral and political principles invited exoneration or revision, further inspiring women writers from Elizabeth Tollet to Esther Lewis. To a surprising extent, eighteenth-century women learned to imitate Pope's Horatian manner without losing their own poetic identities. Perhaps acute awareness of daily feminine role-playing aided them in fabricating personae: women wrote as women writing as Pope writing as Horace. Their frequent responses to Pope's Horatian poems suggest women's longing for a share of cultural authority. It also discloses their belief in Pope's poems as models for authoritative feminine expression.

~~~ Conclusion: Pope's Influence on Eighteenth-Century Women's Poetry

Pope's influence on women's poems extended far beyond their specific imitations of or replies to his poems. Pope's distinctive style was imitated by men and women throughout the century, but women were usually deprived of the Latin models and formal schooling in rhetoric from which Pope derived his effects. Their dependence on Pope and other accessible English writers was therefore pronounced. In one letter, Anna Seward advised Miss Cayley that she master prosody by imitating Pope, Darwin, and Gray (*Letters*, 3:321–25). Among other techniques, Seward recommended Pope's rhythmic effects to Cayley's attention. Seward's letters demonstrate her painstaking study of Pope's prosody. As her poetic style evolved, she recurred to Pope's couplets for both positive and negative illustrations of her opinions.

Seward's refinements of specific Popeian couplets suggest both her own preferences and the extent of Pope's influence on her style. In another letter, for example, Seward proposed an antislavery poem, envisioning a future "where the swart negroes, 'mid the palmy groves, / Might quaff the citron juice, and woo their sable loves" (*Letters*, 2:112). She offered the couplet as a quotation. In "Windsor Forest," Pope had imagined England's progress "till the freed *Indians* in their native Groves / Reap their own Fruits, and woo their Sable Loves" (409–10). Seward retained Pope's precisely balanced structure but adjusted his imagery toward greater specificity. Pope's "Indians" suited his general reference to the dawning empire but was inappropriate for a poem denouncing African slavery. "Freed Negroes" has obvious disadvantages of assonance; Seward probably chose "swart" as a more specific modifier. "Where . . . swart" restored to Seward's couplet the assonance Pope had created by "Till . . . Indians," amplified by her retention of "woo" in the second line. Seward adjusted Pope's groves from "native" to "palmy," a more specific visual image, and her "citron juice" similarly refines his "Fruits." Seward appreciated the exquisite balance of Pope's couplet but revised it for her context and stylistic preferences.

One other example demonstrates Anna Seward's studious adjustments of Pope's style. "I like the sense to overflow the couplet . . . oftener than it ever does in Pope and Johnson," she remarked in a letter of 1789 (*Letters*, 2:210). Her "Epistle to Cornelia" contains many such couplets, among them a conflation of two famous Popeian phrases (*Works*, 2:110–23).

> Friend of my youth, what Cynic could upbraid
> The laugh of scorn, when in thy tints array'd,
> Those consecrated hours before us roll,
> Their feasts of reason, and their flow of soul?
>
> (25–28)

Seward intended a concise assimilation of herself and Cornelia to Pope's Horatian models. Cornelia becomes a Dr. Arbuthnot, the "Friend to my Life" in Pope's epistle ("Epistle to Dr. Arbuthnot," 27). Their enjoyment of the feast of reason and flow of soul indicates proud isolation from Belinda's fashionable crowd, a feminine version of Pope's retreat with "Statesmen, out of Place" in "Satire Iii." By extending her sense through two couplets, Seward associates her friendship with the range and complexity of Pope's.

But Seward's verses illustrate the pitfalls of evading Pope's model. Pope's adherence to the end-stopped couplet was a deliberate effort to correct Dryden's sloppiness. As Geoffrey Tillotson has observed, the heroic couplet builds readers' confidence through authorial responsibility.[1] First Pope gained readers' trust by fulfilling their expectations, then he capitalized on their confidence by creating surprise. In these particular couplets, Seward not only fails to fulfill expectations but creates confusion. The cynic's laugh could not possibly be directed at the speaker and Cornelia. But four more couplets elapse before Belinda emerges as the object of scorn, her morning toilette contrasted with the friends' conversation. The reader is confused by the delayed clarification rather than pleased or surprised. Though they suit her eloquence, Seward's attempts to expand Pope's couplets are sometimes merely verbose. But she was among the few women poets to articulate her differences with Pope and to conceive of her style as a refinement of his.

Anna Seward confidently experimented with Pope's couplets, but she also imitated his effects. In the first epistle of *Louisa*, especially, she made sounds echo sense (*Works*, 2:219–39). When Louisa plays her lute, a bee "seem'd to prolong, with her assiduous wing, / The soft vibration of the tuneful string" (99–100). Liquid and nasal sounds alternate to suggest the hovering bee. In a closer application of Pope's examples, Louisa surveys the barren landscape while the sun sets "and rushes, with hoarse stream, the mountain rill, . . . dashing, down the lonely vale" (212, 214). Pope had recommended that "the hoarse, rough Verse shou'd like the Torrent roar" ("Essay on Criticism," 369). Seward adds explosive *d* sounds to simulate the rushing stream.

Many women poets experimented with Popeian sound effects. Judith Cowper incorporated advice from the "Essay on Criticism" into her poems. Mary Leapor also imitated one of Pope's examples of onomatopoeia. In the "Essay on Criticism," Pope suggested Camilla's swiftness as she "flies o'er th'unbending corn, and skims along the Main" (373). By eliding vowels and employing vibrant *m*, *n* and *ng* sounds, Pope succeeds in making his alexandrine skim along like the fleet Amazon. Leapor attempts a similar effect in her "Essay on Friendship" (Leapor, 74–80), attacking wits who compare women's friendships to flies that "are hatch'd i' th' morning and at ev'ning die" (10). Leapor's simile compresses eleven syllables, using elision to suggest the brevity of a fly's life. She employs *m*, *n*, and *ng* sounds to simulate insects' humming flight. In "The Vanity of external Accomplishments," Mary Whateley also emulated Pope's Camilla passage, elongated for satiric effect (Whateley, 87–90).

> With manly Stride *Camilla* spurns the Ground,
> Or on the prancing Steed pursues the Hound;
> Thro' Brakes, down Precipices, lo! she speeds,
> Dares the rough Torrent, bounds along the Meads;
> For what? the gentle Fair will blush to hear—
> *With her own Hand* to kill the trembling Deer.
>
> (38–43)

Whateley combines Pope's prescriptions for both skimming flight and rushing torrent to expose her modern Amazon. Though many women emulated Pope's sound-and-sense passage, they did so sparingly, confining the effect (as Pope had done in his "Essay") to a few bravura passages. They apparently intuited the danger—defined by Irvin Eh-

renpreis—that such technical displays risked overwhelming a poem
if not integral to its sense.[2]

Most women imitated the myriad patterns Pope used to balance
his couplets. Although Pope had not invented these, his command
of an immense variety of stress patterns struck contemporaries as
unique and even magical (Tillotson, 64, 68). Pope achieved balance
by orchestrating such techniques as elision, alliteration, chiasmus,
and anaphora. Better poets learned from Pope both variety and restraint, while the less accomplished merely repeated his patterns.
Ann Murry, a better pedagogical writer than poet, illustrates the latter
tendency in the opening lines of "A Familiar Epistle to the Author's
Sister" (*Poems*, 64–65).

> Say, dear Maria! is the modish life
> With sense and reason ever found at strife?
> Say, dear Maria! is the rural seat
> Of Peace and Virtue the secure retreat?
> Then form thy judgment, and declare thy choice,
> Tho' inconsistent with the gen'ral voice.
>
> (1–6)

Murry may have borrowed her opening trochaic construction from
Elizabeth Carter's "To Miss D'aeth" ("Say, dear *Bethia*, can thy gentle
mind," 1), but her second line borrows Pope's remark in the "Essay
on Criticism" that "*Wit* and *Judgment* often are at strife" (82). Though
overtly dependent on these precedents, the pattern is pleasingly conversational. Murry's next couplet, however, is more annoying than
artful; the striking construction of line 1 becomes insistent when
merely repeated. Murry next partly paraphrases a couplet from Pope's
"Essay," precisely repeating the stress pattern. Pope urges daily reading of Homer: "Thence form your Judgment, thence your Maxims
bring, / And trace the Muses *upward* to their Spring" ("Essay," 126–
27). Murry appears an inexperienced poet cobbling her verses together
from recent reading. She lacks the confidence to depart from her
models.

Mary Jones also borrowed a great deal from Pope, but her appropriations seem comparatively purposeful. This impression derives
partly from Jones's superior poetic skill. Jones had read Pope atten-
tively and could apply aspects of his prosody to her own couplets.
In "Of Patience" (Jones, 8–25), she contends,

What though in action brave, unaw'd by fear,
Resolv'd as *Clayton*, or as *Swift* severe,
In diff'rent views their trials, tempers scan,
Ev'n *Swift* can weep, and *Clayton* is a man.

(26–29)

The content of this passage is generally indebted to Pope's discussions of the ruling passion in *Essay on Man* and "To Cobham." But more importantly, Jones creates a brisk, authoritative style simply by using Pope's characteristic techniques. She employs a delayed caesura and secures an antithetical effect for synonymous traits by balancing active and passive voice. Ellipsis creates drama and concision. Jones's caesura neatly splits line 27, further balanced by four stresses. Chiasmus saves the line from monotony. She reverts to delayed balance in line 28, varying her structure with alliteration and inverted syntax. Jones's syntax creates the further Popeian effect of a strong rhyme word. Her final line equally applies Pope's style. Completing her assertion, its balanced order appears serene, conclusive, and unquestionable.

Mary Jones's couplets corroborate Anna Seward's advice to Miss Cayley. Jones had analyzed the techniques Pope used to craft aphorisms about human behavior from generalized characters. The passage about Swift and Clayton supports her poem's argument about the necessity of patience in recognizably Popeian style. Examples of such prosody abound in each of Pope's female imitators' poems, more or less successful according to the poet's control. Elizabeth Boyd and Ann Murry were usually content to borrow, but Mary Leapor and Mary Jones applied Pope's prosody. Because they could duplicate Pope's effects, Leapor and Jones were more successful than most women in adopting the Horatian persona of his mature work. But few eighteenth-century women poets achieved such expertise. Most followed Pope in avoiding expletives and preferring strong rhymes. Alexandrines are rare, used only for special effect, as in Anna Laetitia Barbauld's tribute to Science in "The Invitation" (*Memoir*, 2:1–8). Barbauld promises that the eagle, Science, long checked by "bigot rage," "on sounding pinions yet aloft shall soar, / And through the azure deep untravelled paths explore" (107–8). By reserving the alexandrine for such occasions as this, where it appropriately conveys grandeur and sublimity, women obeyed Pope's strictures in the "Essay on Criticism." They also learned from Pope the dramatic potential of anaphora. Mary Jones was commissioned by Lord Beauclerk's widow to write "In Memory of The Right Hon. Lord Aubrey Beauclerk, Who was slain at Carthagena" (Jones, 36–44). Lord Beauclerk's grisly fate, his legs shot off in battle, justified a dramatic elegy. Jones responded in her best Popeian/Horatian manner.

> 'Virtue!—What is it?—Whence does it arise!'
> Ask of the brave, the social, and the wise;
> Of those who study'd for the gen'ral good,
> Of those who sought, and purchas'd it with blood;
> Of those who build, or plant, or who design,
> Ev'n those who dig the soil, or work the mine.
>
> (79–84)

Not all women poets exercised Jones's restraint in matching dramatic sequence to occasion. In "The Invitation," Anna Laetitia Barbauld used anaphora for eight successive lines (125–32) describing youthful school days ("And spirits light, to every joy in tune, / And friendship ardent as a summer's noon"). The effect is disproportionately enthusiastic, but Barbauld (who displayed her usual control in "The Groans of the Tankard," a parody of heroic verse techniques) rarely succumbed to such rhetorical excess.

Pope's influence, as we have confirmed, extended from details of prosody to choice of subjects. Mary Leapor's "The Temple of Love: A Dream" (Leapor, 162–66) recalls Pope's "The Temple of Fame." But Leapor's poem adapts Pope's structure and content to represent women's vulnerability to romantic love. Although Leapor could have returned to Chaucer for the Temple of Venus Pope had excised from his version of *The House of Fame*, she preferred Pope's baroque church to Chaucer's gothic temple. But while Pope's narrator falls so deeply asleep that "Love it self was banish'd from my Breast" (6), Leapor's autobiographical opening finds her reading *Jane Shore* late at night. Pope provides no rationale for his dream, but Mira's occurs after hours spent pondering Rowe's fallen but saintly heroine. The fabric she beholds rising from the ground is accompanied by timbrels and citterns rather than by Fame's martial trumpet, recalling Dryden's distinction between amorous Egyptians and stern Romans in *All for Love*. While Doric pillars mount the western, classical facade of Pope's edifice, ornate Corinthian pillars uphold Leapor's, although Leapor drew on Pope's descriptions for the jeweled interior of her temple. Pope's Fame is a horrid creature with a thousand eyes, ears, and tongues. In Leapor's temple a realistic painting of Venus with Cupid hangs beneath a sparkling canopy, making her building even more like a baroque church than Pope's. Leapor's temple is a prettier, diminuitive version of Pope's, suitable to a young woman's dream of love. But the illusory nature of the goddess proves ominous. Instead of inscriptions of famous names, Leapor observes insidious tactics, "the Statutes and the Arts of Love," inscribed on the walls (24). A beautiful couple enters, the young lady soon overcome by gifts and flattery. The temple then fills with "shrieks and tumult," and the scene changes to "an abbey and a doleful cell" (64, 70), Leapor's version of the "Temple of Rumor." The "ruin'd Nymph" appears, now doomed to penance for her sin (71). Here she must remain in Eloisa-like seclusion until death, enduring the harrassment of reproach, scandal, and remorse (79–88). Mercifully, Leapor awakens to the rising sun. Her poem has departed from its Popeian precedent, although it is indebted for some details of seduction and punishment to *The Rape of the Lock* and "Eloisa to Abelard." The feminine temple enshrines the specter of lost reputation, as frightful as the visions of lost political honor in Pope's poem. Though Leapor's poem does not answer Pope's, she was inspired to create a feminine equivalent, a temple in which the dangers are manifest but the rewards unclear. As in *Jane Shore*, women are granted one avenue to (illusory) power, leading invariably to ruin. Leapor's temple of love is diminuitive because she fears there is only one dreadful pattern for women lured into it, a fear shared by women of all classes throughout the century.

In "Dorinda at her Glass," Leapor addresses another feminine fear by projecting into the future a version of Pope's Belinda from *The Rape of the Lock* (Leapor, 1–8). Dorinda, "whose shining Eyes a thousand Hearts alarm'd" (3), and who spent hours each day before the mirror, must acknowledge that she is aging. Leapor introduces the wrinkled belle amidst reminders that she is no longer a Belinda. While "Sol thro' white Curtains shot a tim'rous Ray," fearful of disturbing Pope's heroine (*Rape*, 1.13), Leapor's "bright Sol had drove the sable clouds away" from a landscape oblivious to Dorinda's plight (11). She awakens not from dreams of birthnight beaux but from nightmares about wrinkles (19–20). As if fulfilling Clarissa's warning in *Rape* (5.26), Dorinda's "careless Locks upon her Shoulder lay, / Uncurl'd, alas! because they half were gray" (25–26). She approaches her mirror, shuddering because no goddess appears, but "a Spectre" (40). Recalling Belinda's mystic rites before the shrine of beauty, Dorinda sighs, "Now who shall bow before this wither'd Shrine, / This mortal Image that was late divine? / What Victim now will praise these faded Eyes?"

(48–50). Forced to this admission, Dorinda directs to her fellow "ancient maids" (72) an appeal satirically pointed but gentler than Pope's dismissal of the "Ghosts of Beauty" as "Hags" in "Epistle to a Lady" (239, 241). Dorinda's characterizations are funny, but also rather touching. She begs Augusta to change "the lac'd Slipper of delicious Hue / For a warm Stocking, and an easy Shoe" (92–93), and she warns Sylvia that neither her patches nor her laced shoes are becoming now, "since none regard her Forehead, nor her Toe" (103). These images culminate in Pruda, who locks up her daughter rather than compete for attention. All are conventional, but Leapor's characters seem more vulnerable than Pope's. Dorinda's advice adapts a Popeian prescription:

> Thus *Pope* has sung, thus let *Dorinda* sing,
> 'Virtue, brave Boys,—'tis Virtue makes a King.'
> Why not a Queen? fair Virtue is the same
> In the rough Hero, and the smiling Dame:
> *Dorinda*'s Soul her beauties shall pursue,
> Though late I see her, and embrace her too.
>
> (122–27)

Pope's advice—what "every child . . . will sing"—occurs in a satiric passage of the "First Epistle of the First Book of Horace Imitated," addressed to Lord Bolingbroke: "Be this thy Screen, be this thy Wall of Brass, / Compar'd to this, a Minister's an Ass" (91–92, 95–96). Many contemporaries would have recognized the political connotations of Pope's "Virtue" (92). But Leapor, like many other women, either failed to recognize or ignored Pope's political implication. She construed his words literally, as a recommendation appropriate for both genders. Dorinda declares she will follow Pope's advice and practice candor and charity for the rest of her life. Unlike Pope's *Rape*, Leapor redeems her erring heroine. Unlike the "Epistle to a Lady," her satire is comic but gentle, never harsh. As in "The Temple of Love," Leapor has transmuted her Popeian sources into a unique and distinctly feminine poem.

Later in the century, Anna Laetitia Barbauld's "To Mrs. P——. With some Drawings of Birds and Insects" evolved from Pope's discussion of sister arts in his "Epistle to Mr. Jervas, with *Dryden*'s Translation of *Fresnoy*'s *Art* of *Painting*."[3] Barbauld's epigraph, "The kindred arts to please thee shall conspire, / One dip the pencil, and one string the lyre," paraphrases Pope's wish for Jervas's beautiful sitters. Like

Pope's, Barbauld's poem celebrates friendship and opens with a discussion of "the kindred arts two sister Muses guide" (6). Unlike Pope, Barbauld represents both arts; her friend Amanda illustrates her argument like the famous society beauties of Pope's. Barbauld thus rearranges "To Mr. Jervas" while preserving Pope's symmetry. As both painter and poet, she is free to weigh the merits of each art and find poetry "deeper" (11). With a fleeting allusion to Ariel's search through "the close Recesses of [Belinda's] Thought" (*Rape*, 3.140), Barbauld asserts that poetry "can pierce the close recesses of the heart," rousing passion through "well-set syllables" (12, 13). Although each art perfects the other, "[painting] gives Amanda's form, and [poetry] her mind" (18). In Pope's "To Mr. Jervas," Pope, more interested in friendship than in relative value, concluded "Thou but preserv'st a Face and I a Name" (78).

Barbauld's comparison of sister arts introduces her chief topic, word-paintings of various birds and insects (19–120). Through these descriptions, Barbauld demonstrates the power of language to capture essence and form. Her newly hatched insects, for example, tremble

> . . . and scarcely dare
> To launch at once upon the untried air:
> At length assured, they catch the favoring gale,
> And leave their sordid spoils, and high in ether sail.
>
> (81–84)

Line 84, an alexandrine, sails off on high-register vowel sounds. Other descriptions, such as the silver pheasant's capture, the birds that "pour out all their little souls in song," and the glowworms that "guide the Indian to his tawny loves" (47–54, 60, 111), draw from Pope's "Windsor Forest." Barbauld's imagery generally defends her claim that language "breathes . . . spirit" into representation (16). Having illustrated her skill, however, Barbauld declares, "I envy not nor emulate the fame / Or of the painter's or the poet's name" (125–26); she writes or paints merely to amuse her friend. Her disclaimer echoes Pope's "Thou but preserv'st a Face and I a Name," but it rings false after her skillful demonstration. Perhaps Barbauld borrowed Pope's modest pose lest anyone consider her poem too ambitious or opinionated.

"Amanda bids;—at her command again / I seize the pencil" began "To Mrs. P——." Like many women's poems, Barbauld's was occasional. Women tended to write about private occasions, such as birthdays or visits, rather than public events, such as battles or political crises. Deaths were another frequent occasion for women's poems. Taxed with such an emergency, women might find in Pope's epitaphs some inspiration for their own. Mary Jones's "In Memory of the Right Hon. Nevil Lord Lovelace" (Jones, 139–42) contains a passage quite peculiar without its Popeian context. Jones's conclusion refers to Lord Lovelace's sister Martha.

> Oft as she eyes yon bright etherial plain,
> And burns to follow thee, and mix again;
> Some tender friendships, some endearing ties,
> Cling round her heart, and hold her from the skies.
> A little while, and these shall all decay,
> And the free soul emerge to endless day:
>
> . . . .
> Her gentler orb shall round its center move,
> Re-kindled into harmony and love.
>
> (56–61, 64–65)

It is unclear whether the "center" around which Miss Lovelace's soul will revolve is God or her brother. Jones's assumption that Martha will pine away for her brother, despite other relationships, seems extravagant. Jones, however, may have modeled her conclusion on Pope's "Epitaph. On the Monument of the Honble. Robert Digby, and of his Sister Mary." Pope addressed Mary as "Blest Maid! attendant on [Digby's] doom" (11), "Not parted long, and now to part no more! / Go then, where only bliss sincere is known! / Go, where to love and to enjoy are one!" (14–16). Pope composed this epitaph for their anguished father, consoling him with the idea of his children's eternal reunion. Jones may have derived the loverlike image of the sister burning to mix with her brother from Pope's promise that in heaven "to love and to enjoy are one." At any rate, she would have found in Pope the precedent for what at first appears an inappropriate sibling response.

Other women drew from Pope's poems the basis of elegiac characterizations. Eliza Thompson's "An Elegy on [Mr. Andrew Ewart]" (Thompson, 24) exhorts the poor to mourn: "Your husband, father, friend! is from you torn" (2). The phrase recalls Eloisa's plea to her "father, brother, husband, friend" (Pope, "Eloisa to Abelard," 152), by 1787 a poetic commonplace. In Thompson's characterization, Ewart

was a student of the Ruling Passion: "He view'd mankind with philo-
sophic eye, / Their springs of action could with ease descry" (9–10).
Unfortunately, this compound of Abelard and the Man of Ross had
not long to live: "Too eager pressing to the summit given, / [he]
O'erstepped the line, and found himself in heaven" (15–16). Elsewhere, Thompson adapted a Popeian epitaph for her occasional tribute "On the Right Honourable Lady S——r——t" (Thompson, 46–
47). Her assurance that "here concenter'd all perfections meet / To
make the woman and the saint complete" (7–8) echoes Pope's remark
on Mrs. Corbet's cancer: "The Saint sustain'd it, but the Woman dy'd"
(Pope, "Epitaph. On Mrs. Corbet," 10). Pope's somber distinction
between Mrs. Corbet's martyrlike spirit and tormented body becomes
a lighthearted compliment to Lady S——r——t's "form angelic, with
a bounteous heart" (6).

Popeian allusions function in poems by women like the classical
allusions in poems by privileged contemporaries. Samuel Johnson
defended such allusions because "there is a community of mind in
it. Classical quotation is the *parole* of literary men all over the world."[4]
Lacking this pledge of literacy, women (and unlettered men) created
a new parole, intimating thorough knowledge of the principal English
poets. Allusion relates Mary Whateley's "Imitation of the Third Elegy
of the Third Book of Tibullus" with Pope's modern classics (Whateley,
28–30). She borrows Eloisa's complaint from Pope and gives it to her
Roman lover, who exclaims, "But what is Honour, Wealth, or Fame,
to Love?" (26; cf. "Eloisa to Abelard," 80). She would gladly resign
any advantages for a simple life with Philander: "These let Ambition
share, be Peace my Lot; / *Philander* mine, and all beside forgot" (37–
38). The couplet appears to amalgamate "This day, be Bread and Peace
my Lot" from Pope's "Universal Prayer" (45) with Eloisa's envious
remark of the blameless vestal, "the world forgetting, by the world
forgot" ("Eloisa to Abelard," 208). The combination of sources is odd,
but their conjunction is apt in this context, the speaker's wish for
marriage and rural retirement. The concluding couplet of "Imitation
of . . . Tibullus" revisits Whateley's favorite *Pastorals*. "Ah! cease, ye
Sighs, to tear my anxious Breast!" (45) recalls Hylas' plea in Pope's
"Autumn" (39–40). Whateley probably retained many of Pope's couplets in memory, recalling and adapting phrases as she composed. But
her choices were purposeful, in this instance reconciling her speaker's
innocence with her passion.

"The Vanity of external Accomplishments" uses allusion to authorize Whateley's satiric purpose (Whateley, 87–90). Mocking feminine affectations, she announces, "Forgive an artless Maid who boldly tries / To vindicate the notions you despise" (5–6). The reference to *Essay on Man* seems tongue-in-cheek given her professed inconsequence, but it hints the gravity of her subject. The poem, like Mary Leapor's "Dorinda," employs both *The Rape of the Lock* and "Epistle to a Lady." Whateley's opening description of Belinda recapitulates Clarissa's speech, with echoes of Pope's valediction.

> Who wou'd not sigh for that inchanting Air,
> Which speaks *Belinda* fairest of the Fair;
> Which Men of Sense admire, and Beaux adore,
> Did one Charm last when Beauty blooms no more?
> When those resistless Eyes no longer shine,
> And the fresh Roses in those Cheeks decline;
> When Age contracts those gay enliv'ning Airs,
> And that fair Forehead crowns with hoary Hairs.
>
> (7–14)

Having reopened the issue Clarissa failed to resolve, Whateley proceeds to expose women's follies by way of the "Epistle to a Lady" ("Why then is *Delia* by the World admir'd? / Her Talk is trifling, and her Tongue untir'd," 21–22), the "Essay on Criticism" ("Camilla," 36–43), and the *Rape of the Lock*.

In "Vanity," Whateley ultimately blames men for encouraging women's affectations (44–51). She concludes by recommending that women cultivate friendship, useful learning, and "Good Sense and Virtue" (53–59). This list resembles Pope's prescriptions. But beneath the Popeian facade lurks Whateley's feminist intention; women's behavior should not be contingent on masculine approval. Because "from our wise *Lords* [women's affectations] first receiv'd their Birth," women must repudiate men's expectations (49). Instead of flirting and applying cosmetics, they should read and exercise. Whateley's advice is hardly revolutionary, but her indictment of men's influence is acerbic. Even Pope's relatively sympathetic satires placed women's behavior in relation to men: Belinda was threatened with spinsterhood, and Martha's virtues opened in relation to a hypothetical husband. Whateley's Popeian allusions assimilated her poem into this tradition of satires against women, enhancing her authority. But they also helped insure positive reception of her moderate feminist opinions.

American women were no less conversant with Pope's poems, as the writings of two contemporaries of the revolutionary era attest. Ann Eliza Bleecker's poems bristle with a range of allusions.[5] Pope's consolatory power emerges when she quotes his epitaph on Mrs. Corbet in her elegy "On Mrs. Joanna Lupton" (Bleecker, 198–99, lines 11–12). She describes Lupton as "God's steward for the poor" (18), a reference to Pope's "Epistle to Bathurst" (174), and as "Sister and friend, each tender name in one" (23), a chaste version of Eloisa's cry in "Eloisa to Abelard" (154). Pope's phrases occured to Bleecker in moments of sorrow, but she also appropriated them on playful occasions. A tetrameter poem "To [Mr. L——]" (Bleecker, 201–3) refers to his "poetic fit" (*Rape*, 4.60) in which he writes like Donne, "whose prose was verse, and verse was prose" (12): a rare allusion to Pope's *Dunciad* (*Variorum*, 1.228). In another poem to Mr. L——, she denies his accusation of plagiarism and demonstrates that he is the guilty party (Bleecker, 203–5):

> To prove my false accuser guilty,
> Repeat his borrow'd lines I will t'ye:
>
> > 'No goose that swims, but soon or late
> > 'Will find some gander for a mate.'
>
> You'll find this couplet, I'll engage,
> In Wife of Bath, the hundredth page,
> Volume the second,—works of Pope—
> Brother, you're now convinc'd, I hope.
>
> (34–41)

Both poets evidently sprinkled their letters and poems with Popeian allusions, sharing their mutual delight in his verse.

The most poignant evidence of Bleecker's attachment to Pope occurs in "Written in the Retreat from Burgoyne" (Bleecker, 215–17). The poem memorializes the death of Bleecker's youngest daughter, Abella, when a revolutionary campaign forced them to flee their rural home for Albany. "Was it for this, with thee a pleasing load, / I sadly wander'd thro' the hostile wood . . . ?" (1–2). Her question's origin in Thalestris's petulant speech in *The Rape of the Lock* ("Was it for this you took such constant Care?" 4.97) heightens by contrast Bleecker's despair for her genuine loss. She describes the auspicious beginning of her journey to rescue her children "from the scalper's pow'r" (8). She rested beneath a tree, Abella playing on the grass, while her sister, "unconscious of her danger, laughing rove[d], / Nor dread[ed] the painted savage in the groves" (13–14). Bleecker's reference to Pope's imaginary Indians in their groves ("Windsor Forest," 409), while describing her flight from brutal scalpers, suggests his poetry influenced the way she interpreted experience.

Bleecker even casts her resignation in terms of Pope's "Satire IIii." She writes, "What tho' my houses, lands, and goods are gone, / My babes remain—these I can call my own" (21–22). Pope referred to legal penalties that dispossessed many Catholic families: "My lands are sold, my Father's house is gone; / I'll hire another's, is not that my own . . . ?" (155–56). Although contemporary English Catholics suffered severe inequities, Pope had carved a satisfactory life for himself and his parents. His Horatian complacency was justified and appropriate. But for a woman whose home has become a battlefield, fleeing with her children from soldiers and savages, Pope's sentiment seems inadequate. The allusion is that of a woman groping for words to describe her ordeal, recalling phrases that formerly illuminated her life. That her Popeian allusions ring false renders Bleecker's attempt even more poignant. She evidently never reconciled herself to Abella's death ("Her spirit fled and left me ghastly clay!" 31). Bleecker's recourse to Pope in the midst of tragedy confirms his shaping power over women readers' perceptions.

Pope also shaped Phillis Wheatley's perceptions of the Revolution. Julian Mason believes that Wheatley adopted Pope's neoclassical style not only because it was fashionable and available to her but because "Homer's heroes [tugged] on her impressionable young mind," inspiring her conceptions of revolutionary generals Lee and Washington (Wheatley, 16). Wheatley's "To His Excellency General Washington" (Wheatley, 164–67), composed in October 1775 before he drove the British from Boston (164 n. 38), casts Washington as the Achilles of a modern Trojan War.

> Celestial choir! enthron'd in realms of light,
> Columbia's scenes of glorious toils I write.
> While freedom's cause her anxious breast alarms,
> She flashes dreadful in refulgent arms.
> See mother earth her offspring's fate bemoan,
> And nations gaze at scenes before unknown!
>
> (1–6)

As the Greeks once looked to Achilles for salvation, so Americans now solicit Washington: "Hear every tongue thy guardian aid implore!" (26).

In "On the Capture of General Lee," Wheatley marvelously interprets the general's ironic capture by his former British regiment as an episode reminiscent of the Trojan War (Wheatley, 67–70). Lee is approached by his former comrade, a "latent foe to friendship" (3), who requests, "Vouchsafe thy presence as my honour'd guest: / From martial cares a space unbend thy soul / In social banquet, and the sprightly bowl" (12–14). In true epic fashion, Lee replies, "Ill fits it me, who such an army guide" to relax while "this day important, with loud voice demands / Our wisest Counsels, and our bravest hands" (16, 19–20). This poem, including an exchange between Lee and his captor that is worthy of Agamemnon and Achilles, is outrageous outside the context of Wheatley's Popeian/Homeric model. But in that context, it remains an imaginative attempt to ennoble what was at the time a doubtful contest. Working with little knowledge of the actual event or personalities (Wheatley, 167 n. 41), Wheatley construed Lee's embarrassing capture as a display of American intrepidity. Taunted by his captors, Lee prophesies American victory in terms characteristic of Pope's Achilles or Hector but not likely to have been tolerated by a real adversary: "Find in your train of boasted heroes, one / To match the praise of Godlike Washington" (65–66).

Mason observes that "On the Capture of General Lee" remained unpublished until the late nineteenth century, probably because Lee's animosity toward Washington—of which Wheatley was unaware—made his speech unlikely. But at this distance, Wheatley's revolutionary poems appear literary examples of the phenomenon Simon Schama observed in Benjamin West's painting of "The Death of General Wolfe."[6] Like West, Wheatley cast modern soldiers in classical configurations. She adjusted real incidents, such as Lee's capture or Washington's assumption of command, to Pope's version of ancient heroism. Although Wheatley was evacuated from her home during the siege of Boston, thus suffering the hardships of war like Ann Eliza Bleecker (albeit to a less tragic extent), Pope's translations of Homer sufficed her imagination and buoyed her through the experience.

Although Homer was her preeminent influence, Wheatley was familiar with Pope's canon. His phrases glimmer throughout her poems. "Thoughts on the Works of Providence" thanks God for His mercy "when wants and woes might be our righteous lot, / Our God forgetting, by our God forgot!" (Wheatley, 67–71, lines 103–4). Wheatley plucked from "Eloisa to Abelard" its evocation of the blameless vestal's lot (208), resetting it in her religious meditation. "On Imagination" briefly (and appropriately) evokes Belinda's toilette in *The Rape of the Lock*, as Wheatley hails the "imperial queen": "Thy wond'rous acts in beauteous order stand" (Wheatley, 78–80, line 3). "A Funeral Poem on the Death of C. E. an Infant of Twelve Months" echoes both the *Essay on Man* and the *Dunciad*, as Wheatley imagines the baby's flight to heaven.

> Enlarg'd he sees unnumber'd systems roll,
> Beneath him sees the universal whole,
> Planets on planets run their destin'd round,
> And circling wonders fill the vast profound.
>
> (Wheatley, 80–81, lines 3–6)

In *Essay on Man*, Pope had reminded Bolingbroke that "thro' worlds unnumbered tho' the God be known," humans must trace Him in this (1.21). Perhaps a clue would appear if he "observe[d] how system into system runs" (1.25). Wheatley's infant is no longer confined to speculation as he flies among "growing splendors" (8). But "the vast profound" he witnesses was originally Lewis Theobald's (or Colley Cibber's) mind in Pope's *Dunciad*, where the hero sat "sinking from thought to thought, a vast profound!" (*Variorum*, 1.112). Further, when Wheatley's C. E. arrives in heaven, he exclaims, "Thanks to my God, who snatch'd me to the skies" (14), an allusion to Pope's "Elegy to the Memory of an Unfortunate Lady" ("Fate snatch'd her early to the pitying sky," 24). From such disparate sources, Wheatley composed a poem to console the bereaved parents. Perhaps, if this poem was commissioned for C. E.'s funeral, Wheatley wrote in haste, Popeian recollections occuring as she sought phrases to describe the infant's heavenward flight. The phrases she chose, even the mock-Miltonic "vast profound," were suitably elevated and dignified when removed from their original contexts. Wheatley, like other women poets, had learned to transmute even Pope's witty or gothic modes for her Christian tributes. When she exhorts "Captain H——D, of the 65th Regiment," "Go, hero brave, still grace the post of fame, / And add new glories to thine honour'd name" (Wheatley, 82, lines 7–8), buried under her new martial context is Pope's salute to Belinda's hair (*Rape*, 5.142).

Phillis Wheatley appropriately concludes my study. Like many women writers, she overcame obstacles to literary achievement, although hers were arguably the cruelest. Some eighteenth-century women writers were self-taught laborers, but Wheatley alone experienced slavery. The Wheatleys treated Phillis kindly, educating her and encouraging her writing. But despite her education, Wheatley, more than other women, endured having her gift treated as a phenomenon, the effusions of a "young untutored African."[7] Despite her bondage, Wheatley received an education more typical of privileged women. Besides the Bible, she read classical authors, such as Homer, Virgil, and Horace, in translation. Though not composed of the Greek and Roman texts reserved for males, Wheatley's reading resembled that of, for example, Fanny Burney.

One other aspect renders Wheatley representative. Of British writers, Mary Wheatley introduced Phillis probably to Milton and certainly to Pope (Wheatley, 4). Though some scholars have wondered what predecessors Wheatley's verse would have reflected had she survived into the Romantic era, and Julian Mason wishes she had been earlier acquainted with Milton (Wheatley, 16–17), Pope manifestly influenced her poems. In "To Maecenas," her description of Homer's *Iliad* really fits Pope's (Wheatley, 49–51).

> While *Homer* paints lo! circumfus'd in air,
> Celestial Gods in mortal forms appear;
> Swift as they move hear each recess rebound,
> Heav'n quakes, earth trembles, and the shores resound.
> . . . .
> When gentler strains demand thy graceful song,
> The length'ning line moves languishing along.
> When great *Patroclus* courts *Achilles*' aid,
> The grateful tribute of my tears is paid;
> Prone on the shore he feels the pangs of love,
> And stern *Pelides* tend'rest passions move.
>
> (7–10, 15–20)

Wheatley's Popeian style denotes her source. The bounding stresses of line 9 ("hear each recess rebound"), followed by a majestic alexandrine marking the gods' flight, imitate Pope's interpretations of Homeric effects. Wheatley continues to use onomatopoeia in "the length'ning line" of Homer's "gentler strains." The entire passage recalls Pope's demonstration in the "Essay on Criticism" almost as much as his *Iliad*.

Her climactic image, Patroclus's appeal to Achilles, confirms not only Wheatley's poetic indebtedness to Pope but her response as his reader. Pope courted sentimental responses in his *Iliad* translation. In book 16, he discerned in the heroes' interview "the softer Parts of [Achilles'] Character" (*Poems*, 8:234 n. 8). He extended Achilles' comparison of Patroclus to a weeping girl, including Achilles himself as an indulgent mother (16.9–16, *Poems*, 8:235 n. 11). Through such techniques, Pope hoped to please all genteel readers, but especially women. Near the end of the century, Phillis Wheatley's response suggests the continued appeal to women of Pope's Homeric translations. Pope's gods fired her imagination, but his heroes wrung tears. This combination of majesty and sentiment inspired Wheatley as she composed her elegies and panegyrics and emulated Popeian virtuosity. She may not have conquered Parnassus, but Wheatley's reading of Pope inspired her to attempt the climb.

Like no writer before him, Pope moved eighteenth-century women readers to respond. Some used his poems as masks for their enactments of feminine passion. Others converted his poems into didactic texts. Still others emulated his persona or his prosody. Most women expressed or implied some ambivalence about writing, not to mention publishing, in what was traditionally an aristocratic men's genre. But whether angry or inspired, moved or amused, critical or emulative, women gradually followed Pope into the marketplace, where the rest is women's literary history.

As a group, Pope's eighteenth-century women readers suggest a model of fearless critical reading. Few of these women identified with Pope's constructions of femininity. Instead, women appropriated and revised Pope's images to suit their own contexts, whether more genteel, more devout, or more feminist. Current analyses implying that contemporary women were somehow victimized by Pope's gendered rhetoric should reconsider the critical acuity with which his female audience often read. Such a consideration necessarily extends the horizon of meanings we can assign to Pope's work at its earliest reception and the horizon of cultural perceptions we may assume available to eighteenth-century women readers.

As women eagerly sought to articulate their experiences in literary genres sanctioned by an exemplar of their male-dominated culture, their writings formed a subversive coda to Pope's canon. As Anne Ingram, Lady Irwin, commented in her "Epistle to Mr. Pope" (1736):

By custom doom'd to folly, sloth and ease,
No wonder, Pope such female triflers sees:
But would the satyrist confess the truth,
Nothing so like as male and female youth;
Nothing so like as man and woman old;
Their joys, their loves, their hates, if truly told.

(1–6)

Eighteenth-century women, trained to think of themselves as "the sex," nevertheless intuited the feminist principle that men and women are not essentially different. They read Pope as women but recognized the ease with which his "masculine" verse could often be altered to include, or articulate, the feminine point of view. Where his opinions seemed dangerous or inimical to women, they published their misgivings. Through their prose criticism and poetic revisions, Pope's women readers appropriated his texts' themes and images to express their own opinions, and versions, of experience: "Their joys, their loves, their hates . . . truly told."

Notes
Bibliography
Index

Notes

Introduction: Alexander Pope, Literary Creativity, and Eighteenth-Century Women

1. Laura Brown, *Alexander Pope* (Oxford: B. Blackwell, 1985); Ellen Pollak, *The Poetics of Sexual Myth: Gender and Ideology in the Verse of Swift and Pope* (Chicago: University of Chicago Press, 1985).

2. Ruth Salvaggio, *Enlightened Absence: Neoclassical Configurations of the Feminine* (Urbana: University of Illinois Press, 1988).

3. Penelope Wilson, "Engendering the Reader: 'Wit and Poetry and Pope' Once More," in *The Enduring Legacy: Alexander Pope Tercentenary Essays*, ed. G. S. Rousseau and Pat Rogers (Cambridge: Cambridge University Press, 1988), 63, 64–65.

4. Valerie Rumbold, *Women's Place in Pope's World* (Cambridge: Cambridge University Press, 1989); Maynard Mack, *Alexander Pope: A Life* (New York: W. W. Norton, 1986).

5. Donna Landry, *The Muses of Resistance: Laboring-Class Women's Poetry in Britain, 1739–1796* (Cambridge: Cambridge University Press, 1990).

6. Alexander Pope, "A Hymn Written in Windsor Forest," in Pope, *The Poems of Alexander Pope*, ed. John Butt et al., 10 vols. (London: Methuen, 1967), 6:194. All further quotations of Pope's poems will be taken from this edition.

7. Maynard Mack discusses possible creative implications of Pope's garden and grotto in *Pope*, 358–66.

8. Maynard Mack recounts the sad fate of Pope's villa and grounds in *The Garden and the City: Retirement and Politics in the Later Poetry of Pope, 1731–1743* (Toronto: University of Toronto Press, 1969), 283 n. 9. Appendix E, "The Legendary Poet," contains a selection of contemporary poems by male admirers celebrating the garden and grotto (266–71).

9. Maynard Mack reprints part of chant 3 of Jacques Delille's "Les Jardins" (1801) in *Garden*, 270–71.

10. Lady Mary Wortley Montagu to the Countess of Mar, April

1722, in *The Complete Letters of Lady Mary Wortley Montagu*, ed. Robert Halsband, 3 vols. (Oxford: Clarendon, 1965), 2:15.

11. Lady Mary Wortley Montagu, "Her Palace placed beneath a muddy road," in *Essays and Poems and Simplicity, A Comedy*, ed. Robert Halsband and Isobel Grundy (Oxford: Clarendon, 1977), 247–51.

12. Elizabeth Carter's report to Rev. Nicolas Carter is quoted by Sylvia Harcstark Myers in *The Bluestocking Circle: Women, Friendship, and the Life of the Mind in Eighteenth-Century England* (Oxford: Clarendon, 1990), 48.

13. Samuel Johnson, "Ad Elisam Popi Horto Lauros Carpentum," in *Gentleman's Magazine* 8 (1738): 372.

14. *Gentleman's Magazine* 8 (1738): 429 features "The *Latin* Epigram . . . Englished" by "Alexis," an "Imitation of the Latin, by Mr. S[tephe]n D[uc]k," and "Another" by "Urbanus" (Johnson). Carter's three answers to Johnson's Latin epigram appear on the same page as these tributes.

15. Claudine Herrman describes this as an inevitable aspect of women's writing in a patriarchal culture. See *Les Voleuses de langue* (Paris: des Femmes, 1976).

16. Worried that Pope and Carter might become friends as the result of her Crousaz translation, Sir George Oxenden warned her father, "there is hardly an instance of a woman of letters entering into an intimacy of acquaintance with men of wit and parts, particularly poets, who were not thoroughly abused and maltreated by them, in print, after some time; and Mr. Pope has done it more than once." See Carter, *Memoirs of the Life of Mrs. Elizabeth Carter, With A New Edition Of Her Poems . . . To Which Are Added, Some Miscellaneous Essays In Prose*, ed. Rev. Montagu Pennington (London: F. C. Rivington and J. Rivington, 1807), 29–30. Carter, working among the writers at St. John's Gate, was probably well aware of Pope's propensity to insert "dunces" into successive editions of the *Dunciad*. Crousaz duly appeared in *Dunciad* 4.198 (1742).

17. Jael Henrietta Pye, *A short account, of the principal seats and gardens, in and about Twickenham* (London, 1760), vii–viii.

18. Hannah More to Mrs. Gwatkin from Hampton Court, in William Roberts, *Memoirs of the Life and Correspondence of Mrs. Hannah More*, 2 vols. (New York: Harper and Brothers, 1851), 1:34–35. Maynard Mack speculates that Pope's house may have been extended by June 1760, when Horace Walpole mentions Stanhope's alterations in a letter (*Garden*, 282 n. 8).

19. The remains of Pope's grotto may still be seen today, by private arrangement with the Sisters of St. Catherine's Convent of Mercy, which occupies the property. When I visited in 1987, the grotto was

virtually a dark, dank tunnel, with few traces remaining of Pope's sparkling inset minerals.

20. Ann Yearsley, "Written on a Visit," in *Poems on Various Subjects* (London: G. G. J. Robinson and J. Robinson, 1787), 139–43.

21. Anna Seward to Mrs. Childers, 30 March 1804, in Seward's *Letters of Anna Seward: Written Between the Years 1784 and 1807*, 6 vols. (Edinburgh: A. Constable, 1811), 6:144–46.

22. In his *Eighteenth-Century Women Poets: An Oxford Anthology* (Oxford: Oxford University Press, 1989), Roger Lonsdale speculates that Seward's *Original Sonnets* (1799) included poems dated from the 1770's that were "reworkings in the increasingly popular sonnet form of earlier poems" (312). Based on its mature technique, I agree with Lonsdale that if Seward wrote this poem in her youth, she probably recast it, after thorough revision, as a sonnet.

23. I paraphrase Anne Finch, countess of Winchilsea, in "The Introduction": "Alas! a woman that attempts the pen, / Such an intruder on the rights of men, / Such a presumptuous Creature, is esteem'd, / The fault, can by no vertue be redeem'd" (9–12). See Finch, *Selected Poems of Anne Finch, Countess of Winchilsea*, ed. Katherine M. Rogers (New York: F. Unger, 1979), 5–7.

24. Joseph Wittreich, *Feminist Milton* (Ithaca: Cornell University Press, 1987). Wittreich's argument refers not only to women's reception but to ideas about women that Milton placed in the more conservative context of his milieu. Pope's feminine constructions, by contrast, were never deemed revolutionary.

25. Had I attempted a definitive study, this book would have been much longer. Students of eighteenth-century women writers will recognize various omissions, particularly of women playwrights. Discussions of other figures are brief because they have already been treated at length elsewhere. For example, Ann Messenger included a chapter on "Arabella Fermor, 1714 and 1769: Alexander Pope and Frances Moore Brooke" in *His and Hers: Essays in Restoration and Eighteenth-Century Literature* (Lexington: University Press of Kentucky, 1986), 148–71. Although my opinion of Brooke's novel differs from Messenger's, my discussion of *The History of Emily Montague* is brief so that I may concentrate on less familiar prose responses. Similarly, Valerie Rumbold treats Mary Wollstonecraft's Popeian allusions in *A Vindication of the Rights of Woman*; see Rumbold, *Women's Place*, 265–68. Donna Landry discusses Mary Leapor's second volume in relation to Pope (78–119) and Ann Yearsley's sometimes subtle references (120–85). I hope my study will stimulate further research on all these figures and on the relations between women's and men's poetry and literary criticism in the eighteenth century.

26. William K. Wimsatt reproduces and describes the portrait, probably painted between 1717 and 1720, in *The Portraits of Alexander Pope* (New Haven: Yale University Press, 1965), 20–23, plate 3.2. Maynard Mack reproduces and discusses the painting in *Pope*, 341–43.

27. See, for example, Addison's *Spectator* 10 (12 March 1711), where he describes his ideal: women who "join all the Beauties of the Mind to the Ornaments of Dress, and inspire a kind of Awe and Respect, as well as Love, into their Male-Beholders." See Addison et al., *The Spectator*, ed. Donald F. Bond, 5 vols. (Oxford: Clarendon, 1965), 1:46–47.

1. *"Appeals to the Ladies":* *Pope and His* Iliad *Readers*

1. Samuel Johnson, "Pope," in Johnson, *Lives of the English Poets*, ed. George Birkbeck Hill, 3 vols. (Oxford: Clarendon, 1905), 3:240.

2. Aaron Hill, "The Progress of Wit: A Caveat," in *Popeiana X: The Dunciad and Other Matters, 1730* (New York: Garland, 1975), 15, line 2.

3. In *Pope*, Laura Brown argues that Pope's imperialist ideology is directly linked to his trivialization of Belinda (18–21) and to the "misogyny" of the "Epistle to a Lady" (101). Ellen Pollak states there is no question that "the texts of [Swift and Pope] are misogynist," because they are "products of a phallocentric culture and its authorizing sign-systems and codes" (181–82). In "'The Point Where Sense and Dulness Meet': What Pope Knows About Knowing and About Women," *Eighteenth-Century Studies* 19 (2): 206–34, Carol Virginia Pohli notes that "discreet misogyny is a disguised but observable feature of Pope's work" (208). She concludes that "the instances of misogyny" are sometimes intended as an Augustan critique of the "human penchant for coping with mystery by denying or scorning it" (233).

4. Hans-Robert Jauss, "Literary History as a Challenge to Literary Theory," in *Toward an Aesthetic of Reception*, trans. Timothy Bahti (Minneapolis: University of Minnesota Press, 1982), 3–45.

5. Lawrence Echard, *Prefaces to Terence's Comedies and Plautus's Comedies*, ed. John Barnard (1694; reprint, Los Angeles: Augustan Reprint Society, 1968), xvii–xviii.

6. James Winn drew my attention to Dryden's "Discourse Concerning the Original and Progress of Satire," which confirms Dryden's awareness of his female audience. Dryden explains that he and his colleagues have translated Juvenal and Persius "for the Pleasure and Entertainment, of those Gentlemen and Ladies, who tho they are not Scholars are not Ignorant," that is, for readers curious about whether

the satirists' wit equals their fame. See Dryden, *The Works of John Dryden*, ed. H. T. Swedenberg, Jr., et al., 20 vols. (Berkeley: University of California Press, 1956–89), 4:87.

7. John Dryden, "Dedication of the *Aeneis*," *Works*, 5:327–28.

8. Alexander Pope, *The Iliad of Homer*, ed. Maynard Mack, in Pope, *Poems*, vols. 7 and 8, 7:25 n. 2.

9. Alan Roper describes this episode in his exhaustive commentary on Dryden's *Virgil*; see Dryden, *Works*, 6:1114, n. 810:29–35. James Winn discusses the quarrel in *John Dryden and His World* (New Haven: Yale University Press, 1987), 475–84. An older account is Harry M. Geduld's in *Prince of Publishers: A Study of the Work and Career of Jacob Tonson* (Bloomington: Indiana University Press, 1969), 73.

10. John Dryden, *The Letters of John Dryden with Letters Addressed to Him*, ed. Charles E. Ward (Durham: Duke University Press, 1942), 80.

11. In *Pope's Once and Future Kings: Satire and Politics in the Early Career* (Knoxville: University of Tennessee Press, 1978), John Aden argued that Pope's emphasis on compassion and empathy, especially in the later books of the *Iliad* and throughout the *Odyssey*, reflected his concern over the vindictive Whig policies that had imprisoned Oxford and driven Bolingbroke into exile. Brean Hammond tempers this account in *Pope and Bolingbroke: A Study of Friendship and Influence* (Columbia: University of Missouri Press, 1984), 36, 40. But Matthew Hodgart, comparing the subscription lists for the *Iliad* and *Odyssey*, concludes that after the *Iliad*, even Walpole felt "that Pope was now not only politically safe but had even become a national monument." See Hodgart, "The Subscription List for Pope's *Iliad*, 1715," in *The Dress of Words: Essays in Restoration and Eighteenth Century Literature in Honor of Richmond P. Bond*, ed. Robert B. White, Jr. (Lawrence: University of Kansas Press, 1978), 34.

12. Stephen N. Zwicker, *Politics and Language in Dryden's Poetry* (Princeton: Princeton University Press, 1984), 187. See also Winn, *Dryden*, especially 484–92.

13. James Winn drew my attention to the political tension between Tonson and Dryden; Tonson altered the translation's plates so that Aeneas's profile resembled William's, but Dryden refused to dedicate the work to William (see Roper's commentary in Dryden, *Works*, 6:871–72). In the translation, Dryden clearly intends Aeneas's banishment to recall James's.

14. Jean H. Hagstrum, *Sex and Sensibility: Ideal and Erotic Love from Milton to Mozart* (Chicago: University of Chicago Press, 1980), 70. See also, however, Hagstrum's discussion of Dryden's treatment of Dido, 102–12.

15. Bezaleel Morrice, "Satire I. On the *English* Translations of Homer," in *Popeiana II: Pope's Homer, 1714–1719* (New York: Garland, 1975), 8, line 47.

16. Pat Rogers, "Pope and his Subscribers," *Publishing History* 3 (1978): 22–23.

17. See Maynard Mack's introduction to Pope's *Iliad*, in Pope, *Poems*, 7:xxxvi n. 5.

18. Although Pope includes one entry under "Anger" in his index "of the internal Passions" at the end of the epic—and two each under "Fear" and "Revenge"—by far the greatest emphasis is placed on the more tender passions, such as "Grief" ("Grief in a fine woman," "Grief in two parents in tenderness for their Child"), which merits ten entries, and "Love" ("Love of a Mother to her Son," "Brotherly Love"), which garners six. Pope evidently compiled his index according to the passions he thought either would or should most interest his readers. See *Poems*, 8:602–3.

19. Grover Cronin, Jr., and Paul A. Doyle, eds., *Pope's Iliad: An Examination by William Melmoth* (Washington, D.C.: Catholic University Press, 1960), 28.

20. Richmond Lattimore, trans., *The Iliad of Homer* (Chicago: University of Chicago Press, 1976), book 6, lines 479–81.

21. Anne Dacier, trans., *L'Iliade d'Homere, traduit en françois avec des remarques*, 3 vols., 1st ed. (Paris: chez Rigaud, Directeur L'Imprimerie Royale, 1711), 1:270–71. Hector begs "mighty Jupiter, and all you other gods of Olympus," that when "his people see [Astyanax] return from vanquishing his enemies, and bearing the bloody spoils of their brave chiefs, they will cry as he passes that the prince is much more valiant than his father, and that his mother, when she hears their praises, will feel all the joy of having a son so great and so virtuous" (my trans.).

22. For Chetwood's version of book 6 see Pope, *Poems*, 10: app. F.

23. See Hagstrum, chapter 7, for a discussion of this evolving role. For a feminist analysis of the consequences of this "bourgeois myth of woman," see Pollak, chapters 1 and 2.

24. John Ogilby, trans., *Homer His Iliads* (London: Printed for T. Roycroft, 1660), 11.243–44.

25. George Chapman, trans., *Chapman's Homer*, ed. Allardyce Nicoll, 2 vols. (New York: Pantheon, 1969), 11.194–95.

26. Catherine Talbot to Elizabeth Carter, 31 October 1746, in Carter, *A Series of Letters between Mrs. Elizabeth Carter and Miss Catherine Talbot, From the Year 1741 to 1770. . . . . ,* ed. Rev. Montagu Pennington, 4 vols. (London: F. C. Rivington and J. Rivington, 1809), 1:171.

27. Dacier, *The Iliad of Homer, with notes . . . by Madam Dacier. Done*

from the French by Mr. Ozell . . . . , trans. John Ozell, 5 vols. (London: B. Lintot, 1712), 2:136 n. 1. Although Ozell frequently compressed Dacier's prose translation to fit his loose blank verse, he faithfully translated her remarks. Pope quotes Ozell's translation of Dacier's "Remarques" throughout his *Iliad* commentary, and he refers to these passages as Dacier's without noting that his source is not the original text but the English version.

28. Howard Weinbrot discusses contemporary hostility toward Homer in *"The Rape of the Lock* and the Contexts of Warfare," in Rousseau and Rogers, 22–30.

29. Laura Brown, "The Defenseless Woman and the Development of English Tragedy," *Studies in English Literature* 22 (1982): 429–43.

30. Kathryn Shevelow, *Women and Print Culture: The Construction of Femininity in the Early Periodical* (London: Routledge, 1989). See especially chapter 4, "'A Sort of Sex in Souls': The *Tatler* and the *Spectator*," 93–145.

31. See particularly Salvaggio, chapter 1, "Histories, Theories, Configurations," 3–28.

32. Anne Dacier, *Des Causes de la Corruption du Goust* (Paris: Au Dêpens de Rigaud Directeur de l'Imprimerie Royale, 1714), 467. Dacier claims that Helen's self-accusations demonstrate "an excellent moral: she sees the horror of her crime, she detests it, and she attributes it to her lack of virtue" (my trans.).

33. Felicity Nussbaum has traced its origin to male fears of chaos after the Civil War. See *The Brink of All We Hate: English Satires on Women, 1660–1750* (Lexington: University Press of Kentucky, 1984). Chapter 2, "Rhyming Women Dead: Restoration Satires on Women," 8–42, illuminates this phenomenon.

34. Mary Astell, *Reflections Upon Marriage*, 3d ed. (London: R. Wilkin, 1706), preface.

35. Of a couplet in "To a Young Lady, with the Works of Voiture" ("Still in Constraint your suff'ring Sex remains, / Or bound in formal, or in real Chains"), Mack remarks, "No twentieth-century feminist could have said it better" (*Pope*, 241).

36. Jervas's portrait is reproduced as plate 30 in Mack, *Pope*, 246, and in color as plate 19 in Elizabeth Einberg, ed., *Manners and Morals: Hogarth and British Painting 1700–1760* (London: Tate Gallery, 1987). In *Dress in Eighteenth-Century Europe, 1715–1789* (New York: Holmes and Meier, 1985), Aileen Ribeiro describes the "closed robe" as "a popular form of undress for the first half of the eighteenth century" (33). In an earlier study, Ribeiro speculates that the wrapped robe in which Michael Dahl painted Henrietta, Countess Ashburnam, in 1717 may represent a "nightgown" or "bedroom gown" before the night-

gown had evolved into a formal, open robe; see Ribeiro, *A Visual History of Costume: The Eighteenth Century*, (London: B. T. Batsford, 1983), plates 16, 28. Einberg describes the same costume, reproduced as plate 18 in *Manners and Morals*, as Knelleresque classical drapery (46). Contemporaries, then, seem to have associated ladies' undress robes with classical garments.

37. Richard Steele et al., *The Guardian*, 2 vols. (London: C. Bathurst et al., 1795), 2:103. I attribute these essays to Addison on the authority of Peter Smithers, who discusses Addison's contributions to *The Guardian* in *The Life of Joseph Addison* (Oxford: Clarendon, 1968), 279–83.

38. See Pope, *The Correspondence of Alexander Pope*, ed. George Sherburn, 5 vols. (Oxford: Clarendon, 1956), 1:307.

39. James Winn, *A Window in the Bosom: The Letters of Alexander Pope* (Hamden, Conn.: Archon, 1977), 63–69.

40. See, for example, Pope's letter of 19 July 1713 to Mrs. Marriot (*Corr.*, 1:180–82), in which he first thanks her for her "very witty Epistle" but then confesses "a little Truth. Faith, Madam, I have never seen or read your Letter . . . but find I must see your Letter or dye."

41. John Dennis, *Remarks upon Mr. Pope's Translation of Homer. With Two Letters concerning Windsor Forest and the Temple of Fame*, in *Popeiana II*, 72–73.

42. Thomas Burnet and George Duckett, *Homerides; or, A Letter to Mr. Pope, by Sir Iliad Doggerel*, in *Popeiana II*, 7, 10, 15.

43. Perhaps the most exhaustive treatment of this relationship is still Norman Ault's chapter on "Pope and Addison" in *New Light on Pope* (1949; reprint, Hamden, Conn.: Archon, 1967), 101–27. Maynard Mack includes a judicious discussion of their quarrel in *Pope*, 272–82.

44. Joseph Addison, *The Freeholder, or, Political Essays* (1716; reprint, Ann Arbor, Mich.: University Microfilms, 1967), 143–44.

45. Charles Gildon, *A New Rehearsal*, in *Popeiana I: Early Criticism, 1711–1716* (New York: Garland, 1975), 8.

46. Sir Richard Steele et al., *The Tatler*, ed. Donald F. Bond, 3 vols. (Oxford: Clarendon, 1987), 1:15.

47. Ault quotes Burnet in *Light*, 115 n. 5.

48. Edward Ward, "Durgen or, a Plain Satyr upon a Pompous Satyrist," in *Popeiana VIII: The Dunciad, 1729* (New York: Garland, 1975), 53–54, lines 930, 956.

49. Aaron Hill, 15, lines 1–4.

50. Anne Dacier, "Reflexions sur la premiere Partie de la Preface de M. Pope," in *L'Iliade d'Homere, traduit en françois, avec des remarques*, 3 vols., 2d ed. (Paris: Au Dêpens de Rigaud Directeur de l'Imprimerie Royale, 1719), vol. 3. The quotation appears on pp. 10–11 of the

"Reflexions," an unpaginated appendix. Madame Dacier complains, "I protest I never expected to see myself attacked by Mr. Pope, in a preface in which I expected some little mark of recognition, or perhaps some words of approbation because of my having had the good fortune to think as he does about many things, for example, about ancient morals, after having said in my preface that the princes watched their flocks, that the princesses drew water from the fountain" (my trans.).

51. [Edmund Curll, ed.], *The Popiad* (London: E. Curll, 1728), 29.

52. *L'Iliade*, 2d ed., app., 15–16. Dacier remarks that "a man so useful should not content himself with perfecting the art of epic poetry; that would be too small a thing; he should perfect the art of politics, much more worthy and important than that of poetry; a man capable of correcting Homer will be capable of shaping men—here is a great benefit for a nation!" (my trans.).

53. *L'Iliade*, 2d ed., app., 16. Alcibiades exclaims, "What, My friend! You are capable of correcting Homer, and you amuse yourself with teaching children, instead of occupying yourself with shaping men!" (my trans.).

54. Martin C. Battestin describes Lady Mary's early assistance in Battestin and Battestin, *Henry Fielding: A Life* (London: Routledge, 1989), 56. Lady Mary continued to aid and influence Fielding's career; for example, he sent her his fragmentary satire of Pope's *Dunciad* in 1729—at the same time that Lady Mary composed "Her Palace plac'd beneath a muddy road"—his satire apparently evoked by Pope's insulting reference to his second cousin (78).

55. Miriam Kramnick briefly discusses Lady Mary in her preface to Mary Wollstonecraft's *Vindication of the Rights of Woman* (New York: Penguin, 1983), 39.

56. See Robert Halsband, ed., *Court Eclogs Written in the Year, 1716: Alexander Pope's autograph manuscript of poems by Lady Mary Wortley Montagu* (New York: New York Public Library, 1977).

57. Mary Delany, *The Autobiography and Correspondence of Mrs. Delany. . .* , ed. Sarah Chauncey Woolsey, 2 vols. (1861–62; reprint, Boston: Roberts Brothers, 1879), 1:95. Eliza Haywood's translation of *La Belle Assemblée: or, the Adventures of Six Days. Being a Curious Collection of Remarkable Incidents which happen'd to some of the First Quality in France*, by Madeleine de Gomez (London: Printed for D. Browne, Jr., and S. Chapman) had first appeared in 1724–25; a second edition was published in 1728. Evidently quite popular, Haywood's translation merited an eighth edition in 1765.

58. Carter refers, of course, to Henry Fielding's hog-keeping Parson Trulliber in *Joseph Andrews*.

59. Sylvia Harcstark Myers describes Bishop Thomas Secker as

Catherine Talbot's virtual "foster father," although of Catherine, her mother, and the Seckers, none used the term (62–63).

60. The correspondence, for example, of Pope's *Odyssey* collaborators indicates that William Broome and Elijah Fenton worried incessantly about the epic's lack of decorum. "How I shall get over the bitch and her puppies, the roasting of the black puddings . . . and the cowheel that was thrown at Ulysses' head, I know not," moans Fenton in a typical letter (*Corr.*, 2:233).

61. Elizabeth Carter, trans., *All the Works of Epictetus* (London, 1752), *The Moral Discourses of Epictetus* (1910; reprint, London: J. M. Dent, 1928), 54.

62. Hester Thrale Piozzi, *Thraliana: The Diary of Hester Lynch Thrale (Later Mrs. Piozzi)*, ed. Katherine Balderston, 2 vols. (Oxford: Clarendon, 1951), 1:34. For a perceptive account of Thrale's relation to Pope, see William McCarthy, *Hester Thrale Piozzi: Portrait of a Literary Woman* (Chapel Hill: University of North Carolina Press, 1985), especially 10–15, 54–57, 77–79.

63. See, for example, verses Thrale claims to have written when 13, "Forrester; or, the old Hunter's Petition for Life addressed to Sir Thomas Salusbury. 1758," in *Thraliana*, 1:37–40. Lines 10–11, "Tell me Philosophers why Man was made / Lord of the Wood and Tenant of the Shade?" paraphrase *Essay on Man* 3.152. William McCarthy recently published Thrale's translation of Louis Racine's "Epitre I sur l'Homme," which he interprets as Thrale's Bloomian gesture of rivalry with Pope. See William McCarthy, "A Verse 'Essay on Man' by H. L. Piozzi," *The Age of Johnson* 2 (1989): 375–420.

64. Felicity Nussbaum, "Eighteenth-Century Women's Autobiographical Commonplaces," in *The Private Self: Theory and Practise of Women's Autobiographical Writings*, ed. Shari Benstock (Chapel Hill: University of North Carolina Press, 1988), 166.

65. Joseph Warton is generally recognized as the first critic to popularize the notion that Pope was not a poet of the first rank, as well as the judgment that "though Dryden be the greater genius; yet Pope is the better artist"; see Warton, *Essay on the Genius and Writings of Pope*, 2 vols. (1756–82; reprint, New York: Garland, 1974), 2:411. Throughout the epistolary debate over their respective merits in *Gentleman's Magazine*, Warton's suggestions are developed, and Joseph Weston finally identifies Dryden with "Beef and Pudding" and Pope, with "Sweetmeats" (23 December 1790); see Gretchen M. Foster, ed., *Pope Versus Dryden: A Controversy in Letters to The Gentleman's Magazine, 1789–1791* (Victoria, B. C.: University of Victoria Press, 1989), 125. Foster includes a valuable analysis of middle to late eighteenth-century attitudes toward Pope.

66. Anonymous, "On one of the Admirers of that Translation, who said, *There was a great deal of Wit in Homer,*" *The Flying Post*, 13 April 1728; reprinted in *Popeiana VI: The Dunciad I, 1728* (New York: Garland, 1975), 32–33, lines 21–22, 25–26.

67. Judith Cowper's verses "To Mr. Pope—Written in his Works" (1717) contain eight couplets praising Pope's *Homer*, but the poem remained in manuscript for many years (*The Cowper Anthology*, MS. 28101, Addison Collection, British Library, London). See chapter 3, "Women's Poetic Addresses to Pope."

68. [Elizabeth Tollet], *Poems on Several Occasions. With Anne Boleyn to King Henry VIII. An Epistle.* (London: J. Clarke, 1724), 52.

69. Pope's note to *Iliad* 17.57, on Menelaus's slaughter of Euphorbus, mentions Pythagoras's notion "that his Soul transmigrated to him from this Hero" as a "Conceit . . . famous in Antiquity," but he does not mention Pythagoras's birth on the Isle of Samos (*Poems*, 8:290 n. 57). Tollet's epithet "Samian Sage" originated therefore in her independent knowledge of the philosopher, not merely in her acquaintance with Pope's translation.

70. Elizabeth Tollet, *Poems on Several Occasion. With Anne Boleyn to King Henry VIII. An Epistle.* 2d ed. (London: T. Lownds, [1756?]), preface, i.

71. Julian D. Mason, in his introduction to her poems, affirms that Phillis Wheatley's "favorite volumes are reported to have been the Bible, a collection of tales from mythology, and Pope's Homer," and that the greatest influences on her poetry were religion and neoclassicism. See Phillis Wheatley, *The Poems of Phillis Wheatley*, ed. Julian D. Mason, Jr. (Chapel Hill: University of North Carolina Press, 1989), 15–16.

72. Helen Maria Williams, *Peru*, in Williams, *Poems, by Helen Maria Williams*, 2 vols. (London: Thomas Cadell, 1786), 2:45–178. The poem bears no resemblance to Sir William Davenant's late-interregnum propaganda piece, *The Cruelty of the Spaniards in Peru*; see *The Play-House to be Let*, in Davenant, *The Dramatic Works of Sir William D'Avenant With Prefatory Memoir and Notes*, 5 vols. (Edinburgh: W. Paterson, 1872–74), 4:76–94. Williams's situations and speeches, however, may be indebted to John Dryden's *The Indian Queen* (1665) and *The Indian Emperour, or, The Conquest of Mexico by the Spaniards* (1667), both of which were influenced by Davenant's play; see Dryden, *Works*, 8:181–231, 9:1–111. For Dryden's indebtedness to Davenant, see John Loftis's commentary in Dryden, *Works*, 9:309–10. In neither of Dryden's plays, however, is there a scene directly comparable to the parting of Capac from Cora and their infant.

73. Anna Seward, *The Poetical Works of Anna Seward, with extracts*

from her literary correspondence, ed. Sir Walter Scott, 3 vols. (Edinburgh: Ballantyne, 1810).

74. On 24 April 1798, Seward wrote Lady Eleanor Butler and Sarah Ponsonby that "small . . . with connections and correspondence so numerous, is the probability that I shall ever finish an epic poem" (see *Letters,* 5:76–77). She appears to have doubts about proceeding to Telemachus's relation of his adventures: "Whether these incidents, not very interesting from Fenelon's pen, are capable of receiving poetic spirit and animation from mine, remains to be tried" (*Letters,* 5:76).

2. Women's Prose Responses to Pope's Writings

1. Fanny Burney, *Evelina or the History of a Young Lady's Entrance into the World,* ed. Edward A. Bloom (1778; reprint, New York: Oxford University Press, 1989), 182.

2. Ann Radcliffe, *The Mysteries of Udolpho,* ed. Bonamy Dobrée (1794; reprint Oxford: Oxford University Press, 1988), 495.

3. See the discussion of eighteenth-century reading habits in John Barrell and Harriet Guest, "On the Use of Contradiction: Economics and Morality in the Eighteenth-Century Long Poem," in *The New Eighteenth Century,* ed. Felicity Nussbaum and Laura Brown (New York: Methuen, 1987), 133–43. For a slightly later but more appropriate example, see Anna Laetita Barbauld, *The Female Speaker; or, Miscellaneous Pieces, in Prose and Verse, Selected from the Best Writers, and Adapted to the Use of Young Women,* 2d ed. (London: Baldwin, Cradock, and Jay, 1816), first printed in 1811. Barbauld's writers range from Shakespeare and Milton to Benjamin Franklin and Maria Edgeworth. She rarely specifies the texts from which the extracts are taken. Exceptions are her citations for Glaucus's comparison of mortality to autumn leaves (*Iliad* 6.181–86) under "Select Sentences" (8), and for the portrait of Nausicaa from Pope's *Odyssey* 6.85–116 and the comparison of the Trojan fires to the moon and stars (*Iliad* 8.687–98) under "Descriptive and Pathetic" (238, 268). Barbauld does not intimate book or line numbers; young ladies were evidently expected merely to know that the images were from Pope's *Homer.*

4. Frances Burney, *The Early Journals and Letters of Fanny Burney,* ed. Lars E. Troide, 2 vols. (Oxford: Clarendon, 1988), 1:40. Troide states that Burney presumably read her father's copy of Pope's *Iliad* and his set of Pope's *Odyssey* and of the 1751 *Works* (1:37 n. 4). In 1771, Burney described the "exquisite delight" with which she read the works of Pope, "a darling Poet of our Family" (1:177).

5. In *Evelina,* vol. 2, letter 11, Evelina says of Mr. Smith "that I should prefer the company of *dullness* itself, even as that goddess is

described by Pope, to that of this *sprightly* young man" (178). In vol. 2, letter 15, she intimates that Vauxhall Gardens would have been more pleasing "had it consisted less of strait walks, where 'Grove nods at grove, each alley has its brother' " (193); see Pope's "Epistle to Burlington," 117. In *Cecilia, or Memoirs of an Heiress* (1782; reprint, New York: Penguin, 1986), the narrator alludes to the "Epistle to Dr. Arbuthnot," lines 37–38 (726). In *Camilla, or A Picture of Youth*, ed. Edward A. Bloom and Lillian Bloom (1796; reprint, Oxford: Oxford University Press, 1983), Sir Sedley Clarendel alludes to *Dunciad* 1.19–20 (65), Mrs. Arlbery argues with Pope's assertions in lines 1–4 of the "Epistle to a Lady" (398), and Camilla is described in terms of Pope's description of "her celebrated namesake" in the "Essay on Criticism," 370–73 (849); the editors speculate that Pope's verses inspired Burney's choice of her heroine's name (929 n. to page 8.1). In *The Wanderer; or, Female Difficulties*, ed. Margaret Anne Doody, Robert L. Mack, and Peter Sabor (1814; reprint, Oxford: Oxford University Press, 1991), "Ellis" demonstrates her taste and intelligence by reading Boileau, Pope, Racine, and Shakespeare (116). Elsewhere in *Wanderer*, Burney alludes to "Epistle to Dr. Arbuthnot," the *Odyssey*, "Epistle to Cobham," "Epistle to a Lady," the *Iliad*, the prologue to Addison's *Cato*, and the *Essay on Man* (231, 929, 932, 937, 950, 951, 954).

6. Rhoda L. Flaxman, "Radcliffe's Dual Modes of Vision," in *Fetter'd or Free?: British Women Novelists, 1670–1815*, ed. Mary Anne Schofield and Cecilia Macheski (1986; reprint, Athens, Ohio: Ohio University Press, 1987), 124–33. Flaxman argues that at their best, Radcliffe's "word-paintings" achieve "an interplay between narrative and descriptive modes" (132).

7. Penelope Wilson complains that the volume of *Critical Heritage* devoted to Pope contains only one or two women's responses besides those of Anne Dacier and Lady Mary Wortley Montagu (64).

8. Margaret J. M. Ezell, *The Patriarch's Wife: Literary Evidence and the History of the Family* (Chapel Hill: University of North Carolina Press, 1987), 84.

9. In *Augustan England: Professions, State and Society, 1680–1730* (London: Allen and Unwin, 1982), Geoffrey Holmes attests that writers achieved professional status much later than, for example, apothecaries and attornies (32).

10. See, for example, Mitzi Myers, "Hannah More's Tracts for the Times: Social Fiction and Female Ideology," in Schofield and Macheski, 264–84. Myers argues the importance of *More's Cheap Repository Tracts* (1795–98) as didactic literature, noting that "educational genres . . . were female specialties" (264).

11. See Hertford, *Correspondence Between Frances, Countess of Hertford,*

and Henrietta Louisa, Countess of Pomfret, Between the Years 1738 and 1741, ed. William Bingley, 3 vols. (London: R. Phillips, 1805), 1:93.

12. Helen Sard Hughes, *The Gentle Hertford: Her Life and Letters* (New York: Macmillan, 1940), 296.

13. See Henry F. Stecher, *Elizabeth Singer Rowe, the Poetess of Frome: A Study in Eighteenth-Century English Pietism* (Frankfurt: H. Lang, 1973), 142.

14. Elizabeth Singer Rowe, *The Miscellaneous Works in Prose and Verse of Mrs. Elizabeth Rowe*, 2 vols. (London: R. Hett and R. Dodsley, 1739), 2:178.

15. Elizabeth Singer Rowe, *Friendship in Death* (1728; reprint, New York: Garland, 1972), 180–82. The 1728 edition included *Twenty Letters from the Dead to the Living*, *Thoughts on Death*, and *Letters Moral and Entertaining I*.

16. Harold Bloom's theory of poetic influence is developed in *The Anxiety of Influence: A Theory of Poetry* (London: Oxford University Press, 1973). I use Bloom's terms advisedly, although other feminist scholars have rightly criticized his failure to consider the female poet in his theory of influence. Nevertheless, a modified version of his paradigm is especially useful in discussing the relation of eighteenth-century women writers to Pope.

17. Baroness Mary Lepel Hervey, *Letters of Mary Lepel, Lady Hervey* (London: J. Murray, 1821), 129.

18. Hester Mulso Chapone, *The Works of Mrs. Chapone: Now First Collected*, 4 vols. (London: J. Murray, 1807), 1:24 (10 January 1750). Mrs. Chapone paraphrases Pope's "Epistle to Dr. Arbuthnot," 148.

19. Charlotte Ramsay Lennox, *Shakespear Illustrated: or the Novels and Histories, On which the Plays of Shakespear Are Founded, Collected and Translated from the Original Authors*, 3 vols. (1753; reprint, New York: AMS, 1973), 1:iv. Of *Cymbeline's* indebtedness to a story in Boccacio's *Decameron*, Lennox remarks, "As Mr. *Pope* observes, little more than the Names in this Play is historical" (1:166).

20. Elizabeth Montagu, *An essay on the writings and genius of Shakespear, compared with the Greek and French dramatic poets* (London: Printed for J. Dodsley et al., 1769). For the prologue to *Cato*, lines 1–4 and 26, see p. 30; for "Eloisa," lines 169–70, see p. 146; for "To Arbuthnot," lines 199–200, see p. 200; and for "Essay on Criticism," lines 326–27, see p. 226.

21. McCarthy, *Piozzi*. See especially his discussion of Piozzi's relations to male precursors as she chose to work in traditionally male genres (54–57).

22. Hester Thrale Piozzi, *British Synonymy*, 2 vols. (1794; reprint, Menston, England: Scolar, 1968), 1:176.

23. In *A Dictionary of the English Language: in which The Words are deduced from their Originals. . . .* (1755; reprint, London: Times, 1979), Johnson had defined *eloquence* as "the power of speaking with fluency and elegance; oratory," illustrated with a quotation from *Coriolanus*, and as "elegant language uttered with fluency"—illustrated ironically from *The Taming of the Shrew*. The third denotation of *voluble*, however, is "nimble; active. Applied to the tongue," illustrated with an Addisonian reference to the "*voluble* and flippant" female tongue. Johnson's fourth definition, "Fluent of words," is illustrated by Iago's description of Cassio as "a knave very voluble."

24. Piozzi was three when Pope died and could have had no personal experience of Pope's "conversation powers." She must have followed Johnson's opinion, expressed in "Pope," that "in familiar or convivial conversation it does not appear that [Pope] excelled" (3:201). She may also have inferred her estimate of Swift from Johnson's suggestion in "Swift" that the dean aggrandized himself by taking nearly unbearable liberties with his superiors (see, for example, 3:61).

25. Sarah Fielding, *The Adventures of David Simple: containing an account of his travels through the cities of London and Westminster in the search of a real friend*, ed. Malcolm Kelsall (1744; reprint, Oxford: Oxford University Press, 1987).

26. Sarah Scott, *A Description of Millenium Hall and the Country Adjacent Together with the Characters of the Inhabitants And such Historical Anecdotes and Reflections as May excite in the Reader proper Sentiments of Humanity, and lead the Mind to the Love of Virtue*, ed. Jane Spencer (1762; reprint, New York: Penguin, 1986); *The History of Sir George Ellison*, 2 vols. (London: A. Millar, 1766).

27. Frances Brooke, *The History of Emily Montague*, 4 vols. (1769; reprint, New York: Garland, 1974).

28. Charlotte Smith, *Emmeline, The Orphan of the Castle* (1788; reprint, London: Pandora, 1988), 7.

29. Charlotte Smith, *The Old Manor House*, ed. Anne Henry Ehrenpreis (1793; reprint, Oxford: Oxford University Press, 1989), 182.

30. See Catherine Talbot to Elizabeth Carter on 16 August 1751 (Carter, *Letters*, 2:46–47): "At some uncharitable moments one can scarce help looking upon all those eloquent expressions of benevolence as too much parade." See also Fanny Burney's entry in December 1771 (*Journals*, 1:179): "The reading of Pope's Letters has made me quite melancholy. He laments with such generous sorrow the misfortunes of his friends, that every Line I read, raises his Character higher in [m]y estimation."

31. In *Pursuing Innocent Pleasures: The Gardening World of Alexander Pope* (Hamden, Conn.: Archon, 1984), Peter Martin notes Pope's de-

light in the "associative Gothic atmosphere of shade and antiquity" (115); see also Martin's account of Pope's visit to Netley Abbey as "a sort of Gothic dream-come-true for Pope" (192–93). Not only women associated Pope with the gothic fashion. Women's familiarity with Pope's work enabled comments on cultural excesses. In Elizabeth Sheridan, *Betsy Sheridan's Journal: Letters from Sheridan's Sister 1784–1786 and 1788–1790*, ed. William LeFanu (London: Eyre and Spottiswoode, 1960), Betsy Sheridan recounts a visit in 1786 to "a rude Cave where it seems Mr. Thickness chose to bury his Daughter." At the entrance to the ivy-covered grotto, "there is a little Female figure and over it an Inscription taken from Pope's Lines on the Death of an Unfortunate Young Lady 'What tho' no sacred Earth allow thee room, etc. etc.' but as Miss Thickness did not destroy herself I can not say I thought the selection judicious. This strange scene is immediately under the House and we saw Thickness and a party of ladies walking past with as much unconcern as they looked on any other garden ornament" (89).

32. Samuel Richardson, *The Correspondence of Samuel Richardson . . . Selected From The Original Manuscripts, Bequeathed By Him To His Family*, ed. Anna Laetitia Barbauld, 6 vols. (1804; reprint, New York: AMS, 1966) 3:39–40. I am indebted to Professor Robert Folkenflik of University of California, Irvine, for calling this exchange to my attention.

33. G. Douglas Atkins compares evidence from Pope's writings with contemporary deism and argues convincingly that the poet was never a deist. See Atkins, "Pope and Deism: A New Analysis," in *Pope: Recent Essays by Several Hands*, ed. Maynard Mack and James Winn (Hamden, Conn.: Archon, 1980), 392–415. The *Essay on Man*, for example, contains sufficient evidence of Pope's mistrust of reason as a sufficient guide. Such contemporaries as Richardson's correspondent, however, worried about the heterodox implications of certain passages lifted out of context. Perhaps this phenomenon resulted from reading each book of the *Essay* separately (as in the *Gentleman's Magazine* serialization) or from reading only extracts of the poem. In either case, contemporary reading habits facilitated analyses suspicious of Pope's orthodoxy.

34. Thomas Kaminsky, *The Early Career of Samuel Johnson* (New York: Oxford University Press, 1987), 76–77. Oddly, Curll later reissued his edition of Charles Forman's version of Crousaz's commentary (published anonymously) to swell the pages of the late Lady Margaret Pennyman's *Miscellanies in Prose and Verse . . . To which are annexed, Some other curious Pieces* (London: E. Curll, 1740). Pennyman had died in 1733 (see preface to *Miscellanies*), but could Curll have wished to create a fleeting impression that he, too, had employed a female

translator of Crousaz? For Forman's authorship see Maynard Mack's note in Pope, *Poems*, 3i:xx n. 4.

35. Jean Pierre de Crousaz, *An Examination of Mr. Pope's Essay on Man. Translated from the French*. . . . , trans. Elizabeth Carter (London: A. Dodd, 1739), 67. Carter's extenuating notes are actually few, but they consistently observe Crousaz's critical deficiencies. Curll's version of the *Commentaire* was equally skeptical of Crousaz's accuracy.

36. See McCarthy's analysis of Piozzi's translation (*Piozzi*, 11–15) and his "A Verse 'Essay.' "

37. Brean Hammond traces this interpretation of the Pope/Bolingbroke relationship to Owen Ruffhead and Joseph Warton (70). He argues against such proponents of Pope's originality in the *Essay* as Maynard Mack (in his preface to *Poems*, 3i:xxix–xxxi) and Douglas H. White, in *Pope and the Context of Controversy: The Manipulation of Ideas in "An Essay on Man"* (Chicago: University of Chicago Press, 1970). Hammond establishes Pope's indebtedness to Bolingbroke in the *Essay*, but his study of the course of their friendship dispels the myth of Bolingbroke's complete ascendancy over Pope. For an example of a twentieth-century female biographer seemingly infatuated with a frail, tormented Pope, see Edith Sitwell, *Alexander Pope* (London: Faber and Faber, 1930). Sitwell confesses, "I am moved almost to tears when I see Richardson's portrait of Pope in the National Gallery—the wide, visionary eyes, that have a look of almost childish anguish and loneliness, the wide and beautiful brow, the worn cheek-bones, and the sensitive pain-stricken mouth" (10).

38. In his edition of Pope's *Correspondence*, George Sherburn declines to print this as a letter of 1716 to Edward Blount, explaining that it was more probably a letter of 1735 to John Caryll (1:337). Mack may have preferred the 1716 date because it better defends his argument that Pope's ideas in the *Essay* were little indebted to Bolingbroke.

39. Catherine Macaulay Graham, *Letters on Education. With Observations on Religious and Metaphysical Subjects* (London: C. Dilly, 1790), 360–61.

40. "For should you attempt to persuade a man, who is naturally avaricious, cruel, insensible of the feelings of sympathy, and attached to all the interests of self gratification, that his greater interests lie in the pleasure which he receives from the indulgence of his more beneficent affections; should you endeavour to engage him to cultivate the opposite means of self good, he will answer you, that his conceptions of self good are different from yours; and that every man has his peculiar taste" (Macaulay Graham, 409).

41. Arthur O. Lovejoy, *The Great Chain of Being: A Study of the History*

of an Idea (1936; reprint, Cambridge: Harvard University Press, 1973), 59.

42. See Catherine Macaulay, *The History of England from the Accession of James I to that of the Brunswick Line*, 8 vols. (London: J. Nourse et al., 1763–83), introduction. For example, she complains that her contemporaries "have lost a just sense of . . . men that, with the hazard and even the loss of their lives, attacked the formidable pretensions of the Stewart family, and set up the banners of liberty . . . and this by the exertion of faculties, which, if compared to the barren produce of modern times, appear more than human" (viii–ix).

43. Hannah More, *The Works of Hannah More*, 2 vols. (New York: Harper and Brothers, 1835), 1:365. Valerie Rumbold (265–68) has discussed Wollstonecraft's objections to Pope in her *Vindication of the Rights of Woman*.

44. Eliza Haywood, *The Female Spectator*, 4 vols., 7th ed. (London: H. Gardner, 1771).

45. Laetitia Pilkington, *Memoirs of Mrs. Laetitia Pilkington, Wife to the Rev. Mr. Matthew Pilkington, Written by Herself*, 3 vols. (London: R. Griffiths and G. Woodfall, 1748–54), 3:2.

46. Mary Deverell, "An Apology to the Public," in *Sermons on the Following Subjects. . . .* (Bristol: S. Farley et al., 1774), vii.

47. Ann Murry, *Mentoria; or, the young ladies instructor in Familiar conversations on moral and entertaining subjects. . . .*, 6th ed. (1778; reprint, London: C. Dilly, 1791), 126.

48. Antonia Forster, "Mr. Pope's Maxims," *Age of Johnson* 2 (1989): 65–89. Forster argues that where his critical opinions were concerned, the eminently quotable Pope "had to wait less than ten years after his death before achieving something like 'the dignity of an ancient' " (86).

49. In *Millenium Hall*, Sarah Scott invokes *Essay* 3.152 to describe the unmolested lives of birds and animals in the Hall's wood (17). In a later chapter, a parish minister uses arguments drawn from the *Essay* to convert Mr. Selvyn from freethinking (157). In her *Observations and Reflections Made in the Course of a Journey Through France, Italy, and Germany*, ed. Herbert Brown (1789; reprint, Ann Arbor: University of Michigan Press, 1967), Hester Thrale Piozzi quotes many of Pope's poems in passing as she describes foreign cultures. For example, she concludes a meditation on the demise of the Jesuits in Italy (291) by quoting *Essay* 2.134–37, where Pope speculates that "man perhaps the moment of his breath / Receives the lurking principle of death."

50. Elizabeth Montagu, *The Letters of Mrs. Elizabeth Montagu, with some of the letters of her correspondents*, ed. Matthew Montagu, 4 vols. (London: T. Cadell and W. Davies, 1809), 1:193.

51. [Eliza Bromley], *Laura and Augustus, An Authentic Story*, 3 vols. [1784], 1:18. Compare with *Essay on Man* 4.1, 8.

52. Mary Hays, *Memoirs of Emma Courtney*, ed. Sally Cline (1796; reprint, London: Pandora, 1987), 12.

53. Maria Edgeworth also alludes principally to Pope and Rousseau in *Belinda*, ed. Eva Figes (1801; reprint, London: Pandora, 1986), but as opposing influences. Clarence Hervey's plot to duplicate St. Pierre's *Paul and Virginia* in his own life is disastrous; although he escapes marriage with Rachel Hartley, she has been damaged by her Rousseau-ian education. "Wicked" Lady Delacour, however, quotes Pope (her unregenerate counterpart, Harriet Freke, *mis*quotes Pope), as does the narrator. Lady Delacour's reformation in the course of the novel suggests that sparkling wit is compatible with moral growth while Rousseau's doctrines are merely debilitating.

54. Mary Jones, *Miscellanies in Prose and Verse* (Oxford: Dodsley et al., 1750).

55. See Margaret Anne Doody, "Swift Among the Women," *Yearbook of English Studies* 18 (1988): 83–87, for an appreciative discussion of Jones's Swiftian poems.

56. Roger Lonsdale, 155–56. I am frequently indebted to Lonsdale's introductory biographies throughout and to entries in Janet Todd's invaluable *A Dictionary of British and American Women Writers, 1660–1800* (Totowa, N.J.: Rowman and Littlefield, 1987).

57. See Sandra M. Gilbert and Susan Gubar, *The Madwoman in the Attic: The Woman Writer and the Nineteenth-Century Literary Imagination* (New Haven: Yale University Press, 1979), 3–7.

58. See, for example, Pope, *Corr*, 1:84, 94, 111.

59. Mary Jones, 403. See Harriet Guest, "A Double Lustre: Femininity and Sociable Commerce, 1730–60," *Eighteenth-Century Studies* 23 (1990): 479–501, especially 479–81, 491–94, 500–501.

60. Lonsdale, 156.

61. Pilkington admitted that her husband had found her alone in a room with a gentleman, but she swore she was only reading a book the man owned and would not lend her. The charge was sufficient, however, to obtain the adulterous Reverend Pilkington his divorce and to have Laetitia Pilkington declared unfit to raise her children.

62. Hesketh Pearson, *The Swan of Lichfield, being a Selection from the Correspondence of Anna Seward* (London: H. Hamilton, 1936), 9–10.

63. For Seward's estimate of Hayley, see *Letters*, 1:189 (to George Hardinge, 7 October 1786): "Hayley is a true poet; he has the fire and invention of Dryden, without any of his absurdity, and he has the wit and ease of Prior. If his versification is a degree less polished than Pope's, it is more various."

64. Bertrand H. Bronson, "The Trough of the Wave," in *England in the Restoration and Early Eighteenth Century: Essays on Culture and Society*, ed. H. T. Swedenberg, Jr. (Berkeley: University of California Press, 1972), 197–226.

3. Women's Poetic Addresses to Pope

1. In *Alexander Pope and the Traditions of Formal Verse Satire* (Princeton: Princeton University Press, 1982), Howard D. Weinbrot compares Pope's "Epistle to a Lady" with satires by Boileau and Young and finds the "Epistle" relatively constructive and conciliatory (189–91). Felicity Nussbaum defines the danger of Pope's satires on women: though not misogynist, they promoted a desexualized ideal of femininity (*Brink*, 154–58). Her conclusion is well supported, but many contemporary women espoused with relief his images of ordinary women, influential and beloved without reference to their sexuality.

2. For example, Dryden's "Eleonora: A Panegyrical Poem Dedicated to the Memory of the Late Countess of Abingdon" celebrated the deceased lady as "the wife, the mother, . . . the friend" (161), albeit in the extravagant terms appropriate to the genre (*Works*, 3:231–46). In such poems as "To the Lady Castlemaine, upon Her Incouraging His First Play" (*Works*, 1:45–46) and "Prologue to the Duchess, on Her Return from Scotland" (*Works*, 2:195–96), Dryden acknowledges the ladies' patronage of the arts and legitimate political influence, respectively. Jean Hagstrum has identified Dryden as a precursor of the cult of sensibility (50–71).

3. For example, by the end of the century, the editors of *The Beauties of Pope, or, Useful and Entertaining Passages selected from the Works of that Admired Author; as well as from his Translation of Homer's Iliad and Odyssey, &c.*, 2 vols. (London: G. Kearsley, 1796), boasted that they had expanded their previous version to include Pope's translations of Homer.

4. Charles Yorke, "To A Lady, With A Present of Pope's Works," in *A Select Collection of Poems: With Notes, Biographical and Historical*, ed. John Nichols, 8 vols. (London: J. Nichols, 1780), 6:301–2, lines 5–12. The poem was written some time after Pope's death and was first published after Yorke's death in 1770.

5. Robert Halsband, *The Life of Lady Mary Wortley Montagu* (Oxford: Clarendon, 1957), *passim*; see especially 129–32 for their mysterious quarrel. Mack speculates about their break (*Pope*, 553–62 and *passim*). Rumbold, 133–45 and *passim*.

6. See Lady Mary's letter to Lady Mar of 1 April 1717, in Lady Mary Wortley Montagu, *Letters*, 1:327.

7. Cynthia Lowenthal, "The Veil of Romance: Lady Mary's Embassy Letters," *Eighteenth-Century Life* 14 (1990): 79.

8. See Rumbold, 155–61. Halsband also addresses the disparity between Lady Mary's character and Pope's memorable slander (*Life*, 152).

9. See Lady Mary Wortley Montagu, *Essays*, 247, 280.

10. Colonel Henry Desaulnais, or Disney, was called "Duke" by his friends.

11. In the absence of contrary evidence, I accept the claims that the two anonymous poems mentioned in the following discussion were written by women. The style of "Advice to Sappho" suggests Elizabeth Boyd as the author; its mildly erotic imagery resembles that in poems by Mary Leapor and Elizabeth Bentley, which Donna Landry considers characteristic of women's praise of Pope. As for "The Neuter," I cannot imagine a male writer's motive for ascribing this satire—not particularly "feminine"—to a lady, but there were women writers capable of joining in the pamphlet war generated by the *Dunciad*.

12. *Advice to Sappho. Occasioned by her Verses on the Imitator of the First Satire of the Second Book of Horace*, by a Gentlewoman (London: J. Roberts, 1733).

13. *The Neuter: or, a Modest Satire on the Poets of the Age*, by a Lady (London: T. Osborne, [1733]).

14. Lady Mary's contempt is exemplified by her famous dismission of Swift and Pope (to Lady Bute, 23 June 1754): "It is pleasant to consider that had it not been for the good natures of [the] very mortals they contemn, these two superior Beings were entitl'd by their Birth and hereditary Fortune to be only a couple of Link Boys" (*Letters*, 3:57).

15. See Falconer Madan, *The Madan Family* (Oxford: Clarendon, 1933), 85. "To Mr. Pope" and the other poems cited in the text are preserved in *The Cowper Anthology*, MS. 28101, Addison Collection, British Library, London. In my text, I quote the poem as included by Pope in his *Miscellany Poems*, vol. 1, 5th ed. (London: B. Lintot, 1736), assuming Judith Cowper's approval of this published version.

16. Pohli observes that Pope's "polite gibes" are "made possible by the disparity in their talents and fame" (230), but that Pope was also aware of the "essential difficulty of trying to gauge someone's worth or thoughts" (231).

17. I am grateful to James Winn for pointing out the gallant signification of Pope's remark, though I persist in finding his metaphor ambivalent.

18. [Bonnell Thornton and George Colman, eds.], *Poems by Eminent Ladies*, 2 vols. (London: R. Baldwin, 1755), 2:136. I quote from this

edition, a printed version of that in the British Library (MS. 28101, Addison Collection). A pirated copy appeared in *The Poetical Works of Mr. William Pattison*, 2 vols. (London: H. Curll, 1728), 1:66–77, leading to confusion over the poem's authorship. As Rumbold observes (146), Lawrence Wright was apparently unaware of the manuscript version when he wrote "Eighteenth-Century Replies to Pope's Eloisa," *Studies in Philology* 31 (1934): 519–33. Wright persisted in attributing the poem to Pattison based on its posthumous appearance in a Curll publication, rather than accepting as Cowper's a poem printed several times under her name during her lifetime, constituting her acknowledgment of authorship.

19. Pope, *The Unfortunate Lovers; Two Admirable Poems. Extracted out of the celebrated Letters of Abelard and Eloisa* (London: Pamphlet Shops, 1756), 13–18, contains a botched version of "Lady M——'s" poem; lines 119–46 are inserted after line 174.

20. In her essay on "Gender and Reading," Elizabeth A. Flynn deduces from a study of male and female undergraduates that the conventions that make women hesitant speakers may render them effective readers. Assigned unfamiliar stories, the women were characteristically "able to resolve the tensions in the stories and form a consistent pattern of meaning" (272). See Elizabeth A. Flynn and Patrocinio P. Schweickart, eds. *Gender and Reading: Essays on Readers, Texts, and Contexts* (Baltimore: Johns Hopkins University Press, 1986): 267–88. The other essays in this volume coincide with Flynn's generalization.

21. See "Miss Cowper to ——," 18, in Lady Mary Wortley Montagu, *Essays*, 227–30. Lady Mary must have read "Abelard to Eloisa" in manuscript.

22. Judith Cowper Madan, "The Progress of Poetry" (London: J. Dodsley, 1783). I quote from this, the unrevised version of the poem, because it represents the youthful Cowper's vision of a literary tradition culminating in Pope.

23. See, for example, "An Ode Composed in Sleep" and "To Lysander. October 3, 1726," in Lonsdale, 95–96.

24. *The Flower-Piece: A Collection of Miscellany Poems. By Several Hands* (London: J. Walthoe, 1731): "To the Memory of Mr. Hughes," pp. 21–24; "The Progress of Poetry," pp. 130–40; "To the ingenious Lady, Author of the Poem entitled, *The Progress of Poetry*," pp. 141–44.

25. "Thy Pen, Great Pope! the wonder of the Age," MS. 4456, f. 97, Birch Collection, British Library, London.

26. The Countess of Suffolk, for example, pronounced herself unwilling to inquire about Pope's pursuits. She wrote Gay on 22 August 1730: "I hear Mr. Pope is now writing Characters; but as he did not tell me himself of it, I would not ask him; so I do not know if this is

true"; *Letters to and from Henrietta, Countess of Suffolk, and her second husband, The Hon. George Berkeley; from 1712 to 1767,* 2 vols. (London: J. Murray, 1824), 1:386. Valerie Rumbold speculates that Teresa Blount, a competent writer who sometimes composed verse, might have impressed Pope with her disinterest in literature "to excuse her from expressing an admiration of *his* writings which would enmesh her further in a problematic relationship" (117).

27. See Sandra M. Gilbert and Susan Gubar, eds. *The Norton Anthology of Literature by Women* (New York: W. W. Norton, 1985), 105; Rumbold, 152–53.

28. Anne Finch, "The Answer," in Finch, 82–83, lines 1–2.

29. See Norman Ault, ed., *Pope's Own Miscellany: Being a reprint of Poems on Several Occasions 1717, containing new poems by Alexander Pope and others* (London: Nonesuch, 1935), 79. As Rumbold observes, Pope probably concealed Lady Winchilsea's name to prevent suspicion that she had been the object of his satire (154).

30. See "To Mr. *Pope,* By the Right Honourable Anne Countess of Winchilsea," in Pope, *The Works of Mr. Alexander Pope* (London: B. Lintot, 1717).

31. Katherine Rogers, in her introduction to Finch's *Poems,* describes the identification of Clinket with Finch as "far-fetched," discredited by modern scholarship (xiii). Rumbold also disputes Pope's intention to satirize Lady Winchilsea in *Three Hours After Marriage* (153–54). The allegation persists, however, even in such sources as Leo Manglaviti's entry for Lady Winchilsea in Todd, 328–29. During his lifetime, the charge denoted Pope's lack of gratitude to titled patrons rather than his misogyny. Similar aspersions greeted his "Epistle to Burlington," thought to satirize the duke of Chandos's estate, Cannons.

32. Mary Barber, *Poems on Several Occasions* (London: C. Rivington, 1734), 173–76.

33. Margaret Anne Doody discusses Barber's relationship with Swift in "Swift," 73–75.

34. Anne Ingram, Viscountess Irwin, "An Epistle to Mr. Pope. Occasioned by his Characters of Women," *Gentleman's Magazine* 6 (1736): 745. A portion of Lady Irwin's poem is anthologized in Lonsdale, 150–51. Rumbold discusses the poem briefly, 264–65.

35. In an untitled poem in *London Magazine* 5 (1736): 515, "A. Z." hopes that when modern ladies read Pope's *Iliad* and learn "what lives the ancient ladies us'd to lead; / Perhaps to imitate they may begin, / And learn of chaste *Andromache* to spin" (10–12).

36. [Sarah Dixon], *Poems on Several Occasions* (Canterbury: J. Abree, 1740), 54.

37. Elizabeth Boyd, *Don Sancho: or, the Students Whim, A Ballad Opera in Two Acts.* London: E. Boyd, 1739.

38. [Elizabeth Boyd], *Variety: A Poem, In Two Cantos* (Westminster: T. Warner, 1727), and Boyd, "Truth, A Poem" (London: E. Boyd, 1740).

39. [Elizabeth Boyd], *Admiral Haddock: or, The Progress of Spain* (London: J. Applebee, 1739). "Truth, A Poem" was addressed to Lord Harrington.

40. Mary Leapor, "On Mr. Pope's Universal Prayer," in Leapor, *Poems Upon Several Occasions* (London: J. Roberts, 1748), 142, lines 1–10.

41. See the biographical preface to Mary Leapor's poems in [Thornton and Colman], 2:16.

42. Betty Rizzo, "The Patron as Poet Maker: The Politics of Benefaction," *Studies in Eighteenth-Century Culture* 20 (1990): 241–66.

43. Betty Rizzo identifies Bridget Freemantle as the author of "To the Reader" in her entry for Leapor in Todd, 192.

44. Roger Lonsdale uses the same phrase to describe both women; due to dependence on Pope, their poetry "would eventually have come to seem old-fashioned" (156, 195).

45. Elizabeth Bentley, *Genuine Poetical Compositions, on Various Subjects* (Norwich: Crouse and Stevenson, 1791), 2, lines 7–8.

46. Landry discusses Bentley's "self-effacing homage" (51–52). Laboring women ravish Pope's texts even as they are ravished by them. Earlier, Landry argues that "for the female laboring poet, transference on to a poetic text often involves a class-conscious dynamic compounded of ambition and humility, eroticism and homage. Ravished by the beauty of a poetic discourse which is alien to her, and from which she is often specifically excluded, yet ironically aware of the space occupied within that discourse by subservient female figures in the form of muses, she raids and ravishes by both praising and appropriating what she admires" (46).

47. For example, Susanna Highmore (mother of poet Susanna Highmore Duncombe) supplied a mocking riposte to an epigram mistakenly attributed to Pope. (Nichols, 8:61–62, prints both epigrams; for the misattribution, see Pope, *Poems*, 6:459). Highmore evidently found "On An Old Gate Erected in Chiswick Gardens" bathetic. The gate in Pope's epigram solemnly announces that "Inigo Jones put me together. / Sir Hans Sloane / Let me alone: / Burlington brought me hither." The little poem is weighed down by low-pitched vowel sounds intimating solemn praise. In her extempore reply, "On Seeing a Gate Carried by Two Men Through Lincoln's Inn Fields," Highmore

asks the gate where it is going. "But it was not so knowing / As yonder Gate / That talk'd of late. / So on it went, without reply; / At least I heard it not, not I!" By replacing the epigram's sonority with sharp, high-pitched sounds, Highmore mocks its pretension. Perhaps her choice of this slight, but witty, genre emboldened Highmore to puncture the gravity characteristic of Pope's tributes in letters and formal satires and of this spurious epigram.

4. Eighteenth-Century Women and Pope's Early Poetry

1. Janet Little, "Given to a Lady who asked me to write a Poem," in *The Poetical Works of Janet Little, the Scotch Milkmaid* (Air: J. Wilson and P. Wilson, 1792), 113–15, line 7.

2. "To a Lady who desir'd her to write an Epithalamion," by a Lady, P. A. Taylor Papers, Vol. 3, MS. 37,684, f. 78–80, lines 23–28, Addison Collection, British Museum, London.

3. Mary Deverell, *Miscellanies in Prose and Verse, mostly written in the Epistolary Style, chiefly upon moral subjects, and particularly calculated for the Improvement of Younger Minds*, 2 vols. ([London?]: J. Rivington, 1781).

4. Mary Anne Bendixen, in her entry for Deverell in Janet Todd's *Dictionary*, notes that Samuel Johnson, Hannah More, and Hester Lynch Thrale subscribed to Deverell's sermons (1774), which were popular with both gentry and clergy. She also cites a reviewer's opinion that the poetry in Deverell's *Miscellanies* had not the "ease" of her epistolary style (102).

5. Esther Lewis, *Poems Moral and Entertaining, Written long since by Miss Lewis, then of Holt, Now, and for almost Thirty Years past, the Wife of Mr. Robert Clark, of Tetbury* (Bath: S. Hazard, 1789), 145–46.

6. Roger Lonsdale describes Dr. Samuel Bowden's strong support (225–26). A note on the title page of Lewis's *Poems Moral and Entertaining* explains the book was "Published at the Request of her Husband, for the Benefit of the Infirmary at Glocester, the Hospital at Bath, and the Sunday Schools at Tetbury."

7. Priscilla Pointon, "Reply to Mr. Jones of Kidderminster . . . written *Extempore*," in *Poems on Several Occasions* (Birmingham: T. Warren, 1770), 5, line 27.

8. Catherine Upton, "A Letter from the Authoress in London to her Father in Nottingham," in *Miscellaneous Pieces, in Prose and Verse* (London, 1784), 9–12, lines 48–51, 54–55.

9. Mary Masters, "To the Right Honourable the Earl of Burlington,"

in *Poems on Several Occasions* (London: T. Browne, 1733), 6–7, lines 21–25.

10. See "Letter XVIII, 'To ——,' " in Masters, *Familiar Letters and Poems on Several Occasions* (London: D. Henry and R. Cave, 1755), 77–78, lines 5–6.

11. Andrew V. Ettin, *Literature and the Pastoral* (New Haven: Yale University Press, 1984), 149. Ettin discusses the dearth of women's pastorals in chapter 8, "Pastoral Society and Ethics," 146–49.

12. Women frequently lamented the constraints on feminine education and social intercourse that hampered them as authors. In the preface to her *Essays upon Several Subjects in Prose and Verse* (London: R. Bonwicke et al., 1710), Lady Mary Chudleigh explains, "Politeness is not my Talent; it ought not to be expected from a Person who has liv'd almost wholly to her self, who has but seldom had the Opportunity of conversing with ingenious Company, which I remember Mr. *Dryden*, in the Preface to one of his *Miscellanies*, thinks to be necessary toward the gaining of Fineness of Stile" ("To the Reader," iv).

13. Mary Whateley, "Dedication to the Hon. Lady Wrottesley, at Perton," in *Original Poems on Several Occasions. By Miss Whateley* (London: R. Dodsley and J. Dodsley, 1764), v.

14. Ann Curtis, *Poems on Miscellaneous Subjects: By Ann Curtis, Sister of Mrs. Siddons* (London: J. Bowen, 1783), iii.

15. Anne Francis, "The Sylph," in *Miscellaneous Poems by Anne Francis* (Norwich: T. Becket and R. Baldwin, 1790), 262–68, lines 132–33, 144, 118.

16. See Whateley Darwall, *Poems on Several Occasions. By Mrs. Darwall. (Formerly Miss Whateley.)*, 2 vols. (Walsall: F. Milward, 1794). Popeian echoes linger, however, as in "Doris, A Pastoral. Inscribed to Mr. Y——" (2:8–13) and "Epilogue Written for a Favourite Actress, and Spoken on Her Benefit Night, *At Walsall*" (2:76–78).

17. Charlotte Ramsay, "To Mira. Inviting her to a Retreat in the Country," in Ramsay Lennox, *Poems on Several Occasions* (London: S. Paterson, 1747), 67–71, lines 15–17.

18. Anne Penny, "Amyntas," in *Poems* (1771; reprint, London, 1780), 51–54.

19. Ann Murry, "Damon and Thyrsis," in *Poems on Various Subjects* (London: 1779), 10–16.

20. Geoffrey Tillotson's introduction to "Eloisa to Abelard" in Pope, *Poems* 2:275–93, establishes the poem's context, Pope's sources, and the extent of his originality.

21. "Sonnet I," in Charlotte Smith, *Elegiac Sonnets, by Charlotte Smith*, 6th ed. (Dublin: B. Dornin, 1790), 1, lines 13–14.

22. Hughes, 420. "The Story of Inkle and Yarrico. A most moving Tale from the Spectator" and "An Epistle from Yarrico to Inkle, After he had left her in Slavery" were published together (London: J. Cooper, 1738).

23. Ramsay's choice of "Moneses," a single-blossomed herb named from the Greek *monos* (alone) + *esis* (delight), for her hero's name also suggests that he is forbidden to Ardelia, a delight she must covet in solitude, best left alone, or perhaps already "one" with a spouse. There is no precedent in the *Heroides* for Ramsay's heroic epistle, or in the *Metamorphoses* for her suggestively named addressee; Ramsay's subtitle may merely signal her poem's generic origin.

24. Jael Henrietta Pye, "Elgiva to Edwy," in *Poems, by Mrs. Hamden Pye*, 2d ed. (London: J. Walter, 1772), 87–95. Odo's motive is described on page 88.

25. Margaret Anne Doody discusses Burney's tragedy in *Frances Burney: The Life in the Works* (New Brunswick: N.J.: Rutgers University Press, 1988), 179–83.

26. Susan Staves has argued that contemporaries admired Home's play not for traditional tragic qualities but for its moving portrait of conjugal and filial devotion. As the embodiment of maternal tenderness, Lady Matilda Randolph, not the play's eponymous hero, most fascinated early audiences. See Staves, "Douglas's Mother," in *Brandeis Essays in Literature*, ed. John H. Smith (Waltham, Mass.: Brandeis University, 1983), 51–67.

27. Vladimir Propp has suggested that fairy tales are constructed from a finite set of character "functions." Some functions may be absent or disguised, but the set appears in every culture, and the functions always occur in the same order (e.g., "One of the members of a family absents himself from home"; "An interdiction is addressed to the hero"; etc.). Propp, *Morphology of the Folktale*, trans. Laurence Scott, ed. Louis A. Wagner, 2d ed. (Austin: University of Texas Press, 1968), chapter 3, "The Functions of Dramatis Personae," 25–65.

28. Maria Falconer, "Alfred and Ethelinda, a Ballad," in *Poems, by Maria and Harriet Falconer*, by Maria Falconer and Harriet Falconer (London: J. Johnson, 1788), 1–22.

29. Susanna Blamire, "The Nun's Return to the World," in *The Poetical Works of Miss Susanna Blamire, "The Muse of Cumberland,"* collected by Henry Lonsdale, preface, memoir, and notes by Patrick Maxwell (Edinburgh: J. Menzies, 1842), 77–86.

30. Elizabeth Hands, "On reading Pope's Eloiza to Abelard," in *The Death of Amnon. A Poem, with an Appendix: containing Pastorals, and other Poetical Pieces* (Coventry: N. Rollason, 1789), 114.

31. Two poems in Hands's *The Death of Amnon*, "A Poem, On the Supposition of an Advertisement appearing in a Morning Paper, of the Publication of a Volume of Poems, by a Servant Maid" and "A Poem, On the Supposition of the Book having been Published and Read" (47–55) suggest Hands's apprehension of genteel readers, despite her satirical reports of their imagined reactions. "'Some whimsical trollop most like,' . . . / Has been scribbling of nonsense, just out of a whim," says a Miss Prim in "On the Supposition of an Advertisement," lines 41–42.

32. Anna Seward, *Louisa, A Poetical Novel. In Four Epistles*, in Seward, *Works*, 2:219–39. The poem went through five editions. Her twentieth-century biographers have dismissed *Louisa*, contemptuous of both the poetical novel and its cultural context. See E. V. Lucas, *A Swan and Her Friends* (London: Methuen, 1907), 52–58, and Margaret Ashmun, *The Singing Swan* (New Haven: Yale University Press, 1931), 124–31.

33. A less discernable influence in Seward's *Louisa* is Matthew Prior's "Henry and Emma, A Poem, Upon the Model of The Nut-Brown Maid," in *The Literary Works of Matthew Prior*, ed. H. Bunker Wright and Monroe K. Spears (Oxford: Clarendon, 1959), 1:278–300. In Prior's poem, Henry tests his beloved's fidelity by inventing a tale of his disgrace, to which Emma responds credulously, offering to accompany him into impoverished exile. Louisa's anguish results from Eugenio's tragic, but honorable, choice of another bride. Seward must have found Henry disingenuous and Emma's trial inconsequential.

34. Lady Sophia Burrell, *Poems. Dedicated to the Right Honourable the Earl of Mansfield*, 2 vols. (London: J. Cooper, 1793), 1:12–16. See also Wright.

35. Jonathan Culler, "Reading as a Woman," in *On Deconstruction: Theory and Criticism after Structuralism* (Ithaca: Cornell University Press, 1982), 43–64.

36. Susan Schibanoff, "Taking the Gold Out of Egypt: The Art of Reading as a Woman," in Flynn and Schweickart, 83–106.

37. I presume that Ramsay was familiar with a translation of the *Heroides*, such as *Ovid's Epistles: with his Amours, translated into English verse, by the most eminent hands* (London: J. Tonson and R. Tonson, 1736). Pope's "Sapho to Phaon" (pp. 5–13) had first appeared in the 1712 edition of this translation.

38. Likewise, Ramsay may have been familiar with *Ovid's Metamorphoses in Latin and English, Translated by the Most Eminent Hands*, 2 vols., trans. Sir Samuel Garth et al. (1717; reprint, Amsterdam: Wetsteins and Smith, 1732), to which Pope also contributed.

5. Pope and Women's Poems "Something like Horace"

1. For these general remarks on Horatian satire, I am indebted to Howard D. Weinbrot, *Pope*, especially 105–9 and 170–200.

2. Bruce Redford has discussed letter writing as a distinct art form in *The Converse of the Pen: Acts of Intimacy in the Eighteenth-Century Familiar Letter* (Chicago: University of Chicago Press, 1986), 1–15. Ruth Perry has found the epistolary mode most characteristic of middle-class eighteenth-century English women in *Women, Letters, and the Novel* (New York: AMS, 1980), 166–67. Patricia Meyer Spacks has elucidated the strategies of eighteenth-century women letter-writers in "Female Rhetorics," in Benstock, 177–91.

3. Jane Brereton, "On Mr. Nash's Picture at full Length, between the Busts of Sir Isaac Newton, and Mr. Pope," in *Poems on Several Occasions: By Mrs. Jane Brereton. With Letters to her Friends, and An Account of Her Life* (London: E. 1744), 121–22, lines 13–16. Earlier, Brereton published *The Fifth Ode of the Fourth Book of Horace, Imitated and Apply'd to the King* (London: W. Hinchcliffe, 1716). Written shortly after the Treaty of Utrecht and the Hanoverian accession, Brereton's ode implies that the Princess of Wales's virtue has made the seas safe for merchants: "The Merchant o'er the Ocean sails, / To fetch us rich Brocades / While *Carolina*'s Pow'r prevails, / And virtuous Life persuades" (21–24).

4. My information about Mary Chandler's life is from Todd's *Dictionary* and Roger Lonsdale's *Eighteenth-Century Women Poets*, supplemented by the account written by her brother in Robert Shiels, *The Lives of the Poets of Great Britain and Ireland*, 5 vols. (1753; reprint, Hildesheim: G. Olms Verlagbuchhandlung, 1968), 5:345–54, and from "Some Literary Celebrities of Bath of the Last Century," *The Bath and County Graphic* 2 (October 1897): 65–66.

5. Mary Chandler, *The Description of Bath . . . With Several Other Poems*, 8th ed. (London: H. Leake, 1747). In her title poem, for example, Chandler explains that "Could I, like tuneful Pope, command the Nine" (317), she could properly eulogize Ralph Allen (p. 17).

6. Donna Landry remarks that Leapor's second volume (1751) contains poems more "critical of [both] contemporary sexual relations" and "the whole tradition of misogynist verse" than her first (82). It is probably not coincidence that the poems expressing Leapor's admiration of Pope were included in the first, more decorous volume I have quoted throughout this study. But Pope's influence remains strong in the second volume, even (as in "Crumble-Hall") where Leapor moves toward a distinctive point of view (see Landry, 110–12).

7. I thank Eric Andrew Lee, a graduate student in my seminar on Eighteenth-Century Women Writers in fall 1990, for calling my attention to Nichols's assertion. Tollet's poem also appears in *Poems*, 2d ed., 99–108.

8. Henry Baker, "The Universe. A philosophical poem. Intended to restrain the pride of man . . ." (London: J. Worral, [1734]).

9. Elizabeth Carter, "In Diem Natalem," in *Poems on Several Occasions*, 2d ed. (London: J. Rivington, 1762), 1–4.

10. For Sappho, see my discussion of Lady Mary Wortley Montagu in chapter 3. "Eliza"/Eliza Haywood appears in *The Dunciad Variorum* (1728), 2.149–58, as the first prize in the dunces' pissing contest. Of Aphra Behn, Pope commented in his "First Epistle of the Second Book of Horace Imitated" (1737), "The stage how loosely does Astraea tread, / Who fairly puts all Characters to bed" (290–91).

11. Eliza Thompson, "Advice to a *Friend*, sent on Valentine's Day," in *Poems on Various Subjects* (London: Denew and Grant, 1787), 19–22, line 52.

12. Paul Gabriner has traced the Opposition significance of "Virtue" in Pope's poems and in contemporary usage. Gabriner, "Pope's 'Virtue' and the Events of 1738," in Mack and Winn, 585–611.

13. Anne Steele, "Imitation of Mr. Pope's Ode on Solitude," in *The works of Mrs. Anne Steele . . . Comprehending poems on subjects chiefly devotional: and miscellaneous pieces in prose and verse*, 2 vols. (Boston: Munroe, Francis, and Parker, 1808), 1:186–87.

14. Henrietta Knight, Lady Luxborough, "Written at a *Ferme Ornée* near Birmingham, August 7th, 1749," in *A Collection of Poems in Four Volumes. By Several Hands* (London: R. and J. Dodsley, 1755), 4:317.

15. Anna Laetita Barbauld, "On the Classics," in *A Memoir of Mrs. Anna Laetita Barbauld, with many of her letters*, ed. Grace A. Ellis, 2 vols. (Boston: J. R. Osgood, 1874), 2:292.

16. Catherine Talbot, "Elegy," in *The Works of the late Miss Catherine Talbot*, 7th ed., ed. Rev. Montagu Pennington (London: F. C. Rivington and J. Rivington, 1809), 423–24.

Conclusion: Pope's Influence on Eighteenth-Century Women's Poetry

1. Still a valuable introduction to Pope's prosody is Geoffrey Tillotson's "On Versification," in *Pope: A Collection of Critical Essays*, ed. J. V. Guerinot (Englewood Cliffs, N.J.: Prentice-Hall, 1972), 50–76. Tillotson discusses Pope's pursuit of correctness (50–58). I am indebted to Tillotson's cogent exposition throughout my discussion of women and Pope's prosody.

2. Irvin Ehrenpreis discussed the strengths and liabilities of Pope's couplet art in "The Style of Sound: The Literary Value of Pope's Versification," *The Augustan Milieu: Essays Presented to Louis A. Landa,* ed. Henry Knight Miller, Eric Rothstein, and G. S. Rousseau (Oxford: Clarendon, 1970), 232–46.

3. Barbauld's "Epistle to Mrs. P——" was first published in 1773, but the account of her activities in *A Memoir of Mrs. Anna Laetitia Barbauld* suggests the poem dates from a 1769 visit to Dr. and Mrs. Priestly at Leeds (1:33–35).

4. Samuel Johnson to John Wilkes, 8 May 1781, recorded by James Boswell in *Boswell's Life of Johnson, Together with Boswell's Journal of a Tour to the Hebrides and Johnson's Diary of a Journey into North Wales,* ed. George Birkbeck Hill, rev. L. F. Powell, 6 vols. (Oxford: Clarendon, 1934), 4:102.

5. Ann Eliza Bleecker died in 1783. Her daughter collected her writings and published them with her own in Bleecker, *The Posthumous Works of Ann Eliza Bleecker, in Prose and Verse, To which is added, A Collection of Essays, Prose and Poetical, by Margaretta V. Faugères* (New York: T. Swords and J. Swords, 1793).

6. In *Dead Certainties (Unwarranted Speculations)* (New York: Alfred A. Knopf, 1991), 21–39, Simon Schama describes the critical acclaim accorded Benjamin West for eschewing classical drapery but evoking a variety of classical-Christian associations in the figures and composition of "The Death of General Wolfe."

7. See the review in *London Magazine* 42 (1773): 456, quoted in Wheatley, 24. Such notices commonly greeted her work.

Bibliography

Addison, Joseph. *The Freeholder, or, Political Essays*. 1716. Reprint. Ann Arbor, Mich.: University Microfilms, 1967.

Addison, Joseph, et al. *The Spectator*. Edited by Donald F. Bond. 5 vols. Oxford: Clarendon, 1965.

Aden, John. *Pope's Once and Future Kings: Satire and Politics in the Early Career*. Knoxville: University of Tennessee Press, 1978.

Advice to Sappho. Occasioned by her Verses on the Imitator of the First Satire of the Second Book of Horace, by a Gentlewoman. London: J. Roberts, 1733.

Alexis [pseud.]. "The *Latin* Epigram [on Elizabeth Carter] Englished." *Gentleman's Magazine* 8 (1738): 429.

Ashmun, Margaret. *The Singing Swan*. New Haven: Yale University Press, 1931.

Astell, Mary. *Reflections Upon Marriage*. 3d ed. London: R. Wilkin, 1706.

Atkins, G. Douglass. "Pope and Deism: A New Analysis." In Mack and Winn, 392–415.

Ault, Norman. *New Light on Pope*. 1949. Reprint. Hamden, Conn.: Archon, 1967.

———, ed. *Pope's Own Miscellany: Being a reprint of Poems on Several Occasions 1717, containing new poems by Alexander Pope and others*. London: Nonesuch, 1935.

Baker, Henry. "The Universe. A philosophical poem." London: J. Worral, [1734].

Barbauld, Anna Laetitia. *The Female Speaker; or, Miscellaneous Pieces, in Prose and Verse, Selected from the Best Writers, and Adapted to the Use of Young Women*. 2d ed. London: Baldwin, Cradock, and Jay, 1816.

———. *A Memoir of Mrs. Anna Laetita Barbauld, with many of her letters*. Edited by Grace A. Ellis. 2 vols. Boston: J. R. Osgood, 1874.

Barber, Mary. *Poems on Several Occasions*. London: C. Rivington, 1734.

Barrell, John, and Harriet Guest. "On the Use of Contradiction: Economics and Morality in the Eighteenth-Century Long Poem." In Nussbaum and Brown, 133–43.

Battestin, Martin C., and Ruthe R. Battestin. *Henry Fielding: A Life*. London: Routledge, 1989.

The Beauties of Pope, or, Useful and Entertaining Passages selected from the Works of that Admired Author; as well as from his Translation of Homer's Iliad and Odyssey, &c. 2 vols. London: G. Kearsley, 1796.

Benstock, Shari, ed. *The Private Self: Theory and Practise of Women's Autobiographical Writings*. Chapel Hill: University of North Carolina Press, 1988.

Bentley, Elizabeth. *Genuine Poetical Compositions, on Various Subjects*. Norwich: Crouse and Stevenson, 1791.

Blamire, Susanna. "The Nun's Return to the World." In *The Poetical Works of Miss Susanna Blamire, The Muse of Cumberland*, collected by Henry Lonsdale, preface, memoir, and notes by Patrick Maxwell, 77–86. Edinburgh: J. Menzies, 1842.

Bleecker, Ann Eliza. *The Posthumous Works of Ann Eliza Bleecker, in Prose and Verse, To which is added, A Collection of Essays, Prose and Poetical, by Margaretta V. Faugères*. New York: T. Swords and J. Swords, 1793.

Bloom, Harold. *The Anxiety of Influence: A Theory of Poetry*. London: Oxford University Press, 1973.

Boswell, James. *Boswell's Life of Johnson, Together with Boswell's Journal of a Tour to the Hebrides and Johnson's Diary of a Journey into North Wales*. Edited by George Birkbeck Hill. Revised by L. F. Powell. 6 vols. Oxford: Clarendon, 1934.

[Boyd, Elizabeth.] "Admiral Haddock: or, The Progress of Spain." London: J. Applebee, 1739.

Boyd, Elizabeth. *Don Sancho: or, the Students Whim, A Ballad Opera of Two Acts*. London: E. Boyd, 1739.

———. "Truth, A Poem." London: E. Boyd, 1740.

[———.] *Variety: A Poem, In Two Cantos*. Westminster: T. Warner, 1727.

[Brereton, Jane.] *The Fifth Ode of the Fourth Book of Horace, Imitated and Apply'd to the King*, by a Lady. London: W. Hinchcliffe, 1716.

[———.] "On Mr. Nash's Picture at full Length, between the Busts of Sir Isaac Newton, and Mr. Pope." In *Poems on Several Occasions: By Mrs. Jane Brereton. With Letters to her Friends, and An Account Of Her Life*, 121–22. London: E. Cave, 1744.

[Bromley, Eliza.] *Laura and Augustus, An Authentic Story*. 3 vols. [1784].

Bronson, Bertrand H. "The Trough of the Wave." In Swedenberg, 197–226.

Brooke, Frances. *The History of Emily Montague*. 4 vols. 1769. Reprint. New York: Garland, 1974.

Brown, Laura. *Alexander Pope*. Oxford: B. Blackwell, 1985.

———. "The Defenseless Woman and the Development of English Tragedy." *Studies in English Literature* 22 (1982): 429–43.

Burnet, Thomas, and George Duckett. *Homerides; or, a Letter to Mr. Pope, by Sir Iliad Doggerel*. In *Popeiana II*.

Burney, Frances. *Camilla, or A Picture of Youth*. Edited by Edward A. Bloom and Lillian Bloom. 1796. Reprint. Oxford: Oxford University Press, 1983.

———. *Cecilia, or Memoirs of an Heiress*. 1782. Reprint. New York: Penguin, 1986.

———. *The Early Journals and Letters of Fanny Burney*. Edited by Lars E. Troide. 2 vols. Oxford: Clarendon, 1988.

———. *Evelina or the History of a Young Lady's Entrance into the World*. Edited by Edward A. Bloom. 1778. Reprint. New York: Oxford University Press, 1989.

———. *The Wanderer; or, Female Difficulties*. Edited by Margaret Anne Doody, Robert L. Mack, and Peter Sabor. 1814. Reprint. Oxford: Oxford University Press, 1991.

Burrell, Lady Sophia. *Poems. Dedicated to the Right Honourable the Earl of Mansfield*. 2 vols. London: J. Cooper, 1793.

Carter, Elizabeth [Eliza, pseud.]. "Answers to the said Epigram [on Elizabeth Carter]." *Gentleman's Magazine* 8 (1738): 429.

Carter, Elizabeth. *Memoirs of the Life of Mrs. Elizabeth Carter, With A New Edition Of Her Poems . . . To Which Are Added, Some Miscellaneous Essays In Prose*. Edited by Rev. Montagu Pennington. London: F. C. Rivington and J. Rivington, 1807.

———. *Poems on Several Occasions*. 2d ed. London: J. Rivington, 1762.

———. *A Series of Letters between Mrs. Elizabeth Carter and Miss Catherine Talbot, From the Year 1741 to 1770. . . .* Edited by Rev. Montagu Pennington. 4 vols. London: F. C. Rivington and J. Rivington, 1809.

———, trans. *All the Works of Epictetus*. London, 1752. *The Moral Discourses of Epictetus*. 1910. Reprint. London: J. M. Dent, 1928.

Chandler, Mary. *The Description of Bath . . . With Several Other Poems*. 8th ed. London: H. Leake, 1747.

Chapman, George, trans. *Chapman's Homer*. Edited by Allardyce Ni-
    coll. 2 vols. New York: Pantheon, 1969.
Chapone, Hester Mulso. *The Works of Mrs. Chapone: Now First Collected*.
    4 vols. London: J. Murray, 1807.
Chudleigh, Lady Mary. *Essays Upon Several Subjects In Prose and Verse*.
    London: R. Bonwicke et al., 1710.
The Cowper Anthology. MS. 28101, Addison Collection. British Library,
    London.
Cowper Madan, Judith. "The Progress of Poetry." London: J. Dodsley,
    1783.
Cronin, Grover, Jr., and Paul A. Doyle, eds. *Pope's Iliad: An Examination
    by William Melmoth*. Washington, D.C.: Catholic University Press,
    1960.
Crousaz, Jean Pierre de. *An Examination of Mr. Pope's Essay on Man.
    Translated from the French. . . .* Translated by Elizabeth Carter.
    London: A. Dodd, 1739.
Culler, Jonathan. "Reading as a Woman." In *On Deconstruction: Theory
    and Criticism after Structuralism*, 43–64. Ithaca: Cornell University
    Press, 1982.
[Curll, Edmund, ed.] *The Popeiad*. London: E. Curll, 1728.
Curtis, Anne. *Poems on Miscellaneous Subjects: By Ann Curtis, Sister of
    Mrs. Siddons*. London: J. Bowen, 1783.
Dacier, Anne. *Des Causes de la Corruption du Goust*. Paris: Au Dêpens
    de Rigaud Directeur de l'Imprimerie Royale, 1714.
———. *The Iliad of Homer, with notes . . . by Madam Dacier. Done from
    the French by Mr. Ozell. . . .* 5 vols. London: B. Lintot, 1712.
———, trans. *L'Iliade d'Homere, traduit en françois avec des remarques*. 3
    vols. 1st ed. Paris: Chez Rigaud, Directeur de l'Imprimerie Royale,
    1711.
———, trans. *L'Iliade d'Homere, traduit en françois, avec des remarques*. 3
    vols. 2d ed. Paris: Au Dêpens de Rigaud Directeur de l'Imprimerie
    Royale, 1719.
Davenant, Sir William. *The Dramatic Works of Sir William D'Avenant
    With Prefatory Memoir and Notes*. 5 vols. Edinburgh: W. Paterson,
    1872–74.
Delany, Mary. *The Autobiography and Correspondence of Mrs. Delany.
    . . . Edited by Sarah Chauncey Woolsey*. 2 vols. 1861–62. Reprint.
    Boston: Roberts Brothers, 1879.
Dennis, John. *Remarks upon Mr. Pope's Translation of Homer. With Two*

Letters concerning Windsor Forest and the Temple of Fame. In *Popeiana II.*

Deverell, Mary. *Miscellanies in Prose and Verse, mostly written in the Epistolary Style, chiefly upon moral subjects, and particularly calculated for the Improvement of Younger Minds.* 2 vols. [London?]: J. Rivington, 1781.

———. *Sermons on the Following Subjects. . . .* Bristol: S. Farley et al., 1774.

[Dixon, Sarah.] *Poems on Several Occasions.* Canterbury: J. Abree, 1740.

Doody, Margaret Anne. *Frances Burney: The Life in the Works.* New Brunswick, N.J.: Rutgers University Press, 1988.

———. "Swift Among the Women." *Yearbook of English Studies* 18 (1988): 68–92.

Dryden, John. *The Letters of John Dryden with Letters Addressed to Him.* Edited by Charles E. Ward. Durham: Duke University Press, 1942.

———. *The Works of John Dryden.* Edited by H. T. Swedenberg, Jr., et al. 20 vols. Berkeley: University of California Press, 1956–89.

[Duck, Stephen.] "Imitation of the Latin [Epigram on Elizabeth Carter]." *Gentleman's Magazine* 8 (1738): 429.

Echard, Lawrence. *Prefaces to Terence's Comedies and Plautus's Comedies.* Edited by John Barnard. 1694. Reprint. Los Angeles: Augustan Reprint Society, 1968.

Edgeworth, Maria. *Belinda.* Edited by Eva Figes. 1801. Reprint. London: Pandora, 1986.

Ehrenpreis, Irvin. "The Style of Sound: The Literary Value of Pope's Versification." In *The Augustan Milieu: Essays Presented to Louis Landa,* ed. Henry Knight Miller, Eric Rothstein, and G. S. Rousseau, 232–46. Oxford: Clarendon, 1970.

Einberg, Elizabeth, ed. *Manners and Morals: Hogarth and British Painting 1700–1760.* London: Tate Gallery, 1987.

Ettin, Andrew V. *Literature and the Pastoral.* New Haven: Yale University Press, 1984.

Ezell, Margaret J. M. *The Patriarch's Wife: Literary Evidence and the History of the Family.* Chapel Hill: University of North Carolina Press, 1987.

Falconar, Maria. "Alfred and Ethelinda, a Ballad." In *Poems, by Maria and Harriet Falconer,* by Maria Falconer and Harriet Falconer, 1–22. London: J. Johnson, 1788.

Fielding, Sarah. *The Adventures of David Simple: containing an account* of his travels through the cities of London and Westminster in the search of a real friend. Edited by Malcolm Kelsall. 1744. Reprint. Oxford: Oxford University Press, 1987.

Finch, Anne, Countess of Winchilsea. *Selected Poems of Anne Finch, Countess of Winchilsea*. Edited by Katherine M. Rogers. New York: F. Unger, 1979.

Flaxman, Rhoda L. "Radcliffe's Dual Modes of Vision." In Schofield and Macheski, 124–33.

The Flower-Piece: A Collection of Miscellany Poems. By Several Hands. London: J. Walthoe, 1731.

Flynn, Elizabeth A., and Patrocinio P. Schweickart, eds. *Gender and Reading: Essays on Readers, Texts, and Contexts*. Baltimore: Johns Hopkins University Press, 1986.

Forster, Antonia. "Mr. Pope's Maxims." *Age of Johnson* 2 (1989): 65–89.

Foster, Gretchen M. *Pope Versus Dryden: A Controversy in Letters to The Gentleman's Magazine, 1789–1791*. Victoria, B. C.: University of Victoria Press, 1989.

Francis, Anne. "The Sylph." In *Miscellaneous Poems by Anne Francis*, 262–68. Norwich: T. Becket and R. Baldwin, 1790.

Gabriner, Paul. "Pope's 'Virtue' and the Events of 1738." In Mack and Winn, 585–611.

Geduld, Harry M. *Prince of Publishers: A Study of the Work and Career of Jacob Tonson*. Bloomington: University of Indiana Press, 1969.

Gilbert, Sandra M., and Susan Gubar. *The Madwoman in the Attic: The Woman Writer and the Nineteenth-Century Literary Imagination*. New Haven: Yale University Press, 1979.

———, eds.*The Norton Anthology of Literature by Women*. New York: W. W. Norton, 1985.

Gildon, Charles. *A New Rehearsal*. In *Popeiana I*.

Guest, Harriet. "A Double Lustre: Femininity and Sociable Commerce, 1730–60." *Eighteenth-Century Studies* 23 (1990): 479–501.

Hagstrum, Jean H. *Sex and Sensibility: Ideal and Erotic Love from Milton to Mozart*. Chicago: University of Chicago Press, 1980.

Halsband, Robert. *The Life of Lady Mary Wortley Montagu*. Oxford: Clarendon, 1957.

———, ed. *Court Eclogs Written in the Year, 1716: Alexander Pope's autograph mauscript of poems by Lady Wortley Montagu*. New York: New York Public Library, 1977.

Hammond, Brean. *Pope and Bolingbroke: A Study of Friendship and Influence*. Columbia: University of Missouri Press, 1984.

Hands, Elizabeth. *The Death of Amnon. A Poem, with an Appendix: containing Pastorals, and other Poetical Pieces*. Coventry: N. Rollason, 1789.

Hays, Mary. *Memoirs of Emma Courtney*. Edited by Sally Cline. 1796. Reprint. London: Pandora, 1987.

Haywood, Eliza. *The Female Spectator*. 4 vols. 7th ed. London: H. Gardner, 1771.

————, trans. *La Belle Assemblée: or, the Adventures of Six Days. Being a Curious Collection of Remarkable Incidents which happen'd to some of the First Quality in France*, by Madeleine de Gomez. London: Printed for D. Browne, Jr., and S. Chapman, 1724–25.

Herrmann, Claudine. *Les Voleuses de langue*. Paris: des Femmes, 1976.

Hertford, Frances Seymour, Countess of. *Correspondence Between Frances, Countess of Hertford, and Henrietta Louisa, Countess of Pomfret, Between the Years 1738 and 1741*. Edited by William Bingley. 3 vols. London: R. Phillips, 1805.

[Hertford, Frances Seymour, Countess of.] "The Story of Inkle and Yarrico. A most moving Tale from the Spectator" and "An Epistle from Yarrico to Inkle, After he had left her in Slavery." London: J. Cooper, 1738.

Hervey, Baroness Mary Lepel. *Letters of Mary Lepel, Lady Hervey*. London: J. Murray, 1821.

Hill, Aaron. "The Progress of Wit: A Caveat." In *Popeiana X*.

Hodgart, Matthew. "The Subscription List for Pope's *Iliad*, 1715." In *The Dress of Words: Essays in Restoration and Eighteenth-Century Literature in Honor of Richmond P. Bond*, ed. Robert B. White, Jr., 25–34. Lawrence: University of Kansas Press, 1978.

Holmes, Geoffrey. *Augustan England: Professions, State and Society, 1680–1730*. London: Allen and Unwin, 1982.

Hughes, Helen Sard. *The Gentle Hertford: Her Life and Letters*. New York: Macmillan, 1940.

Ingram, Anne, Viscountess Irwin. "An Epistle to Mr. Pope. Occasioned by his Characters of Women." *Gentleman's Magazine* 6 (1736): 745.

Jauss, Hans-Robert. "Literary History as a Challenge to Literary Theory ." In *Toward an Aesthetic of Reception*, translated by Timothy Bahti, 3–45. Minneapolis: University of Minnesota Press, 1982.

Johnson, Samuel. "Ad Elisam Popi Horto Lauros Carpentum." *Gentleman's Magazine* 8 (1738): 372.

———. [Urbanus, pseud.]. "Another [Translation of the Epigram on Elizabeth Carter]." In *Gentleman's Magazine* 8 (1738): 429.

———. *A Dictionary of the English Language: in which The Words are deduced from their Originals. . . .* 1755. Reprint. London: Times, 1979.

———. *Lives of the English Poets.* Edited by George Birkbeck Hill. 3 vols. Oxford: Clarendon, 1905.

Jones, Mary. *Miscellanies in Prose and Verse.* Oxford: Dodsley et al., 1750.

Kaminsky, Thomas. *The Early Career of Samuel Johnson.* New York: Oxford University Press, 1987.

Knight, Henrietta, Lady Luxborough. "Written at a *Ferme Ornée* near Birmingham, August 7th, 1749." In *A Collection of Poems in Four Volumes. By Several Hands*, 4:317. London: R. Dodsley and J. Dodsley, 1755.

Landry, Donna. *The Muses of Resistance: Laboring-Class Women's Poetry in Britain, 1739–1796.* Cambridge: Cambridge University Press, 1990.

Lattimore, Richmond, trans. *The Iliad of Homer.* Chicago: University of Chicago Press, 1976.

Leapor, Mary. *Poems Upon Several Occasions.* London: J. Roberts, 1748.

Lewis, Esther. *Poems Moral and Entertaining, Written long since by Miss Lewis, then of Holt, Now, and for almost Thirty Years past, the Wife of Mr. Robert Clark, of Tetbury.* Bath: S. Hazard, 1789.

Little, Janet. *The Poetical Works of Janet Little, the Scotch Milkmaid.* Air: J. Wilson and P. Wilson, 1792.

Lonsdale, Roger, ed. *Eighteenth-Century Women Poets: An Oxford Anthology.* Oxford: Oxford University Press, 1989.

Lovejoy, Arthur O. *The Great Chain of Being: A Study of the History of an Idea.* 1936. Reprint. Cambridge: Harvard University Press, 1973.

Lowenthal, Cynthia. "The Veil of Romance: Lady Mary's Embassy Letters." *Eighteenth-Century Life* 14 (1990): 66–82.

Lucas, E. V. *A Swan and Her Friends.* London: Methuen, 1907.

Macaulay, Catherine. *The History of England from the Accession of James I to that of the Brunswick Line.* 8 vols. London: J. Nourse et al., 1763–83.

Macaulay Graham, Catherine. *Letters on Education. With Observations on Religious and Metaphysical Subjects.* London: C. Dilly, 1790.

McCarthy, Willam. *Hester Thrale Piozzi: Portrait of a Literary Woman*. Chapel Hill: University of North Carolina Press, 1985.

———. "A Verse 'Essay on Man' by H. L. Piozzi." *The Age of Johnson* 2 (1989): 375–420.

Mack, Maynard. *Alexander Pope: A Life*. New York: W. W. Norton, 1986.

———. *The Garden and the City: Retirement and Politics in the Later Poetry of Pope, 1731–1743*. Toronto: University of Toronto Press, 1969.

Mack, Maynard, and James Winn, eds. *Pope: Recent Essays by Several Hands*. Hamden, Conn.: Archon, 1980.

Madan, Falconer. *The Madan Family*. Oxford: Clarendon, 1933.

Martin, Peter. *Pursuing Innocent Pleasures: The Gardening World of Alexander Pope*. Hamden, Conn.: Archon, 1984.

Masters, Mary. *Familiar Letters and Poems on Several Occasions*. London: D. Henry and R. Cave, 1755.

———. "To the Right Honourable the Earl of Burlington." In *Poems on Several Occasions*, 5–7. London: T. Browne, 1733.

Messenger, Ann. *His and Hers: Essays in Restoration and Eighteenth-Century Literature*. Lexington: University Press of Kentucky, 1986.

Montagu, Elizabeth. *An essay on the writings and genius of Shakespear, compared with the Greek and French dramatic poets*. London: J. Dodsley et al., 1769.

———. *The Letters of Mrs. Elizabeth Montagu, with some of the letters of her correspondents*. Edited by Matthew Montagu. 4 vols. London: T. Cadell and W. Davies, 1809.

Montagu, Lady Mary Wortley. *The Complete Letters of Lady Mary Wortley Montagu*. Edited by Robert Halsband. 3 vols. Oxford: Clarendon, 1965.

———. *Essays and Poems and Simplicity, A Comedy*. Edited by Robert Halsband and Isobel Grundy. Oxford: Clarendon, 1977.

More, Hannah. *The Works of Hannah More*. 2 vols. New York: Harper and Brothers, 1835.

Morrice, Bezaleel. "Satire I. On the *English* Translations of Homer." In *Popeiana II*.

Murry, Ann. *Mentoria; or, the young ladies instructor in Familiar conversations on moral and entertaining subjects. . . .* 6th ed. 1778. Reprint. London: C. Dilly, 1791.

———. *Poems on Various Subjects*. London: 1779.

Myers, Mitzi. "Hannah More's Tracts for the Times: Social Fiction and Female Ideology." In Schofield and Macheski, 264–84.

Myers, Sylvia Harcstark. *The Bluestocking Circle: Women, Friendship, and the Life of the Mind in Eighteenth-Century England*. Oxford: Clarendon, 1990.

The Neuter: or, a Modest Satire on the Poets of the Age, by a Lady. London: T. Osborne, [1733].

Nichols, John, ed. *A Select Collection of Poems: With Notes, Biographical and Historical*. 8 vols. London: J. Nichols, 1780.

Nussbaum, Felicity A. *The Brink of All We Hate: English Satires on Women, 1660–1750*. Lexington: University Press of Kentucky, 1984.

———. "Eighteenth-Century Women's Autobiographical Commonplaces." In Benstock, 147–71.

Ogilby, John, trans. *Homer His Iliads*. London: T. Roycroft, 1660.

Ovid. *Ovid's Epistles: with his Amours, translated into English verse, by the most eminent hands*. London: J. Tonson and R. Tonson, 1736.

———. *Ovid's Metamorphoses in Latin and English, Translated by the Most Eminent Hands*. 2 vols. Translated by Sir Samuel Garth et al. 1717. Reprint. Amsterdam: Wetsteins and Smith, 1732.

Pattison, William. *The Poetical Works of Mr. William Pattison*. 2 vols. London: H. Curll, 1728.

Pearson, Hesketh. *The Swan of Lichfield, being a Selection from the Correspondence of Anna Seward*. London: H. Hamilton, 1936.

Penny, Anne. "Amyntas." In *Poems*, 51–54. 1771. Reprint. London, 1780.

Pennyman, Margaret. *Miscellanies in Prose and Verse . . . To which are annexed, Some other curious Pieces*. London: E. Curll, 1740.

Perry, Ruth. *Women, Letters, and the Novel*. New York: AMS, 1980.

Pilkington, Laetitia. *Memoirs of Mrs. Laetitia Pilkington, Wife to the Rev. Mr. Matthew Pilkington, Written by Herself*. 3 vols. London: R. Griffiths and G. Woodfall, 1748–54.

Piozzi, Hester Thrale. *British Synonymy*. 2 vols. 1794. Reprint. Menston, England: Scolar, 1968.

———. *Observations and Reflections Made in the Course of a Journey Through France, Italy, and Germany*. Edited by Herbert Brown. 1789. Reprint. Ann Arbor: University of Michigan Press, 1967.

———. *Thraliana: The Diary of Mrs. Hester Lynch Thrale (Later Mrs. Piozzi)*. Edited by Katherine Balderston. 2 vols. Oxford: Clarendon, 1951.

Pohli, Carol Virginia. "'The Point Where Sense and Dulness Meet':

What Pope Knows About Knowing and About Women." *Eighteenth-Century Studies* 19 (2): 206–34.

Pointon, Priscilla. "Reply to Mr. Jones of Kidderminster . . . Written *Extempore.*" In *Poems on Several Occasions*, 5. Birmingham: T. Warren, 1770.

Pollak, Ellen. *The Poetics of Sexual Myth: Gender and Ideology in the Verse of Swift and Pope*. Chicago: University of Chicago Press, 1985.

Pope, Alexander. *The Correspondence of Alexander Pope*. Edited by George Sherburn. 5 vols. Oxford: Clarendon, 1956.

———. *Miscellany Poems*. Vol. 1. 5th ed. London: B. Lintot, 1736.

———. *The Poems of Alexander Pope*. Edited by John Butt et al. 10 vols. London: Methuen, 1967.

———. *The Works of Mr. Alexander Pope*. London: B. Lintot, 1717.

Pope, Alexander, et al. *The Unfortunate Lovers; Two Admirable Poems. Extracted out of the celebrated Letters of Abelard and Eloisa*. London: Pamphlet Shops, 1756.

Popeiana I: Early Criticism, 1711–1716. New York: Garland, 1975.

Popeiana II: Pope's Homer, 1714–1719. New York: Garland, 1975.

Popeiana VI: The Dunciad I, 1728. New York: Garland, 1975.

Popeiana VIII: The Dunciad, 1729. New York: Garland, 1975.

Popeiana X: The Dunciad and Other Matters, 1730. New York: Garland, 1975.

Prior, Matthew. "Henry and Emma, A Poem, Upon the Model of the Nut-Brown Maid." In *The Literary Works of Matthew Prior*, edited by H. Bunker Wright and Monroe K. Spears, 2 vols., 1:278–300. Oxford: Clarendon, 1959.

Propp, Vladimir. *Morphology of the Folktale*. Translated by Laurence Scott. Edited by Louis A. Wagner. 2d ed. Austin: University of Texas Press, 1968.

Pye, Jael Henrietta. "Elgiva to Edwy." In *Poems, by Mrs. Hampden Pye*, 2d ed., 87–95. London: J. Walter, 1772.

———. *A short account, of the principal seats and gardens, in and about Twickenham*. London, 1760.

Radcliffe, Ann. *The Mysteries of Udolpho*. Edited by Bonamy Dobrée. 1794. Reprint. Oxford: Oxford University Press, 1988.

Ramsay Lennox, Charlotte. *Poems on Several Occasions*. London: S. Paterson, 1747.

———. *Shakespear Illustrated: or the Novels and Histories, On Which the Plays of Shakespear Are Founded, Collected and Translated from the Original Authors*. 3 vols. 1753. Reprint. New York: AMS, 1973.

Redford, Bruce. *The Converse of the Pen: Acts of Intimacy in the Eighteenth-Century Familiar Letter*. Chicago: University of Chicago Press, 1986.

Ribeiro, Aileen. *Dress in Eighteenth-Century Europe, 1715–1789*. New York: Holmes and Meier, 1985.

———. *A Visual History of Costume: The Eighteenth Century*. London: B. T. Batsford, 1983.

Richardson, Samuel. *The Correspondence of Samuel Richardson . . . Selected From The Original Manuscripts, Bequeathed By Him To His Family*. Edited by Anna Laetitia Barbauld. 6 vols. 1804. Reprint. New York: AMS, 1966.

Rizzo, Betty. "The Patron as Poet Maker: The Politics of Benefaction." *Studies in Eighteenth-Century Culture* 20 (1990): 241–66.

Roberts, William. *Memoirs of the Life and Correspondence of Mrs. Hannah More*. 2 vols. New York: Harper and Brothers, 1851.

Rogers, Pat. "Pope and His Subscribers." *Publishing History* 3 (1978): 7–36.

Rousseau, G. S., and Pat Rogers, eds. *The Enduring Legacy: Alexander Pope Tercentenary Essays*. Cambridge: Cambridge University Press, 1988.

Rowe, Elizabeth Singer. *Friendship in Death*. 1728. Reprint. New York: Garland, 1972.

———. *The Miscellaneous Works in Prose and Verse of Mrs. Elizabeth Rowe*. 2 vols. London: R. Hett and R. Dodsley, 1739.

Rumbold, Valerie. *Women's Place in Pope's World*. Cambridge: Cambridge University Press, 1989.

Salvaggio, Ruth. *Enlightened Absence: Neoclassical Configurations of the Feminine*. Urbana: University of Illinois Press, 1988.

Schama, Simon. *Dead Certainties (Unwarranted Speculations)*. New York: Alfred A. Knopf, 1991.

Schibanoff, Susan. "Taking the Gold out of Egypt: The Art of Reading as a Woman." In Flynn and Schweickert, 83–106.

Schofield, Mary Anne, and Cecilia Macheski. *Fetter'd or Free?: British Women Novelists, 1670–1815*. 1986. Reprint. Athens, Ohio : Ohio University Press, 1987.

Scott, Sarah. *A Description of Millenium Hall and the Country Adjacent Together with the Characters of the Inhabitants And such Historical Anecdotes and Reflections as May excite in the Reader proper Sentiments of Humanity, and lead the Mind to the Love of Virtue*. Edited by Jane Spencer. 1762. Reprint. New York: Penguin, 1986.

——. *The History of Sir George Ellison*. 2 vols. London: A. Millar, 1766.

Seward, Anna. *Letters of Anna Seward: Written Between the Years 1784 and 1807*. 6 vols. Edinburgh: A. Constable, 1811.

——. *The Poetical Works of Anna Seward, with extracts from her literary correspondence*. Edited by Sir Walter Scott. 3 vols. Edinburgh: Ballantyne, 1810.

Sheridan, Elizabeth. *Betsy Sheridan's Journal: Letters from Sheridan's Sister 1784–1786 and 1788–1790*. Edited by William LeFanu. London: Eyre and Spottiswoode, 1960.

Shevelow, Kathryn. *Women and Print Culture: The Construction of Femininity in the Early Periodical*. London: Routledge, 1989.

[Shiels, Robert.] *The Lives of the Poets of Great Britain and Ireland*. 5 vols. 1753. Reprint. Hildesheim: G. Olms Verlagbuchhandlung, 1968.

Sitwell, Edith. *Alexander Pope*. London: Faber and Faber, 1930.

Smith, Charlotte. *Emmeline, The Orphan of the Castle*. 1788. Reprint. London: Pandora, 1988.

——. *The Old Manor House*. Edited by Anne Henry Ehrenpreis. 1793. Reprint. Oxford: Oxford University Press, 1989.

——. "Sonnet I." In *Elegiac Sonnets, by Charlotte Smith*, 6th ed., 1. Dublin: B. Dornin, 1790.

Smithers, Peter. *The Life of Joseph Addison*. Oxford: Clarendon, 1968.

"Some Literary Celebrities of Bath of the Last Century." *The Bath and County Graphic* 2 (October 1897): 65–66.

Spacks, Patricia Meyer. "Female Rhetorics." In Benstock, 177–91.

Staves, Susan. "Douglas's Mother." In *Brandeis Essays in Literature*, edited by John H. Smith, 51–67. Waltham, Mass.: Brandeis University, 1983.

Stecher, Henry F. *Elizabeth Singer Rowe, the Poetess of Frome: A Study in Eighteenth-Century English Pietism*. Frankfurt: H. Lang, 1973.

Steele, Anne. "Imitation of Mr. Pope's Ode on Solitude." In *The works of Mrs. Anne Steele . . . Comprehending poems on subjects chiefly devotional: and miscellaneous pieces in prose and verse*, 2 vols., 1:186–87. Boston: Munroe, Francis, and Parker, 1808.

Steele, Richard, et al. *The Guardian*. 2 vols. London: C. Bathurst et al., 1795.

——. *The Tatler*. Edited by Donald F. Bond. 3 vols. Oxford: Clarendon, 1987.

Suffolk, Henrietta Howard, Countess of. *Letters to and from Henrietta,*

Countess of Suffolk, and her second husband, The Hon. George Berkeley; from 1712 to 1767. 2 vols. London: J. Murray, 1824.

Talbot, Catherine. "Elegy." In *The Works of the late Miss Catherine Talbot*, 423–24. 7th ed. Edited by Rev. Montagu Pennington. London: F. C. Rivington and J. Rivington, 1809.

Thompson, Eliza. *Poems on Various Subjects*. London: Denew and Grant, 1787.

[Thornton, Bonnell, and George Colman, eds.] *Poems by Eminent Ladies*. 2 vols. London: R. Baldwin, 1755.

"Thy Pen, Great Pope! the wonder of the Age." MS. 4456, f. 97, Birch Collection. British Library, London.

Tillotson, Geoffrey. "On Versification." In *Pope: A Collection of Critical Essays*, ed. J. V. Guerinot, 50–76. Englewood Cliffs, N.J.: Prentice-Hall, 1972.

"To a Lady who desir'd her to write an Epithalamion." By a Lady. P. A. Taylor Papers, vol. 3. MS. 37,684, f. 78–80, Addison Collection. British Library, London.

Todd, Janet, ed. *A Dictionary of British and American Women Writers, 1660–1800*. Totowa, N.J.: Rowman and Littlefield, 1987.

[Tollet, Elizabeth.] *Poems on Several Occasions. With Anne Boleyn to King Henry VIII. An Epistle*. 1st ed. London: J. Clarke, 1724.

Tollet, Elizabeth. *Poems on Several Occasions. With Anne Boleyn to King Henry VIII. An Epistle*. 2d ed. London: T. Lownds, [1756?].

Upton, Catherine. "A Letter from the Authoress in London to her Father in Nottingham." In *Miscellaneous Pieces, in Prose and Verse* , 9–12. London, 1784.

Ward, Edward. "Durgen or, a Plain Satyr upon a Pompous Satyrist." In *Popeiana VIII*.

Warton, Joseph. *Essay on the Genius and Writings of Pope*. 2 vols. 1756–82. Reprint. New York: Garland, 1974.

Weinbrot, Howard D. *Alexander Pope and the Traditions of Formal Verse Satire*. Princeton: Princeton University Press, 1982.

———. "*The Rape of the Lock* and the Contexts of Warfare." In Rousseau and Rogers, 22–30.

Whateley, Mary. *Original Poems on Several Occasions. By Miss Whateley*. London: R. Dodsley and J. Dodsley, 1764.

Whateley Darwall, Mary. *Poems on Several Occasions. By Mrs. Darwall. (Formerly Miss Whateley.)*. 2 vols. Walsall: F. Milward, 1794.

Wheatley, Phillis. *The Poems of Phillis Wheatley*. Edited by Julian D. Mason, Jr. Chapel Hill: University of North Carolina Press, 1989.

White, Douglas H. *Pope and the Context of Controversy: The Manipulation of Ideas in "An Essay on Man."* Chicago: University of Chicago Press, 1970.

Williams, Helen Maria. *Peru.* In *Poems, by Helen Maria Williams*, 2 vols, 2:45–178. London: T. Cadell, 1786.

Wilson, Penelope. "Engendering the Reader: 'Wit and Poetry and Pope' Once More." In Rousseau and Rogers, 63–76.

Wimsatt, William K. *The Portraits of Alexander Pope.* New Haven: Yale University Press, 1965.

Winn, James. *John Dryden and His World.* New Haven: Yale University Press, 1987.

———. *A Window in the Bosom: The Letters of Alexander Pope.* Hamden, Conn.: Archon, 1977.

Wittreich, Joseph. *Feminist Milton.* Ithaca: Cornell University Press, 1987.

Wollstonecraft, Mary. *Vindication of the Rights of Woman.* Edited by Miriam Kramnick. New York: Penguin, 1983.

Wright, Lawrence S. "Eighteenth-Century Replies to Pope's Eloisa." *Studies in Philology* 31 (1934): 519–33.

Yearsley, Ann. "Written on a Visit." In *Poems on Various Subjects*, 139–43. London: G. G. J. Robinson and J. Robinson, 1787.

Yorke, Charles. "To a Lady, With A Present of Pope's Works." In Nichols, 6:301–2.

Z., A. Untitled Poem. *London Magazine* 5 (1736): 515.

Zwicker, Stephen N. *Politics and Language in Dryden's Poetry.* Princeton: Princeton University Press, 1984.

Index

"Abelard to Eloisa" (Burrell), 185–88
"Abelard to Eloisa" (Cowper), 132–35, 137, 139
Achilles (*Iliad*), 54–55
Addison, Joseph. *See* Addison's and Steele's publications
Addison's and Steele's publications: as arbiters of taste, 26, 34, 35, 48; attacks on Pope, 45–47; fashion in, 38, 39; ideas about women in, 37–38, 40–41, 43, 44–45, 55, 150, 252n.27; and Lady Montagu, 35, 52; on women's education, 17, 141
Aden, John, 23, 253n.11
"Admiral Haddock: or, The Progress of Spain" (Boyd), 220–21
Adventures of David Simple, The (Fielding), 79
"Advertisement" (Jones), 204, 207, 208
"Advice to a *Friend*, sent on *Valentine*'s Day" (Thompson), 221
"Advice to Sappho" (anonymous), 129, 269n.11
Aeneid, 24, 26
Alexander Pope (Brown), 1
Alexander Pope: A Life (Mack), 2
"Alfred and Ethelinda" (Falconer), 180–81
All for Love (Dryden), 232
All the Works of Epictetus (Carter), 57
Amazons (*Iliad*), 44
"Amyntas" (Penny), 172–73
Andromache (*Iliad*), 38, 43–44
Anecdotes of Dr. Johnson (Thrale), 60

"Anne Boleyn to King Henry VIII" (Tollet), 175, 192
"Another Epistle to Nell" (Little), 224–25
"Answer, The" (Finch), 140–41
Anxiety of Influence: A Theory of Poetry, The (Bloom), 262n.16
Astell, Mary, 37
Athenian Mercury (Dunton), 35
Austen, Jane, 65

Baker, Henry, 209
Barbauld, Anne Laetitia, 223–24, 231, 232, 234–36
Barber, Mary, 145–46, 158
Beauclerk, Lady. *See* Lovelace, Martha
Behn, Aphra, 35, 120, 167, 188, 278n.10
Belinda (Edgeworth), 267n.53
Bendixen, Mary Anne, 273n.4
Bentley, Elizabeth, 157, 158, 159, 269n.11, 272n.44, 272n.46
Bermor, Belle, 42
Birch, Thomas, 86, 138
Blamire, Susanna, 181–83, 192
Bleecker, Ann Eliza, 239–40
Bloom, Harold, 65, 262n.16
Blount, Martha, 16, 39, 41–42, 82, 149, 190. *See also* "Epistle to a Lady"
Blount, Teresa, 39, 41–42
Bolingbroke, Lord, 75, 87, 90–91, 265n.37. *See also* Essay on Man, An
Bowden, Samuel, 164, 273n.6

Bowyer, Lady, 102
Boyd, Elizabeth, 152, 158–59, 220,
    231
Brereton, Jane, 195, 277n.3
British Synonymy (Thrale), 76–79, 88,
    90, 94, 108
Bromley, Eliza, 98–99
Bronson, Bertrand, 111
Brooke, Frances, 81–82
Broome, William, 22, 36, 258n.60
Brown, Laura, 1, 20, 35, 252n.3
Burke, Edmund, 76
Burnet, Thomas, 45, 48
Burney, Fanny, 68, 69–70, 71, 177–
    78, 260n.4, 260–61n.5; on Pope's
    correspondence, 83, 107
Burns, Robert, 171, 224
Burrell, Lady Sophia, 185–88
Burton, Hezekiah, 94

Caesar, Mary, 130
Cambridge Platonists, 89–90
"Camilla" (Whateley), 238
Carter, Elizabeth, 98; career of, 85–
    86; Crousaz translation, 7, 86,
    212, 250n.16, 265n.35; and *An Es-
    say on Man*, 86–87, 88, 211–16,
    225; and Johnson, 19, 40, 86; and
    The Rape of the Lock, 190; re-
    sponse to *Iliad* translation, 55–58,
    66, 257n.58; style, 230; and
    Twickenham, 6–8, 15
Cato (Addison), 52
Cave, Edward, 86
Cavendish, Margaret, 202
"Celadon to Mira" (Leapor), 156,
    158
Chandler, Mary, 195–99, 225,
    277n.5
Chapman, George, 32
Chapone, Hester Mulso, 75
Chetwood, Knightly, 29
Christianity, 36, 222–23. *See also Es-
    say on Man, An*
Chudleigh, Lady Mary, 274n.12
Cibber, Colley, 26, 110
Civil War, 255n.33

Clark, Robert, 164
Collier, Arthur, 87
Collins, William, 171
Colman, George, 132
Commentaire (Crousaz), 86, 264–
    65n.34
Contemporary ideas about women:
    education, 17, 40–42, 44–45, 55,
    141, 148, 163; and *Iliad* transla-
    tion, 40–42, 146, 271n.35; sexual-
    ity, 134; sympathy, 118, 268n.2;
    women's rights, 93
Contemporary women writers'
    lives: and ambition, 205; ambiva-
    lence, 160–65; criticism of, 139;
    laboring-class, 10–13, 154–55,
    157–58; and patronage, 208; and
    poetry, 120–21, 123–24, 142; pub-
    lishing, 70–71, 85, 124, 142, 189;
    and pursuit of money, 105–6; re-
    strictions, 17, 106–7, 168,
    252n.27, 274n.12
Cowper, Judith, 130–39, 158, 229,
    259n.67
Cowper, William, 168
Crousaz, Jean Pierre de, 7, 212,
    250n.16, 264–65n.34, 265n.35
Culler, Jonathan, 188
Curll, Edmund, 86, 264–65n.34
Curtis, Ann, 168, 179–80, 192

Dacier, Anne: and Fielding, 52,
    257n.54; *Iliad* translation, 27–28,
    33, 34, 36–37, 38, 39, 254n.21,
    254–55n.27, 255n.32; response to
    Pope's *Iliad* translation, 49–52,
    66, 256–57n.50, 257n.52
Dahl, Michael, 255n.36
"Damon and Thyrsis" (Murry), 173
Darwin, Erasmus, 114
Death of Ammon, The (Hands),
    276n.31
Delany, Mary, 55
"Delia, A Pastoral" (Whateley), 168,
    169–70
Dennis, John, 44, 47, 48

Des Causes de la Corruption du Goust (Dacier), 36

Description of Bath . . . With Several Other Poems, A (Chandler), 196

Description of Millenium Hall, A (Scott), 79–80

"Deserted Village, The" (Goldsmith), 171

Deverell, Mary, 97, 161–63, 273n.4

Dictionary of the English Language: in which The Words are deduced from their Originals, A (Johnson), 77, 263n.23

"Discourse Concerning the Original and Progress of Satire" (Dryden), 194, 252–53n.6

Dixon, Sarah, 150–51, 158

Dodsley, Robert, 4

Don Sancho: or, the Students Whim (Boyd), 152

Doody, Margaret Anne, 101, 105, 178

"Dorinda at her Glass" (Leapor), 233–34, 238

Douglas (Home), 179, 275n.26

Dryden, John, 113, 232; and Pope's *Iliad* translation, 22–26, 27, 28, 59, 252–53n.6, 253n.13; on satire, 194, 252–53n.6; style, 228; sympathy with women, 118, 268n.2

Duck, Stephen, 6

Duckett, George, 45

Dunciad, 86, 152, 278n.10; allusions to, 69, 242; and Twickenham, 5–6, 124–25; and women's emulation, 103, 107

Dunton, John, 35

"Durgen" (Ward), 48–49

Echard, Lawrence, 22, 25

Edgeworth, Maria, 267n.53

Edwards, Thomas, 83, 84–85

Ehrenpreis, Irvin, 229–30

Einberg, Elizabeth, 256n.36

Elegaic Sonnets (Smith), 174–75

"Elegy" (Talbot), 225–26

"Elegy on a much lamented Friend" (Whateley), 169

"Elegy on [Mr. Andrew Ewart]" (Thompson), 236–37

"Eleonora: A Panegyrical Poem Dedicated to the Memory of the Late Countess of Abingdon" (Dryden), 268n.2

"Elgiva to Edwy" (Pye), 177–79, 192

Emmeline (Smith), 82

"Engendering the Reader: 'Wit and Poetry and Pope' Once More" (Wilson), 1–2

Enlightened Absence (Salvaggio), 1, 188

"Epistle from Eloisa to Abelard," women's responses to, 82, 83, 174–88, 190, 236; allusions, 237, 239, 242; Burrell, 185–88; Cowper, 132–35, 137, 139; Hertford, 72–73, 175–76; Leapor, 233; Macaulay Graham, 91; Elizabeth Montagu, 75; novelists, 98, 99, 100; and Pope's ideas about women, 85, 120, 191, 192–93; revision, 183–84; Seward, 110–11, 184–85, 192, 276n.32; Smith, 174–75; and women's sexuality, 176–83, 187–88

"Epistle from Fern-Hill" (Jones), 101

"Epistle from Yarico to Inkle, An" (Hertford), 72

"Epistle to a Lady," women's responses to, 85, 127, 151, 190, 203, 238; Brooke, 81, 82; Carter, 212–13, 214, 215; Irwin, 147, 148–49, 150; and Pope's ideas about women, 101, 118–19, 215, 218, 219; Seward, 217–20; and women's ambivalence, 163

"Epistle to a Lady, An" (Leapor), 199–201

"Epistle to a Physical Devine, who requested the author to write poetry, An" (Deverell), 161–62

"Epistle to Burlington," 80, 147, 223, 224, 271n.31; Burney's response to, 69–70; Jones' response to, 204, 206

"Epistle to Cornelia" (Seward), 217–20, 228

"Epistle to Dr. Arbuthnot," 4, 60, 152, 160, 168. *See also* "Epistle to Dr. Arbuthnot," women's responses to

"Epistle to Dr. Arbuthnot," women's responses to, 73, 75, 198, 214, 228; Jones, 102, 204, 205, 206, 207, 208; Leapor, 201, 202; Talbot, 225–26

"Epistle to Lady Bowyer, An" (Jones), 204–9

"Epistle to Moneses. In Imitation of Ovid" (Ramsay), 176–77, 179, 191–92, 275n.23

"Epistle to Mr. Pope. Occasioned by his Characters of Women, An" (Irwin), 85, 146–50, 244–45

Épitre I sur l'Homme (Racine), 87

"Essay on Criticism, An," 12, 162, 163, 189, 204; on style, 229, 231, 243. *See also* "Essay on Criticism, An," women's responses to

"Essay on Criticism, An," women's responses to, 62, 149–50, 152, 238; Cowper, 130–31, 135, 136, 137, 229; Leapor, 153–54, 229; Elizabeth Montagu, 75, 76; Thrale, 59, 77–78, 94

"Essay on Friendship" (Leapor), 201–4, 229

"Essay on Homer" (Parnell), 62

Essay on Man, An: Crousaz on, 7, 250n.16; on education, 148; heterodoxy of, 84–85, 264n.33. *See also Essay on Man, An,* women's responses to

Essay on Man, An, women's responses to, 83–101, 180; allusions, 79, 96–98, 242, 266n.49; Boyd, 220–21; Carter, 86–87, 88, 211–12, 214–15; Irwin, 146, 147, 149; Jones, 102, 208–9, 231; Leapor, 152–54, 157, 202; Lewis,

165, 221–22; Macaulay Graham, 90–93, 94, 95, 96, 100–101, 265n.40; male attention to, 83–85; Lady Montagu, 126–27; More, 93–96, 100–101; novelists, 98–101, 267n.53; and pastorals, 172, 174; Thrale, 87–90, 94, 96, 97, 266n.49; Tollet, 209–11

Essay on the Writings and Genius of Shakespear (Elizabeth Montagu), 75

Ettin, Andrew V., 167–68

Evelina (Burney), 68, 260–61n.5

Examination of Mr. Pope's Essay on Man, An (Crousaz), 7, 86, 212, 250n.16, 265n.35

Ezell, Margaret, 70, 85

Fairy tales, 275n.27

Falconer, Maria, 180–81

"Familiar Epistle to the Author's Sister, A" (Murry), 230

Fashion, 38–39, 255–56n.36

Female Spectator, 96

Feminist criticism, 1, 7, 21, 262n.16

Feminist Milton (Wittreich), 118

Fenton, Elijah, 22, 258n.60

Fielding, Henry, 52, 257n.54, 257n.58

Fielding, Sarah, 71, 79

Finch, Anne, 140, 163, 188, 190, 251n.23

Flaxman, Rhoda, 70

Flower-Piece, The (Cowper), 138

Flynn, Elizabeth A., 270n.20

Forster, Antonia, 97, 266n.48

Foster, Gretchen M., 64

Francis, Ann, 168

Freeholder, The, 46, 47

Freemantle, Bridget, 154

French Revolution, 183

"Funeral Poem on the Death of C. E. an Infant of Twelve Months, A" (Wheatley), 242

Gay, John, 26, 52

Gentleman's Magazine, 86, 113, 114

Gilbert, Sandra M., 105, 188

Gildon, Charles, 47

"Given to a Lady who asked me to write a Poem" (Little), 224

Goldsmith, Oliver, 171

"Goliath of Gath" (Wheatley), 62–63

Gothic style, 83, 263–64n.31

"Groans of the Tankard, The" (Barbauld), 232

Guardian, 37, 40

Gubar, Susan, 105, 188

Guest, Harriet, 105

Hagstrum, Jean, 25, 29, 268n.2

Halsband, Robert, 121, 125

Hammond, Brean, 51, 265n.37

Hands, Elizabeth, 183, 191, 192, 276n.31

Hardinge, George, 113

Hayley, William, 111, 112, 115, 267n.63

Hays, Mary, 99–101, 106

Haywood, Eliza, 96

"Heart Unfathomable, The" (Lewis), 165

Hector (*Iliad*), 27–29

Helen (*Iliad*), 25, 34, 36–37, 255n.32

"Henry and Emma, A Poem, Upon the Model of the Nut-Brown Maid" (Prior), 276n.33

"Her Palace placed beneath a muddy road" (Montagu), 5

Hertford, Lady, 71–73, 74, 150, 175–76, 214

Hervey, Baroness Mary Lepel, 75

Hervey, Lord, 124, 125

Highmore, Susanna, 272–73n.47

Hill, Aaron, 49

History of Emily Montague, The (Brooke), 81–82

History of England from the Accession of James I to that of the Brunswick Line (Macaulay Graham), 92, 266n.42

History of Sir George Ellison, The (Scott), 79–81

History of the Works of the Learned (Warburton), 89

Hobbes, Thomas, 32

Hodgart, Matthew, 253n.11

Hogarth, William, 218–19

Holmes, Geoffrey, 261n.9

"Holt Waters" (Jones), 101

Home, John, 179, 275n.26

Homer, 136–37, 240–41. *See also Iliad* translation by Pope; *Odyssey* translation by Pope

Homerides; or, A Letter to Mr. Pope, by Sir Iliad Doggerel (Burnet and Duckett), 45

Homosexuality, 169

Horatian satires, women's responses to, 75, 149, 194–226, 278n.10; Barbauld, 223–24; Boyd, 220–21; Carter, 211–16, 225; Chandler, 195–99, 225, 277n.5; Jones, 204–9, 225; Leapor, 199–204, 225, 277n.6; Little, 224–25; Lady Montagu, 125, 126, 128–29; Seward, 217–20, 225; Steele, 222–23. *See also Essay on Man, An,* women's responses to; *specific works*

Howard, Henrietta, 130

Howe, Sophia, 4

Hughes, Helen Sard, 175

"Hymn Written in Windsor Forest," 115, 130, 227, 235, 240; and Twickenham, 3, 4, 10, 11; and women's pastorals, 169, 170, 171

"Hypatia" (Tollet), 67

Iliad translation by Pope, 19–67; and contemporary ideas about women, 40–42, 146, 271n.35; criticisms of Pope's appeals to women, 20, 21, 45–49; and Dryden compared, 22–26, 27, 28, 252–53n.6, 253n.13; encouragement of women's classical reading, 15, 17, 20, 67; and expanded reading public, 25–26; extracts, 69, 260n.3; facetious tone in, 42–

44; fashion in, 38–39, 43–44; Johnson's criticism of, 19–20, 21, 58, 66; political context, 23–24, 34, 253n.11, 253n.13; and Pope's ideas about women, 15, 24, 25, 35–38, 118; and readers' expectations, 20–21, 65–66; refinement in, 33–35; sentimentality in, 26–33, 67, 254n.18, 254n.21; and woman's point of view, 189. *See also Iliad* translation by Pope, women's responses to

Iliad translation by Pope, women's responses to, 15–16, 130; allusions, 68–70, 81, 260–61n.5; Carter, 55–58, 66, 257n.58; Dacier, 49–52, 66, 256–57n.50, 257n.52; emulation, 62–65, 66, 130–31, 259n.66, 259n.67, 260n.74; Lady Montagu, 52–55, 66; Thrale, 19, 58–61, 66, 67; Tollet, 61–62, 66, 192, 259n.69; Wheatley, 243–44

"Imitation of Mr. Pope's Ode on Solitude" (Steele), 223

"Imitation of the Third Elegy of the Third Book of Tibullus" (Whateley), 237

"In Diem Natalem" (Carter), 211–12

Ingram, Anne. *See* Irwin, Lady

"In Memory of The Right Hon. Lord Aubrey Beauclerk, Who was slain at Carthagena" (Jones), 231–32

"In Memory of the Right Hon. Nevil Lord Lovelace" (Jones), 236

"Invitation, The" (Barbauld), 224, 231

Iphidamus (*Iliad*), 30–33

Irwin, Lady, 85, 146–50, 157–58, 244–45

Jane Shore (Rowe), 26, 34, 35, 233

Jauss, Hans-Robert, 20–21

Jervas, Charles, 16–18, 39

Johnson, Samuel, 48, 116, 137, 237; and Carter, 6–7, 19, 40, 86; on Pope's *Iliad* translation, 19–20,

21, 58; and Thrale, 61, 66, 77, 263n.23, 263n.24

Jones, Mary, 57, 236; emulation of Pope, 101–6, 114, 155; and *Essay on Man, An,* 102, 208–9, 231; and Horatian satires, 195, 204–9, 225; style, 230–32

Jones, Oliver, 102

Joseph Andrews (Fielding), 257n.58

Juno (*Iliad*), 36, 38, 43

Juvenal, 194, 195

Kingsborough, Lord, 110

Knight, Henrietta. *See* Luxborough, Lady

Kramnick, Miriam, 53

Landry, Donna, 2, 158–59, 183, 188–89, 269n.11, 273n.46, 277n.6

Lattimore, Richmond, 27, 28, 32

Laura and Augustus (Bromley), 98–99

Leapor, Mary, 231, 232–34, 238, 272n.44; and "Essay on Criticism, An," 153–54, 229; and Horatian satires, 199–204, 225, 277n.6; poetic addresses to Pope, 152–57, 158, 159, 269n.11

Lennox, Charlotte, 19, 71, 75

"Letter II: To a Young Lady" (Deverell), 162–63

Letters . . . by Sir Thomas Fitzosborne, Bart. (Melmoth), 27

Letters from the Dead to the Living (Rowe), 74, 124, 156

Letters Moral and Entertaining (Rowe), 74

Letters on Education (Macaulay Graham), 90–93, 100–101

"Letter to the Right Honourable the Lady Russel, A" (Chandler), 196–99

Lewis, Esther, 163–65, 221–22, 273n.6

Life of Cowley (Johnson), 116

Life of Pope (Johnson), 48, 58

"Literary History as a Challenge to Literary Theory" (Jauss), 21

Literature and the Pastoral (Ettin), 167
Little, Janet, 160, 224–25
Locke, John, 88, 116
Lonsdale, Roger, 101–2, 174, 251n.22, 272n.44, 273n.6
Louisa, A Poetical Novel (Seward), 110–11, 184–85, 229, 276n.32, 276n.33
"Louisa to Emma" (Seward), 184–85
"Love Elegies and Epistles" (Seward), 110
Love in Several Masques (Fielding), 52
Lovelace, Martha, 102, 103, 105
Love's Last Shift (Cibber), 26
Lowenthal, Cynthia, 123
Luxborough, Lady, 223, 225
Lyrical Ballads (Wordsworth), 67

Macaulay Graham, Catherine, 90–93, 94, 95, 96, 100–101, 265n.40, 266n.42
McCarthy, William, 76, 77, 79, 87, 89, 90
"MacFlecknoe" (Dryden), 59
Mack, Maynard, 2, 4, 37, 42, 89–90, 121, 128, 255n.35, 265n.37
Madan, Falconer, 135
Madan, Judith Cowper. *See* Cowper, Judith
Manglavati, Leo, 271n.31
Manley, Delarivière, 35
"Man more happy than Beasts" (Lewis), 165
Marriage, 29–30, 33
Marriots, 42, 256n.40
Marxist criticism, 1, 2
Mason, Julian, 240, 241, 243
Master, Mary, 166
"*Mastif* and *Curs*, A Fable inscrib'd to Mr. Pope, The," (Winchilsea), 144–45
Melmoth, William, 27, 66
Memoirs (Pilkington), 106–10
Memoirs of Emma Courtney (Hays), 99–101, 106
Mentoria; or, the young ladies instructor (Murry), 97, 119, 173, 221

Metamorphoses (Ovid), 192, 276n.38
Meyers, Sylvia Harcstark, 214
"Microcosm, The" (Nichols), 209–11
Millenium Hall (Scott), 97, 266n.49
Milton, John, 15, 118, 243, 251n.24
Miscellanies in Prose and Verse (Jones), 101, 102, 105–6, 204
Miscellanies in Prose and Verse . . . To which are annexed, Some other curious Pieces (Pennyman), 264–65n.34
Miscellany Poems (Finch), 140
Misogyny, 1, 20, 37–38, 51–52, 252n.3, 255n.33. *See also* Contemporary ideas about women
Montagu, Elizabeth, 75–76, 97–98
Montagu, Lady Mary Wortley, 121–30, 158, 269n.14; and Addison's and Steele's publications, 35, 52; antiromanticism of, 122–23; and Cowper, 133; and "Epistle from Eloisa to Aberlard," 175; and *An Essay on Man*, 126–27; and Horatian satires, 125, 126, 128–29; and *Iliad* translation, 52–55, 66; Pope's attachment to, 3, 4, 42, 121–22, 130; restrictions on, 123–24; and Twickenham, 3, 4–6, 13–14, 15, 124–25
More, Hannah, 9–10, 15, 93–96, 100–101
Murry, Ann, 97, 120, 173, 221, 230, 231
Muses of Resistance: Laboring-Class Women's Poetry in Britain, 1739–1796, The (Landry), 2
Myers, Sylvia Harcstark, 257–58n.59
Mysteries of Udulpho, The (Radcliffe), 69

"Nell's Answer" (Little), 224
Neuter: or, a Modest Satire on the Poets of the Age, The (anonymous), 129, 269n.11
New Rehearsal (Gildon), 47
Nichols, John, 209

"Niobe in Distress for her Children Slain by Apollo" (Wheatley), 63

"Now with fresh vigour Morn her Light displays" (Lady Montagu), 124–25

"Nun's Return to the World, by the Decree of the National Assembly of France, February, 1790, The" (Blamire), 181–83

Nussbaum, Felicity, 60, 255n.33, 268n.1

Observations and Reflections Made in the Course of a Journey Through France, Italy, and Germany (Thrale), 60, 97, 266n.49

"Ode on Melancholy" (Carter), 214

"Ode to Wisdom" (Carter), 214

Odyssey translation by Pope, 26, 258n.60; collaboration in, 21–22, 52; women's responses to, 33, 56, 57, 65, 73, 110

"Of Desire: An Epistle to the Honourable Miss Lovelace" (Jones), 209

"Of Patience: An Epistle to the Right Hon. Samuel Lord Masham" (Jones), 208–9, 230–31

Ogilby, John, 32–33

Oldisworth, William, 36

Old Manor House, The (Smith), 82–83

"On a Poem of the Right Honourable Lady Mary Wortley Montagu in Mr. Hammond's Miscellany" (Tollet), 61

"On Hearing Miss Lynch Sing" (Carter), 190–91

"On Imagination" (Wheatley), 242

"On Mr. Nash's Picture at full Length, between the Busts of Sir Isaac Newton, and Mr. Pope" (Brereton), 195, 277n.3

"On Mr. Pope's Homer" (Tollet), 61–62

"On Mr. Pope's Universal Prayer" (Leapor), 152–54

"On Mrs. Joanna Lupton" (Bleecker), 239

"On Reading A Description of Pope's Gardens at Twickenham" (Seward), 13–15, 251n.22

"On Reading Mr. Pope's Poems" (Bentley), 158

"On reading Pope's Eloiza to Abelard" (Hands), 183, 191

"On Seeing a Gate Carried by Two Men Through Lincoln's Inn Fields" (Highmore), 272–73n.47

"On the Capture of General Lee" (Wheatley), 241

"On the Classics" (Barbauld), 223–24

"On the Death of a justly admir'd Author" (Leapor), 155

"On the Death of Her Sacred Majesty Queen Caroline" (Carter), 87

"On the Death of Mrs. Rowe" (Carter), 214–16

"On the Loss of Stella's Friendship" (Dixon), 150–51

"On the Right Honourable Lady S_____r_____t" (Thompson), 237

Ovid, 192, 276n.38

Oxenden, Sir George, 250n.16

Ozell, John, 20, 34, 36, 60, 125, 254–55n.27

Paris (*Iliad*), 34

Park, Thomas, 113

Parker, William, 87

Parnell, Thomas, 62

"Pastoral from the Song of Solomon, A" (Ramsay), 172

Patriarch's Wife, The (Ezell), 70

Pearson, Hesketh, 111

Penny, Anne, 172–73

Pennyman, Lady Margaret, 264–65n.34

Persius, 194

Philips, Katherine, 74

Phillips, Teresia Constantia, 109

Philosophical Inquiry (Burke), 76
Pilkington, Laetitia, 96–97, 106–10, 120, 267n.61
Pilkington, Matthew, 107, 108, 267n.61
Piozzi, Hester Thrale. *See* Thrale, Hester Lynch
"Poem, On the Supposition of an Advertisement appearing in a Morning Paper, of the Publication of a Volume of Poems, by a Servant Maid, A" (Hands), 276n.31
"Poem, On the Supposition of the Book having been Published and Read, A" (Hands), 276n.31
Poems (Gay), 26
Poems (Williams), 63–64
Poems by Eminent Ladies (Thornton and Colman), 132
Poems Moral and Entertaining (Lewis), 163–65, 273n.6
Poems on Several Occasions (Barber), 145
Poems on Several Occasions (Pointon), 166
Poems on Several Occasions (Ramsay), 172
Poems on Several Occasions, With Anne Boleyn to King Henry VIII (Tollet), 61, 175
Poems on Subjects Chiefly Devotional (Steele), 222–23
Poems on Various Subjects (Murry), 173, 221
Poetics of Sexual Myth: Gender and Ideology in the Verse of Swift and Pope, The (Pollak), 1
Pohli, Carol Virginia, 131, 252n.3, 269n.16
Pointon, Priscilla, 166
Politics, 73–74, 220–21, 255n.33; and criticisms of Pope's appeals to women, 45–47, 48; and *Iliad* translation, 23–24, 34, 51, 253n.11, 253n.13
Pollak, Ellen, 1, 20, 42, 252n.3

Pope, Alexander: ambivalence of, 160; Jervas portrait, 16–17; personal relationships with women, 3–5, 41–42, 66, 121–30, 175; physical appearance, 42. *See also specific topics.* Works: "Advertisement," 73; "Autumn," 169, 170; correspondence, 83, 103–4, 107, 121–22, 263n.30; "Dull, Stupid, Heavy," 77; "The Dying Christian to His Soul," 73; "Elegy to the Memory of an Unfortunate Lady," 83; "Epilogue to the Satires," 72, 160, 195, 203, 220; *Epistles to Several Persons*, 195; "Epistle to Bathurst," 80, 145, 147, 203, 208, 239; "Epistle to Cobham," 109, 147, 148, 231; "Epistle to Miss Blount, with the Works of Voiture," 1, 41, 118, 119; "Epistle to Mr. Jervas, with *Dryden's* Translation of *Fresnoy's Art* of *Painting*," 131, 234–35; "Epistle to Mr. [John] Gay," 3, 4, 5, 6; *The Garden and the City*, 128; "Impromptu, to Lady Winchilsea," 140; "Moral Essays," 148, 149; "Ode for Musick, on St. Cecilia's Day," 215; "Ode on Solitude," 171, 222–23; "On An Old Gate Erected in Chiswick Gardens," 272–73n.47; "On the Use of Riches," 200; *Pastorals*, 10, 167–74, 190, 237; *Poems on Several Occasions*, 142, 145; *Satire on Women*, 93; "Sober Advice," 72; "Spring," 170, 173–74; "Summer," 169; "The Temple of Fame," 232; *Three Hours After Marriage*, 144, 271n.31; "To a Lady. Of the Characters of Women," 41; "To Lady ——, from a Sylph," 74; "Universal Prayer," 152–54, 237; "Winter," 169, 170. *See also Dunciad*; "Epistle from Eloisa to Abelard"; "Epistle to a Lady," women's responses to; "Epistle to

Burlington"; "Epistle to Dr. Arbuthnot"; "Essay on Criticism,
An"; *Essay on Man, An;* Horatian
satires; "Hymn Written in Windsor Forest"; *Iliad* translation by
Pope; *Odyssey* translation by
Pope; *The Rape of the Lock*
Pope's ideas about women, 2, 3–4,
189, 251n.24, 268n.1; encouragement of reading, 41–42; and
"Epistle from Eloisa to Abelard,"
85, 120, 191, 192–93; and "Epistle
to a Lady," women's responses
to, 101, 118–19, 215, 218, 219; in
An Essay on Man, 93; facetious
tone, 42, 256n.40; as feminist, 37,
255n.35; and Horatian satires,
201–2; and *Iliad* translation, 15,
24, 25, 35–38, 118; Irwin's response to, 85, 146–50; and marriage, 29–30, 33; as misogynist,
1, 20, 37–38, 51–52, 252n.3; wom-
en's welcome of, 118, 268n.1
Pope's women readers: access, 119–
20; contemporary criticisms of
Pope's appeals to, 20, 21, 45–49,
60, 66, 258n.65; effectiveness of
reading, 270n.20; importance of,
1–2; and Jervas portrait, 16–18;
Pope's writings as sanction for,
75–76, 165–66. *See also* Contemporary women writers' lives; Wom-
en's responses to Pope's writings; *specific works*
"Power of Destiny, The" (Whateley), 168–69
*Practical Piety, or the influence of the
Religion of the Heart on the Conduct
of Life* (More), 94–96, 100–101
Prior, Matthew, 276n.33
"Progress of Poetry, The" (Cowper), 135–37
"Progress of Wit: A Caveat, The"
(Hill), 49
"Prologue to the Duchess, on Her
Return from Scotland" (Dryden),
268n.2

Propp, Vladimir, 179, 275n.27
"P——— to Bolingbroke" (Lady
Montagu), 126, 128
Pye, Jael Henrietta, 8–9, 177–79, 192

Racine, Louis, 87
Radcliffe, Ann, 68, 69, 70, 71, 83
Rake's Progress, The (Hogarth), 218–
19
Ramsay, Charlotte, 172, 176–77,
179, 191–92, 275n.23, 276n.37,
276n.38
Rape of the Lock, The, 5, 19–20; and
"Epistle from Eloisa to Abelard,"
134; facetious tone in, 42–43;
fashion in, 38, 39; ideas about
women in, 81, 82, 85, 118, 120,
140, 147; women's allusions to,
10, 74, 81, 82, 130, 156, 235, 238,
239, 242; and women's educa-
tion, 41, 55; women's responses
to, 140, 144, 147, 190–91, 207,
217, 233
*Reflections Concerning Innate Moral
Principles* (Bolingbroke), 90–91
Reflections Upon Marriage (Astell), 37
*Remarks upon Mr. Pope's Translation
of Homer* (Dennis), 47
Rémond, Nicolas-François, 124
"Resolution, A" (Lewis), 163–64,
165
Ribeiro, Aileen, 255–56n.36
Richardson, Samuel, 83–84, 154, 214
Rizzo, Betty, 154
Roberts, William, 9
Rogers, Katherine, 271n.31
Rogers, Pat, 26
Rousseau, Jean Jacques, 85
Rowe, Elizabeth Singer, 93, 145,
156, 190; Carter on, 214–16; and
politics, 71, 73–74; and women's
publishing, 85, 124
Rowe, Nicholas, 26, 34, 35, 233
Ruffhead, Owen, 265n.37
"Ruined Cottage, The" (Words-
worth), 171
Rumbold, Valerie, 2, 20, 42, 121,

123, 130, 131, 132–33, 135, 138, 140, 145, 150, 271n.29
"Rural Happiness. To a Friend" (Whateley), 170–71

Salusbury, Hester. See Thrale, Hester Lynch
Salvaggio, Ruth, 1, 35, 188, 189
Schama, Simon, 241
Schibanoff, Susan, 188
Scott, Sarah, 71, 79–81, 97, 266n.49
Scott, Sir Walter, 64–65
Secker, Thomas, 56, 257–58n.59
Select Collection (Nichols), 209
Seneca, 94
Serle, John, 6
Several Discourses (Burton), 94
Seward, Anna, 267n.63, 276n.33; emulation of Pope, 14–15, 64–65, 110–17, 260n.74; and "Epistle from Eloisa to Abelard," 110–11, 184–85, 192, 276n.32; and Horatian satires, 217–20, 225; and Iliad translation, 64–65, 66, 67; style, 227–29; and Twickenham, 13–15
Seymour, Frances. See Hertford, Lady
Shadwell, Thomas, 59
Shakespear Illustrated (Lennox), 75
Sherburn, George, 54
Shevelow, Kathryn, 35, 188
Shiels, Robert, 196
Short account, of the principal seats and gardens, in and about Twickenham, A (Pye), 8–9
"Slander Delineated" (Lewis), 164, 165
Smith, Charlotte, 71, 82–83, 120, 174–75
Southey, Robert, 111, 114–15
Spectator. See Addison's and Steele's publications
Staves, Susan, 275n.26
Steele, Anne, 222–23
Steele, Richard. See Addison's and Steele's publications

Strictures on the Modern System of Female Education (More), 93
"Strong Box, The" (Dixon), 151
Swift, Jonathan, 106, 107, 108, 110, 146, 269n.14
Sykes, Richard, 112
"Sylph, The" (Francis), 168

"Taking the Gold Out of Egypt: The Art of Reading as a Woman" (Schibanoff), 188
Talbot, Catherine, 214, 257–58n.59; and Horatian satires, 225–26; and Iliad translation, 33, 55–57, 66; on Pope's correspondence, 83, 263n.30
Tatler, The. See Addison's and Steele's publications
"Temple of Love: A Dream, The" (Leapor), 232–33, 234
Terence's Comedies and Plautus's Comedies (Echard), 22
Thomas Aquinas, Saint, 94
Thompson, Eliza, 221, 236–37
Thomson, James, 171
Thornton, Bonnell, 132
"Thoughts on the Works of Providence" (Wheatley), 241–42
Thrale, Henry, 61
Thrale, Hester Lynch, 76–79, 108, 263n.24; and An Essay on Man, 87–90, 94, 96, 97, 266n.49; and Iliad translation, 19, 58–61, 66, 67
Thraliana (Thrale), 58–61, 67, 76
Tickell, Thomas, 48
Tillotson, Geoffrey, 174, 175, 228, 230
"To His Excellency General Washington" (Wheatley), 240–41
Tollet, Elizabeth, 61–62, 66, 67, 175, 192, 209–11, 259n.69
"To Maecenas" (Wheatley), 243–44
"To Mira" (Ramsay), 172
"To Miss D'aeth" (Carter), 212–14, 230
"To Mr. Duck, Occasioned by a

Present of His Poems" (Carter), 87

"To [Mr. L⸺]" (Bleecker), 239

"To Mr. *Pope*" (Finch), 143–44

"To Mr. *Pope*: Intreating him to write Verses to the Memory of *Thomas*, late Earl of Thanet" (Barber), 145–46

"To Mr. Pope—Written in his Works" (Cowper), 130–31, 133

"To Mrs. P⸺. With some Drawings of Birds and Insects" (Barbauld), 234–36

Tonson, Jacob, 23, 253n.11

"To the ingenious Lady, Author of the Poem entitled, *The Progress of Poetry*" (anonymous), 138

"To the Lady Castlemaine, upon Her Incouraging His First Play" (Dryden), 268n.2

To the Lighthouse (Woolf), 58–59

"To the Memory of Mr. Hughes" (Cowper), 138

"To the Muse" (Dixon), 151

Town Eclogues (Lady Montagu), 52

"Triumvirate of Poets, The" (Tollet), 62

"Truth" (Boyd), 152

Twickenham garden and grotto, 3–4, 250–51n.19. *See also* Twickenham garden and grotto, women's responses to

Twickenham garden and grotto, women's responses to, 4–16; deference, 6–8; disillusionment, 9–10; identification, 8–9, 13–15; laboring-class, 10–13; rejection, 4–6, 124

"Universe, The" (Baker), 209

"Upon the Death of her Husband" (Rowe), 145

Upton, Catherine, 166

"Vanity of external Accomplishments, The" (Whateley), 229, 237–38

Variety (Boyd), 152

"Verses Address'd to the Imitator of the First Satire of the Second Book of Horace" (Lady Montagu), 125, 129

Virgil, 22–23

Warburton, William, 89

Ward, Edward, 48–49

Warton, Joseph, 258n.65, 265n.37

"Way of the World, The" (Leapor), 201

Weinbrot, Howard, 44, 195

West, Benjamin, 241

Weston, Joseph, 20, 64, 114

Whateley, Mary, 168–71, 229, 237–38

Wheatley, Phillis, 62–63, 163, 240–44, 259n.71

Williams, Helen Maria, 63–64, 183

Wilson, Bernard, 87

Wilson, Penelope, 1–2, 261n.7

Winchilsea, Lady, 140–45, 251n.23

Winn, James, 42, 121, 252–53n.6, 253n.13

Wittreich, Joseph, 15, 118, 251n.24

Wollstonecraft, Mary, 37, 93, 99, 183, 188

"Woman's Frailty" (Lewis), 164, 165

Women and Print Culture (Shevelow), 35, 188

Women's allusions to Pope's writings, 79–83, 237–42, 266n.48; *An Essay on Man*, 79, 96–98, 242, 266n.49; *Iliad* translation, 68–70, 81, 260–61n.5; *The Rape of the Lock*, 10, 74, 81, 82, 130, 156, 235, 238, 239, 242

Women's emulation of Pope, 74, 101–17, 166–67, 262n.16; Cowper, 130–32; and *Iliad* translation, 62–65, 66, 130–31, 259n.66, 259n.67, 260n.74; Jones, 101–6, 114, 155; Leapor, 155, 166; *Pastorals*, 167–74, 190; Pilkington, 106–10; Pope's rejection of, 131–32; Seward, 14–15, 64–65, 110–

17; and style, 227–32, 240–41,
243. *See also* "Epistle from Eloisa
to Abelard," women's responses
to
Women's Place in Pope's World (Rumbold), 2, 20
Women's poetic addresses to Pope,
118–59, 270–71n.26, 272–73n.47;
Barber, 145–46, 158; Bentley, 157,
158, 159, 166, 272n.46; Boyd,
152, 158–59; Cowper, 130–39,
158; Dixon, 150–51, 158; Irwin,
146–50, 157–58; Leapor, 152–57,
159; and Pope's sympathy with
women, 118–19; Winchilsea,
140–45, 271n.29, 271n.31. *See also*
Montagu, Lady Mary Wortley
Women's responses to Pope's writings: and ambivalence, 160–65;
antagonism, 4–6, 76–79, 87–96,
107–10, 124; choice of subject,
232–37; critical analysis, 70, 83–
84, 261n.7; deference, 7–8; identification, 8–9, 13–15, 87–88, 160–
61, 189, 265n.37; importance of,
2–3; and influence, 74, 262n.16;
laboring-class, 10–13, 154–55,
157–58, 272n.46; and politics, 73–

75; Pope's correspondence, 83,
107, 263n.30; and religion, 71–73,
83–85; and woman's point of
view, 188–93, 244–45; and wom-
en's publishing, 70–71. *See also*
Women's allusions to Pope's writ-
ings; Women's emulation of
Pope; Women's poetic addresses
to Pope; *specific works*
Woolf, Virginia, 58–59
Wordsworth, William, 67, 168, 171
Wright, Lawrence, 185
"Written at a *Ferme Ornée* near Bir-
mingham, August 7th, 1749"
(Luxborough), 223
"Written in the Retreat from Bur-
goyne" (Bleecker), 239–40
"Written on a Visit" (Yearsley), 10–
13
Wroth, Lady Mary, 167
Wycherley, William, 132

Yearsley, Ann, 10–13, 14, 15
Yorke, Charles, 119
Young, Edward, 109, 171

"Zelida to Irena" (Curtis), 179–80
Zwicker, Stephen, 24

Claudia N. Thomas is an associate professor of English at Wake Forest University, where she teaches Restoration and eighteenth-century British literature. Her articles have appeared in *Eighteenth-Century Life, The Age of Johnson,* and the *South Central Review.*